ENGLAND IN THE AGE
OF THE AMERICAN
REVOLUTION

ENGLAND IN THE AGE OF THE AMERICAN REVOLUTION

BY
SIR LEWIS NAMIER

SECOND EDITION

MACMILLAN

First edition 1930
Second edition 1961
Reprinted 1974

Published by
THE MACMILLAN PRESS LTD
London and Basingstoke
Associated companies in New York
Dublin Melbourne Johannesburg and Madras

SBN (boards) 333 05559 4
(papers) 333 09278 3

Printed in Great Britain by
REDWOOD BURN LIMITED
Trowbridge & Esher

PREFACE TO SECOND EDITION

THIS book has had to be reprinted in a form resembling its first edition much more closely than was the case with *The Structure of Politics*. When the second editions of both were first thought of, my husband's intention was to make in the second book corrections and alterations like those he had made in the first. He died with the task barely begun.

But while at work on it in the last weeks of his life, he was veering to the opinion that alterations like those in *The Structure of Politics* would not do for *England in the Age of the American Revolution*. On the one hand he felt them to be less necessary here, on the other he saw that, if made, they would have to be much greater — notably in some of the lists. Burdened as he was with other work he realised there was neither time nor strength for so vast an undertaking.

As to deletions, on some he had made up his mind. And those which he had clearly pointed out, to Mr. John Brooke or to me, have been made with one exception only : certain asides, in the text or footnotes, which reveal Lewis himself — be it his life or his character, his mind or his extraneous pre-occupations at the time of writing — have been left to stand because of their enhanced biographical value.

Allusions to political or social events widely known in the nineteen-twenties have been retained where still compre-hensible. Others, rendered cryptic by the passing of time, have been omitted — which accords with the author's inten-tions in his last days. In short, the new edition is the 1930 book slightly emended, in the last resort by Mr. Brooke and me.

JULIA NAMIER

NOTE TO FIRST EDITION

I BEG leave to record my humble thanks to His Majesty the King for permission to make use of the papers of George III at Windsor Castle.

I have further to thank the Marquess of Bute, K.T., Mr. William Godsal, the Marquess of Lansdowne, the Earl of Minto, and the Earl of Sandwich, for having allowed me to use their collections of manuscripts ; the Rhodes Trustees, for another grant towards my research work ; the friend, who now, as when I published my former book, wishes to remain anonymous, for further financial help ; Mr. C. G. Stone and Mr. R. R. Sedgwick, for having read the manuscript of this book, and made many valuable suggestions.

L. B. NAMIER

15 GLOUCESTER WALK
  LONDON, W.8
    5 *May* 1930

BIBLIOGRAPHICAL NOTE

1. All references to *The Structure of Politics at the Accession of George III* are to the second edition, published in 1957.

2. Since the publication of the first edition of *England in the Age of the American Revolution*, the letters of George III to Lord Bute have been edited by Mr. Romney Sedgwick and are referred to in this volume by their dates.

CONTENTS

BOOK I

GOVERNMENT AND PARLIAMENT UNDER THE DUKE OF NEWCASTLE

THE SOCIAL FOUNDATIONS

THE SOCIAL FOUNDATIONS

THE UNREFORMED HOUSE OF COMMONS

THE social history of England could be written in terms of membership of the House of Commons, that peculiar club, election to which has at all times required some expression of consent on the part of the public. At no time was the House truly unrepresentative ; for with us the result of elections does not primarily depend on constituencies or electorates. Live forces break through forms, and shape results to suit requirements. Were it decided that the 615 heaviest men in the country should constitute the House of Commons, the various interests and parties could be trusted to obtain their proportionate weight in it. But the idea of representation and the nature of the body politic vary from age to age, and with them varies the social structure of the House of Commons.

In its origin the House of Commons was akin to the jury, and the representative character and functions of the two were in a way cognate ; from an intimate knowledge of conditions, the House declared the sense of the commonalty on questions which most patently and directly concerned them, but did not pronounce sentence and did not meddle with matters of government or 'mysteries of State'. Attendance at it was truly a service. But as the position and prestige of Parliament increased, and seats in the House of Commons began to be prized, it came to represent, not so much the sense of the community, as the distribution of power within it — the two developments being necessarily and inevitably correlated. The leading territorial families, and even the gentry of lesser rank, now invaded the borough representation ; and the Crown attempted to secure seats in the House of Commons for its servants and dependants — if a true equation of forces was to

3

be attained, the executive, centring in the King and as yet extraneous to the Commons, had to receive its own representation in the House. As make-weight in favour of stable government, the royal influence in elections continued to be worked after the Revolution of 1688. When the struggle commenced between George III and his grandfather's political 'undertakers', an outcry was raised against 'prerogative' — the term was still current by force of ideological and linguistic survival ; for ideas outlive the conditions which gave them birth, and words outlast ideas. In reality, George III never left the safe ground of Parliamentary government, and merely acted the *primus inter pares*, the first among the borough-mongering, electioneering gentlemen of England. While the Stuarts tried to browbeat the House and circumscribe the range of its action, George III fully accepted its constitution and recognised its powers, and merely tried to work it in accordance with the customs of the time.

The demoralising influence of the eighteenth-century electoral system is obvious, and its nonsensical features are only too patent ; its deeper sense and its usefulness are less apparent. The rotten boroughs were a necessary part of the eighteenth-century organisation of the British Government, while corruption in populous boroughs was the effect of citizen status in an electorate not fully awake to national interests ; even so, it was a mark of English freedom and independence, for no one bribes where he can bully. Without those boroughs the House of Commons in 1761 would practically have represented one class only, the landed interest, and in the first place those independent country gentlemen who in fact supplied most of the knights of the shires ; this might possibly have sufficed for a self-centred nation, never for an Empire. A careful student of Parliamentary history gives the following description of the fifteen knights of the shire who represented Devonshire between 1688 and 1761, and ten of whom belonged to three families : 'Of nearly every one we might say : he belonged to a well-known Devon family ; while in Parliament he made no speeches, held no office, and achieved no distinction of any sort ; but whenever he is known to have recorded a vote, it was given against

the government then in office'.[1] The most respectable constituencies in Great Britain returned the dullest members ; they
did not supply the architects and craftsmen of government and
administration. The boroughs under Government management, or acquired by the Government at the time of the election,
opened the gates of the House to budding statesmen and to
hard-working civil servants, the permanent secretaries of
Government departments (who were not as yet disqualified
from sitting in it), to various law officers of the Crown, to
admirals and pro-consuls ; in short, to the men who had the
widest and most varied experience of administrative work ;
while the promising young men and the 'men of business' of
the Opposition were similarly provided for by its borough
patrons. Since 1832 the party organisations have tried to fill
the place of patrons or the Government in providing for men
who are required in the House but are not of sufficient fame,
wealth, or popularity to secure them seats. These endeavours
have not been altogether successful — in 1873 Lord Lytton
wrote in a novel about a rising politician : 'In the old time,
before the first Reform Bill, his reputation would have secured
him at once a seat in Parliament ; but the ancient nurseries of
statesmen are gone, and their place is not supplied'.[2] Even
now the safest, richest, and therefore most independent Conservative constituencies elect mainly local worthies, while able
young men have to be sent by headquarters to doubtful constituencies, dependent on financial support from the party
organisation, and succumb at a landslide.

Yet another function was discharged by the corrupt and
the rotten boroughs : through them the *nouveaux-riches* in
every generation were able to enter the House of Commons ;
and this occurred with such regularity that by tracing the
history of these new men one could follow the rise and fall of
various branches of commerce, the development of modern
finance, and the advance of capitalist organisation in industry,
and measure the relative importance of the West and East

[1] J. J. Alexander, 'Devon County Members of Parliament', *Reports and
Transactions of the Devonshire Association*, vol. 49, p. 368.
[2] *The Parisians*, vol. i, p. 120.

Indies. Thus even a good deal of the economic and colonial history of England could be written in terms of membership of the House of Commons.

THE SOCIAL STRUCTURE

The fact that in England money was allowed to play a great part in the selection of the governing body (much greater than in Scotland and Wales) was the result and expression of the peculiar character of English society, civilian and plutocratic, though imbued with feudal habits and traditions.

England knows not democracy as a doctrine, but has always practised it as a fine art. Since the Middle Ages, no one was ever barred on grounds of class from entering the House of Commons, and in the House all Members have always sat on equal terms ; as between freemen, England never knew a rigid distinction of classes. Still, there has been throughout an element of heredity in the membership of the House, largely connected with property in land, but at no time resulting in the formation of close castes ; England's social structure to this day retains more traces of feudalism than that of any other country, but it has never been hierarchical. Trade was never despised, and English society has always shown respect for property and wealth. The financial expert, usually a 'moneyed' man, was valued in the House, and the Treasury has for centuries held a pre-eminent position in the Government. St. Matthew vi. 21 was quoted by the English mediaeval author of the *Dialogus de Scaccario* to prove by the authority of Christ that the King's heart was, where his treasure was, in the Exchequer ; and there the heart of the nation has been ever since — which accounts for the paramount importance of Budget nights and for the excellence of British public finance.

The social history of nations is largely moulded by the forms and development of their armed forces, the primary aim of national organisation being common defence. The historical development of England is based on the fact that her frontiers against Europe are drawn by Nature, and cannot be the subject of dispute ; that she is a unit sufficiently small for coherent government to have been established and maintained even under very primitive conditions; that since 1066 she has never suffered serious invasion; that no big modern armies have succeeded her feudal levies; and that her senior service is the navy, with which foreign trade is closely connected. In short, a great deal of what is peculiar in English history is due to the obvious fact that Great Britain is an island.

Encroachments on frontier provinces were never possible in the case of England (the Scottish and Welsh Borders may be here left out of account); a conquest had to be complete or could not endure. Frontier encroachments are apt to produce chaos, whereas complete conquests tend to establish strong governments. In anarchical conditions those who bear arms obtain an ascendancy over the other classes, and usually form themselves into a close, dominant caste; while a strong central government, such as was established in England after 1066, was in itself a check on class privileges. Where armies serve as 'expeditionary forces' militarism has little chance to permeate the life of the nation; and there is more of the knight-errant in a merchant-adventurer than in an officer of the militia.

Feudalism was a system of social organisation whereby both army service and administrative functions were bound up with the holding of land. When a change supervened in armament and methods of fighting, on the European Continent a new type of royal army took the place of feudal levies, and the administrative structure of Continental countries was adjusted to the requirements of the new military organisation. Rank and caste were not eliminated, but they were no longer bound up with property in land. An army is necessarily built up on gradations of rank, and universal military service has imbued the Continental nations with hierarchical conceptions; even posts in the civil service were in many countries assimilated to ranks in the army. Society became sharply divided into those who were trained for officers and those who could not claim commissioned rank; and 'honour', implying the right to fight duels, was restricted to members of the officer-class.

If the compelling, uncompromising exigencies of military

organisation are sufficient to override tradition, war is in itself revolution ; it results in a destruction of existing forms, carried out by military organisations in accordance with an accepted code. Regard for property and law can hardly be maintained in war ; invasion and conquest do away with prescriptive rights. The fine growth of English Conservatism is due, in a high degree, to the country having been free from the revolutionary action of war within its borders, and of militarism within its social organisation. The true Conservative is not a militarist.

Feudalism in England, divested of its military purpose, and not supplanted by any new military establishment on a national scale, survived in local government and social relations, continuing to rest on property in land ; but as there was no sharp division of classes, based on the use of arms, and no subject of the King was debarred from holding land, the new civilian feudalism — a peculiarly English product — necessarily bore a plutocratic imprint. Primogeniture, feudal in origin, survived, and titles retained a territorial character, with the result that there can be but one holder of a title. This restriction has allowed more room for new creations, while the position of younger sons has similarly worked against a sharp division of classes.

The younger sons of country gentlemen, and even of peers, went into trade without thereby losing caste ; the eldest son inherited the family estates, the second, third, or even fourth, were placed in the Church, in the army or navy, at the bar, or in some government office ; but the next had usually to be apprenticed to a merchant, and, however great the name and wealth of the family, the boy baptised Septimus or Decimus was almost certain to be found in a counting-house ; only courtesy lords were precluded by custom from entering trade. 'Trade in England', wrote Defoe in 1726, 'neither is or ought to be levell'd with what it is in other countries ; or the tradesmen depreciated as they are abroad. . . . The word tradesman in England does not sound so harsh, as it does in other countries; and to say a gentleman-tradesman is not . . . nonsense. . . .' [1]

[1] *The Complete English Tradesman*, p. 380.

'Were it not for two articles, by which the numbers of the families of gentlemen are recruited . . . when sunk and decayed . . . this nation would, in a few years, have very few families of gentlemen left ; or, at least, very few that had estates to support them.' [1]   But 'the gentry are always willing to submit to the raising their families, by what they call City fortunes',[2] while 'the rising tradesman swells into the gentry'.

Trade is so far here from being inconsistent with a gentleman, that in short trade in England makes gentlemen, and has peopled this nation with gentlemen ; for . . . the tradesmen's children, or at least their grand-children, come to be as good gentlemen, states-men, Parliament-men, privy-counsellors, judges, bishops, and noblemen, as those of the highest birth and the most antient families. . . .

We see the tradesmen of England, as they grow wealthy, coming every day to the Herald's Office, to search for the coats of arms of their ancestors, in order to paint them upon their coaches, and en-grave them upon their plate, embroider them upon their furniture, or carve them upon the pediments of their new houses; and how often do we see them trace the registers of their families up to the prime nobility or the most antient gentry of the Kingdom ?

In this search we find them often qualified to raise new families, if they do not descend from old. . . .[3]

The first Lord Craven, whose father had been a wholesale grocer, 'being upbraided with his being of an upstart nobility, by the famous Aubrey, Earl of Oxford, who was himself of the very antient family of the Veres, Earls of Oxford', replied that he would 'cap pedigrees with him' ; 'he read over his family thus ; I am William Lord Craven, my father was Lord Mayor of London, and my grandfather was the Lord knows who. . . .'[4]

If anyone about 1760 could be named as prototype of the country gentleman it would be the Tory squire, Sir John Hinde Cotton, M.P., of Madingley Hall, Cambridgeshire, 4th baronet. The Cottons had been settled for centuries at Mad-ingley, and had sat in Parliament in the fourteenth and sixteenth centuries ; the father of Sir John had represented the County,

[1] Daniel Defoe, *A Plan of the English Commerce* (1728), p. 81.
[2] *Ibid.*, p. 13.
[3] Defoe, *The Complete English Tradesman* (1726), pp. 376-7.
[4] *Ibid.* pp. 377-8.

and so did he himself. But his paternal grandmother was Elizabeth, daughter of John Sheldon, Lord Mayor of London ; and his mother, Lettice, daughter of Sir Ambrose Crowley, the famous Durham ironmaster, whose warehouse in Upper Thames Street bore the sign of the 'Leathern Doublet', to commemorate the dress in which he had come to London. 'No gent., nor any pretence to arms' was the description given of his Quaker father,[1] and Ambrose Crowley himself, as Jack Anvil, transformed into Sir John Enville, appears in Addison's *Spectator* (No. 299) as the type of the self-made man, 'bent upon making a family' with 'a dash of good blood in their veins'. Sir John Hinde Cotton married his cousin Anne, daughter of Humphrey Parsons, Lord Mayor of London, by Sarah, another daughter of Sir Ambrose Crowley ; and his sister Mary married Jacob Houblon, the son of a merchant and a descendant of the *Pater Bursae Londoniensis*. Elizabeth, a third daughter of Crowley, married John, 10th Lord St. John of Bletso ; one of Crowley's granddaughters married Sir William Stanhope, M.P., brother of the famous Lord Chesterfield, and another, 'with a fortune of £200,000', John, 2nd Earl of Ashburnham.

Illustrations of this kind could be multiplied indefinitely, but even a dozen examples, though, in their accumulation, subconsciously reassuring to the reader, do not prove a thesis, and the subject is too vast and complex for an exhaustive statistical examination ; an analysis of the House of Commons, that invaluable microcosmic picture of England, will, however, supply a certain amount of evidence.

Wealth amassed in trade was laid out in landed estates and used to secure seats in the House of Commons, for both helped to lift their holders into a higher social sphere.

A merchant may be Member of Parliament . . . and shall sit in the House of Commons, with the sons of peers. . . . This equality it is . . . which can alone preserve to commerce its honor, and

---

[1] See Peter Le Neve's *Pedigrees of Knights*, ed. by G. W. Marshall, *Harleian Society Publications* (1873), p. 495. See further 'Pedigree of the Family of Crowley', by G. W. Marshall, in *The East-Anglian* (1867), vol. iii. pp. 95-8 ; about Ambrose Crowley and his ironworks, see also William Hutchinson, *History of Durham* (1787), vol. ii. pp. 441-3, and Surtees, *History of Durham* (1820), vol. ii. pp. 272-3.

inspire to those who profess it, an esteem for their condition. . . .
The lords can have no contempt for the usefull professions of their
fellow subjects, who are their equals, when assembled to regulate
the public affairs of the nation.[1]

Naturally purchases of landed estates by men enriched in
trade were most frequent in the neighbourhood of London,
though the process is noticeable also round secondary centres
such as Bristol, Liverpool, Norwich, or Hull, and in industrial
districts, *e.g.* the wool-manufacturing counties of the West and
the iron districts of the Western Midlands ; 'new men rooted
themselves upon old acres'.

As early as 1576, William Lambard wrote in his *Perambula-
tion of Kent* :

The gentlemen be not heere (throughout) of so auncient stockes
as else where, especially in the partes nearer to London, from whiche
citie (as it were from a certeine riche and wealthy seedplot) courtiers,
lawyers, and merchants be continually translated, and do become
new plants amongst them.[2]

And Defoe in 1728 :

I dare oblige my self to name five hundred great estates, within
one hundred miles of London, which within eighty years past, were
the possessions of the antient English gentry, which are now bought
up, and in the possession of citizens and tradesmen, purchased fairly
by money raised in trade ; some by merchandizing, some by shop-
keeping, and some by meer manufacturing ; such as clothing in
particular.[3]

In the local histories of the home counties published between
1760 and 1830, such as Lysons, Hasted, Manning and Bray,
Horsfield, Dallaway, Clutterbuck, Morant, etc., one can watch
this process continue and expand, though it is no longer specific-
ally mentioned, having become obvious and ordinary. The following account appears in the genealogical volume of the *Victoria
County History* dealing with *The Landed Houses of Hertfordshire*:[4]

In some counties the origin of their modern landed houses can be
traced in many cases to great local industries ; Hertfordshire, rather

---

[1] See Sir John Nickolls, *Remarks on the Advantages and Disadvantages
of France and of Great Britain with respect to Commerce* (1754), p. 110.
'Sir John Nickolls' is a pseudonym — the author was a Frenchman, Plumard
de Dangeul. [2] P. 10.
[3] *A Plan of the English Commerce*, pp. 83-4. [4] P. 4.

an agricultural and residential than an industrial county, is not without its distinctive note, though this is of a different character. Banking
and brewing, chiefly in London, are responsible for the rise and
wealth of a quite exceptional proportion of families in this county.

To pursue this county, as an example, in the microcosmos
of the House of Commons — these were the six Hertfordshire
Members returned at the general election of 1761 : *Hertford
County* : Thomas Plumer Byde — a squire in Hertfordshire
and a merchant in London,[1] descended on both sides from
families aldermanic in origin, subsequently Parliamentary ; and
Jacob Houblon, the owner of large landed estates, son of Charles
Houblon, a Portugal merchant, by Mary, daughter of Daniel
Bate, London merchant and vintner.[2] *Hertford Town* : John
Calvert, a London brewer possessed of an estate in Hertford-
shire ; [3] and Timothy Caswall, an officer in the Guards, grandson of Sir George Caswall, a London banker of South Sea
notoriety, nephew of John Caswall, also a London banker, and,
on his mother's side, nephew of Nathaniel Brassey, another
London banker, who had preceded Timothy Caswall as
Member for Hertford, and had in 1761 secured his nephew's
election for the borough.[4] *St. Albans* : James West, barrister

[1] T. P. Byde unsuccessfully contested Cambridge as an Opposition
candidate in 1774 and 1776, and became bankrupt in 1779 (see *Gentleman's
Magazine*, 1779, p. 272) ; he died at Naples in 1789 'reduced to the most
abject condition, after all his visionary speculations in his own country,
and the unjustifiable means he pursued to realise them' (*Gentleman's
Magazine*, 1789, vol. i. p. 575, and vol. ii. p. 669). William Baker, M.P.,
wrote to his mother-in-law, Lady Juliana Penn, on 13 November 1778 :
'By the folly and knavery of my neighbour Mr. Byde our whole county,
and particularly his own district, is involved in the utmost confusion and
distress. . . . Hardly a farmer in his neighbourhood, but has suffered by
placing money in his hands. . . . In short it is easier to conceive than
describe all the distress which this impudent and wicked man has occasioned'
(Baker MSS.).
[2] About Jacob Houblon and his ancestry, see Lady A. Archer Houblon,
The Houblon Family (1907).
[3] About the Calvert family, see *The Landed Houses of Hertfordshire* in
the *V.C.H.*
[4] See letter from Nathaniel Brassey to the Duke of Newcastle, 5 October
1760, Add. MSS. 32912, f. 387 ; and from T. Caswall to the same, 3 November 1760, Add. MSS. 32914, f. 56 : 'Mr. Brassey has serv'd long in Parliament and may continue so to do, or his substitute for him'. Caswall was
brought in at the general election of 1761 as that 'substitute'. The daughter
and heiress of N. Brassey married Thomas Dimsdale, doctor and subsequently banker, M.P. for Hertford, 1780–90, the founder of a well-known

and civil servant, the Duke of Newcastle's faithful Secretary to the Treasury, of a Warwickshire family, married to Sarah, daughter and heiress of Sir James Steavens, a Bermondsey timber merchant ; [1] and George Simon, Lord Nuneham, eldest son of Simon, 1st Earl Harcourt, by Rebecca, daughter of Charles Samborne Le Bas, and granddaughter of Sir Samuel Moyer, 1st bart., a Turkey merchant.[2]

In short, the representation of this county, even though it had neither rotten boroughs, pocket boroughs, nor boroughs under Government management, fills in the detail of the picture given above of social amalgamation between the landed nobility or gentry and those who, as a class, have to be described by a foreign term — the big *bourgeoisie*.

THE UPPER CLASSES

Trade was not despised in eighteenth-century England — it was acknowledged to be the great concern of the nation ; and money was honoured, the mystic, common denominator of all values, the universal repository of as yet undetermined possibilities. But what was the position of the trader ? There is no one answer to this question. A man's status in English society has always depended primarily on his own consciousness ; for the English are not a methodical or logical nation — they perceive and accept facts without anxiously inquiring into their reasons or meaning. Whatever is apt to raise a man's self-consciousness — be it birth, rank, wealth, intellect, daring, or achievements — will add to his stature ; but it has to be translated into the truest expression of his sub-conscious self-valuation : uncontending ease, the unbought grace of life. Classes are the more sharply marked in England because there is no single test for them, except the final, incontestable result ;

Hertford Parliamentary 'dynasty'; see Clutterbuck, *History of Hertford-shire*, vol. ii. p. 35.

[1] The Duke of Newcastle, in a letter to Lord Rockingham, put her fortune at £100,000 ; see Add. MSS. 32968, f. 264.

[2] Lord Nuneham's maternal grandfather, Charles Samborne Le Bas, was descended from John Le Bas, of Caen, Normandy, who in the beginning of the seventeenth century had married Anne, daughter of Richard Samborne, an English merchant settled at Caen (see *The Genealogist*, vol. i. pp. 218-19).

and there is more snobbery than in any other country, because the gate can be entered by anyone, and yet remains, for those bent on entering it, a mysterious, awe-inspiring gate. The Chinese used to ennoble a great man's ancestors ; Menelaus greeted Telemachus as a son of 'god-born kings', for no man who was 'low born' could have been his father ; and Sir James Barrie's 'Admirable Crichton', when master of the lonely island, remembered that he had been 'a king in Babylon'. All stars appear higher to man than they are in the skies ; for while the line of light curves, the human eye follows the tangent to the last short span of the distant road which the ray has traversed ; the past is always seen on the line of the present. No 'Admirable Crichton', Beau Nash, or Brummel is asked for his genealogical credentials ; they are taken for granted (or dispensed with) even in the leisurely life of ease, where there is more scope for fastidiousness and distinctions than in the serious work of the nation. In the phylogenetic history of the Englishman the Oxford undergraduate of my own time corresponded to the eighteenth-century man, and with him nearly foremost among social qualifications was that a man should be amusing. Anyone can enter English society provided he can live, think, and feel like those who have built up its culture in their freer, easier hours.

English civilisation is essentially the work of the leisured classes. We have no word to render the German idea of *Wissenschaft*, and we restrict the term of 'science' to branches in which (alas !) the necessary labour and laboratories cannot be hidden. The German prefaces his monumental work by long chapters on methodology, and hesitates ever to take down the scaffolding which he has erected, for fear people might think the building had grown by itself. We prefer to make it appear as if our ideas came to us casually — like the Empire — in a fit of absence of mind. *Literae Humaniores*, the most English of schools, goes back to the all-round man of the Renaissance. For specialisation necessarily entails distortion of mind and loss of balance, and the characteristically English attempt to appear unscientific springs from a desire to remain human. It is not true that Englishmen have little respect for mental achievements. Whereas on the Continent scholarships rank as poor relief, at Oxford or Cambridge the scholar holds a privileged position, coveted as a distinction. More intellectual work is done by aristocrats in England than anywhere else, and, in turn, scientists, doctors, historians, and poets have been made peers — to say nothing of the discipline most closely connected with the State, law, where peerages have for centuries been the regular and almost unavoidable prizes for the leaders of the profession ; but no German *Gelehrter* was ever made a baron or a count. What is not valued in England is abstract knowledge as a profession, because the tradition of English civilisation is that professions should be practical and culture should be the work of the leisured classes.

The English landowners, for centuries past, have not tilled their land ; they had no serfs to work it, nor did they do so with hired labour ; they leased it out to small farmers. In the eighteenth century, in some Continental countries estates were measured by the number of 'souls' (serfs attached to their soil), in others by the number of 'smokes' (chimneys — homesteads), yet in others by their acreage ; in England alone they were described in terms of their rental. The work of the owner on an English landed estate was, and remains, primarily administrative ; but, though more exacting than it may seem to outsiders, it has always left the owners a fair amount of leisure for social administration and for political work, for literary and scientific pursuits, for agricultural experiments on the home farm, for 'improvements' (the building of mansions, the laying out of gardens, the developing of mines and various industrial enterprises on their estates, the making of roads and canals, etc.), for outdoor sports and recreations, for social intercourse, for life in town, and for foreign travel. The one thing never mentioned in the sketch of Sir Roger de Coverley or of Squire Western is agricultural work, such as was done until recently on big estates in Central and Eastern Europe under the immediate supervision of their owners ; nor is it obvious nowadays in the life of the average English country house. But primarily on the rental of England were raised her political system and lore, and her civilisation.

This civilisation is neither urban nor rural ; the English ruling classes have for centuries been amphibious. In Germany there has always been a sharp division between the towns and the 'land' outside ; many towns for a long time preserved an independence which emphasised still more the division, but the political power in the big Germanic States was in the hands of the 'agrarians', who, except for a small circle of Court aristo-cracy, lived on their land. In Italy during the Renaissance, the cities were dominant, and the big landowners inhabited them, as they did in ancient Greece and Rome ; in some places (*e.g.* at Treviso) they were even forbidden by law to live outside the city walls. In eighteenth-century England the ruling classes lived neither in fortified castles, nor in agrarian manor-houses, nor in town palaces, but in palatial mansions planted out on their estates (the suburban system of our time is merely a replica of that amphibious life, democratised and rendered accessible to a large part of the nation). Few attempts at out-side architecture have been made by the English aristocracy in their town houses ; no Chatsworth, or Longleat, or Harewood was ever built in Bloomsbury, Piccadilly, or Mayfair. But in the country the atmosphere and character of town civilisation clings to their houses ; they certainly are neither primitive nor rustic.

In style the English country house is not the product of the English countryside ; some old Tudor or Jacobean mansions may still pass as autochthonous ; the Georgian house bears witness to the classicism of the English mind ; the pseudo-Gothic 'castle', or a mansion Palladian in front and Gothic at the back, to a 'grand tour' gone wrong. The English country house dominates its surroundings ; no old forest reaches its doors, as in America ; nor does it, like an Ukrainian manor-house, hide in a 'yar' (cañon), from fear of the endless steppes above, and of the sharp winds which sweep them. Its civilising influence spreads over the lawns which surround it, over the turf and trees in the park ; they are not much interfered with nowadays, and yet bear such a peculiarly well-groomed appearance.

But the eighteenth century, with its exuberant zeal and

ingenious conceit, did not allow parks to live their own lives ;
the *furor hortensis*, the passion for landscape gardening, reigned
supreme.   Chatham on one occasion, when summoned on
urgent business to London, mapped out a garden for a friend
by torchlight ; and Thomas Whately, M.P., Secretary to the
Treasury, who had a prominent share in drafting the American
Stamp Act, was best known to his own generation as the
author of *Observations on Modern Gardening* — he could not
leave things alone.   England offers exceptional facilities for
landscape gardening ; no dominant natural features, 'absolutely
vertical' or 'absolutely horizontal' — high mountains, wide
plains, or great rivers — interfere with the fancies of men.
Within the limited space, closed in by hills and mists, noble
views can be opened up and pointed with pleasing objects.
Here is the story of William Shenstone, an eighteenth-century
poet, and of rural taste as then conceived :

> In 1745 he took possession of his paternal estate, when his delight
> in rural pleasures, and his ambition of rural elegance was excited;
> he began from this time to point his prospects, to diversify his
> service, to entangle his walks, and to wind his waters ; which he did
> with such judgement, and such fancy, as made his little domain the
> envy of the great and the admiration of the skilful; a place to be
> visited by travellers and copied by designers. . . .
> He spent his estate in adorning it, and his death was probably
> hastened by his anxieties.   He was a lamp that spent its oil in
> blazing.[1]

The zeal and conceit of the upper classes of eighteenth-
century England, which spent much of its best oil 'in blazing',
have been paid for heavily, in matters small and great ; but it
was thus that Englishmen learnt to leave things well alone —
to refrain from drawing up elaborate, artificial, naive schemes
for parks or Empires.   The self-restraint and conscious rectitude
of a neo-Puritanism, 'undemonstrative, gentlemanlike, and
reasonable', had to be superimposed on the curious, voracious,
acquisitive, utterly egotistic, and amoral energy of the
eighteenth century, before the Englishman could change from

---

[1] A MS. note on William Shenstone by Elizabeth Gulston (presumably
the sister of Joseph Gulston, M.P., the print collector), inserted in a copy
of his letters to Lady Luxborough, now in the British Museum.

a rover into a ruler. The eighteenth century was the childhood of Imperial Britain.

The Land as Basis of Citizenship

The relations of groups of men to plots of land, of organised communities to units of territory, form the basic content of political history. The conflicting territorial claims of communities constitute the greater part of conscious international history ; social stratifications and convulsions, primarily arising from the relationship of men to land, make the greater, not always fully conscious, part of the domestic history of nations — and even under urban and industrial conditions ownership of land counts for more than is usually supposed. To every man, as to Brutus, the native land is his life-giving Mother, and the State raised upon the land his law-giving Father ; and the days cannot be long of a nation which fails to honour either. Only one nation has survived for two thousand years, though an orphan — my own people, the Jews. But then in the God-given Law we have enshrined the authority of a State, and in the God-promised Land the idea of a Mother-Country ; through the centuries from Mount Sinai we have faced Arets Israel, our land. Take away either, and we cease to be a nation ; let both live again, and we shall be ourselves once more.

When a tribe settles, membership in the tribe carries the right to a share in the land. In time the order becomes inverted : the holding of land determines a man's position in the community. There is some well-nigh mystic power in the ownership of space — for it is not the command of resources alone which makes the strength of the landowner, but that he has a place in the world which he can call his own, from which he can ward off strangers, and in which he himself is rooted — the superiority of a tree to a log. In land alone can there be real patrimony, and he who as freeman holds a share in his native land — the freeholder — is, and must be, a citizen. Wealth consists of an accumulation, or the command, of goods and chattels ; the idea of inalienable property, cherished beyond its patent value, arises from the land. Throughout the

centuries rich English business men have therefore aimed at
acquiring landed estates and founding 'county families' — they
have commuted wealth into property, be it at a loss of revenue.
Even the tiny garden at the back of the workman's house is a
'corner of his own', for which the clean courtyard of model
buildings is no compensation ; and in the most reduced, im-
poverished form the 'corner of one's own' still appeared until
recently, as a qualification for full citizenship, in the latchkey
franchise.   It was not in rental and leisure alone that the
superiority of the landed classes was grounded in eighteenth-
century England, but even more in the ease of the well-balanced
existence of men who had their share in the land and the State.

In the eighteenth century this connexion between ownership of land and a share in the State was acknowledged and
upheld by Tories and Whigs alike.   Swift claimed that 'law in
a free country is, or ought to be, the determination of the
majority of those who have property in land',[1] while Defoe
considered that in case of a dissolution of government the power
would devolve on the freeholders, 'the proper owners of the
country', the other inhabitants being 'but sojourners, like
lodgers in a house'.   'I make no question but property of land
is the best title to government in the world'.[2]   And on the
very eve of the American Revolution, constitutional right, as
arising from the ownership of land, was pleaded by the Continental Congress in the address *To the People of Great Britain*,
voted at Philadelphia on 5 September 1774 : 'Are not the
proprietors of the soil of Great Britain lords of their own
property ?   Can it be taken from them without their consent ? . . . Why then are the proprietors of the soil of America
less lords of their property than you are of yours ?'

English history, and especially English Parliamentary
history, is made by families rather than by individuals ; for
a nation with a tradition of self-government must have thousands
of dynasties, partaking of the peculiarities which in other
countries belong to the royal family alone.   The English

[1] *Thoughts on Various Subjects*, first edition of his *Works*, 1735, vol. i.
p. 306.
[2] Daniel Defoe, *The Original Power of the Collective Body of the People
of England* (third edition, 1702), p. 16.

political family is a compound of 'blood', name, and estate, this last, as the dominions of monarchs, being the most important of the three ; that is why mansions instead of families are so often the subject of monographs dealing with the history of the English upper classes. The name is a weighty symbol, but liable to variations ; descent traced in the male line only, is like a river without its tributaries ; [1] the estate, with all that it implies, is, in the long run, the most potent factor in securing continuity through identification, the 'taking up' of the inheritance. The owner of an ancestral estate may have far less of the 'blood' than some distant relative bearing a different name, but sprung from a greater number of intermarriages between descendants of the founder of the family ; still, it is he who in his thoughts and feelings most closely identifies himself, and is identified by others, with his predecessors. Primogeniture and entails psychologically help to preserve the family in that they tend to fix its position through the successive generations, and thereby favour conscious identification.

There is a curious interplay between men and land in British history ; interlocked, they seem to compete for dominion — which will stamp the name upon the other ? In eighteenth-century Scotland, the individual was practically nameless between his clan and his land ; men were called by their estates.[2] In England, after a man had founded a family on an estate, the estate would often convey the name of its founder to heirs receiving it through a woman, and sometimes even to heirs unconnected by blood. Thomas Brodnax (M.P. for

[1] Ten generations back, which means, as a rule, less than three centuries, a man has (barring the inevitable repetitions which result from inter-marriages) more than a thousand progenitors ; at the time of the Norman Conquest, this would make about a thousand millions ! The mathematical probability is therefore distinctly in favour of every Englishman being descended from every person who was in this country at the time of the Conquest and has left descendants.

[2] Scotsmen did not even necessarily impose their names on their wives, and their own designation varied with their residence or estate. Gilbert Elliot, in June 1742, thus concluded a letter to William Mure of Caldwell, M.P. : 'Dear Glanderston, adieu' ; to which the editor has added the following explanation : 'Glanderston was an old estate, and frequent residence of the Caldwell family about this period. Hence occasionally preferred to Caldwell as the title of the proprietor'. See *Caldwell Papers* (1854), part ii. vol. i. p. 29.

Canterbury), on inheriting Rawmere in 1727, changed his name to May, but in 1738, on inheriting Chawton in Hampshire, to Knight;[1] William Evelyn (M.P. for Hythe), on marrying Frances, daughter and heiress of William Glanville, assumed her name, but when in 1742, after his wife's death, their only daughter married Admiral Boscawen, and thereby 'carried her estate to that family', William Evelyn 'resumed his original name';[2] and Percy Wyndham, M.P., the second son of the famous Tory leader, William Wyndham, on inheriting estates under the will of Lord Thomond, the husband of his mother's sister, assumed the name of O'Brien, though in no way descended from that family.[3]

Landed property of any kind is called 'realty', all other property being 'personalty'. Under most legal systems the rules of inheritance with regard to 'realty' are determined by its location — it has its own 'nationality'; 'personalty' follows the law and nationality of its owner. British citizenship itself can be derived from men or from land, from the nationality of the parents or the land of birth. The pre-eminent rights of landowners have often been explained by their having 'the greatest stake in the country', and certainly *qua* landowners they cannot withdraw themselves from the burdens which weigh on the permanent territorial framework of the nation — for instance, the national debt or misgovernment; as Locke put it, there was 'always annexed to the enjoyment of land a submission to the government of the country of which that land is a part'.[4] By a logical equation, if one's thinking inclines that way, one may therefore conclude that the men who are most intimately affected by the government have a primary claim to a share in it; in reality this conclusion is based on instincts and modes of thinking much deeper and much more cogent than any conscious reasonings, but into which it is not necessary here to enter.

For centuries a freehold in England has carried with it the

---

[1] See W. A. Leigh and M. G. Knight, *Chawton Manor and its Owners* (1911), pp. 142-3.
[2] See Helen Evelyn, *History of the Evelyn Family* (1915), pp. 561-2.
[3] See G. E. C., *Complete Peerage*, under 'Thomond'.
[4] *Of Civil Government*, § 73.

most signal mark of citizenship, a vote ; estates carried with them seats in the Great Council of the nation ; and these connexions were pressed so far that at times the land of England, rather than her people, seemed to be represented in her Parliament. This was the avowed doctrine when the *barones majores* personally attended it in right of their fiefs. But the interplay between men and land soon attached the writ to the heirs of 'the body', rather than of the land. The House of Lords lost its original basis, but the leading landowners, if not of baronial rank, reappeared in the House of Commons as well-nigh hereditary, though not immovable, representatives of the shires and boroughs in which they held 'the best property'. Still, in the Commons they formed one element only, and in the elections their property was one factor only, supremely important but not exclusive or statutory. The House of Commons became the dominant assembly because it was the most comprehensive ; it did not suffer from any rigid, logical rules, which the English mind abhors, and it had, what Englishmen always try to find, a common practical denominator. 'The Commons in Parliament are not the representative body of the whole Kingdome,' wrote Sir Robert Filmer in 1648 ; 'they do not represent the King, who is the head and principall member of the Kingdome, nor do they represent the Lords. . . .' [1] Whatever the position had been in 1648, Filmer's dictum was patently untrue in the eighteenth century ; through patronage, borough influence, and territorial predominance, both King and Lords were well represented in the Commons, but in terms commensurable with those of the rest of the nation.

This is not the place to discuss the mutual relations of the two Houses, their personnel and the intimate connexions which existed between them in the eighteenth century ; what primarily concerns us here is their connexion with the land of Great Britain. Although the writ to the 'heirs male of the body' had been made the basis of most peerages, the idea of attachment to certain lands continued even in the eighteenth century — witness the revival of numerous peerages in heirs to peers' estates who had no claim to the title ; occasionally a peerage

[1] *The Anarchy of a Limited or Mixed Monarchy*, p. 14.

was revived even in an heir who was in no way connected by blood with his predecessors — Percy (Wyndham) O'Brien, mentioned above, was in 1756 created Earl of Thomond in the peerage of Ireland, thus succeeding even to the title of the husband of his mother's sister, whose estates he had inherited and whose name he had adopted. The possession of estates which had belonged to peers was still always considered to carry with it a certain claim to a peerage ; this is shown, e.g., by the curious phrase which, on 19 May 1756, the Duke of Newcastle used, when conveying to Lord Chetwynd (an Irish peer) the refusal of an English peerage : 'The King makes very few peers at present, and one who is most nearly allied to me, and has, I may say, better pretensions than any body, having the estates of two peers in him, whose peerages are, in a manner, sunk, will not be of the number.'[1]

It is but natural that in the absence of a secret ballot the possession of land in counties or boroughs should have carried with it considerable influence in Parliamentary elections through the pressure which its owners were able to exert on their tenants. But in eighteenth-century England this element of crude pressure shades off by almost imperceptible degrees into a tradition which connected a claim to the representation of certain constituencies even with specific estates, not because of their size or location only, but because of some mysterious tradition which seemed to attach to them and to be conveyed to their owners. To uphold such a tradition was well-nigh a duty incumbent on their possessor. To give one example : the Newport family had long been predominant in Shropshire, and Lord Bath, having purchased the reversion of part of their estates from the mother of the illegitimate son of Henry, 3rd Earl of Bradford, put up his son for Shrewsbury in 1759,

---

[1] Add. MSS. 32865, f. 51. The same case is mentioned in Newcastle's letter to Sir Jacob Downing (22 May 1756 ; Add. MSS. 32865, f. 87) : 'I was forc'd to submit the pretensions of my nephew Watson (who has the estates and, in some measure, the peerages of two peers, who are as it were sunk in him) to His Majesty's favour upon some other occasion'. Lewis (Monson) Watson, second son of John, 1st Lord Monson, inherited the estates of his maternal grandfather, Lewis, 1st Earl of Rockingham: He was Newcastle's nephew by marriage, his wife being a daughter of Henry Pelham. He was created Lord Sondes in 1760.

pleading that this was his 'duty to the Bradford interest' [1] (a conception of duty extraordinary, even as an 'explanation', when professed to an estate which Lord Bath did not as yet own, and of which, indeed, neither he nor his son lived to acquire possession).[2]   But an even more striking 'example of the abiding nature of political tradition which could be furnished only in England' — and one should add, of territorial tradition in politics — was given in a letter from Alfred Robbins in *The Times* on 4 November 1924, after the general election of that year : 'Mr. A. M. Williams, who has won the seat for the Northern Division of Cornwall, is a son of Mr. John Charles Williams . . . who holds the estate of Werrington' ; this, for more than two centuries, 'was considered by electoral managers to carry with it the representation of Launceston, which is the chief town of the Northern Division of Cornwall. . . .'   From 1650 till 1865 the estate of Werrington and the Parliamentary representation of Launceston were held in succession by Sir Francis Drake, the Morices, and the Percys ; in 1865, a Manchester cotton merchant, who had bought Werrington, 'was promptly returned for Launceston' ; in 1874, its next owner, a Cheshire brewer, explicitly claimed that Launceston ought to be represented by him or his nominee — which it was, till disfranchised in 1885 ; 'the long spell of "Werrington influence" politically dominant in the district since 1650, was then broken, only to be revived in 1924'.

In our days a case of this kind, if not accidental, would at least be treated as incidental — interesting but not important. In the eighteenth century the superiority of property, especially of landed property, over men was an acknowledged fact, and to neglect it would be to miss one of the main factors in the political thinking and practice of the age.   The following letter from 'Solomon Seewell', in the *London Chronicle* of 2–4 April 1761, discussing the expected creation of new peers, has a

---

[1] Lord Bath to Robert More, some time in June 1759 ; MS. Top. Salop, c. 3, in the Bodleian Library, at Oxford.

[2] Possession of these estates was acquired by Lord Bath's distant collateral heirs in 1783.   About them see *The Grenville Papers*, vol. i. p. 17 ; Edward Lloyd, *Antiquities of Shropshire* (1844), p. 243 ; H. E. Forrest, 'Some Old Shropshire Houses and their Owners', in the *Transactions of the Shropshire Archaeological Society*, 4th Series, vol. vii. Part ii. (1920), p. 110.

peculiar flavour in its naïve and matter-of-fact treatment of the subject :

It is said many millions of property is going to be added to the weight of the upper house of parliament. If so, it may be proper to consider how much it is likely to weaken the scale of power to the Commons. . . .

Property in counties, as well as boroughs, commands the choice of representatives ; and if the bulk of property should once more get into the hands of members of the upper house, that will secure to them the appointment of the representatives of the people, when their own children and dependents will become the disposers at their pleasure of our liberties and fortunes.

Did then the eighteenth-century Parliament represent the men or the land of Great Britain ? One might as well ask to whom the child owes its life, to the father or the mother ? It represented both ; or to put it more accurately, it represented British men rooted in the soil of Great Britain. Those roaming beyond its borders were not (and are not) represented, while all those within its borders (even if they had no votes) were considered to have been represented, 'virtually' at least, through the land on which they lived.[1] The very definition of 'virtual representation' implicitly declared its character : there was 'not a blade of grass in Great Britain' which was unrepresented in Parliament. But because territorial rather than tribal, the British Parliament could not (and cannot) cover those definitely rooted in other soil, nor 'virtually' represent the 'blades of grass' of other lands, even if inhabited by men of the same stock. The first British Empire suffered disruption because Englishmen failed as yet to distinguish between a 'Mother Country' and a 'native land' ; and between the distant, sublimated authority of the Crown, symbolically 'paternal', and

[1] 'Virtual representation' is no purely British invention, still less a mere ingenious fiction to palliate the absurdities of the unreformed House of Commons. In the seventeenth and eighteenth centuries the Lithuanian Jews had a communal Parliament of their own, called in Hebrew 'Vaad' (Council). Its members were elected by the capital towns alone of the five territorial divisions into which Lithuanian Jewry was divided, but the members of each were deemed to represent all the other communes in their division, even though these had no share in returning them. See article on 'The Lithuanian Vaad' by M. Wischnitzer, in the *Istorya Yevreyskavo Naroda* (*History of the Jewish People*), Moscow, 1914, vol. xi.

the direct governmental power which in a free country is wielded by the sons of the soil. A tribal sovereignty can be common to members of the race scattered through various countries ; the supreme power in a self-governing country must be in those acknowledging it as the mother who gave them birth.

THE STATE

Beginning with God — *abhinu, malkenu* ('our Father, our King') — all authority is paternal, and therefore all authority was deemed to be 'of God'. Kings, as incarnation of authority, have been termed fathers, in Eastern Europe down to our own days ; and the great seventeenth-century English champion of absolute monarchy, 'the learned Sir Robert Filmer, Baronet', summed up his doctrine in *Patriarcha, or the Natural Power of Kings*. 'Even the power which God himself exerciseth over mankind', wrote Filmer, 'is by right of fatherhood ; he is both the King and Father of us all.' [1] 'The subjection of children to their parents is the fountain of all regal authority.' [2] 'It is true, all kings be not the natural parents of their subjects . . . yet in their right succeed to the exercise of supreme jurisdiction.' [3] 'All power on earth is either derived or usurped from the fatherly power.' [4] 'The law which enjoyns obedience to kings is delivered in the terms of Honour thy father.' [5] Similarly John Winthrop, the Puritan Governor of Massachusetts, a contemporary of Sir Robert Filmer, but who could not have been acquainted with Filmer's works and certainly would not have accepted his conclusions, declared, when arguing against democracy, that to allow it in Massachusetts would be 'a manifest breach of the 5th Commandment'.[6]

From the paternal and quasi-divine character of authority, Filmer drew conclusions to suit his own instincts and inclinations : that government should be monarchical and absolute.

---

[1] 'Directions for Obedience to Government in Dangerous and Doubtful Times', published as an appendix to *Observations touching Forms of Government*, edition of 1696, p. 159.
[2] *Patriarcha*, p. 12.   [3] *Ibid.* p. 19.
[4] *Observations*, p. 158.   [5] *Patriarcha*, p. 23.
[6] See R. C. Winthrop, *Life and Letters of John Winthrop* (1867), p. 430.

These conclusions he fortified with twisted Biblical quotations and a mass of cumbrous learning. John Locke destroyed Filmer's superstructure in his famous *Two Treatises of Government*, in fine language and with irresistible logic, both, so far as Filmer was concerned, misdirected to a futile purpose. Were one roughly to sum up the essence of their respective arguments, one might describe Filmer's thesis as a postulate that the 'political child' should never grow up at all — and in fact vast numbers of individuals and even whole nations never do grow up ; while Locke's fundamental assumption is that the 'political child', having attained manhood, discards all the memories and instincts of its childhood, which, though possibly desirable, never is, nor can be, achieved. Still, after having destroyed Filmer's arguments and made great play with the inclusion of the mother in the Fifth Commandment, Locke finished by admitting the paternal origin, and implicitly the paternal character, of government :

. . . it was easy, and almost natural for children by a tacit and scarce avoidable consent to make way for the father's authority and government. They had been accustomed in their childhood to follow his direction, and to refer their little differences to him ; and when they were men, who fitter to rule them ? . . . 'Tis no wonder that they made no distinction betwixt minority and full age ; nor looked after one-and-twenty or any other age that might make them the free disposers of themselves and fortunes, when they could have no desire to be out of their pupilage. . . .
Thus the natural fathers of families by an insensible change became the politic monarchs of them too. . . .[1]

Whether the theory of an actual paternal origin of government is a correct phylogenetic or logical inference, or merely a psychological delusion, we shall probably never know ; but this much is certain, that it is an assumption natural to us all. Correct perception of a psychological fact underlay Sir Robert Filmer's theory : all authority is to human beings paternal in character, for they are born, not free and independent as some of Filmer's opponents would have it, but subject to parental authority ; in the first place, to that of their fathers. The

[1] *Of Civil Government*, §§ 75 and 76.

development of every man, in his individual life, obviously
proceeds from subjection to freedom, and it proves arrested
growth if full freedom is never reached, and if inwardly he
carries on the revolutionary (or counter-revolutionary) struggle
long after he himself should have attained uncontending
authority. For in the life of every man comes a night when
at the ford of the stream he has to strive 'with God and with
men'; if he prevails and receives the blessing of the father-
spirit, he is henceforth free and at peace.

Above individual men rises the community, the State.
There the struggle is repeated, on an infinitely wider stage,
in terms similar to those of man's individual life, and yet in
dimensions which are beyond the understanding of the average
man. For man is able in a quasi-mechanical, agglutinative
manner, to construct monstrous Leviathans which exceed his
consciously regulated norms and his comprehension. A sudden
expansion of the State, whether in territorial size or in the
numbers of individuals which it comprises as active members,
is frequently, and even usually, accompanied by a retrograde
movement in matters of self-government ; at every stage in
social development freedom has to be reconquered.

In absolute monarchies the political child never outgrows
its nonage, and at the utmost changes into a revolutionary.
But there is still a long way from revolution to active self-
government. The essence of our own present system is that
the idea and symbols of authority are raised above the gerents
of power and made inaccessible to them. The fact that the
'paternal' authority of the State centres in the Crown, whose
bearer does not, and must not, in any way personally exercise
it, establishes a psychological equality between the actual rulers
of the State and those governed by them, and between the
winning and the losing side in the political struggle ; it secures
both the idea of authority and the unity of the nation.

Royalty, as the embodiment of the paternal idea, supplies
the most natural and most appropriate expression to tribal
unity, and as such is unrestricted by territorial limits. A compact and centralised national State can form a republic, and a
State comprising vast or diversified but contiguous territories, a

federal republic; the British Empire, united in its origins, racial and ideological, but scattered over various continents, must have for its bond the great royal symbol of paternal authority, divested, however, of executive power, which in free communities has to be with the grown-up children of each land. Benjamin Franklin declared : '. . . the British empire is not a single state ; it comprehends many . . . We have the same King, but not the same legislatures' ; [1] '. . . the Parliament has no right to make any law whatever, binding on the colonies ; . . . the king, and not the king, lords, and commons collectively, is their sovereign'.[2] And he objected to 'a claim of subjects in one part of the King's dominions to be sovereigns over their fellow-subjects in another part of his dominions'.[3] 'Every man in England seems to consider himself as a piece of a sovereign over America ; seems to jostle himself into the throne with the King, and talks of *our subjects in the Colonies.*' [4]

Franklin's thesis was correct, but the constitutional ideas and practice of Great Britain hardly allowed as yet of its application. The King in Parliament and the King as first magistrate — the head of the executive — had to become well-nigh a fiction, a shadow, before he could acquire a free symbolic existence, outside the British Parliament and apart from it. But in eighteenth-century England, the King was still a real factor in Administration.

GOVERNMENT AND TRADE

A State must have a territorial basis, but government can exist without it, for example, in migrating tribes or in armies engaged on distant expeditions, which, having to face new and changing circumstances, require, if anything, more government than a settled nation. Though the State primarily belongs to the owners of the land, it is the circulating part of the nation which is most directly concerned with government;

---

[1] To Barbeu Dubourg, 2 October 1770 ; *The Life and Writings of Benjamin Franklin*, edited by A. H. Smyth (1905-7), vol. v. p. 280.
[2] To William Franklin, 6 October 1773, vol. vi. p. 144.
[3] To Samuel Cooper, of Boston, 8 June 1770 ; vol. v. p. 260.
[4] To Lord Kames, 11 April 1767 ; vol. v. p. 17.

and governments, as all human institutions, are influenced and shaped by those who are willing to work and pay for them, *i.e.* those who need them most. The merchant who moves among strangers requires organised assistance more than the agricultural labourer or the landowner ; moreover, trade is, in its very nature, social, while agriculture starts with self-sufficiency and always retains a considerable measure of it ; consequently trade is at all times much more the subject of legislation than agriculture. The constitutional distinction between internal and external taxation, still accepted in England about 1630, in America about 1760, and in Hungary about 1840, testifies to the direct connexion between the government and the merchant trading with foreign countries. The frontiers are the King's, they belong to the government and to the whole tribe, rather than to the fraction settled within them (the Dominions, as distinguished from the Empire, until recently had no jurisdiction beyond their coast-line). The desert, the sea, and the towns have developed the purest, strongest types of male religion and governments apart from territory. The urban, trading element was for centuries over-represented in the House of Commons ; and even after most of the borough representation had passed into the hands of the aristocracy and landed gentry, trade none the less continued to hold a most conspicuous place in British political thought and action.

Trade is the natural form for the acquisitive endeavours of islanders. But for purposes of trade all shores border on the ships of a seafaring nation ; and water is the earliest high-road in history for the transport of bulky objects, not merely of luxuries. The idea, at one time current among economists, that the profits of trade depended upon the distance covered and the time consumed, crudely expressed facts of common experience. Trade depends on a diversity of produce, which is more likely to be found between distant than between neighbouring countries ; and trade between distant countries is a venture not to be attempted on a small scale, so that it requires considerable capital, and consequently results in more than average profits — up to a certain point the very rate of profits increases with the size of the capital. Trade at great distance and on a considerable scale leads to capitalism with its peculiar 'trading' ideology, very different from, and indeed opposed to, that of militarism. As ships, the carriers of trade, are at the same time the 'wooden walls' of an island, the trading spirit of its population is not checked and countered by militarism, which in France, Italy, and Germany, ultimately engulfed and destroyed the spirit and enterprise of the seaboard. The rise of powerful monarchies on the Continent had by the beginning of the sixteenth century interlocked them in rivalry and war, riveting their attention to the European Continent at the very time when their superior strength expelled England from it. England was forced to remain an island, which Venice and Holland could be only in a very imperfect manner.

Naval power and commerce, 'like twins', are 'born together, and not to live asunder',[1] and oversea trade is a venture never to be despised by an island nation. In the Anglo-Saxon laws it was written that 'if a merchant thrived, so that he fared thrice over the wide sea by his own means [craft], then was he thenceforth of thaneright worthy'.[2] Trade with distant countries, across oceans, along untrodden paths, is something very different from keeping a booth at a country fair. George Cartwright rejoiced when in Labrador he exchanged 'a small ivory comb', which had cost him 'no more than twopence halfpenny' in England, against a silver fox 'worth four guineas';[3] but the hardships braved in the polar region, his refusal of a fine offered by Eskimos in atonement for an attempted theft,[4] in fact, the general character of his ventures, shows that he, the brother of Edmund Cartwright, the inventor, and Major John Cartwright, the reformer, was no mere trader. Continental nations engaged in wars for loot and talked of glory; the English

---

[1] Defoe, *A Plan of the English Commerce*, 3rd edition (1749), p. 150.

[2] *Ancient Laws and Institutes of England*, ed. by B. Thorpe (1840), p. 81.

[3] George Cartwright, *A Journal of Transactions and Events, during a Residence of nearly Sixteen Years on the Coast of Labrador* (1792), vol. i. p. 145.

[4] 'The man . . . returned with a beautiful seal-skin as a present to me; but I would by no means accept of it, making him and the rest understand, that I did not quarrel with him, that he should make me a present to be reconciled; but because he had been guilty of a dishonest action; and that as he now seemed to be sensible of his crime, I was perfectly satisfied' (*op. cit.* vol. i. p. 240).

went out for adventures and talked of trade. But Horace Walpole, a sentimental and unemotional pacifist, shrewdly suspected that 'trade' was often a mere excuse for things which other men explained in different terms.

I am a bad Englishman, because I think the advantages of commerce are dearly bought for some by the lives of many more. . . . But . . . every age has some ostentatious system to excuse the havoc it commits. Conquest, honour, chivalry, religion, balance of power, commerce, no matter what, mankind must bleed, and take a term for a reason.[1]

Still, the terms in which men try to account for their actions are of supreme importance ; every country and every age has dominant terms, which seem to obsess men's thoughts. Those of eighteenth-century England were property, contract, trade, and profits. Locke, its teacher, declared that 'government has no other end but the preservation of property',[2] but under the term 'property' he included a man's 'life, liberty, and estate' ; [3] this was not the narrow 'nightwatchman conception of the State' as developed in the nineteenth century, but a terminology dominated by the sense of ownership.[4] However much Mandeville explained away his *Fable of the Bees*, it was significant that he should have placed moral and economic values, to say the least, on one level. Possibly the reducing of all values to one common money denominator was to some extent stimulated by the discovery of the atom, a common unit in an infinitely diversified creation — social and moral disciplines, having no exact measures of their own and yet trying to simulate precision, are singularly liable to be influenced by terms and conceptions borrowed from science. The quantitative theory of happiness of the English 'utilitarians' was, no doubt, psycho-

[1] To Sir H. Mann, 26 May 1762.
[2] *Of Civil Government*, § 94.   [3] *Ibid.* § 87.
[4] Similarly with the Americans 'property' stood in the centre of their thinking, and 'liberty' itself was merely a function and safeguard of 'property'. It is thus that Abel Stiles, a New Englander, wrote to Ezra Stiles on 18 April 1766, about resistance to the Stamp Act (Stiles MSS., in the Yale College Library, New Haven, Conn.) :

Shall Revelation say stand fast and contend earnestly for the Faith — and doth not the God of Nature, the God of Civil Liberty and property say stand fast. . . . Pray what forbids us to resist even unto blood, where that freedom is in question, the death of which is the death of property, as the pregnant mother's death is fatal to the infant unborn.

logically connected with this habit of reducing moral values to the money unit.

Does this common money denominator signify a peculiarly materialistic turn of mind in the eighteenth century ? It might perhaps be fairer to give the matter a broader basis. The later eighteenth century in England was an eclectic and inquisitive age, inventive in material production and mechanics, in time- and labour-saving devices ; primarily an age of collectors, with a passion for accumulating no matter what — books, prints, manuscripts, shells, pictures, old coins, or the currency of the realm. For at bottom it does not matter much what a man collects — money, buttons, or irrelevant knowledge — it de- notes the same stage in development. But when the collecting habit gets hold of a whole community, the apparent result is materialism ; and trade becomes the great watchword in politics.

The Duke of Newcastle, a year before his death, summed up the record of his life by speaking of his

zealous endeavours to promote, at all times, the true interest of my country, and the security of our religious and civil liberties ; to sup- port the Protestant Succession in His Majesty's Royal Family . . . ; and to contribute all that was in my power to the encouragement and extension of the trade and commerce of these kingdoms.[1]

Lord Hervey wrote in 1734 of 'our trade, which is so much the vital breath of this nation that the one cannot subsist whenever the other is long stopped' ; [2] and George Grenville in 1764 felt flattered when the Spanish ambassador said about him that he 'would lose all he has in the world rather than suffer diminu- tion of the honour of the King his master, or of the commerce of the kingdom' [3] — a juxtaposition typical of eighteenth- century England. Lecky notes with some surprise the mental outlook of the eighteenth-century Parliament :

In very few periods in English political history was the com- mercial element more conspicuous in administration. The prevailing spirit of the debates was of a kind we should rather have expected in a middle-class Parliament than in a Parliament consisting in a

[1] Add. MSS. 32987, f. 204. See also his letter to the Archbishop of Canterbury, 2 February 1766 (Add. MSS. 32973, ff. 342-4) : 'I have been bred up to think, that the trade of this nation is the sole support of it'.

[2] *Memoirs* (ed. Romney Sedgwick), ii. 351.

[3] *The Grenville Papers*, vol. ii. p. 516.

very large measure of the nominees of great families. . . . The questions which excited most interest were chiefly financial and commercial ones. The increase of the National Debt, the possibility and propriety of reducing its interest, the advantages of a Sinking Fund, the policy of encouraging trade by bounties and protective duties, the evils of excise, the reduction of the land-tax, the burden of Continental subsidies, were among the topics which produced the most vehement and the most powerful debates.[1]

His description is accurate. Young, ambitious Members of the gentry class eagerly engaged in the study of trade and finance, and someone in an official position, in 1779, put the following marginal remark on a paper dealing with trade : 'No man sho'd be elligible to sit in the H[ouse] of C[ommons] that has not a competant knowledge in geography and the trade and manufactures of Great Britain'.[2]   Edward Eliot, of Port Eliot, applied to Newcastle for a place at the Board of Trade, because he hoped there to obtain 'such information as may enable some of us young people who act together to put in execution the resolution we have formed, of endeavouring to speak in the House of Commons upon points of business'.[3]   When in 1759 Hans Stanley asked to be made a Lord of the Treasury, he declared to Newcastle : 'The chief employment of my studies has been the revenue and the commercial interests of this country', an assertion amply confirmed by his memoranda on financial subjects. To Charles Jenkinson's studies of these subjects, his papers, now in the British Museum, bear witness. In fact, in the eighteenth century detailed economic information and sound economic speculation is found even in quarters where one would hardly have expected them. In 1754 Newcastle transmitted to William Murray (subsequently Lord Mansfield) two papers on financial matters 'from two country gentlemen, Mr. Campion and Mr. Page . . . the one from an old man of seventy-four who never was above one year and half in busyness and that forty years ago, the other from a clerk

---

[1] *England in the Eighteenth Century*, vol. i. pp. 433-4.

[2] This remark, in the margin of Roberts's MS. 'Observations on the Trade to Africa', appears against a complaint that the 'gentlemen of the landed interest', and others, 'desert the House when Africa is mentioned', though they attend 'many days to late hours, on a dispute about a road, navigation or inclosure bill' (Eg. MS. 1162 A. ff. 55-6).

[3] 5 October 1756 ; Add. MSS. 32868, ff. 96-7.

in the South Sea House in the year 1720, retired, and settled in the country, now for near thirty years ; the last is a master piece'. [1] Adam Smith was not a lonely figure in his time, least of all in 'that part of Britain usually called Scotland', as can be seen from the correspondence of James Oswald, Gilbert Elliot, or William Mure, all three Members of Parliament. The 'trading' spirit was abroad, and men took pride in the record figures of British trade (unless they tried to make the flesh of their fellow-subjects creep with tales of its decay). When, in 1753, Sir George Savile was put up as candidate for Yorkshire, Mr. Thornhagh (subsequently Hewett), M.P. for Nottingham-shire, in supporting his nomination, argued that he was 'the properest candidate for this trading county, as the situation of his property makes the prosperity of trade more immediately his concern' ; [2] and Lord Ducie, when resigning the Lord Lieutenancy of Gloucestershire, spoke of it with pride as 'this great trading county'.[3] The picture which eighteenth-century Englishmen had of their country, and their view of commerce as the dominant factor in its existence, is reflected in a memo-randum drawn up about 1772 by George III, who in many ways was a typical exponent of the doctrines of his time. He thus envisaged an *entente* between Great Britain and France, and distinguished their relative positions :

Commerce the foundation of a marine can never flourish in an absolute monarchy therefore that branch of grandeur ought to be left to England whilst the great army kept by France gives her a natural preeminence on the continent.[4]

The Imperial Problem

No great historic problem has ever been settled by means of a brilliant idea — an invention in the sphere of politics —

[1] Add. MSS. 32736, ff. 591-4 and 477-81. There is another paper on revenue in the Newcastle MSS. from John Page, M.P. for Chichester, drawn up in October 1757 (Add. MSS. 32875, ff. 340-57), which, too, is very sound ; he argues in it, *e.g.*, in favour of taxing property and not pro-duction, and the rental of houses, not their windows.

[2] Andrew Wilkinson to Newcastle ; Add. MSS. 32732, ff. 313-14.

[3] Ducie to Newcastle, 13 September 1758 ; Add. MSS. 32883, f. 442.

[4] *The Correspondence of King George III*, edited by Sir John Fortescue, vol. ii. p. 429.

when its solution was not latent in circumstances, but many a problem has found settlement by not being pressed at such a moment. 'Indolence, when it is not the result of weakness or vice, is a very great virtue', wrote Shelburne in 1801.[1] Restraint, coupled with the tolerance which it implies and with plain human kindness, is much more valuable in politics than ideas which are ahead of their time ; but restraint was a quality in which the eighteenth-century Englishman was as deficient as most other nations are even now.

By the conquests of the Seven Years' War, the British Empire in America had been enlarged and consolidated, and it was generally felt that the time had come for settling it on a more regular basis ; but all conceptions regarding its future turned round questions of trade and finance. 'Happily for this country', wrote in 1764 Thomas Whately, M.P., Joint Secretary to the Treasury, 'the real and substantial, and those are the commercial interests of Great Britain, are now preferred to every other consideration : and the trade from whence its greatest wealth is derived, and upon which its maritime power is principally founded, depends upon a wise and proper use of the Colonies'.[2] These, as Comptroller Weare explained, were

[1] In his autobiography ; Lord Fitzmaurice, *Life of William, Earl of Shelburne* (1912), vol. i. p. 25.

[2] In his pamphlet on *The Regulations lately made concerning the Colonies* ; this pamphlet, ascribed in the British Museum catalogue to John Campbell, LL.D., was by Thomas Whately (see *Bowdoin-Temple Papers, Collections of the Massachusetts Historical Society*, series vi. vol. ix. p. 77). Whately, who was largely responsible for the Stamp Act and was one of the 'men of business' of the Grenville group, was often represented as hostile to America ; he was not. He wrote to J. Temple, Surveyor-General of the Customs for the Northern District of America, on 8 December 1764, while that Act was being prepared : 'I always loved the Colonies, I am, I always was, curious about them, and very happy when I am employed in any business that relates to them. The present circumstances of affairs gives me a great deal in my office, and the House of Commons must be full of the subject. Tho' much is done, much is still to do before that important and now vast object can be properly settled ; but I am confident it will be done right at last. I know that those who are at present in administration are anxious for the prosperity of the Colonies ; and highly sensible of their importance' (*ibid.* p. 38). W. S. Johnson, agent for Connecticut, wrote to Jared Ingersoll about Whately from London on 18 February 1767, that he 'unhappily . . . entertains mistaken principles and ill opinions with respect to the Colonies though I really think him sincere and that he in truth thinks he is aiming at the real interest of both countries' (Bancroft Transcripts in the New York Public Library, *Connecticut Papers*, pp. 95-6).

not 'planted with a view to founding new empires, but for the sake of trade',[1] for England's 'profit, not her glory'.[2] Although British administrative practice was not nearly as callous as British political theory, and sympathetic concern for the Colonies was shown in hundreds of ways, it was not an article of conscious political thinking. 'Nations have affections for themselves, though they have none for one another', wrote an Irish pamphleteer in 1779 ; 'the body politic has no heart. . . . There is no such thing as political humanity, or, if the sentiment did exist, it is not likely to be found in a country of commerce'.[3]

Thus economic considerations impelled British statesmen to take action with regard to the Empire at a time when, even for constitutional reasons, a true settlement could not be attained. In 1760 Great Britain had not reached a stage at which it would have been possible to remodel the Empire as a federation of self-governing States under a Crown detached from the actual government of any of its component parts. Royalty, which is now the bond of the Empire, was still an active factor in British politics, and to eighteenth-century Englishmen any exercise of its attributes apart from the British Parliament would have seemed a dangerous and unconstitutional reversion to 'prerogative'. This junction between King and Parliament in Great Britain was by itself bound to carry the supremacy of the British Parliament into the Colonies ; and the very fact that George III so thoroughly and loyally stood by the constitutional principles of the time rendered a conflict inevitable — had he entertained any idea of power or authority apart from the British Parliament, he might have welcomed the conception of a separate sovereignty in the Colonies. The necessary limitations to the authority of the British Parliament, a territorial assembly, were not as yet understood.

A social contrast is often drawn between an aristocratic or

---

[1] 'A letter to the Right Honorable the Earl of ——' in the *Collections of the Mass. Hist. Soc.*, series i. vol. i. (1792), pp. 66-7.

[2] See Van Schaack's diary, under 8 October 1779, in H. C. Van Schaack, *The Life of Peter Van Schaack* (New York, 1842), p. 243. He was at that time a loyalist refugee in England.

[3] *Considerations on the Expediency*, etc., Dublin, 1779.

oligarchic Great Britain and democratic Colonies, but the true contrast was not altogether what it seemed. English society was never exclusive, in the sense of adhering to standardised ranks — had it been so, it might have been remembered that many of the Colonists were of the best blood of England ; nor were the Colonies by any means as democratic as American orators would make them appear.[1] But the social structure of England, the product of many centuries of close organic growth, was compact and complex, and outsiders, of whatever rank, could not easily fit themselves into it ; while that of the Colonies was comparatively simple, as it always must be in new countries with a vast, empty hinterland and a moving 'frontier'. Nor was the conception of British superiority over the Colonies based on social distinctions, but much rather on the fetishism of places, which ascribes a certain superiority to the inhabitants of the old country over those who have left it, while preserving its language, customs, traditions, and ideas ; and on that curious family hierarchy of Mother Country and 'children' which appears whenever one part of a nation continues in the old country while another forms a new community, leaving its own past in the custody of those who inherit the land of their common ancestors. The eighteenth-century British claim to superiority over the Colonies was largely the result of thinking in terms of personified countries.[2]

[1] The following case, recorded in a letter from G. Lyman to J. Tyng, 23 May 1759, throws a curious light even on New England 'democracy'. When a certain Mr. Phelps of Hadley was appointed to the Commission of Peace of Northampton County in Massachusetts, the other magistrates wrote to the Governor that they 'beg His Excellency's pardon in their desire of resigning their commissions, in case he sets with them', and alleged that he had been put in 'not for any benefit to him ; but to reflect upon the Justices ; because he, the said Phelps, was not a magistrate's son, etc., but a bricklayer till a few years past'. Lyman indignantly repudiated this allegation, pointing out that Phelps was a lawyer (see the *New England Historical and Genealogical Register*, vol. xi. (1857), p. 79). In England no one made any fuss over Sir Robert Darling being returned to Parliament (in 1768), though 'when a boy he used to keep cows', and afterwards had been 'apprentice to a lapidary' (see O. Marsh, *Biography of Bedfordshire* ; Add. MSS. 21067, f. 62). And even the case of 'Bob' Mackreth, who had been a waiter and billiard-marker at White's, but in 1774 became an M.P., caused amusement rather than indignation.

[2] I cannot enter here at length into this matter, with which I shall deal in a later volume, if ever I write it. For the present, see my article on 'The Disinheritance of America' in the London *Nation*, 26 January 1929.

Almost the only men who about 1770 held the modern British view of the Empire were the English Dissenters ; to them alone, who knew no hierarchy either in religion or politics, the Colonists were so many 'congregations of brethren beyond the seas '. In their own depressed condition, they followed the growth of those communities with a sincere and active love, and with a hope that the new England would some day right the wrongs of the old. That friendship was requited by the American Dissenters, and though sympathy with English Nonconformity naturally did not in any way soften their feelings towards Anglicanism, political or religious, it made them think in terms of the British Empire. Ezra Stiles (subsequently President of Yale University) wrote to the Rev. Dr. Fordyce, a Dissenting minister in London, on 22 November 1763 :

Our infant churches from their original plantation in the deserts of America have ever retained an affectionate esteem and respect for their brethren the Dissenting Churches in England and Ireland, and the Established Church of Scotland. The similitude of our doctrines and forms of worship make our cause one, which if cemented by harmonious intercourse might render us at length into a much more respectable body in the British Empire and the Protestant world, than if we continue to subsist disunited, disconnected.[1]

The disruption of the First British Empire, next to the downfall of the Puritan Commonwealth in Great Britain, was the greatest disaster for British Dissent, and the greatest setback for British democracy ; and it is by no means certain that it was conducive to a healthy growth of democracy even in America, where French ideas, adaptable in their rootless superficiality, warped the further growth of the New England Puritan community, intellectually the strongest group on the Continent. In the spirit of the Dissenters alone could a solution of the Imperial problem have been found in 1770, and it seems extremely doubt ful whether Burke and his friends, if in power, would have succeeded in saving the First British Empire. Their ideas were no less hierarchical and authoritarian than those of George III and Lord North, and to them, too, trade was the soul of

---

[1] A draft of this letter is among the Stiles MSS. (Yale College Library) in a leather-bound volume marked 'Letters. IV '.

Empire ; had Burke been in office during the American Revolution, we might merely have had to antedate his counter-revolutionary Toryism by some twenty years.

Why was not representation in the British Parliament — a British Union — offered to the Colonies ? or why, alternatively, was not an American Union attempted, such as had been proposed at the Albany Congress in 1754 ? This might have freed Great Britain from burdens, responsibilities, and entanglements, and paved the way to Dominion status. Both ideas were discussed at great length and with copious repetition, but mechanical devices, though easily conceived on paper, are difficult to carry into practice when things do not, as it were, of their own accord, move in that direction. There is 'the immense distance between planning and executing' and 'all the difficulty is with the last'.

It requires no small labour to open the eyes of either the public or of individuals, but when that is accomplished, you are not got a third of the way. The real difficulty remains in getting people to apply the principles which they have admitted, and of which they are now so fully convinced.[1]

In the end statesmen hardly ever act except under pressure of 'circumstances', which means of mass movements and of the mental climate in their own circles. But about 1770, the masses in Great Britain were not concerned with America, and the mental and moral reactions of the political circles were running on lines which, when followed through, were bound to lead to disaster.

The basic elements of the Imperial Problem during the American Revolution must be sought not so much in conscious opinions and professed views bearing directly on it, as in the very structure and life of the Empire ; and in doing that the words of Danton should be remembered — *on ne fait pas le procès aux révolutions*. Those who are out to apportion guilt in history have to keep to views and opinions, judge the collisions of planets by the rules of road traffic, make history into something like a column of motoring accidents, and discuss it in the atmosphere of a police court. But whatever theories of 'free

[1] Shelburne in his autobiography ; Fitzmaurice, *Shelburne*, vol. i. p. 18.

will' theologians and philosophers may develop with regard to the individual, there is no free will in the thinking and actions of the masses, any more than in the revolutions of planets, in the migrations of birds, and in the plunging of hordes of lemmings into the sea. At the moment of supreme crisis, in March 1778, Governor Thomas Hutchinson, a loyalist refugee in England, wrote in despair : 'It's certain the political clock stands still'. He was wrong ; the political clock of Great Britain was ticking the seconds and striking the hours, as it always does, no slower and no quicker ; it was a clock, and not a seismograph.

GOVERNMENT AND PARLIAMENT UNDER THE DUKE OF NEWCASTLE

I

PROLEGOMENA TO 1760

THE CONSTITUTIONAL POSITION UNDER GEORGE II

THERE is an inherent logic in ideas and institutions, and given certain conditions, be they even only temporary or fortuitous, forms will arise which a later age may reproduce on a different, a solid and permanent, basis; a sudden influx of Arctic air early in autumn will sometimes cover stagnant pools and ponds with a thin surface of ice, long before winter may (or may not) render them suitable for skating — it possibly anticipates things to come; but this first ice is anyhow unfit to stand the test of burdens.[1]

Under the first two kings of the Hanoverian dynasty certain forms and even principles of Cabinet government seemed to have been established. The Government was based on a party majority in the House of Commons, the King had to accept the leaders or makers of that majority, and had to act, and even think, through them — they were already conscious of knowing the King's (constitutional) mind better than he knew it himself. The contrast which the first part of the reign of George III presented to this, in appearance, advanced constitutional period, was, and usually continues to be, ascribed to his personal character and to the principles he is said to have imbibed at Leicester House; whereas the development was in reality the logical outcome of the situation. The early constitutional development under the first two Georges rested on a lop-sided basis, and its inherent weakness is apparent even at the time of the most signal success, in the crises of

---

[1] I have deliberately chosen the comparison of early winter in preference to premature spring, so as not to pander to sentimental imaginations; not every start in the direction of so-called constitutional government need be followed up by solid development, nor, if it comes, is it necessarily 'life-giving'.

1744–46, when George II failed where his grandson was yet to score a (temporary) success.

In November 1744, Lord Granville, usually considered the favourite Minister of George II, was forced to resign, and the Broadbottom Administration was formed.   But the King did not give up the game, and there were 'calculations of strength, and lists of persons . . . making every day . . .' [1]   Lord Chancellor Hardwicke was therefore commissioned by the rest of the Cabinet to speak to the King, and the interview, of which Hardwicke has left a record, took place on 5 January 1744/45 (O.S.) : [2]

K. I have done all you ask'd of me.   I have put all power into your hands and I suppose you will make the most of it.

Ch. The disposition of places is not enough, if Your Majesty takes pains to shew the world that you disapprove of your own work.

K. My work !   I was forc'd — I was threatened.

Ch. I am sorry to hear your Majesty use those expressions.   I know of no force — I know of no threats.   No means were used, but what have been used in all times, the humble advice of your servants, supported by such reasons as convinc'd them that the measure was necessary for your service.

K. Yes, I was told that I should be opposed.

Ch. Never by me, Sir, nor by any of my friends.   How others might misrepresent us I don't pretend to know.   But, whatever had been our fate, and tho' Your Majesty had determin'd on the contrary side to what you did, we would never have gone into an opposition against the necessary measures for carrying on the war and for the support of your Government and Family. . . .

. . . .

Ch. . . . Your Ministers, Sir, are only your instruments of Government.

K. (smiles). Ministers are the Kings in this country.

Ch. If one person is permitted to engross the ear of the Crown, and invest himself with all its power, he will become so in effect; but that is far from being the case now, and I know no one now in Your Majesty's service that aims at it.

The King, however, remained unconvinced and did not desist from dealing with unofficial advisers ; consequently on 10-11 February 1745/6, forty-five of his 'servants' resigned,

---

[1] Andrew Stone to Lord Hardwicke, 30 December 1744 ; Add. MSS. 35408, f. 110.   [2] Add. MSS. 35870, ff. 87-91.

only to be recalled two days later, when the failure of Bath
and Granville had become obvious. George II was now told
that those who were 'only his instruments of Government', had
to be his only instruments.

That His Majesty will be pleas'd entirely to withdraw his confidence and countenance from those persons, who of late have, behind
the curtain, suggested private councills, with the view of creating
difficulties to his servants, who are responsible for every thing, whilst
those persons are responsible for nothing.

That His Majesty will be pleas'd to demonstrate his conviction
of mind that those persons have deceiv'd or misled him by representing that they had sufficient credit and interest in the nation to
support and carry on the public affairs, and that he finds they are
not able to do it.

[Here follow demands for the dismissal of some, and the appointment of others, including Pitt.]

That His Majesty will be pleas'd to dispose of the vacant Garters
in such manner, as to strengthen, and give a public mark of his
satisfaction in, his administration.

That, as to foreign affairs, His Majesty will be pleased not to
require more from His servants than to support and perfect the
plan, which He has already approved.[1]

The constitutional theory underlying these articles was
clearly explained in a letter in which, on 15 February 1745/6,
Charles Yorke sent an account of the crisis to his brother
Joseph, then on active service in Scotland — it can be taken
to sum up the opinions of their father, Lord Hardwicke.

The notion of the Constitution is this, that Ministers are account-
able for every act of the King's Government to the people; if that
be so, they have a right to his confidence, in preference to all others;
else they are answerable for measures not their own. Here is the
security both of the King and of his people. The next great policy of
the Constitution is this, that whatever the King does should seem to
come *ex mero motu*; the result of his own wisdom and deliberate
choice. This gives a grace to Government in the eyes of the people,
and here is the dignity of the Monarchy.[2]

On the surface this looks like the full doctrine of responsible
Parliamentary Government; in reality it merely defines the
constitutional relations between the King and the Ministers he

---

[1] *Ibid.* f. 117.   [2] Add. MSS. 35385, f. 53.

employs, and as such prescribes no more than self-respecting statesmen might expect even under an autocratic, if civilised, system. Hardwicke was right when he told George II that Ministers were not 'Kings' so long as there was no Prime Minister ; for obviously there must be a supreme direction, and this, according to Hardwicke and his contemporaries, had to come from the King. It is not Parliament as such, but the system of firmly organised parties under single leadership, which precludes an active, personal participation of the King in Government. But the ideas held about 1750 concerning the position of the King in the executive, and of parties in Parliament, differed widely from our own, and the events of 1744–46 were an accident rather than the natural consequence of the constitutional ideas held at that time.

The Crown has no choice concerning the set of men to be entrusted with office when there are firmly organised parties and a clear majority ; it has to summon the leaders of the majority, who otherwise, with their entire following, automatically pass into opposition. This was not so about 1750. The same letter of Charles Yorke, containing the constitutional *exposé*, in the account it gives of the conference which Hardwicke had with the King on 14 February 1746 restates once more the doctrine about the iniquitous character of a 'formed opposition'. Hardwicke told the King that if he could not give his full confidence to his old Ministers, he had better 'pursue the new plan', and Hardwicke and his friends would continue 'supporting his government in general and giving ease to it' ;

that for himself especially he would say that as long as he lived he would never enter into a formed opposition to any administration, that he would not undergo the slavery nor would he partake in the guilt of it.

This abhorrence of 'a formed opposition' was not a hollow phrase, nor polite pretence ; it fully reappears in the confidential correspondence between Newcastle, Hardwicke, and Mansfield, when their group was once more out of office. Newcastle and Hardwicke had resigned in November 1756, in consequence of the loss of Minorca, the withdrawal of Fox, and the refusal of Pitt to join them, though at that time 'there was not the least diminution of the King's goodness, affection, and confidence' to them, nor 'the least appearance of any loss of . . . friends in either House of Parliament'.[1] With the Devonshire-Pitt Administration, their immediate successors, they had a tacit understanding, securing the old ministers from prosecution and the new from opposition. But when the King, having dismissed Temple and Pitt, seemed to turn to Fox, at that time the political agent of the Duke of Cumberland, the position changed completely. From Fox, who had been Secretary of State when Minorca was lost, Newcastle had nothing to fear ; Pitt loathed Fox, whom he described as 'the *blackest* man that ever lived',[2] while Leicester House stood in excessive fear of the Duke of Cumberland, who, with his military character, following, and associations, was distrusted and disliked by the majority both of Whigs and Tories. Lord Mansfield, though personally friendly to Fox, told George II, 'there was a general apprehension that the . . . intended administration was founded in violence and would be supported by *violence*'.[3] All the materials for a successful opposition were to hand ; what line was the 'old corps' of Whigs to adopt ?

Newcastle, 'much at a loss', on 8 April 1757 applied to Hardwicke for advice, adding from himself :

I detest in general the thought of Opposition. I have detested and blamed it in *others*, and therefore shall most unwillingly come into it *myself*. But, on the other hand, if *we* support these men and measures, . . . to the publick it is the same as if we were parties to the Administration. For without *us*, this Administration at present cannot go on. . . . Might not there be a middle way . . . might we not . . . act according to events, and as particular questions arise ? This I know will be difficult and possibly in no shape satisfactory to our friends, who from thence may go part to one side and part to the other.[4]

---

[1] The Duke of Newcastle to Lord Bristol, 6 December 1756. Add. MSS. 32869, ff. 257-8.

[2] Fitzmaurice, *Shelburne*, vol. i. p. 61.

[3] Lord Dupplin, presumably to the Duchess of Newcastle, 13 June 1757 ; Add. MSS. 32871, ff. 298-9. See also letter from James Abercromby to Lord Halifax, April 1757, about the feeling in the City 'against Mr. F—x and his Military Administration, which they think stands on an anticonstitutional bottom'; Add. MSS. 32870, f. 372.   [4] *Ibid.* ff. 376-88.

He thus recognised that a party or political group out of office required at least as much organisation as when it had its natural rallying-point in the Government, or was doomed to disintegration. But Hardwicke replied on 9 April 1757 : [1]

For my own part, I am determin'd not to go into a *form'd general opposition*. I have seen so much of them that I am convinc'd they are the most wicked combinations, that men can enter into ; — worse and more corrupt than any Administration, that I ever yet saw, and so they have appear'd in the conclusion. Therefore I see no other way at present, but to keep off from any absolute engagement with either party . . . and to oppose wrong measures, and concur in right ones, as particular questions shall arise, or be foreseen. I am sensible that this is not the political way to keep a party together, but that is not an objection against doing what I think in my own conscience to be right.

Similarly Lord Mansfield, endorsing Lord Hardwicke's opinion, most insistently warned Newcastle against trying, by the help of 'Leicester House and the People', to impose himself on the King, who would then rather forgive his bitterest enemy than one whom he had trusted so long :

To mix in factious opposition, after so many years of honourable service, wou'd blast your fame and reputation for ever. Specious pretences are never wanting ; but in the present distress, it is impossible for any Court, how desperate soever, to make unconstitutional attempts ; if they did, every man ought to oppose such attempts. But I speak of opposition to right or indifferent measures to force a change of hands. I desire for one to subscribe to Lord Hardwicke's declaration as the sentiment of a virtuous and loyal mind, to which I will inviolably adhere. I had much rather not exist than join at this time factiously in opposition to the King, whomsoever he employs. For his sake, for the sake of his successor, for the sake of Government itself I wou'd not do it. [2]

Upbraided in this way by both his trusted friends, Newcastle, in a letter to Hardwicke (15 April 1757) completely receded from his previous suggestion of opposition, very faint though it had been :

I . . . entirely agree with your Lordship not on any account *to enter into a formed General Opposition*; and I thought I had stated

---

[1] Add. MSS. 32870, ff. 395-400.
[2] 15 April 1757 ; Add. MSS. 32870, ff. 427-31.

my objections to it in the strongest manner . . . the *metzo termino* flung out in my letter, I think will be (as things stand at present) the only way; Lord Dupplin made me mention the difficulty of such a conduct in a stronger light than I should otherwise have done.[1]

In short, these men, while at times expounding what would seem the full doctrine of responsible Parliamentary government, had no conception of a party-government unconnected with the King, and hence of a constitutional Parliamentary Opposition. For the King was to them a real factor in government, and not a mere figurehead or an abstract idea; he was a god in politics, not a deity. He was the 'supreme Magistrate', the fountain-head of power and honours, the permanent pivot of the Executive; and the mere conception of a 'Sole Minister', a *de facto* ruler, was indignantly disclaimed by them. It was the King's business to see the government of the nation carried on, and for that purpose he had a right to choose his 'instruments'; and 'support of Government' was considered 'a duty, while an honest man could support it'.[2] To try to impose oneself on the King by means of a systematic opposition, 'to force a change of hands', was considered by them factious and dishonest, and replete with 'guilt'. As the actual person of the King still always stood in the very forefront of politics, all 'formed opposition' was in some measure tainted with disloyalty; for obviously, a regular opposition does aim, not at giving the Executive the best advice, but at impeding its action. And, *vice versa*, because of the very real position still held by the King, every organised political party, aspiring to office, tended to gather to a Royal person: the King in being, 'the King over the water', the King to come (*i.e.* the Prince of Wales), or at least a Royal Highness (*e.g.* the Duke of Cumberland).

[1] *Ibid.* f. 419. A paper of Newcastle's, dated 19 April 1757, 'My present resolution with regard to Administration' (Add. MSS. 32997, f. 135), contains the following paragraph:

Not to enter, on any account, into general opposition; or to attempt by force, in Parliament, to remove or replace Ministers; or, in any degree, to force the King, contrary to his inclination, to admit any persons into his Administration.

[2] Lord Barrington to A. Mitchell, 13 December 1762; Add. MSS. 6834, f. 42.

Prestige and patronage invested the King with considerable power both in Parliament and in the constituencies, and it was Lord Granville's maxim, 'Give any man the Crown on his side, and he can defy everything'.[1] In this conviction he induced George II to make the attempt of February 1746; but when faced with mass resignations, the King, as Lord Shelburne puts it in his autobiography, 'did not choose to try the experiments which his Grandson is about, nor was that time by any means ripe, I believe, for them, though Lord Granville thought otherwise'.[2] Shelburne's view seems the better founded, and not by results alone. The House of Commons at that time can be roughly divided into four groups, though it is not always easy to draw the line between them : the Administration group of placemen and civil servants, of men dependent on whatever Government was in power ; the Whig connexions which had hitherto supported the Government ; the 'flying squadron' of discontented Whigs, men who, having quarrelled with Sir Robert Walpole, the Pelhams, and 'the main body', had entered the orbit of the Prince of Wales ; and the Tories who, whether they had the Jacobite leanings ascribed to them or were merely men of independent character and views, anyhow were not a rock on which to build a government. The Administration group, if united with all the rest of the 'old corps', offered a sufficient basis for a stable government ; but otherwise support would have to be sought from the Prince of Wales since Walpole's old friends, even if successfully detached from the Pelhams, would hardly be sufficient. Rather than submit to that, George II preferred to recall the Pelhams ; it was for this reason that he abandoned the experiment which his grandson was to attempt under fundamentally different conditions.

Thus in 1746 the King had to capitulate before his Ministers because his own person still stood in the centre of political controversy ; what we should now call a 'constitutional' surrender came as the result of a highly unconstitutional situation. The King, as his own Prime Minister, was, or deemed himself,

---

[1] H. Walpole to Horace Mann, 26 November 1744.
[2] Fitzmaurice, *Shelburne*, vol. i. p. 37.

restricted to co-operation with one set of men, and to them he lent his means for recruiting supporters. Their majority rested at least as much on the support of the Crown as on support from the 'public'. No one can deny the apparent resemblance of the events of 1746 with modern practice ; still, of this enforced partnership in government the appearances only were constitutional in the modern sense. The moment the King ceased to deem himself restricted to one group (which intrinsically is a much more constitutional situation), the reality of 'personal government' was bound to reappear. But such a return to earlier forms did not amount to a fundamental change of system, and Newcastle, Hardwicke, etc., so far from being the spiritual ancestors of the Whig Opposition of, say, 1780, were the direct forerunners of Lord North, who served his apprenticeship as the trusted young friend of Newcastle ; and their own families, with a fine instinct for realities, finished by joining North, while many so-called Tories of the reign of George II became Radicals under George III (Beckford, Meredith, Dowdeswell, etc.). The system which existed under George II, when examined in its foundations, is seen to lead up directly to the experiment of the first years of George III's reign, and to the 'stabilisation' under North. There was sound sense in North, Sandwich, George Germaine, etc., never themselves discarding the 'denomination' of Whigs, and in the elder Pitt working with the Tories.

The coming to Court of the Old Tories on the accession of George III marked in a signal manner the extinction of even theoretical Jacobitism, and is usually given prominence in the change of scene. But was it really this official funeral of a dead creed which set the King free to assume the lead and choose his 'servants' ? The conflict between successive generations of the Hanoverian dynasty had for a long time played a much greater part in English (though not in Scottish) politics than the existence of a discredited rival dynasty, alien to the nation in religion and ideas. The struggle between father and son, known in ordinary families, is very much intensified in ruling dynasties, the throne affording room for one only. But in family conflicts, scapegoats are always in demand, against whom an embarrassing hatred is diverted. Parents ascribe everything which does not suit their book to the 'bad influence' of undesirable friends on their presumably feeble-minded progeny ; and sons in opposition to their royal fathers (as also the other 'children' of the King, his subjects) knew the tale about 'wicked advisers' long before a constitutional convention gave it official status. Thus the struggle of the heir to the throne against the monarch becomes coupled with bitter hostility against his ministers. Even in recent times such developments could be observed at some Continental Courts. The Crown Prince Rudolf of Austria, in opposition to his conservative father, the Emperor Francis Joseph I, professed liberal views, indiscreetly criticising the constitutional advisers of his father to ill-chosen confidants. Similarly, the Crown Prince Frederick of Germany, though with more intelligence and discrimination, developed an advanced liberalism in opposition to William I and Bismarck, while his own son in turn sharply opposed the politics of his parents. But having succeeded to the throne, William II, though not a Liberal, felt as irresistibly moved to dismiss Bismarck as if he had come into the views, and not merely into the place, of his father ; just as George III was irresistibly moved to dismiss the Ministers of his grandfather.

With the Hanoverians the conflict between the King and the Heir-Apparent was a regular institution. George II, as Prince of Wales, stood in sharp opposition to George I and Sir Robert Walpole, whose dismissal was universally expected on his accession, and very nearly occurred. In the next reign George II and his Queen, and their son Frederick, Prince of Wales, openly proclaimed their hostility to each other — '. . . whoever goes to pay their Court to their Royal Highnesses, Prince or Princess of Wales, will not be admitted to Their Majesties' presence' (official notice of 12 September 1737) — 'duty on the one side' was considered 'disaffection on the other'.[1] In the lifetime of Frederick, Prince of Wales, the future George III received from both his parents 'treatment

[1] See Dodington's 'Narrative', appended to his *Diary*, p. 452. — A similar prohibition had been issued against George II by his father in 1717.

which went the length of the most decided contempt of him,
if not aversion, setting up his brother the Duke of York's
understanding and parts in opposition to his, and under-
valuing everything he said or did'.[1] But after the death of
Frederick in 1751, the attitude of the Princess to her eldest son
changed completely, and in time he took his father's place at
Leicester House and in opposition to his grandfather, George II.
The usual retribution came for George III in the struggle with
his eldest son, George IV, who, as Prince of Wales, closely
associated with the Whig Opposition in bitter hostility to his
father and his Ministers. It is this struggle of successive
generations which, at a time when the King's person still
stood in the forefront of politics, supplied a rallying-point to
Oppositions, and which, more than Tories or Jacobites, forced
George II into a partnership with the Pelham group.

There is a well-known passage in the *Diary* of Bubb Dodington, under date of 18 July 1749, describing how the Prince
of Wales promised, when King, to bestow a peerage on him
and make him Secretary of State — 'and I give you leave to
kiss my hand upon it, now, by way of acceptance'. Dodington
was thus received into the Shadow Cabinet by the princely
leader of the Opposition to His Majesty. Born in 1691, and
only about eight years younger than the King, he none the less
sold 'spot' (he resigned the office of Treasurer of the Navy) and
bought 'futures', a transaction more obviously justified in
young politicians who were likely to spend the best part of their
lives under the King's successor. 'The Prince of Wales gains
strength in Parliament in proportion as the King grows older'
wrote Lord Chesterfield on 25 April 1749.[2] The death of the
Prince, in 1751, which at first disturbed actuarial calculations,
in the end merely increased the tension : 'The Court was old ;
the Ministry was old ; there was a long generation between
them and the heir apparent'.[3] In 1755 the Duke of Newcastle
explained to the King himself that he found more difficulty
'from the notion of opposition from that quarter [Leicester

[1] Fitzmaurice, *Shelburne*, vol. i. pp. 53-4.
[2] To S. Dayrolles ; see *Letters*.
[3] Fitzmaurice, *Shelburne*, vol. i. p. 52.

House], which affects particularly all the young men, than from all other causes whatever'.[1] 'The influence of the young Court . . . will gather new strength every month after seventy-four' was again Chesterfield's diagnosis of the situation in 1757 [2] (George II was born in 1683).

The situation of George III on his accession differed from that of his predecessors in that he was young and had no competing heir. The Duke of Cumberland, who previously had been looked upon, rightly or wrongly, as the incarnation of what we should call 'Prussianism', and as a menace to the constitution, was soon to become the acknowledged protector of the 'constitutional' Whigs — this was in accordance with the law of conflict between successive generations in the Royal Family. Still, after his recent stroke of palsy, he was a poor substitute for a Prince of Wales — he was not likely to outlive George III and all his brothers. As Hardwicke wrote to Newcastle on 18 April 1761, expressing his doubts whether Pitt and Temple would go into opposition — 'There is now no *reversionary* resource. Instead of an old King, and a young successor; a young healthy King, and no successor in view'.[3]

The peculiarity of an Opposition grouped round the Prince of Wales, especially while there were no clearly defined parties, was that it could hardly expect to establish itself in office in the lifetime of the King, and that its main chance lay therefore, not in a victory in Parliament or at the polls, but in the 'reversion'. Dodington, in the 'Memorial for the Prince', dated 12 October 1749, pointed out the mistake he made in heading an active Opposition, 'carried on for the private preferment of the opposers'. 'Can a Prince of Wales be preferred? — He must be King; and as he can be nothing else, can such an Opposition make him so, one hour before his time?' The Prince himself

---

[1] Add. MSS. 32860, f. 16.
[2] To Newcastle, 8 June 1757; Add. MSS. 32871, f. 244.
[3] Add. MSS. 32922, ff. 40-42. — With this compare the passage about George III's accession in Burke's *Thoughts on the Cause of the Present Discontents* (1770), p. 10: '. . . coming to the throne in the prime and full vigour of youth, as from affection there was a strong dislike, so from dread there seemed to be a general averseness, from giving any thing like offence to a Monarch, against whose resentment opposition could not look for a refuge in any sort of reversionary hope.'

'cannot act at the head of any Administration', and were the
King forced to call in the leaders of the Opposition, they could
not assume office, without ceasing to be followers of the Prince ;
'it is not your interest to drive them from you', nor theirs to
give up the certainty of favour in future 'for the uncertain, ill-
will'd, precarious emoluments which they may snatch, in the
scramble of a new Administration, forced upon the Crown'.
The Prince should aim at becoming 'the sole object of mankind's expectation, for the redress of all the grievances they
feel, and the disposition of all the future benefits they hope
for' ; while his followers should confine themselves to carrying,
one day, his 'great designs into execution'.[1] The death of
George II was obviously to be 'the day' for all those, whether
discontented Whigs or Tories, who were ready to re-enter
active politics, but who during his lifetime had to remain in
the outer darkness.

As the Government party, built up by Walpole and the
Pelhams, owed its large majority in the House of Commons to
the patronage of the Crown, to claim, as is sometimes done,
that it was incumbent on the King to accept their apparent
majority as constitutionally binding on him, is to put the cart
before the horse. Nor, indeed, would such a theory have been
popular at the time. A system had come to be established
under which the Cabinet, to carry on efficiently the King's
business, had to have a majority in Parliament ; but the earliest
outcome of the close linking-up of Executive and Legislature
was the control of 'the Minister' over a House of Commons
which tended to 'degenerate into a little assembly, serving no
other purpose than to register the arbitrary edicts of one too
powerful subject', 'designed', as Pitt went on to say, 'to be an
appendix to — I know not what — I have no name for it'.[2]
Others had supplied names for it in abundance during forty
years of bitter campaigns against 'the Sole Minister', 'the
over-grown Minister', the 'fellow-subject lifted above others'

[1] Cf. also Hervey's advice to Frederick, Prince of Wales. *Memoirs* (ed.
Sedgwick), i. 303-4.
[2] William Pitt in the House of Commons, 26 November 1754 ; see
letter from Henry Fox to Lord Hartington, published in an appendix to
Lord Waldegrave's *Memoirs* (1821), pp. 146-50.

and made into 'a kind of magistrate odious to the English Constitution, who draws everything within the vortex of his own power', 'treasurer, archbishop, judge, and perpetual legislator', etc.

Still, can one wonder at people not having guessed the future of the institution of Prime Minister ? — who, with the patronage of the Crown at his disposal, was almost as permanent as the King, but, having personal connexions of his own and being partly dependent on them, tended to exclude a large, perhaps the larger, part of the political nation from a constructive share in national politics. This seemed a travesty of both Royal and Parliamentary government, combining the disadvantages of both ; and men naturally asked themselves whether 'the management of one man in the character of Prime Minister' was not in the end 'more prejudicial to a country than that of the sovereign himself' — the interests of the King appearing to them more closely identified with those of the nation, and he himself more independent of factions and confederacies of men, and therefore more impartial in judging between them. By 1760 the nation seems to have reached a state of reaction against government by Cabinet and so-called party, and with other paths as yet unexplored was inclined to revert to a rather primitive monarchical idea. A Patriot King, an independent House of Commons composed of Members 'guided only by the dictates of their own judgment and conscience', the enlightened voter moved by pure reason only, were inhuman fictions, 'as much creatures of imagination as griffins or dragons', but had to be tried in turn before the wisest politicians came to accept human absurdities provided they worked. But about 1760, in the thoughts of the nation, the King alone stood above the 'unguarded guardians' ; in the calculations of politicians he alone could give to the excluded a share or turn in the enjoyment of office — and if the old King would not do so, their hopes were pinned on his successor. That the death of the King would naturally imply changes in office had for years been well-nigh an axiom. For had Ministers, placed and maintained in office through the countenance and support of a king, been able to raise a claim to surviving him, had they thus been able to establish a quasi-mortgage on the Crown, they would indeed have been 'mock monarchs', 'a fourth estate, to check, to controul, to influence, nay, to enslave the other three'.[1]   But when in 1770 Burke in his *Thoughts on the Cause of the Present Discontents* expatiated on the 'power arising from connection' — 'the great Whig connections' — as a security 'for the importance of the people', he carefully refrained from stating that the main foundation of their power had been the influence of the Crown.

While the theory of the King's constitutional duty to accept and continue the Ministers of his predecessor was held by no one in 1760, not even by the Ministers themselves, peculiar circumstances at the accession of George III rendered their temporary continuance advisable, or even necessary.   In March 1759, Lord Bute, the Grand Vizier of Leicester House, had affirmed that he 'wished the King's life as much as any subject';[2] which was true, for he dreaded lest the new reign (*ego et rex meus*) should start in the midst of war, and be burdened with the responsibility for negotiating a peace which was bound to arouse much heat and opposition.   The Prince of Wales explicitly stated his fears of such a contingency in a letter written *c.* 2 July 1758, and deprecating further military commitments in Germany — 'if this unhappy measure should be taken we shall be drawn deeper in a Continental War than ever; and when I mount the Throne, I shall not be able to form a M[inistr]y who can have the opinion of the people'. Indeed, it was suggested that 'Mr. Pitt and Mr. Grenville certainly wish'd to continue the War during the King's life; that the Prince of Wales might find the nation in War; and, consequently, that they should be the more necessary'; 'whilst the contrary was the wish and object of Lord Bute'.[3]

---

[1] Phrases and descriptions of this kind are here gathered from various opposition papers and pamphlets published between 1735 and 1761; for most of them it seems unnecessary to give specific references as they were generally current.

[2] Newcastle's memorandum of 22 March 1759; Add. MSS. 32889, ff. 185-7.

[3] See Newcastle's memorandum marked 'C.V.' [minute of a talk with Count de Viry], 16 March 1759, Add. MSS. 32889, ff. 100-5; and also another 'C. V.' memorandum, of 17 March 1759, *ibid.* ff. 121-5.

When it happened as Pitt was alleged to have wished, it seemed expedient to let the late King's Ministers pursue their measures and complete their work. 'If this plan can be carried into execution', wrote an impartial observer a month after the death of George II, 'and all political cabal and contention removed to the less critical time of peace (for this country cannot be altogether free from political strugles), we should, in the main, be happy. . . .' [1] And on 19 December 1760, he again expressed the hope and wish, shared by most people, that 'the present Ministers' should be continued 'so long as the war lasts'. 'When a peace is once secured 'twill be time enough to attend to the insinuations of jealousy and ambition.' [2]

This, of course, was hardly the view of the old men, who for the last ten, twenty, or thirty years had waited for the death of George II ; who in 1737 had thought the King 'in a languishing condition', anyhow unable to 'live many years' ; who in 1749 had seen Frederick, Prince of Wales, 'with one foot on the throne', when in reality it was in the grave ; and who now, having spent very nearly the Biblical term of years in the desert, saw the Promised Land and did not want to die the death of Moses. George III, and perhaps even Bute, might have bided their time, but not the old, ravenous, embittered men. A pamphlet, called *Seasonable Hints from an Honest Man on the present important Crisis of a new Reign, and a new Parliament*, expressed the feelings of many among them besides Lord Bath, who had inspired it. Published anonymously on 16 March 1761, it was the work of his scribe and political agent, John Douglas, D.D. (subsequently Bishop of Salisbury). High wisdom and lofty sentiments are affected, but are continually dimmed by virulent invective and bitter recriminations, till at last an irrepressible, heartfelt cry pierces through all the verbiage — about 'the insatiable thirst of those who, though they have been intoxicated for years, with the most copious draughts of the cup of power, are still so unreasonable as to be craving for more, to the utter exclusion of numbers who have an equal right to taste it in their turn'. In *The London*

---

[1] R. Symmer to Andrew Mitchell, 28 November 1760 ; Add. MSS. 6839, ff. 201-2.   [2] *Ibid*. ff. 203-4.

Chronicle of 9 December 1760, a naïve soul, 'Solomon Sage', having, it seems, genuinely hoped for redress of grievances and 'economic reform' in the new reign, complained that 'we hear of no pensions suspended, nor of any sinecures abolished, or needless officers discharged'. But a wiser man, 'David Simple', on 16 December, gave him the clue to the situation. 'We hope that the cavalry shall never any more be permitted to engage in battle, but shall be entirely reserved to hunt down old Courtiers, good or bad, seeing that we are new Courtiers. . . .' In truth, there were no principles in question — it was a charge of the new courtiers led by the disappointed, embittered failures of the previous reign, by the excluded, the prematurely dead, who now wanted to force their way back to life — Lord Bath, Henry Fox, Bubb Dodington, etc.

Politicians and their quarrels had enjoyed a peculiar longevity in the second half of George II's reign. In 1760 the same seventeenth-century men continued in the forefront of politics who had stood there about 1745. The King, born in 1683, was still on the throne ; the Duke of Newcastle, born in 1693, was still electioneering, distributing jobs, holding levees, and over every trifle 'flinging himself' on the advice and support of his friend Lord Hardwicke (born in 1690) ; the Duke of Argyll, born in 1682, continued as the uncrowned King of Scotland ; Lord Ligonier, born in 1680, was Commander-in-Chief of the Army ; Lord Anson, born in 1697, was First Lord of the Admiralty ; Lord Bath, born in 1684, and Lord Granville, born in 1690, were still overflowing with hostility and contempt for Newcastle and Hardwicke, of whom, in their long lives, though superior in brilliancy and wit, they had never managed to get the better ; and some distance behind them all (to be mentioned as type rather than as individual), Bubb Dodington, born in 1691, was still making 'his ideas consonant to the opinions of those men from whom he expected emoluments'. The new reign, so long awaited or apprehended, had come, and here they were still all present, 'young gentlemen of seventy and upwards'. They remembered William III, had been engaged in politics or professions before Queen Anne died, were elderly men at the fall of Sir Robert

Walpole, and were still active in 1760. The next generation
was similarly complete. There were the Duke of Cumberland,
the Dukes of Bedford and Devonshire, William Pitt, Lord
Temple, George Grenville, Lord Egremont, Lord Granby,
Lord Sandwich, Lord Holdernesse, H. B. Legge, Lord Mansfield, Henry Fox, Charles Townshend, William Beckford,
Charles Yorke, etc. In fact, only two politicians of mark had
died between 1745 and 1760, Frederick, Prince of Wales, and
Henry Pelham. But the death of George II on 25 October 1760
marked the first breach in this seemingly immovable array;
the others, even the prominent men of the younger genera-
tion, followed rapidly. The Duke of Argyll died in 1761, Lord
Anson and Lord Melcombe (Dodington) in 1762, Lord Granville
and Lord Egremont in 1763, Lord Hardwicke, Lord Bath,
H. B. Legge, and the Duke of Devonshire in 1764, the Duke of
Cumberland in 1765, Charles Townshend in 1767, the Duke
of Newcastle in 1768, Lord Ligonier, Lord Granby, William
Beckford, George Grenville, and Charles Yorke in 1770, the
Duke of Bedford in 1771. When Lord North became First
Lord of the Treasury, of those who had been leaders in 1760
and for many years before it, hardly any were alive, and, barring
Chatham and Sandwich, none were any longer active in politics.
It was in these ten years, 1760–70, that the real change
supervened in the political personnel as well as in political
ideas.

The accession of George III did not in itself mark the
advent of any new ideas, nor, except for the disturbing and
ineffective person of Lord Bute, did it immediately bring forth
new men. With change delayed by longevity and now once
more by the war, the new reign presented the extraordinary
sight, both ludicrous and disgusting, of long-repressed, and still
impeded, feuds fought out between men most of whom had
outlived their time — between 'the dead above ground'.
Horace Walpole, who himself half-died with his father and
felt therefore a very old man at forty-four — a detached
observer of a world which did not concern him any longer —
after sixteen years' absence, in March 1761 revisited Houghton.
Sitting in his father's 'little dressing-room', by his scrutoire,

he wrote what is perhaps the deepest, most sincere, and un-
affected letter in the many volumes of his correspondence.
His thoughts that night wandered to the church 'into which I
have not yet had courage to enter', to the time when he himself
would at last be buried in it, to the years when his father was
alive, to the scenes he would witness the next day at Lynn,
where he was to be re-elected to George III's first Parliament
— and he wrote about Sir Robert Walpole and those who had
outlasted him : 'There lies he who founded its [Houghton's]
greatness, to contribute to whose fall Europe was embroiled —
there he sleeps in quiet and dignity, while his friend and his foe,
rather his false ally and real enemy, Newcastle and Bath, are
exhausting the dregs of their pitiful lives in squabbles and
pamphlets !' [1]

Whatever the ingratitude of monarchs may be, they cannot
practise it with the anonymous irresponsibility of assemblies
or nations. George III could not discard those who had
maintained the House of Hanover on the throne, nor the
Emperor William II dismiss the man who had made the
Hohenzollern Empire, with the same ease with which France
dropped Clemenceau after the victory was won. Nor can
monarchs talk about their 'father complex' as voters do about
the 'swing of the pendulum', though probably the two have
much in common (electorates at general elections can realise
the child's dream to wash, with an enormous sponge, the face
of an indignant and protesting nurse).

Monarchs feel constrained to give reasons ; they plead,
therefore, that there had been presumption on the part of the
old retainer, and argue that in reality he had been an overbearing master who had kept the poor old grandpapa in
bondage. It was inconvenient for the new Court (as later on
it would have been for Burke and other opposition writers and
orators) to admit that Newcastle had been only the faithful
servant and political manager of George II. The would-be
heirs and successors of the old Minister worked up lurking
suspicions and provided the necessary arguments. Thus
Dodington, in December 1760, implored Bute 'to recover

[1] Horace Walpole to George Montagu, Houghton, 25 March 1761.

monarchy from the inveterate usurpation of oligarchy',[1] and
sent him some lines, which were not to be seen by anybody,
'unless his lordship has a mind to make the King or the
Princess [of Wales] laugh' :

> Quoth Newcastle to Pitt, 'tis in vain to dispute ;
>   If we'd quarrel in private, we must make room for Bute.
> Quoth Pitt to his Grace, to bring that about,
>   I fear, my dear lord, you or I must turn out.
> Not at all, quoth the Duke, I meant no such thing,
>   To make room for us all, we must turn out the King.
> If that's all your scheme, quoth the Earl, by my troth,
>   I shall stick by my master, and turn ye out Both.

Next, Lord Bath, through his agent Douglas, supplied the
King and the public with very full and serious *Hints* about
past 'iniquities' and the changes which were required. A
knot of Ministers should no longer be allowed 'to grasp
universal influence in domestic business' and dictate whom
the King should employ, and their 'factious connections and
confederations' should be broken up. The King should show
'that we have a monarch on the throne, who, knowing that he
reigns in the hearts of a united people is determined not to
resign himself to the insolent pretensions of any confederacy
of Ministers', and that he will not 'content himself with the
shadow of royalty, while a set of undertakers for his business
intercept his immediate communication with his people, and
make use of the legal prerogatives of their master, to establish
the illegal claims of factious oligarchy'. 'Can there be the
least doubt that the nation, in general, would list itself on his
side . . . when the competition is not between prerogative
and liberty, but between the King and Ministers. . . . ?' If
the King decides to do his own business, 'the over-grown
Minister . . . will soon find that his supposed friends were
only the friends of his power, and will continue firm to him
no longer than while he has possession of the means of gratifying
them. In the age we live in, there are but few retainers of a
Court so little attentive to their interest as to forget that the

---

[1] See *Hist. MSS. Comm.*, *Various Collections*, vol. vi. p. 47, MSS. of
Miss M. Eyre Matcham.

Crown is permanent and administrations temporary.' Indeed, a singularly accurate forecast of things to come.

Sir Robert Walpole had a policy and used the royal patronage to secure it ; under Henry Pelham there was less policy and more patronage ; with the Duke of Newcastle a policy was hardly traceable ; nor did much real opposition remain — the number of 'Whigs' was continually growing, and the difficulty of Administration was merely 'to find pasture enough for the beasts that they must feed'.[1] This the Duke of Newcastle made the task of his life, leaving the work of Government to stronger men, after 1757 to Pitt, who, in his own words, had been 'called to invigorate Government, and to overrule the influences of feeble and shortsighted men'.[2] In his own thinking Newcastle was primarily the servant of George II, whose reign he had to make 'easy', and the chief of a 'connection' of men, for whom he had to provide. As he himself put it in a memorandum of 10 August 1761 his tenure of office was 'for the service of those friends, in whose cause I am, and have ever been, embarked';[3] and a week later, when discussing resignation, he wrote to Hardwicke : 'There is one thing, I own, which does, and will affect me extremely ; and that is the only one. There are some particular friends of mine, both in Church and State, whom I shall be most sorry to leave without prospect of assistance or advancement. . . .'[4] Pitt rightly remarked about him that he had 'two points only in view, viz., the disposal of employments and the confidence of the King'.[5] In neither of these did Pitt mean to give him any disturbance ; for he 'was not ambitious. He was modest or proud, which

---

[1] Lord Chesterfield to S. Dayrolles, 16 November 1753.—Admiral Rodney, in his letter from Martinique, on 10 February 1762, while congratulating the Duke of Newcastle on the conquest of the island and the 'considerable sum' it would annually yield to the Treasury, significantly added : 'I have likewise great satisfaction when I consider that this conquest puts it into your Grace's power to oblige many of your friends by the posts and employments in your Grace's gift, and which are very lucrative in this island. . . .' Add. MSS. 32934, ff. 255-7.

[2] W. Pitt to Gilbert Elliot, 6 October 1761 ; see G. F. S. Elliot, *The Border Elliots* (1897), pp. 366-7.

[3] Add. MSS. 32926, ff. 348-51.

[4] 17 August 1761 ; Add. MSS. 32927, ff. 68-73.

[5] Minute of Newcastle's conversation with Count de Viry, 16 March 1759 ; Add. MSS. 32889, ff. 100-5.

you would. He had taken another turn. He would not be
Disposing Minister, if he could.'[1] The reason which Pitt
gave for remaining in office, was 'the service of the public'.
He was the 'Minister of measures', while Newcastle was the
'Minister of numbers'.[2]

By 1760 Pitt, through his conduct of the war, had earned
a well-deserved, nation-wide popularity, a fact which was
frankly, and even generously, acknowledged by Newcastle.
Thus he recorded in his notes on 4 September 1759 : 'Mr. Pitt
— More popular every day than ever ; even in the country and
with the Old Whigs' ;[3] and in a letter of 27 November 1759
he wrote about Pitt to Granby : 'He is a man. A man of
great merit, weight and consequence. It is for the service of
the publick to be well with him ; to aid and assist him.'[4]
Meantime Newcastle's own thankless task of 'Disposing
Minister' had raised against him a host of enemies among
those who, while not anxious to do real work or bear heavy
responsibilities, felt equal to the distributing or accepting of
places, sinecures, and pensions ; and Pitt did not show as much
understanding for his difficulties as Newcastle showed for Pitt's
greatness. It is characteristic of the situation in 1760 that in
the numerous attacks against the 'confederacy of Ministers'
criticisms of policy seldom occur, but complaints are continually
raised against the monopolising of patronage — this being the
subject of paramount interest to the crowds which did not live
for, but by, politics. Newcastle was the butt of that peculiar
opposition, and in the picture they drew of him, the weak, old,
ill-used man grew into a Herod because of the starved ambitions
and avidities for which he had failed to find room on the
pastures of Government favour.

[1] 'Heads of Mr. Pitt's Conversation', 17 October 1759, noted down by
Newcastle ; Add. MSS. 32897, ff. 173-5. Cf., however, on this point,
Shelburne's remark : 'He [Pitt] did not cultivate men because he felt it an
incumbrance, and thought that he could act to more advantage without the
incumbrance of a party. He told me himself in 1767, that the world were
much mistaken in thinking that he did not like patronage, for he was but
a little man in 1755, and was obliged to act the part he did' (Fitzmaurice,
i. p. 59).
[2] These descriptions of the two are given by Lord Temple in a letter to
John Wilkes, 16 October 1761 ; Grenville Papers, vol. i. p. 405.
[3] Add. MSS. 32895, ff. 155-6.   [4] Add. MSS. 32899, ff. 141-2.

The Duke of Newcastle as First Lord of the Treasury

English constitutional forms are vague, and often ill-defined and contradictory ; much of their contents depends therefore on the personalities of those who work them. During the last years of George II's reign, the Duke of Newcastle stood in the place of the 'over-grown Minister' ; he was First Lord of the Treasury ; he chose and managed the House of Commons ; he was the link between the King and Parliament. In examining his position and ideas it will be found that by 1760 little was left of the Prime Minister of Walpole's time. Pitt did the work of Secretary of State ; otherwise there was no real government.

There are many brilliant, and even correct, descriptions of Newcastle, and perhaps the best and fairest among them are the sketch by Lord Chesterfield, and the account which one can gather from incidental remarks scattered throughout the first part of Lord Shelburne's autobiography. Newcastle's correspondence, which fills hundreds of volumes, fully confirms the character given him by these two contemporaries.

'The public opinion', wrote Chesterfield about Newcastle, 'put him below his level : for though he had no superior parts, or eminent talents, he had a most indefatigable industry, a perseverance, a court craft, and a servile compliance with the will of his sovereign for the time being' ; by which means he achieved success.

He was good-natured, to a degree of weakness, even to tears, upon the slightest occasion. Exceedingly timorous, both personally and politically. . . .

His ruling, or rather his only, passion was the agitation, the bustle, and the hurry of business . . . ; but he was as dilatory in despatching it as he was eager to engage in it. . . .

He was as jealous of his power as an impotent lover of his mistress, without activity of mind enough to enjoy or exert it. . . .

His levees were his pleasure, and his triumph ; he loved to have them crowded, and consequently they were so . . . he accosted, hugged, embraced, and promised every body, with a seeming cordiality, but . . . with an illiberal and degrading familiarity.

He was exceedingly disinterested, very profuse of his own

fortune. . . . He retired from business in the year 1762, above four hundred thousand pounds poorer than when he first engaged in it.

Upon the whole, he was a compound of most human weaknesses, but untainted with any vice or crime.

When Henry Pelham died, 'his poor brother, the Duke of Newcastle', writes Shelburne, 'offered a most inviting object [for attacks] ; "hubble-bubble", busy and unsteady . . . Mr. Fox and Mr. Pitt . . . alternately and separately courted, bullied, and frightened him ; each offering to act under him, in hopes of governing him and through him the country'. 'He had no resolution nor mind of his own.' While he himself did the work of 'a *commis*', his clerks and dependants meddled with policy. 'They took advantage of his good nature, his love of bustle, etc., and left the detail of business to him, which he mistook, as many men are apt to do, for real business.'

In the Coalition of 1757, Pitt allowed 'the Duke of Newcastle the undisturbed enjoyment of the whole patronage of the Crown, the only idea he had of power', and the Duke, 'a very good-humoured man, was abundantly content . . . enjoyed full levees, promised and broke his word, cajoled and flattered all mankind, and, like the fly upon the chariot-wheel, imagined that he carried on the Government' ; and although 'at bottom an honester man' than Pitt, 'he lost the reputation of one by good nature and want of resolution in the conducting the common patronage of the Treasury'.[1]

No biography of the Duke of Newcastle has yet been attempted ; when written, it will have to be in terms of psychopathology. His nature and mind were warped, twisted, and stunted, and his life must have been agony, though perhaps he himself did not clearly realise how much he suffered. He was haunted by fears ; every small incident was the portent of terrible things to come ; every molehill a volcano. With an abundant substratum of intelligence and common sense, he looked a fool, and with an inexhaustible fund of warm human

---

[1] These passages are gathered from the autobiography in Lord Fitzmaurice's *Life of William, Earl of Shelburne*, vol. i. pp. 41, 43, 44, 65, 66, and 69. The order in which they appear there is not adhered to.

kindness and sincere good-will, he acquired a reputation for dishonesty. His thinking was sound, but it was paralysed by fears; unable to stand up to anyone or to refuse a pressing request, he could not keep honest, and the weak resentments of an exasperated coward, who felt constantly bullied and brow-beaten, were bound to create the appearances of treachery. There probably never was another man in a position outwardly so great who felt so wretchedly poor in soul. If he was vain, this was merely a craving for some compensation for the insults and humiliations, real and imaginary, which he daily suffered and which cut him to the heart. He was not equal to greatness and success, and paid a heavy price for them.

While 'in power', Newcastle anxiously looked into the eyes of stronger men to see whether he found favour in them. Here is a minute which he himself put down of a conversation with Count de Viry, on 21 November 1759:

My friend [Viry] had a long conversation yesterday with Mr. Pitt. He found him in the best humour and disposition imaginable towards me and my friends. He told my friend, how well he was satisfied with me; and that, if I continued to act as I did, he would have an absolute confidence in me.[1]

Again, on 23 October 1757, as First Minister, and after having held Cabinet rank for forty years, he thus reported to Hardwicke a visit at Leicester House:

I had a most indifferent and shameful reception. I stood at your Lordship's door, and as soon as the Princess perceived me she turn'd her head to the window and went into the Drawing Room. *She* afterwards spoke to me *very civilly*, but after waiting almost the whole Drawing Room. The Prince of Wales did me the honor *only* to say, Was you at Claremont last week? The same question he asked me yesterday.[2] Lord Bute told me he should know in ten days

---

[1] Add. MSS. 32899, ff. 11-12.

[2] This may have been mere shyness and lack of anything better to say. When, five years later, on 15 May 1762, Newcastle expressed to the King the wish to resign — 'His Majesty ask'd me whether I should go to Clare-mont?' (Add. MSS. 32938, f. 249). George III was notoriously regular in his habits, and on other occasions in the same way asked Hardwicke whether he was 'going to Wimple', or addressed to Pitt 'a civil general question or two, relating to Hayes' (Add. MSS. 32940, ff. 90-1). Even a conversation with Lady Sarah Lennox, a short time after his accession, he started in the same way: 'You are going into Somersetshire; when do you return?' (see *Life and Letters of Lady Sarah Lennox*, p. 27).

whether he should be satisfied with me or not. It is too much to be the first object of the resentment of the Duke [of Cumberland], etc. because *I* have been able to establish a Ministry he does not like; and that he thinks Leicester House does. And to be treated there in this impertinent manner. Something must be done but what I know not. Pray, think of it.[1]

Or again on 14 June 1759, he wrote to Lord Hardwicke much distressed :

I am scarce now consulted in any thing [concerning the Government], except where they want my opinion to make use of to my disadvantage. The Lady [Yarmouth] is quite silent towards me, and I know little of some pretty material occurrences but what the King is so good as to tell me. That is an odd figure for me to make, and I will not make it long. Surely something should be done or said; for things can't remain in this situation.[2]

But a fortnight later the Duke of Newcastle received a reassuring letter from John Roberts, who had previously been secretary to Henry Pelham and had extensive backstairs connexions at Court : [3]

I am commissioned to assure your Grace from *her* 'that your apprehensions were without foundation; that she had the same regard for your Grace as ever, and as you can wish her to have; and that she had wanted the other day to speak to you about some business but could not get an opportunity'.[4]

Still, why wonder if Newcastle rejoiced at Pitt's good humour and noted with grave misgivings inattention on the part of the Prince of Wales, doubts in his favourite, or silence in the King's mistress, when even 'bad humour' in a small dependant of his own was sufficient to upset and scare him ? H. V. Jones, the son of a penurious and ultimately bankrupt solicitor, who had married a sister of Lord Hardwicke while the Yorkes were still very small people,[5] was Newcastle's private secretary. By 1760 the Duke had loaded him with

---

[1] Add. MSS. 32875, ff. 232-3.

[2] Add. MSS. 32892, ff. 58-61.

[3] About John Roberts see my note on 'Three Eighteenth-century Politicians' in the *English Historical Review*, July 1927.

[4] John Roberts to Newcastle, 27 June 1759 ; Add. MSS. 32892, ff. 268-9.

[5] About Charles Valence Jones, the father of H. V. Jones, see P. C. Yorke, *Life of Lord Chancellor Hardwicke*, vol. i. pp. 35 and 40-7.

sinecures to the annual value of £1400 and a reversion of
another £1000 a year ; but when a certain employment 'reputed £2000 a year' fell vacant, Mr. Jones thought he ought
to have that too, and when given a consolation prize of £200
only, became sullen. 'And what is my situation, if Mr. Jones
is not *now* pleased with me ?' wrote Newcastle to Hardwicke.[1]

The Duke of Newcastle 'had no resolution or mind of his
own'. He would always apply for advice to his friends so as
to shift on to them the responsibility for his actions, and to
establish a moral claim to their time and help, if afterwards
anything had to 'be done or said'. 'I fling myself upon my
friends for their advice and assistance' ; 'I hope I shall be
countenanced and assisted by all my great and considerable
friends' ; 'my friends must think for me' ; 'pray pity me and
advise me' ; etc. On account of any trifle he would send
urgent summonses to Hardwicke, Mansfield, or Dupplin if
they happened to be out of town, and reproach them with
coldness and indifference if they did not immediately fly to
his rescue. To Hardwicke he turned like a child to its nurse,
occasionally receiving replies reminiscent of the nursery. What
boy, worried over the well-mannered epistle of thanks which
he has to write to his grandmamma for the lovely birthday
present, has not been told that surely such a big boy will
know how to write a simple letter ? In March 1760 the Town
Clerk of Bristol came up to London with an address conferring
its freedom on Newcastle and Pitt. Newcastle — who by then
had held Cabinet office for forty-three years — applied to
Hardwicke : 'What answer should I give to the inclosed
speech, which is to be made to me by the Town Clerk of
Bristol on Friday morning next ?' He enclosed the draft of
a reply, long, ponderous, and elaborate. 'I leave the whole
to your goodness and friendship — for once put yourself in
my place ; and make an answer for me. I have also put some
queries on the margin to which I hope for an answer from
your Lordship.'[2] 'I am very sure your Grace can want no

---

[1] 13 September 1760 ; Add. MSS. 32911, ff. 272-3.
[2] Newcastle to Hardwicke, 5 March 1760 ; Add. MSS. 32903, ff. 98-9 ;
the draft, ff. 120-1.

F

advice upon the answer to be given to Mr. Townclerk of
Bristol's speech', replied Lord Hardwicke. Still, he answered
the Duke's queries (*e.g.* whether he should consult Mr. Pitt
before answering the Town Clerk ?) and added : '. . . all I can
say to the draught is that, in my humble opinion, it is much
too long'.[1] Thereupon the Duke composed two more drafts,[2]
and finally his labours, which fill some ten pages of foolscap,
resulted in the following reply : 'Mr. Townclerk, I desire you
would return my thanks to the Corporation of Bristol for this
mark of their regard for me. I shall always endeavour to
deserve the continuance of their good opinion.'[3]

Like so many sufferers from obsessionist neurosis, great,
middling, or insignificant, Newcastle wasted his life on trifles,
pursuing them with an intensity which was to hide their
inanity. '*Vive la bagatelle*', wrote Swift ; and Samuel Johnson
remarked on one occasion that 'a man would never undertake
great things, could he be amused with small. I once tried
knotting . . . but I could not learn it.'[4] Still, Johnson himself unconsciously achieved a compromise between the heavy
strain of concentrated, creative work and 'knotting', in his
Dictionary, the sum total of thousands of small stitches, and in
innumerable disconnected dicta. Similarly Newcastle made in
politics disconnected detail his chosen province ; patronage and
the House of Commons, the doling out of financial advantages
to importunate beggars and the engineering of elections, en-
grossed his thinking, which he seldom allowed to rise to the
level of a political idea. Even into foreign politics he managed
to infuse his habits or obsessions ; he insisted on paying
subsidies to petty German States, as useless to England in a
crisis as Newcastle's political retainers were to prove to him ;
and between 1750 and 1753 made the election of the son of the
Empress Maria Theresa, the Archduke Joseph, as King of the

[1] 6 March ; Add. MSS. 32903, f. 128.
[2] *Ibid.* ff. 119, 122, 124, and 116.
[3] To the last draft is added the remark : 'No other answer to be return'd'
(Add. MSS. 32903, f. 116) ; and the paper commemorating the speech
(f. 143) bears a note which anxiously attests that this and nothing else was
the answer given to the Town Clerk in presence of the two Members for
Bristol.
[4] G. B. Hill, Boswell's *Life of Johnson*, vol. iii. p. 242.

Romans 'the great system, the great object' of his labours in foreign affairs.[1] Chesterfield, subtle and ironic, seems to have perceived that this was merely another expression of Newcastle's mania for electioneering, and on 26 June 1752, thus instructed his son :

> . . . as soon as you are upon a foot of talking easily to him, tell him *en badinant*, that his skill and success in thirty or forty elections in England leave you no reason to doubt of his carrying his election for Frankfort, and that you look upon the Archduke as his Member for the Empire.

Newcastle retained the leading position, which nominally was his, by reducing it to his own dimensions. He acted the part of what was subsequently known as 'the patronage secretary of the Treasury', but being a duke, possessed of great wealth and connexions, he was called First Lord of the Treasury. The three hundred volumes of his papers and correspondence in the British Museum are a monumental dictionary, exhaustive and indiscriminate, of jobs and job-hunters, and of the ways in which places and pensions were solicited, promised, assigned, and obtained. Tide-waiters, riding-officers, surveyors of window lights, postmasters, or parsons, occupied Newcastle's attention as much as those who were to fill high office in the Cabinet and at Court, bishoprics, seats at departmental boards, etc. — they were sand and mortar, pillars and beams for his political edifice. In the summer of 1754 he is found writing seven letters about a postmaster at Midhurst in Sussex [2] — but Midhurst was a Parliamentary borough, and the Duke's correspondents were Lord

---

[1] Newcastle to Henry Pelham, 29 September (O.S.) — 10 October (N.S.) 1750 ; see Coxe's *Pelham Administration*, vol. ii. p. 121. '. . . I told his Majesty . . . that if he could make a King of the Romans, it would be the greatest honour to him in the world' (to Pelham, 2 June 1750, N.S. ; vol. ii. p. 340). 'If the election is dropt, or should miscarry, I think the honour and reputation of the King and country will be in a great measure lost . . .' (to Hardwicke, 29 June 1752 ; vol. ii. p. 432), etc. He continued spending English money on this election when Maria Theresa herself no longer cared about it.

[2] Letters from Newcastle on the subject : Add. MSS. 32735, ff. 392, 421, 455, and 609, and Add. MSS. 32736, ff. 143, 145, and 147 ; letters to Newcastle on the same subject : Add. MSS. 32735, ff. 242, 411, 429, 464, and 593, and Add. MSS. 32736, ff. 5, 81, and 166.

Montague, its patron, and John Peachey, one of its Members ; and the House of Commons would have to be called the crowning part of Newcastle's political edifice, had there ever been such a building. But it did not exist ; there were materials in profusion — majorities in the House of two hundred and above — which their helpless maker tried to guard against decay and pilfering, but with which he himself could do nothing ; he had neither plan nor idea — all trace of architectural design was wanting. In the eighteenth century men could muddle on by such methods, but even then could not govern ; while a man with personality and ideas could obtain a hold on the crowd in the House of Commons, no less than on the masses out of doors, and could lead without bribing. Pitt, intractable, moody, and overbearing, and therefore bad at dealing with individuals, none the less gained an ascendancy over Parliaments of which Newcastle was the maker and patron, a fact which Newcastle himself had to acknowledge.

This is Newcastle's own minute of a conversation with the King, on 6 June 1757,[1] prior to the formation of the coalition with Pitt :

'I can't come in without bringing in my enemy, Mr. Pitt. He turn'd me out. But I can't serve without my enemy.'
'He will be unreasonable.'
'He is, Sir !'
'Beat him as low as I [you] can.'
'If Your Majesty won't approve it, I can't come in alone.'

And again, on 25 October 1759 :

I ask'd His Majesty, suppose Mr. Pitt should quit now, how does Your Majesty propose to have your affairs carried on ? He said, you can do it ; you have the majority of the House of Commons. I replied, it would be betraying Your Majesty, if I flattered you with the possibility of my being able to do it. No one will have a majority at present, against Mr. Pitt. No man, Sir, will, in the present conjuncture, set his face against Mr. Pitt in the House of Commons.[2]

What profit, then, had Newcastle from all his labour wherein he laboured under the King ? Chesterfield says, as did most contemporaries, that 'his levees were his pleasure,

[1] Add. MSS. 32871, f. 224.
[2] Newcastle to Hardwicke, 25 October 1759 ; Add. MSS. 32897, f. 375.

and his triumph'; but Shelburne significantly adds that Newcastle 'cajoled and flattered all mankind', not that he was
flattered by them.   Indeed, if the levees bore any resemblance
to his correspondence, one wonders how they could have given
him pleasure.   Sir Robert Walpole before him, and Lord Bute
after him, learnt the invidious character of patronage work,
which for Newcastle was made even worse by his way of
transacting business.   'He was as dilatory in despatching it as
he was eager to engage in it'; so that favours were usually
delayed till they earned him not gratitude but reproaches.

To take one extreme example : Charles Jenkinson (subsequently 1st Earl of Liverpool) had been, since 1756, an un-
paid clerk in the office of Lord Holdernesse, then Secretary of
State.   On 15 December 1758 he reported to his patron,
George Grenville, that Legge would speak to Newcastle about
a pension for him, and on 26 December, that the Duke himself
had told him he would be glad to do anything for him.[1] Besides
Grenville, Lord Harcourt and Lord Portsmouth engaged on
behalf of Jenkinson ; and the following entry appears in Newcastle's 'Memorandums for the King' of 19–20 February 1759 :

> Mr. Jenkinson to have a pension of £200 p.a. He is now in my
> Lord Holdernesse's office till he can have an establishment there or
> somewhere else.

On 26 March Harcourt wrote again to the Duke, and entries
about Jenkinson's pension reappear in the Memoranda of
29 March and 4 and 5 April.   On the 7th Jenkinson learns
'that the Duke of Newcastle had not spoken to the King
yesterday, but that he had engaged before Lady Yarmouth
to return an answer by the middle of the week'; on the 10th,
that the Duke is to speak to the King 'this morning', but by
the 12th Jenkinson has heard nothing further about it.   New
entries in the Memoranda on 11 May and 10 June — and on
14 June, Jenkinson again reports assurances from Newcastle
to Harcourt 'that he would certainly do my affair'.   On 1 July

---

[1] The letters from Charles Jenkinson here quoted are all to George
Grenville and have been published in the *Grenville Papers*, vol. i., where they
can be easily traced by their dates ; no references to pages are therefore
given.   The 'Memorandums for the King' and other letters quoted above
are in Add. MSS. 32887-32901 ; these too can be traced by their dates.

another letter from Harcourt, and a new entry on 13 July. 'Every time I see his Grace he still repeats to me the same promises,' writes Jenkinson on 26 July ; West and Jones urge him, but it avails nothing. On 6 August : 'His Grace of New-castle is resolved upon the present occasion to show the plenitude of his power, and that no circumstance or considera-tion shall oblige him to perform even a promise, where, at the same time that he passed his word, his inclination was not with it'. New entries in the Memoranda (9 and 26 September, and 26 October), a letter from Lord Portsmouth on 1 Novem-ber, and another from Harcourt on 4 November : 'It is now more than twelve months that your Grace promised to do something for Mr. Jenkinson. . . .' In the course of two months, 9 November 1759 — 9 January 1760, Jenkinson's pension is mentioned fifteen times in Newcastle's Memoranda. On 25 December, Jenkinson writes that the Duke 'vowed' to Lord Portsmouth and himself 'in the most solemn manner, that he would fulfil his promise to me' ; and on 29 December : 'I am very much of your opinion in relation to the only motive that will operate on the *vis inertiae* of the Duke of Newcastle : I have long thought that force is the only true way of working, and by the alarm I can visibly distinguish that any application on my affair always puts him into, I am convinced that it would succeed'. On 14 March 1760, a last letter from Har-court, and on the 17th a last entry, 'Mr. Jenkinson — £250 p.a.' The settling of it had thus required sixteen months, twenty-seven entries in Memoranda, many letters, innumer-able personal reminders, and it finished by producing only irritation, annoyance, and contempt. A year later Charles Jenkinson became Under-Secretary to Lord Bute, and after-wards one of George III's chief favourites.

But not many applicants had Harcourt's urbane manners. Here are examples of the way in which they would address Newcastle : 'Give me leave to acquaint your Grace that it is not with smooth words and fair promises only that men of my rank expect to be treated'.[1] '. . . I can no longer forbear to

---

[1] Lord Denbigh to the Duke of Newcastle, 13 July 1758 ; Add. MSS. 32881, f. 299.

put your Grace in mind that I do expect at this time a performance of the repeated promises you have given me and which
you must be conscious of : I have been your faithful friend
and cannot now be amused by specious words. To be neglected
I neither deserve, or can I submit to it. Your Grace's answer
will determine me.' [1] 'I am heartily sorry to be so obscure
that even your own promise . . . could not call to your
remembrance one who . . . on the faith of your promise',
etc., etc.[2] 'I waited so often about the affair your Grace
promised me last year, without any success, that . . . without
some further encouragement I am convinced it will be needless
to trouble your Grace any more.' [3] 'I desire *to stake my whole
credit* (for the present and to come) with your Grace *on this
point*, and I shall make it my final criterion whereby to judge
of your Grace's intentions towards me.' [4] 'I have been too
long acquainted with Ministers, my Lord, to be turn'd off to
Commanders in Chief, Memorials, &c. I shall apply to no
body but your Grace, if I succeed the merit shall be all your
own, if I do not, I shall know with how much zeal I ought to
be, my Lord, your Grace's most obedient &c.' [5] Or again, a
request from a small man for 'an explicit answer from the
Duke' was accompanied by the following remark : '. . . for
if it be in the negative I shall not trouble his Grace any more,
which next to granting my request is the greatest favour he can
do me'.[6] But hardly ever was rudeness visited by Newcastle
on its author ; more often than not it served its purpose and
was paid for by the object desired. And Newcastle was
'abundantly content with the whole patronage being left to
him'.

[1] John Frederick, M.P., to Newcastle, 27 May 1757 ; Add. MSS. 32871,
f. 149.
[2] Peter Burrell to Newcastle about a seat in Parliament, 27 December
1756 ; Add. MSS. 32869, f. 404.
[3] Thomas Watson, M.P., to Newcastle, 19 July 1757. Add. MSS.
32872, f. 267.
[4] Edward Eliot, M.P., to Newcastle, when asking for a place at the
Board of Admiralty, 15 May 1759 ; Add. MSS. 32891, f. 142.
[5] Colonel William A'Court, M.P., to Newcastle, 5 March 1759 ; Add.
MSS. 32888, f. 344.
[6] Joseph Gulston, M.P., to James West, Secretary to the Treasury,
6 November 1755 ; Add. MSS. 32860, f. 393.

Slighted, disregarded, and snubbed, sore from the many rebuffs he received, Newcastle discovered them even where none was meant.   He invited attacks and expected them, and found his only profit in despairing complaints.   These, no doubt, were often exaggerated — none the less they expressed a subjective truth.   Feeling deserted and profoundly unhappy, he was always on the point of resigning, but somehow could not do it.   '*Ingratitude* or (what is much worse) *being suspected* I meet with every day from those of whom I deserve it the least . . .' he wrote to his late secretary, Andrew Stone, on 25 June 1756.   '*Friends and enemies* will force me out of employment.' [1]   And to Hardwicke : 'Every day convinces me that it is impossible for *me* almost to oblige anybody ; or to avoid being suspected of falsity and duplicity, even to those for whom I have, and have always profess'd, the greatest friendship.' [2]

Again, on 21 May 1757, to his nephew, Lord Lincoln : [3]

I am without advisers. . . . I am at a loss what to do, I am amused by my imperious enemies, unassisted by my friends, courted and tricked by those who mean only to cheat and supplant me.

Here again is a memorandum of 27 August 1759, marked 'Business with my Lord Hardwicke' :

My own situa- tion.	It is necessary to determine whether I should go on or not. In what manner, if I was to go out. Can I stay in, unsupported by any one man in office ? [4]

And on 4 November 1759 :

My situation.	Lord Hardwicke withdraws himself from business — alone — with these two Secretaries [Pitt and Holdernesse] — taking advantage of every thing they can. Carrying on every thing of real consequence, in some measure, without me. It is not safe for me to go on. Christmas will be the proper time to go out, with the least inconvenience to the King's affairs.

[1] Add. MSS. 32865, f. 430.   [2] 25 June 1756 ; *ibid.* f. 434.
[3] Add. MSS. 32871, ff. 113-14.   [4] Add. MSS. 32894, f. 479.

My situation   The King, the only person from whom I can ever
at Court.   expect any countenance.

               His Majesty has been extremely good to me, but I
feel an alteration arising from my not being able to
give His Majesty hopes of what he desires [concern-
ing Hanover at the peace conference]. False hopes
would be treachery. Real hopes untrue.

               If Mr. Pitt was to know I had done so, he would
make it a strong article of (possibly publick) accusa-
tion against me.[1]

Nor is it true that he occupied a great and dominant position
with George II. Contemporaries knew better ; Chesterfield
speaks of his 'servile compliance with the will of his sovereign
for the time being', Bute, about his 'pusillanimity in the
closet' during George II's reign.[2] Even in matters of preferments George II was not Newcastle's mere 'rubber-stamp', as
he is sometimes represented. Here is Newcastle's own account
to Hardwicke of a scene which occurred over a minor recommendation (a K.B. for George Warren, M.P.) :

His Majesty flew into a passion. . . . *What, do you think I dote ?
Pray, don't come to me with such propositions as these.* I bow'd and
said little. . . . How can I make any proposition to him after this ?
What shall I do ? Pray, send me your thoughts upon it.[3]

And nine days later he wrote again :

My situation, *thought* a favorite in the closet, with power to do
but a few things there, and scarce daring to do even those few things ;
my situation, I say, puts me in the power of almost every body to
hurt me every hour of the day — alone and unsupported in the
Administration — attack'd daily with offensive speeches, or, if I

[1] 'Memorandums for the King', 4 November 1759 ; Add. MSS. 32898,
ff. 81-2. Pitt was in the habit of threatening and bullying Newcastle, who
feared him. When, for instance, Newcastle, in reference to his private
correspondence with Joseph Yorke, assured Pitt that he never thought of
entering into any separate peace negotiations, 'he then said, *not very politely*,
if I did, I should not be able to walk the streets without a guard' (Newcastle
to Hardwicke, 31 October 1759 ; Add. MSS. 32897, ff. 512-26).
   [2] 'Heads of Lord Bute's Letter to Mr. Grenville', 13 October 1761 ;
Grenville Papers, vol. i. pp. 395-7.
   [3] 16 October 1759 ; Add. MSS. 32897, f. 148. For Warren's application see Add. MSS. 33055, f. 281. Warren put forward his £16,000 p.a.
as one of his chief claims to the distinction, and Newcastle accepted his
'immense estate' for a valid qualification.

escape them at Court, have some letters of reproach or menace the next morning.[1]

Afraid of the King, Newcastle sought consolation and support with the King's mistress, Lady Yarmouth. 'What has she to do with these things ?' was on one occasion the King's protest against this method of approaching him.

The only comfortable two hours I have in the whole day, are those I pass there; and you are always teazing her with these things. — Because, Sir, I thought it the most respectful way of conveying them to Your Majesty.[2]

Even the King's leave to go away for a week-end, the First Lord of the Treasury would occasionally receive through her :

Le Roi m'ordonne de vous dire, qu'il vous accordai la permission d'aller jusqu'à lundi à Claremont, et qu'il étoit content des arangemens que vous avés pris. . . .[3]

This was the great man who afterwards was accused of having ruled, run, and exploited George II.

No better was his position in the Government. It was his continual (and no doubt justified) complaint that on the most important matters he was not consulted, and that his own measures at the Treasury were not properly supported in Parliament by the other Ministers. He lived in constant fear of attacks from Pitt, and many a time, in his anxious imagination, saw himself on the point of being impeached. The fact that about the middle of the eighteenth century there was no joint Cabinet responsibility, and that Ministers could oppose each other in Parliament, and speak and vote on opposite sides, is too well known to require elaboration ; and Newcastle, helpless, timid, and utterly dependent on others, felt most severely the incoherence which in the Government under his nominal headship had reached a fantastic degree.

At all times methodical and harmonious conduct of administration is much more difficult than is generally supposed. During the last war, in the Political Intelligence Department

---

[1] Newcastle to Hardwicke, 25 October 1759 ; Add. MSS. 32897, f. 374.
[2] Newcastle to Hardwicke, 27 September 1759 ; Add. MSS. 32896, f. 136.
[3] Lady Yarmouth to Newcastle 18 April 1760 ; Add. MSS. 32904, f. 430.

of the Foreign Office, where we studied the affairs of foreign
countries, we often felt that the most useful and arduous work
was left undone : to find out what was happening in London,
in our own Government. About 1760 there was a man whose
business it seems to have been to serve as such an Intelligence
Officer between the various Ministers and groups, and he makes
indeed an interesting figure in the history of that time. This
man was Count de Viry, the Sardinian Minister to the Court
of St. James's, a peculiar intriguer, an ample talker, assiduous,
inscrutable, secretive, and yet plausible, who carried information or tales from Newcastle to Pitt, from Pitt to Bute, from
Bute to Newcastle (the reader may complete for himself the
permutations). It was Viry who informed Newcastle that Pitt
was satisfied with him ; [1] with him Newcastle discussed his
own position and those of his fellow Ministers ; to him Pitt
aired his views about Leicester House or Newcastle, and Bute
about Newcastle, Pitt, Grenville, etc. ; [2] to him, in November
1759, George II sent a paper explaining his plans concerning
Hanover at the coming peace conference, and only from him
did Newcastle obtain knowledge of its contents.[3] It was he
who explained to the First Lord of the Treasury the foreign
policy of the Secretary of State : 'My friend [Viry] told
me . . . Mr. Pitt's scheme of foreign politicks, which is,
above all, to cultivate and gain, if possible, the Court of Peters-
burgh as a check, etc.' ; [4] and in July 1760 he claimed to have
been asked by Pitt 'to sound the sentiments of Leicester House
with regard to peace and the terms and conditions of it, and
particularly to learn their thoughts as to Spain . . .' [5] In
October 1759, the King said to Newcastle in reference to the
two Secretaries of State : 'I hate and detest Holdernesse, as

[1] See above, p. 69.
[2] See, for instance, Add. MSS. 32908, ff. 342-4, and Add. MSS. 32890,
ff. 7-9. One might suspect that Viry made up many of the confidential talks
which he reported ; still, sometimes, where his accounts can be verified
from other sources, they are found to have a substratum of fact ; see, for
instance, Newcastle's 'Minutes of a conversation with Lord Bute', 11 April
1759, which confirm the account given on the same day by Viry to Newcastle
of his own conversation with Bute.
[3] Memorandum of 22 November 1759 ; Add. MSS. 32899, ff. 35-6.
[4] 21 November 1759 ; ibid. ff. 11-12.
[5] Add. MSS. 32908, ff 342-3.

much as you do, *I don't know what to do with him* — let Viry
endeavour to set Pitt against him'. [1] With Viry, Bute discussed
the general election of 1761 and who should nominate to
Government boroughs ; it was through him that Bute's
assumption of office was negotiated ; it was again from Viry
that, in March 1762, Newcastle learned Bute's 'notions upon
the terms of peace'. [2] And it was through Viry that the preliminary negotiations for the Peace of Paris were carried on.
Anyone who wants to fathom the whole depth of Newcastle's
ludicrous position in the Government should read the many
minutes in his papers marked 'C. V.' and note his attitude
towards that quaint foreign intriguer.[3]

Newcastle frequently referred to himself as a 'galley-slave'
— why then did he remain in office ? Men are said to seek
pleasure and shun pain ; but as 'there is no accounting for
tastes', the statement is tautological — they seek what they
seek. It was proudly believed in the past that the earth was the
centre of the universe ; that man was created on a different
day from other animals ; that he was a reasonable being, 'the
captain of his soul'. Men still cling to this last fundamental
belief and they continue to give 'reasonable' explanations for
their actions, *i.e.* to 'rationalise' them. Disraeli and his wife

---

[1] 31 October 1759 ; Add. MSS. 32897, ff. 512-26.
[2] Newcastle to Hardwicke, 8 March 1762 ; Add. MSS. 32935, ff. 249-51.
[3] By 1758 Viry had become so indispensable a part of the British Governmental machine, that when his recall was mooted at Turin, all the powers
that were in London with one voice cried out against it. 'I entirely agree
with you', wrote Newcastle to Pitt, on 17 March 1758, 'as to the necessity of
stopping the most unjust recall of that honest man, M. Viri . . .' (*Chatham
Correspondence*, vol. i. p. 302). Next day Viry informed Bute that the
King had instructed Pitt to prevent his recall (Add. MSS. 36796, f. 28),
and Pitt wrote to Bute on the same subject (*ibid.* f. 35). An equal degree
of harmony in action was seldom, if ever, shown by the rulers of Great
Britain in that period. — It seems an appropriate sequel to Viry's English
career that his grandson, Francis Joseph Marie Henry, Baron de la Perrière,
born in this country but owing allegiance to the King of Sardinia (in 1813
he succeeded his father as Comte de Viry), should have sat in the British
Parliament (1790–96) under the assumed name of Henry Speed ; he had
married Augusta Montagu, the natural daughter of John, 4th Earl of Sandwich, and Martha Ray, was practically disowned by his father, and was
returned to Parliament for Huntingdon by his father-in-law. The correspondence which passed over that marriage between Lord Sandwich and
Comte de Viry (the son of Newcastle's friend) was published by the present
Earl of Sandwich in *The Times* on 10 October 1928.

themselves finished by accepting the story that he had married her for her money, though circumstances clearly prove that this was not the case ; and Nietzsche's 'pale murderer' robbed his victim in order to provide an explanation plausible to himself and to others. There are men who crave for mortification ; 'la mia allegrez' è la maninconia'. But unless this desire assumes a standardised religious form — hair-shirt or hermit's hut — and can be represented as a profitable bargain for another world, men dare not admit it, not even to themselves. If proved beyond doubt, it is described as madness ; educated men may become monks, but must not enlist as privates in the Army. 'Why dost thou deprive thyself of the joys of this world, if thou dost not hope to gain eternal joy ?' asks, in *Thaïs* Paphnucius the anachorete, of Timocles the stoic. But no true ascetic has ever practised his creed for a bargain ; and Paphnucius, who tried it, finished with the devil.

There was unconscious self-mortification in Newcastle's tenure of office. In the lifetime of George II he explained his service as a duty to the King. When Pitt hinted at resigning together — 'I told him my case was different. I had so many obligations to the King that I had no choice, but one part to take.' [1] At the opening of the new reign, Newcastle declared his intention to resign ; and then remained. People thereupon concluded that his intention had never been serious ; but all one can say is that he was unable voluntarily to leave his treadmill.

The King to Come

1. *The Education and Character of the Prince*

It is usually alleged that George III was brought up in 'autocratic notions'. But there is nothing to show, either in his words or acts, that he ever aimed at being more than what the self-contradictory constitutional theory and practice of the time made him — the hereditary, irresponsible head of the executive in a Parliamentary State. So far from being taught

[1] 'Heads of Mr. Pitt's Conversation', 17 October 1759 ; Add. MSS. 32897, ff. 173-5.

les of prerogative, he was nurtured on constitutional
ides which he duly copied, adorning them with the
nt verbiage about virtue and liberty.

The obligation of each Briton to fulfil the political duties, receive a vast accession of strength when he calls to mind of what a
noble and well balanced constitution of government he has the
honor to belong; a constitution of free and equal laws, secured
against arbitrary will and popular licence, a constitution in fine the
nurse of heroes, the parent of liberty, the patron of learning and
arts, and the dominion of laws.[1]

Indeed, he believed as firmly as any of his contemporaries
in 'our happy settlement' and the 'balance of our most excellent constitution', he beheld with the greatest enthusiasm 'the
beauty, excellence and perfection of the British constitution
as by law established', and he abhorred 'despotism'. He
would declare that he could only accept the Crown 'with the
hopes of restoring my much loved country to her antient
state of liberty; of seeing her in time free from her present
load of debts and again famous for being the residence of
true piety and virtue'. Otherwise (in the best eighteenth-
century style) — 'I should with an eye of pleasure look on
retiring to some uninhabited cavern that would prevent me
from seeing the sufferings of my countrymen and the total
destruction of this Monarchy'. In short, he talked flapdoodle
of the most innocent kind — and the danger was only in what
a man might not do who talked such flapdoodle.

No doubt he was continually reminded by his guardians
and teachers of the high station to which fate had predestined
him — what prince is not? Still, he was brought up not so
much in particularly high notions of royalty as in an atmosphere
of dynastic opposition, both his mother and Lord Bute confirming him in his hatred and contempt of the King, his grandfather. He was encouraged to hate before he could think, and
a cleavage developed in his feelings which made him see himself surrounded by devils and angels, all the devils at St.
James's and all the angels at Leicester House; the neurotic
boy, bitter in soul and mentally underdeveloped, concentrated

[1] This essay is among the Bute MSS.

on the King the hostility of the heir and rival, while his love went out to Lord Bute, to him the incarnation of a tutelary paternal spirit. When he reached the age of eighteen, George II proposed to settle him at Kensington Palace and St. James's, and thus, if possible, to withdraw him from the influences to which he had hitherto been subjected ; and Lord Waldegrave was instructed to explain to the Prince of Wales and his mother that 'the King looked upon my Lord Bute as closely connected with Mr. Pitt and the Opposition, and that therefore His Majesty did not think him a proper person to be put about His Royal Highness'.[1] Threatened by separation the Prince sent Bute the following paper :

KEW. *June* 31 [*sic*], 1756.

MY DEAR LORD — I have had the pleasure of your friendship during the space of a year, by which I have reap'd great advantage, but not the improvement I should if I had follow'd your advice ; but you shall find me make such a progress in this summer, that shall give you hopes, that with the continuation of your advice, I may turn out as you wish.

It is very true that the Ministers have done everything they can to provoke me, that they have call'd me a harmless boy, and have not even deign'd to give me an answer when I so earnestly wish to see my friend about me. They have also treated my Mother in a cruel manner (which I will neither forget nor forgive to the day of my death) because she is so good as to come forward and to preserve her son, from the many snares that surround him. My Friend is also attack'd in the most cruel and horrid manner, not for anything he has done against them, but because he is my Friend, and wants to see me come to the Throne with honor and not with disgrace and because he is, a friend to the bless'd liberties of his country and not to arbitrary notions. I look upon myself as engag'd in honor and justice to defend these my two Friends as long as I draw breath.

I do therefore here in the presence of Our Almighty Lord promiss, that I will ever remember the insults done to my Mother, and never will forgive anyone who shall offer to speak disrespectfully of her.

I do in the same solemn manner declare, that I will defend my Friend and will never use evasive answers, but will always tell him whatever is said against him, and will more and more show to the world the great friendship I have for him, and all the malice that can be invented against him shall only bind me the stronger to him.

[1] Newcastle to Hardwicke, 12 June 1756 ; Add. MSS. 32865. ff. 277-86.

I do further promise, that all the allurements my enemies can think of, or the threats that they may make pour out upon me, shall never make me in the least change from what I so solemnly promiss in this paper.

I will take upon me the man in every thing, and will not shew that indifference which I have as yet too often done.

As I have chosen the vigorous part, I will throw off that indolence which if I don't soon get the better of will be my ruin, and will never grow weary of this, tho' —— [George II] should live many years.

I hope my dear Lord you will conduct me through this difficult road and will bring me to the gole. I will exactly follow your advice, without which I shall inevitably sink.

I am young and unexperienc'd and want advice. I trust in your friendship which will assist me in all difficulties.

I know few things I ought to be more thankfull for to the Great Power above, than for its having pleas'd Him to send you to help and advise me in these difficult times.

I do hope you will from this instant banish all thoughts of leaving me, and will resolve, if not for my sake for the good of your country to remain with me. I have often heard you say, that you don't think I shall have the same friendship for you when I am married as I now have. I shall never change in that, nor will I bear to be in the least depriv'd of your company. And I shall expect that all my relations shall show you that regard which is due to the Friend of the whole family.

I sign my name with the greatest pleasure to what I have here written which is my firm and unalterable resolution.

GEORGE P.

Meantime the Prince begged the King's permission to remain at Kew with his mother — 'this point is of too great consequence to my happiness for me not to wish ardently Your Majesty's favour and indulgence in it'; and, determined not to let himself 'be in the least deprived' of Bute's company, he continued to urge as his 'most ardent request' and the 'only one' with regard to his establishment, that Bute 'be plac'd in some principal situation' about his person.[1] And as the position

---

[1] The Prince of Wales to the King, 12 July 1756; Add. MSS. 32684, ff. 92-3. Two days later the Prince wrote to Bute:

The K—— and those he has consulted have treated [me] with less regard than they would have dared to have done any Member of Parliament; I hope you will agree with me in thinking that if this just request is refused, that for my honour, dignity and character, I may keep no

of the Government in the country had become precarious and attempts to buy off Bute had failed,[1] Newcastle and Fox, afraid of the Opposition, prevailed on the King to grant the Prince's request.

The letter written by the Prince of Wales to Lord Bute in June 1756 deserves close examination; it is not that of a normal youth of eighteen. It starts with a confession of his own insufficiency and a promise of 'progress' in the future. After that it plunges into accusations tinged with persecution mania and expressed in soaring terms which fall quite flat. Perhaps the opening words, 'It is very true that . . .', supply the key; with deep conviction the boy seems to repeat phrases which upset and terrify him, but which he probably has not coined himself. Next, he breaks out into new confessions and vows — 'I will take upon me the man in everything', etc., and the point directed against his grandfather, the King, appears: he will never 'grow weary of this tho' —— should live many years'; the wish that he should not is fairly obvious. On this follows adoration of Bute, the God-sent man, without whose friendship and guidance he would 'inevitably sink', and the fear that Bute might leave him — like a poor young girl he is afraid of being deserted; this is coupled with such a consciousness of his own unworthiness that it is the good of the country which he has to plead. And finally comes the surprising discussion of what change marriage would work in his feelings — no, even this shall not shake his dependence on Bute. The letter, full of the will to be a man and of confessions to the contrary, thus closes with an unconscious assurance that he will never grow

measures with these counsellors who have not prevented the K—— treating me with such unheard of contempt, the longer I live the more I shall see how little any trust can be placed in most men except yourself.

[1] The Duke of Argyll, Bute's uncle, was used as intermediary. 'He said he had wished for years to have connected Ld. B. with the Administration to which Ld. B. was himself extreamly well disposed, but the being slighted and passed over had wrought and might still work upon his passions. Other things at present must operate too; therefore he declared he cou'd not so much as guess what effect his endeavours wou'd have' (William Murray to Newcastle, 10 July 1756; Add. MSS. 32866, ff. 111-12). On sounding Bute the Duke of Argyll found that he would not accept any place to compensate him for that in the Prince's household, and that he was much mortified by the King's refusal (same to same, 25 August 1756; Add. MSS. 32867, ff. 46-7).

up into one. It is a pathetic human document, which circumstances endow with high historic importance.

The painful impression is deepened by other letters. They are full of the same exasperating consciousness of his own insufficiency, the same honest will to 'improve' and despairing doubt as to whether he can, the desire to become worthy of the station 'it has pleased Almighty Providence to place' him in, and the fear of making in it but 'a very poor and despicable figure'; and the letters present throughout the same picture of mental and moral underdevelopment. He will 'act the man in every thing'; and how will he do it ? By *repeating* whatever he *is to say* with spirit ! How is his growth to be secured ? By Bute examining 'at least once a week' what he has done ! This from a youth of about twenty, in an age when men matured quicker than they do now. Here are two more of these letters :

SAVILE HOUSE,
March 25th.

MY DEAR LORD — I have had your conversation of Wednesday night ever since in my mind; it greatly hurts me, that I cannot make an excuse for myself. I am conscious of my own indolence which none but so sincere a friend as you, could so long have borne with. I do here in the most solemn manner declare that I will entirely throw aside this my greatest enemy and that you shall instantly find a change; my negligence which I reckon as belonging to indolence is very great but shall absolutely be for ever laid away.

I will employ all my time upon business, and will be able for the future to give you an account of everything I read.

As to what you mention'd in your note of last night concerning F—x [Fox] it has made me strictly examine myself; and I do now here tell you that I am resolv'd in myself to take the resolute part, to act the man in everything, to repeat whatever I am to say with spirit and not blushing and afraid as I have hitherto, I will also never shew the least irresolution, and will not from being warm on any subject, by degrees grow quite indifferent about it, in short my conduct shall convince you that I am mortified at what I have done, and that I despise myself as every body else must, that knows how I have acted; I hope that by altering now, I shall be able to regain your opinion which I vallue above everything in this world.

I beg you will be persuaded that I will constantly reflect whether what I am doing is worthy of one who is to mount the Throne, and who owes everything to his friend.

I will by my behaviour shew that I know, if I in the least deviate from what I here promise and declare, I shall loose the greatest of stakes my Crown and what I esteem far beyond that, my friend, I hope this will persuade you not to leave me, when all is at stake, when nobody but you can steer me thro' this difficult, tho' glorious path.

I am, my dear Lord, with very great sincerity, your most oblig'd friend,   GEORGE P.

½ past eight.

MY DEAREST FRIEND — My heart was so full with the many truths you told me last night that I was not then able to express my thoughts to you; I, therefore, take this method of laying them before you; but at the same time what hopes can I have that you will credit any resolution that I make when you cannot help remembering that as many as I have made, I have regularly broke; my dearest friend the considering of how little effect my promises have as yet been will be one of the strongest motives to rouse me to act with the greatest minuteness up to what I now promise.

All I beg of you is that you would have a little patience and judge by my actions whether my words are not my firm and unalterable resolutions.

I mean from the present hour to apply with the greatest assiduity to attempt if it be possible to regain the many years I have fruitlessly spent; I will engage that you shall find a very visible alteration in me, the thoughts of what I ought to be shall ever be in my mind, and that added to my desire of making a good figure in the station it has pleased Almighty Providence to place me in, will make me spare no pains to accomplish this, though I own I am of such an unhappy nature that if I cannot in a good measure alter that, let me be ever so learned in what is necessary for a King to know, I shall make but a very poor and despicable figure. My dearest friend the only small return I can make you for your unwearied pains for my future quiet and honour, and the happiness of this my dear country is the making it appear that the many things you have said in my favour are not entirely void of truth.

I therefore desire that we may regulate my studies, and that you would at least once a week examine what I have done.

The more I consider how I have thrown away my time, the more I am surprised at the greatness of your indulgence, that you have been able to prevail upon yourself to remain with me.

I might add various other things, but they shall remain till I see you alone, when if you please we will talk the matter thoroughly over.

There is another letter, dated 25 September 1758, again most contrite in tone, admitting the 'many truths' Bute had told him :

. . . they have set me in a most dreadful light before my own eyes ; I now see plainly that I have been my greatest enemy ; for had I always acted according to your advice, I should now have been the direct opposite from what I am. . . .

If you should now resolve to set me adrift, I could not obraid you, but on the contrary look on it as a natural consequence of my faults, and not want of friendship in you.

I say if you shall ever think fit to take this step, my line of action is plain : for though I act wrong in most things, yet I have too much spirit to accept the Crown and be a sypher, and too much love for my countrymen to mount this Throne and be their detestation ; I would therefore in such an unhappy case retire to some distant region where in solitude I might for the rest of my life remain, and think on the various faults I have committed that I might repent of them. . . .

What mental diagnosis can be drawn from these letters for one who finally had to be diagnosed as hopelessly insane ? Sensitive and brought up under abnormal conditions ; imbued with high moral principles and paralysed by an overwhelming consciousness of guilt ; and yet all the time reminded of the high place he would some day have to fill ; a youth who had never been allowed to be young and who had not managed to grow up ; not diverted from serious work by passions or pleasures, but sinking helplessly into sad indolence ; perceiving such a distance between what he felt himself to be and what he wanted to become, that he was bound to seek refuge in dissimulation ; ready to resign his will completely to the man in whom he believed to have found his ideal ; and yet, in that self-imposed bondage, yearning after great achievements.

There was another serious peculiarity in this unbalanced, tortured mind. There is no 'sinner' with a 'cosmic' consciousness of guilt who does not call on others to repent, and does not invoke punishment on them if they seem normally cheerful ; who does not extend to others his severe moral self-depreciation, and does not despise them with a tinge of self-elevation. At the age of twenty, the Prince of Wales was

firmly convinced of the utter unworthiness of all men except
Bute : 'As to honesty, I have already lived long enough to
know you are the only man I shall ever meet with who possesses
that quality'. In fact, practically everybody was to him ungrateful, faithless, and corrupt, and this poor, immature boy,
in speaking of the oldest and most distinguished statesmen of
the age, would say how some day he would treat them 'according to their deserts', make them 'smart', etc. From morbid
self-abasement he would pass to exultation such as that of the
Emperor William II, and feel himself in a partnership with
God ; only in the case of George III, even for that partnership
Bute was indispensable. The following letter, written on 20
August 1758, may serve as an example :

Near eleven.

My DEAR FRIEND — I fear this check will prevent General Aber-
crombie's pushing towards Crown Point, but in this as well as every
thing else I entirely rely on the Almighty who best knows what is
fit for us ; the assistance he has given us at Louisburgh makes me
hope we shall receive further marks of His goodness ; [1] I am certain
that by trusting in him ; and attempting with vigour to restore religion and virtue when I mount the Throne this great country will
probably regain her antient state of lustre ; I have no fears with
regard to a future day provided you keep your health. Adieu, best
of friends.

And in November 1757, when trying to ward off 'black
thoughts' concerning the future of this country, he concluded
the letter : 'If you are but well and Providence assists us,
England may yet be free and happy'.

Of his honest good-will and his high moral purpose, there
can be no doubt. Here is a letter to Bute, written in the
winter 1759–60 — how worthy in sentiment and how flat in
expression !

You have often accused me of growing grave and thoughtful, it
is entirely owing to a daily encreasing admiration of the fair sex,

[1] But occasionally the Prince took a different view of victories when won
for his grandfather and his Government ; in October 1760 he wrote to Bute
about the fall of Montreal :

I wish my dearest friend joy of this success, but at the same time, I
can't help feeling that every such thing raises those I have no reason
to love.

which I am attempting with all the phylosophy and resolution I am capable of to keep under, I should be asham'd after having so long resisted the charms of those divine creatures now to become their prey; Princes when once in their hands make miserable figures, the annals of France and the present situation of Government in the Kingdom I the most love, are convincing proofs of; when I have said this you will plainly feel how strong a struggle there is between the boiling youth of 21 years and prudence, the last I hope will ever keep the upper hand, indeed if I can weather it, but a few years, marriage will put a stop to this combat in my breast, I believe you will agree that application is the only aid I can give to reason, that by keeping the mind constantly employ'd is a likely means of preserving those passions in due subordination to it; believe me I will with the greatest assiduity attempt to make all that progress which your good counsels, if properly attended to have reason to expect.

Bute's reply to this letter provoked another, so extraordinary in style as to require no comment:

On receiving your note I find my dearest friend intimates something I did not mean in my letter this morning; you seem to think of the most important step to my happiness, but I can never agree to alter my situation whilst this old man [George II] lives; I will rather undergo anything ever so disagreeable than put my trust in him for a single moment in an affair of such delicacy; my dearest friend will, I am sure, entirely agree with me, I shall therefore, only add that I hope the dose you are taking to-night will have its desired effect.

Looking at George III, one can merely wonder whether his becoming a prey to 'the charms of those divine creatures' would not have been preferable to the qualms of a diseased conscience, and whether it would not have been better for England had the Prince of Wales had a gay mistress instead of a sententious preceptor, wrongly described as a 'favourite'. The biggest blunders in the world are committed by men with serious faces who feel uncomfortable in their own minds, talk a great deal, and never enjoy themselves.

A picture which the Prince of Wales drew of his own position, and the programme for his future reign, are contained in an 'Essay on King Alfred', written presumably some time between 1755 and 1758 ; [1] he appears in it as the strong man he wished to be, reproving and correcting others (those

[1] In the Bute MSS.

'myrmidons of the blackest kind' who served his grandfather),
himself noble and virtuous, in close and natural partnership
with the 'Almighty Power' :

> . . . He had the happiness of being bred up in the school of ad-
versity . . . excellent were his laws, and vigorously kept to ; for he
examined into everything himself, impenetrable in his secrets. . . .
> . . . When Alfred mounted the Throne, there was scarce a man
in office that was not totally unfit for it, and generally extremely
corrupt in the execution of it . . . he got rid of the incorrigible,
reclaimed others, and formed new subjects for to raise his own glory
and with it the glory and happiness of his country. . . . When all
this is carefully examined, we may safely affirm that no good and
great Prince born in a free country and like Alfred fond of the cause
of liberty, will ever despair of restoring his country to virtue, freedom
and glory, even though he mounts the Throne in the worst corrupted
times, in storms of inward faction and the most threatening circumstances without.
> Let him be but true to himself, true to religion, virtue, honour,
freedom ; such a Prince has a right to expect, and will most certainly
have the support of that Almighty Power that decides the fate of
kingdoms, and baffles all the black designs and wrecks the cunning
of proud, ambitious and deceitful men.

2. *Newcastle, Pitt, and Leicester House*

How did meantime the 'proud, ambitious and deceitful
men', presumably in the first place the poor old Duke of Newcastle, the King's 'knave and counsellor', prepare for the
coming reign of virtue ? For sooner or later, the Prince of
Wales would be King, with Lord Bute for Minister. Newcastle, in his own style, adjusted himself beforehand to a future
in which, as to office, he claimed to be uninterested ; and while
George II was still alive, and on very indifferent terms with
Leicester House, Newcastle was none the less prepared to
admit the influence of the Prince of Wales and Bute in the
Government. But about 1757, William Pitt was still their
chosen champion, and Bute, in his stilted letters, addressed Pitt
as his 'dearest friend' and signed himself 'your most affectionate
friend and devoted servant'. Even if public opinion were
against Pitt, wrote Bute to him on 2 March 1757:

I am certain the firm support and countenance of *him* who is some day to reap the fruits of my friend's unwearied endeavours for the public safety, would make him perfectly easy under the frowns of prejudiced, deluded, fluctuating men.[1]

In the spring of 1757, during the confusion which followed on the dismissal of Pitt and Temple, Bute took a prominent part in the negotiations for a new Government. There was danger of the Duke of Cumberland and Henry Fox gaining control ; 'Leicester House', wrote Newcastle to Mansfield on 13 April 1757, 'is so much frighten'd with this new Administration, that they wish to make up with me. . . .'[2] Meetings were arranged between Newcastle and Bute, Hardwicke and Pitt. 'You must, if you come in at all,' wrote Chesterfield to Newcastle, who complained of their excessive terms, 'come in with a strength of your own, that may curb the influence of the Duke of Cumberland and his party, and you only can have that strength by bringing the Prince and Princess of Wales along with you.'[3] With the active help and full approval of Bute, the coalition was formed between Newcastle and Pitt.

Henceforth Newcastle was careful to comply with Bute's wishes and opinions. In January 1758, when urging Lord Dupplin to become Chancellor of the Exchequer, he quoted Bute as one of those who considered Dupplin the proper man for the post.[4] Having been told by Legge that Bute had a candidate for Sheriff-Depute of the County of Lothian,[5] he thanked Legge effusively for this opportunity 'of shewing that person how desirous I am to obey his commands. . . .'[6] When, in February 1758, a Commissionership of the Excise fell vacant and Bute informed Newcastle that the Prince of Wales wished it for his old preceptor, G. L. Scott, Newcastle, though he had previously obtained the King's consent to the appointment of a distant cousin, Henry Pelham, replied that

---

[1] *Chatham Correspondence*, vol. i. pp. 223-4.
[2] Add. MSS. 32870, ff. 411-12.
[3] Newcastle to Chesterfield, 7 May 1757, Add. MSS. 32871, f. 39 ; Chesterfield to Newcastle, same day, *ibid.* f. 45.
[4] Newcastle to Dupplin, 10 January 1758 ; Add. MSS. 32877, f. 86.
[5] H. B. Legge to Newcastle, 9 June 1758 ; Add. MSS. 32880, f. 373.
[6] Newcastle to H. B. Legge, 9 June 1758 ; *ibid.* f. 375.

he would not allow a relation of his to stand in the way of a recommendation from the Prince of Wales. 'I have already acquainted the King with the state of the case ; and hope very soon to receive His Majesty's orders for the appointment of Mr. Scott.' [1] Not that the King relished such compliance with the wishes of his expectant heir — this is Newcastle's account of the audience :

> When I came to mention the affair of the Commissioner of the Excise, and the message from my Lord Bute, We [the King] took fire immediately : '*What has he to do with it ?*' And I am sorry to say, I hear'd a language, which I have not hear'd before, since I came in last. *That* deserves serious consideration.[2]

But Newcastle's eager subserviency to Leicester House made no material difference in their attitude towards him — it was one of cold and haughty contempt. 'The Prince', wrote Bute in reply to Newcastle's zealous assurances, 'interested himself in that affair no otherways than as thinking derogatory to his dignity to suffer a person to remain unprovided for, who once had the honour of being concern'd in his education.' [3]

If Newcastle was despised, Pitt soon came to be hated at Leicester House. Dodington's view proved accurate, that a follower of the Prince of Wales, when turned minister of the King, was bound to abandon his previous connexions. In December 1758 the Prince wrote to Bute :

> I am certain he [Pitt] has given himself up to the K. —— or the D of N. —— or else he could not act the infamous and ungrateful part he now does.

And on 30 July 1759 :

> I am not surpriz'd at this insolence of Pitt's, he has long shown a want of regard both of you, my dearest friend, and consequently of myself.

---

[1] Newcastle to Bute, 8 February 1758 ; Add. MSS. 32877, ff. 382-3. G. L. Scott was appointed.

[2] Newcastle to Hardwicke, 4 February 1758 ; *ibid*. f. 350.

[3] 9 February 1758 ; *ibid*. ff. 408-9. Even so, Scott was not exactly 'unprovided for' ; he was in receipt of a secret service pension of £600 p.a. ; see my book on *The Structure of Politics at the Accession of George III*, pp. 230 and 446-8.

Again, on 23 December 1759, after Legge had refused to comply with the commands of Leicester House with regard to the Hampshire election, the Prince wrote to Bute :

. . . my dearest friend, we must look out for new tools, our old ones having all deserted us ; if I am but steady and have your assistance, we may make them all smart for their ingratitude.

Pitt's presence in the Government failed to provide Leicester House with the patronage they seem to have expected — as Viry reported to Newcastle on 6 October 1758, Bute considered that Pitt left it too much to Newcastle. 'That Lord B.—— wish'd only such a conduct towards me as might *faire aller la machine* : but that Mr. P.—— gave up all recommendations to employments etc. to me. . . .'[1]   But even about measures, Pitt seems not to have informed or consulted Leicester House as they wished, and had expected.   Viry alleged that Pitt's colleague, Holdernesse, was making his court to Lord Bute (which was probably true) ; and whenever the post came in, sent him the most minute accounts that could be collected. 'The other Secretary is not so minute and that does not please.'

Nobody wishes more than I do [Pitt explained to Viry] that the King would order his servants to communicate his business to the Prince of Wales, and even to order His Royal Highness to assist at Council : but, since that was not the King's pleasure, he did not think it was right for any of the King's servants to inform His Royal Highness of the King's business.[2]

[1] Newcastle to Hardwicke, 5 October 1758 ; Add. MSS. 32884, ff. 259-67. A year earlier there is an entry about the same matter in the 'Register of Lord Bute's Correspondence' (Add. MSS. 36796, f. 23) : 'Count Viry to the Earl of Bute (22 October 1757) : The Duke is determined to have in his power all the Government situations. That Mr. Pitt will be obliged to resign. The Duke of Newcastle.' Naturally no conclusions can be ventured on the basis of mere headings — one can merely regret being deprived of the amusement which a comparison of the reports made by Viry on the same matter to different people would undoubtedly afford.

[2] 'C. V.', 10 November 1759 ; Add. MSS. 32898, ff. 204-5. If this was Pitt's line, he was in this, as in so many other things, ahead of his time ; *e.g.*, Newcastle could not in fairness have condemned Holdernesse. He himself, after he had resigned office in November 1756, had invited and received communications about official business from Holdernesse ; 'I am infinitely obliged to you for the continuance of your confidence', Newcastle wrote to him on 12 December 1756, 'of which you need never apprehend any ill consequences' (Add. MSS. 32869, f. 351). And in 1762, while still in office, Newcastle sent full accounts of despatches received to the Duke of Cumberland.

The way in which the Prince of Wales took Pitt's reserve can be seen from a letter which he wrote to Bute on 8 December 1758:

> I suppose you agree with me in thinking that as Mr. P. does not now chuse to communicate what is intended to be done, but defers it till executed, he might save himself the trouble of sending at all, as I should hear only a few days later, as well as other people, what measures have been taken.
>
> Indeed my dearest friend he treats both you and me with no more regard than he would do a parcel of children, he seems to forget that the day will come, when he must expect to be treated according to his deserts.

3. *The Future Government*

Late in 1758 discussions were started concerning the Government to be formed on the accession of the Prince of Wales. To him Bute was naturally the man predestined to be 'the Minister' of his reign, and as appears from the letters given below, in 1756 Bute had agreed to assume the Treasury on the Prince's accession, obviously counting on having Pitt for his Secretary of State ; now, with Pitt estranged from him and in coalition with Newcastle, and the country at war, he hesitated. The following letter is undated, but seems to have been written in December 1758 :

> *9 o'clock.*
>
> I have pretty much turned over in my thoughts the idea you had the other night, of not accepting the Treasury in a future day : the more I reflect upon it, the more I with horror see the inevitable mischiefs that would arise from your taking such a step, to this poor country, and consequently to myself; for I fear I should not only find how differently that board would be managed but also that you would give me less of that holsome advice that alone can enable me to make this great nation happy.
>
> I cannot help differing with you in the reasons you gave for thinking of this; are not Legge, Lord George [Sackville], Lord Halifax, Conway, and more that could [be] nam'd equal in abilities to these great Greenvilles ? for as to honesty, I think all sets of men seem equaly to have thrown that aside, and if you should agree with me in this, why cannot we embark with the above men, or some others, in case the great men should prove themselves, what I begin to think them. . . .

The next letter is again undated, but its first sentence seems to refer to the preceding : the Prince's programme of giving 'puts off' to his Ministers until he has consulted Bute was to be duly carried out on his accession :

MY DEAREST FRIEND — Since I wrote yesterday to you, I have turn'd over in my mind the various reasons that can urge you to harbour that most destructive thought to me, of refusing the Treasury. I immagine 'tis owing to some diffidence of me, for when I compare the many things I have heard you say on the subject, I feel that that alone can be the reason for this alteration in your opinion. You are, I believe, sensible that besides having the greatest opinion of your worth and judgment, I also have the greatest love and friendship for you ; the latter would alone be sufficient to put me on the rack at your seeming determin'd to leave me, but when I add the former to it, 'tis too much for mortal man to bear, I should look upon it as the greatest instance of your friendship if you would tell me what it is that makes you so extremely doubtful of accepting the office you yourself consented to two years ago, that I might convince you that you may with safety rely on my conduct. Perhaps it is the fear you have I shall not speak firmly enough to my Ministers or that I shall be stagger'd if they say anything unexpected ; as to the former I can with great certainty assure [you] that they, nor no one else shall see a want of steadiness either in my manner of acting or speaking, and as to the latter, I may give fifty sorts of puts off till I have with you thoroughly considered what part will be proper to be taken ; indeed, my dearest friend, the more I think of it the more I see my certain ruin if you should take that step. Do not imagine that what I alledge with regard to my own conduct is the mere dictates of a hasty thought, it is my firm resolve, after mature deliberation.

Meantime Bute engaged in conversations with Pitt about the future Government, from which the idea of himself at the Treasury does not seem to have been absent. They were reported by Viry to Newcastle whose minute, dated 19 December 1758, is reproduced here with all due reserve ; Viry undoubtedly heard and knew a great deal, but it must be borne in mind that it was not his only, or even his chief, aim to supply Newcastle (and future historians) with accurate information.

. . . then my Lord Bute enter'd upon a more material conversation, vizt. what it might be proper to do hereafter in case of an accident to the King.

Mr. Pitt said that he thought, in such case, everything should be done in concert with the Duke of Newcastle considering his long experience in business, his credit, his reputation *abroad*, and his constant zeal for the present Royal Family. To which Lord Bute replied, What ! The Duke of Newcastle to continue Minister, as he is, and (I think) in the office he is in ? That can't be. All sorts of regard should be paid to the Duke of Newcastle, his friends should be consider'd and supported ; and proper management should be had for him ; but he was not to continue to be *what he is now*.

Mr. Pitt replied that he did not mean to mark out any particular station, but that in general there should be a concert with the Duke of Newcastle ; that, very probably, the Duke of Newcastle might himself not desire to continue in the hurry of business, etc. My Lord Bute said the Prince of Wales would be very glad of Mr. Pitt's service ; but he must not expect to assign this man this employment, and another another. Mr. Pitt said that was far from his thoughts — he should be very ready to do the best service he could — that what he had said about the Duke of Newcastle was not at all with any such view. They parted well, and all seems made up for the present.[1]

Under date of 20 December 1758, appears a continuation of Viry's report to Newcastle, purporting to be Pitt's own account of the results of the above conversation :

That it was decided that the Duke of Newcastle was the Minister at present ; and that he had told my Lord Bute that he thought the Duke of Newcastle should be un bon parti dans le Ministère à l'avenir. Lord Bute said, to be Minister of this country hereafter, was what the Duke of Newcastle could not be. But Mr. Pitt did not say, what answer his Lordship made to that he said of *un bon parti* dans le Ministère.[2]

During the next months negotiations seem to have taken place between Leicester House and Henry Fox, who apparently spoke in the name of the Cumberland group, but probably in the first place pursued his own aim — to secure for himself a return to active politics on the death of the King [3] (a return which he ultimately achieved, without, and even against, his principal, the Duke of Cumberland). Leicester House thereupon approached the Duke of Newcastle with an inquiry which,

[1] Add. MSS. 32886, ff. 384-6.   [2] *Ibid*. f. 411.
[3] About earlier 'overtures' made by Fox to Leicester House, see Viry's talk with Lord Royston ; Royston to Hardwicke, 18 March 1758, Add. MSS. 35352, ff. 1-2.

together with his own reply, he placed on record in a memorandum dated 'Claremont, 18 March 1759':

My Lord Lincoln having acquainted me that in a conversation with my Lord Bute, his Lordship expressed a great desire on the part of the Prince of Wales, to know what part the Duke of Newcastle and his friends would take in case of the demise of the Crown; and shewing a great inclination to have a connection and assurance from them; when great applications were making to them from certain quarters; which would be immediately rejected if they were sure of the Duke of Newcastle's concurrence and assistance; that he, Lord Bute, did not know whether the Duke of Newcastle had any thoughts of continuing Minister; that if he had not, the Duke of Newcastle might be assured of having the Prince of Wales's confidence, and all possible regard for himself and his friends, but that they wished to know, what the Duke of Newcastle's intentions and those of his friends were, insinuating, that upon that must depend their resolutions with regard to other people. My Lord Bute always expressed the same regard for my Lord Hardwicke and distant expressions of respect and consideration for my Lord Mansfield without naming him.

I having consulted my Lord Hardwicke, whether any thing, or what it might be proper to say in answer, my Lord Hardwicke and I have agreed that for the ease and success of the King's affairs, for His Majesty's happiness and tranquillity, and for the welfare and peace of the Kingdom, it would be proper that my Lord Lincoln should verbally return the answer in the margin to my Lord Bute. *N.B.* His Lordship lamented the paring down the prerogative and the low state to which the House of Lords was at present reduced.

The Answer

That the —— [Duke of Newcastle] and his friends have the greatest zeal for the King, and his Royal Family, and have the most ardent wishes that, when the unhappy event of the King's death shall happen, H.R.H. the Prince of Wales may succeed to the Crown with the greatest glory, and in such a situation, as shall leave his hands free, and enable him to form his plan of Government with advantage. That Lord Bute may be assured that the —— and his friends have nothing more at heart than, when that unfortunate event shall happen, to support H.R.H.'s Government and to prevent his being overruled, or constrained by any faction, or combination of men whatsover.

I have desired my Lord Lincoln to make my Lord Bute all the proper compliments from me, of my regard for his Lordship, in return to the many civil things which he said upon my subject.

And my Lord Lincoln may say that he knows enough of my way of thinking, that nothing would engage me in another reign to undergo the fatigue and trouble of a Minister; which my personal duty to the King (whom I have served such a number of years, and from whom I had received so many marks of goodness and confidence), and the consideration that in the present circumstances, and the difficult situation of affairs, I might be of some service to the King, his Royal Family and the publick, make me even at present submit to. Tho' the not being in the situation of a Minister will have no influence upon my conduct in every thing that relates to the support of the Government.[1]

Lord Bute and the Prince declared themselves satisfied with the answer, which they seem to have taken at its face value ; they now assumed that Newcastle would withdraw at the accession of the Prince, and from his retirement support the new Government, receiving honours and profits in compensation for power. A rough, undated draft of the letter which Bute wrote to Lincoln, obviously on receipt of Newcastle's reply, is preserved among the papers of George III at Windsor :

I have reported to H.R.H. what your Lordship communicated to me, I inform'd him that y.L. was authorized from the D. of N. to declare that H[is] G[race] &c.

I am now my Lord commanded by the P[rince] to desire y.L. to assure the D. of N., that nothing can give him more real satisfaction than H.G. declarations of the zealous and cordial support of himself and friends to his future plan of Government, when he shall have the great misfortune of loosing the K[ing] his grandfather ; H.R.H. is also sensible to the confidence plac'd in him by the D. of N. in explaining his present uneasy situation, and his resolution of retiring from the weight of Ministerial office at the K.'s demise.

H.R.H., my Lord, is pleas'd to declare that the attachment and affection shown him on this occasion make the deepest impressions, such as cannot fail of proving agreable to his Grace and his friends.

Meantime Bute declared that he would do all in his power to shut the door against certain people (Fox, etc.),[2] and on 3 April 1759, Viry told Newcastle that an end had been made of the negotiations with the Cumberland group ; that Leicester

---

[1] Add. MSS. 32889, ff. 136-7.
[2] Memorandum of 22 March 1759 ; Add. MSS. 32889, ff. 185-7.

House 'had return'd for answer, that the Prince of Wales could not enter into any resolution or promise with regard to future times ; that His Royal Highness should then act as he should see proper ; and gave them to understand that he desir'd to have no more applications of that sort'. To the Duke of Cumberland, reported Viry, the Prince of Wales would always show due regard, but 'the Duke was not to expect to have any share in affairs. To which I [Newcastle] ask'd, whether that related to the army. My friend seem'd to think, it did; as the army would give great power in the House of Commons.' [1]

The relations of the Prince of Wales to the King and his Ministers were embittered still further when, in July 1759, the Prince's request for permission to join the Army was refused. The King, on receipt of his letter, said nothing about it to the two Secretaries [2] but showed it to Newcastle, and, as he reported to Hardwicke on 20 July, asked him

what answer he should return; and said, he wants to be rising; monter un pas. . . . I told His Majesty that I hoped he would return a kind answer; that the letter was very respectful and submissive. The King then said that he would call my Lord Pembroke in and say 'The time was not yet come, that the case [a French invasion] did not yet exist'.

Newcastle dissuaded him from an answer which would have given publicity to the matter, and advised him to reply that he would consider the request. 'Tho' the Command in Chief was not named, or any thing like it, the King took it to mean *that* ; and indeed that did seem to be the purport of the letter.' Lady Yarmouth concluded that 'the fear of the Duke' [of Cumberland] was behind it ; 'and in that I agreed with her'.[3] So did Hardwicke — he thought that the person who had

---

[1] Add. MSS. 32889, ff. 348-9.

[2] Pitt seems to have first received a copy of the Prince's letter from Bute, with a covering letter dated 25 July 1759. 'I hope', wrote Bute, 'it will appear full of duty and respect ; but the more it is so, the more I fear the consequences of a refusal ; I make no doubt but my worthy friend will see the propriety, I had almost said, the necessity of indulging His Royal Highness in so noble and reasonable a request, and that he will as far as the circumstances of his situation permit, endeavour to procure it a favorable answer' (Add. MSS. 36797, f. 44).

[3] Add. MSS. 32893, ff. 172-3.

advised the letter did not really expect a favourable reply, 'but rather that the P. of W., having made such an offer, if it is not accepted, may make it more difficult to bring the Duke into that situation'. He, too, favoured a non-committal answer.[1]

Finally Newcastle persuaded the King to show the letter to Pitt, but even then the King gave Pitt no opportunity to offer an opinion. When the reply to be sent to the Prince was discussed by the Ministers, Pitt warmly espoused the Prince's cause and the ultimate draft was a compromise;[2] also afterwards Pitt insisted on minor concessions being made to the Prince.[3] But neither Newcastle nor Pitt ever received from the Prince any credit still less thanks, for their endeavours, the one to remove all asperity from the reply, the other to render it favourable to him. On receiving the King's letter, the Prince wrote to Bute (28 July 1759):

> You will see by H.M. letter how shuffling it is and unworthy of a British Monarch; the conduct of this old K—— makes me asham'd of being his grandson; he treats me in the same manner, his knave and counsellor, the D. of N——, does all people. For this answer by some may be look'd upon as agreeing to my petition, by those who think further, as an absolute refusal.
>
> I am going to carry a copy of this unworthy letter to my mother.

On 7 August Bute wrote to Pitt in reply to a letter in which Pitt regretted 'his inability to impart anything satisfactory in reference to the subject they had been conversing upon':[4]

> I am extrem'ly concerned to observe by your letter that all endeavours have proved hitherto unsuccessful in regard to a business the Prince has so much at heart; I need not tell you that he complains bitterly of the extreme neglect he ever meets with, in any matter (be it what it will) that immediately concerns himself; the most gentle, patient dispositions may be at last so soured that all the prudential reasons and arguments in the world will not prevent very bad effects, very pernicious consequences; nothing shall be wanting on my part to preserve peace and good humour, but at the same time

---

[1] 21 July 1759; *ibid.* ff. 202-3.

[2] Newcastle to Hardwicke, 27 July, *ibid.* ff. 318-19.

[3] See Newcastle's letter to Andrew Stone, 1 August 1759, *ibid.* ff. 408-9; and his memoranda for Hardwicke and the King, *ibid.* ff. 425 and 432.

[4] Summary of Pitt's letter of August 6, in the 'Register'; Add. MSS. 36796, f. 39.

I will not be answerable for the consequences of this treatment; tho' I am certain that in whatever resolutions His Royal Highness shall take, whatever measures he shall think necessary for his own honor to pursue at this crisis, he will do nothing unworthy of himself, or that he shall think disrespectful to the King.[1]

In the spring of 1760 the question of the Government to be formed on the accession of the Prince was discussed once more, and Bute attempted a reconciliation with Pitt, which would have enabled him to assume the Treasury. The negotiations were carried on through Gilbert Elliot, M.P., a friend to both, who fully understood how much the public interest demanded their co-operation ; an account of these negotiations survives in the copy which Elliot made of a letter addressed to him by Bute, and in Elliot's notes of his subsequent conversation with Pitt.[2] Bute wrote to Elliot on 30 April 1760 :

As I am not well and may be gone into the country to morrow before you get hither, I think it best to send you in a letter all I had to say on the subject we lately talked of, when I flung out to you my thoughts concerning Mr. Pitt. I was aware that you from publick motives, as well as from private friendship, might wish to impart to him the substance of our discourse, you accordingly did so, and you found me pleas'd with it, having in some measure obtain'd all the end I propos'd by it, your conveying to Mr. Pitt's mind the personal regard I have ever had for him, unshaken by the long chain of unfortunate circumstances, that have gradually brought on the distance now subsisting, and on the other side, I think I perceive from you that Mr. Pitt's ideas and mine coincide in this great essential. The longer I reflect on what you repeated of the conversation in St. James Square,[3] the more I perceive my character, my views, my way of thinking greatly mistaken, I hope I may say without meaness or vanity that the clearing up of these matters would prove beneficial to Mr. Pitt as well as myself, and be perhaps of some utility to the publick. The odd appearances some time past in the House of Com-

---

[1] Add. MSS. 36797, ff. 44-5.

[2] These papers are in the possession of the Earl of Minto, at Minto House, Hawick. They are bound in a volume marked 'MSS. vol. VII', and excerpts from them have been published by Mr. G. F. S. Elliot, in his book on The Border Elliots (1897), pp. 362-5. Mr. Elliot has carefully arranged and annotated these MSS., and anyone who now studies them must feel grateful to him for his work.

[3] Pitt lived at that time at 10 St. James's Square, which is still called Chatham House, and now belongs to the Royal Institute of International Affairs.

mons, and the language Mr. Pitt has held upon them are to me by no means indifferent, and the less so, that I am tempted to think few or none of these things would have happened had the same fraternal union still remained that once existed between him and me, I go further, I believe that could this be once more renewed these appearances would diminish if not entirely cease. Such were the thoughts [which] produced our first conversation, and full of the same impressions at this minute, I without hesitation impower you to communicate the contents of this to Mr. Pitt, when a proper opportunity offers, and if you please, you may tell him, that on the strictest search I can discover no one idea in my mind, that opposes tying the knot of union as tight as ever; if he is able to say as much the business is in a manner done. As to the mode of meeting, the matter proper to be discussed betwixt us etc., these come not one minute into my consideration, explanations also should be unnecessary to those who wish the subject they are made on bury'd in oblivion, but if they cast up in discourse, they would be treated by the temper I describe without repugnance or reserve. A cordial interview with these similar ideas cannot fail to remedy past errors, and prevent future ones, but suffer me also to add one word of caution, that with the best intentions you may not deceive yourself; if contrary to what I have been saying you perceive on further conversation that either passion, plan, disinclination, or apprehension is likely to obstruct the renewal of our former union, it will be fruitless, and therefore better avoided, and in that case, be assur'd that whatever interpretations may be given to the openings I here wish you to make for me, I never shall repent them, I feel in my own breast the generous publick principle I act on, and that rewards, let what will happen.

With this letter Elliot went to Pitt, whose reply was summarised by him in rough notes. It would seem that the opening part of the account is missing, for the extant notes start abruptly with a sentence which obviously refers to the forming of a Government without Newcastle and Hardwicke:

The droping of one or two of the principal actors make a great change in the scene — favour not every thing in this country — a high, imperious tone, the singleing of confidence into one hand to the exclusion of all mankind, the flippant use of the P[rince's] name gives disgust: talking tauntingly of my progress at Court, and in certain quarters of it. I own placed there a bulwark against the D[uke of Cumberland], to contend with the intrigue and favour of the D[uke] of N[ewcastle], with the K[ing] hardly speaking to me, I have practis'd L[ady] Y[armouth], and with success, I have found her a very fair honest woman and well disposed to aid every measure for the interest of this country. But in such circumstances to be continually met with obstruction instead of support from Leister House, to be ground between two Courts is too much : has he forgot how we came first together, then feeling the disadvantage of his situation as a S.P. [Scottish peer ?] talking of our generosity since they had nothing to bestow, that all would be in our hands in a future day, after some interval told shortly that he himself was destined for the Treasury, that he agreed to it mostly on my account, as every other person in that situation would sap and undermine me, he would only act as my friend and throw all into my hands : these expressions not be sure taken in their full extent flowing from not so much the effusions of the heart, yet tho not meaning all, surely meaning something : now every one more at home at Leister House than I, different lines at different times entered into almost with every quarter, persons talked of to day as the lowest and most unable of men, to morrow caressed and confidentially used : I have never gone into these representations of men's characters knowing how changes come about : a root of umbrage in that mind which nothing can remove or draw in

aut calidus sanguis, aut inscitia rerum.[1]

As one connection been made, can he suffer any other person to make one, who might do it. I have purposely avoided it feeling the jealousy it would occasion. As to want of confidence and communication so much complained of : I have acted upon the concerted plan, I have effectually barred the entrance to those who were meant to be excluded, carried on the war on its plan, armed the country even Scotland when every other Minister threw out suspicions on that quarter, but have not carefully transmitted every little scrap of paper, all the little paltry detail, I have not waited for direction and approbation, but seized the moment when I could to secure these measures : my health, infirmity's, temper dont admit of making such court : neither would ; I would never have been Minister to act in collusion with any P[rince] and M[inister]. I will not be rid with a check rein, nor postpone measures or delay business till I hear from [the] K[ing] : such being the case I know it is impossible for me to act in a responsible ministerial office with L[ord] B[ute] ; he has all confidence, all habitude, gives hourly indications of an imperious nature, I cant bear a touch of command, my sentiments in politicks like my religion are my own, I cant change them, I'll controvert them with any Minister and the Sovereign must judge betwixt us : the rights of my office are not enough to me, if I am to be in a responsible

---

[1] The line is from Horace, *Ep.* i. 3. 33, and should run :
Seu calidus sanguis seu rerum inscitia vexat.

situation ; I cannot be dictated, prescribed to etc. : neither acting as a friend can I then contend for the closet or drive measures by national weight, as I do at present, when I pretend not friendships to the Ministers with whom I act : [1] my age, infirmitys, turn of mind make it impossible for me to undertake new [2] oppositions, the heats and colds of the House of Commons are too much for me, neither will I retire peevish and discontented but recur to the P[rince] and Lord Bute friendships to put me in some honourable bystanding office where I have no responsibility but aid counsels if called upon. I will even make way for his greatness, assist it, only I cannot make part of it.[3]

Let me conclude with saying, by distrusting his friends he'll become dependent on his enemys.

The concluding part of these notes is scribbled on the wrapper of a letter addressed to Elliot, and there is moreover, one disconnected sentence jotted down on it, which is probably Pitt's description of Bute :

'Excelent parts, ornamental talents, capacity to govern a nation, not temper, experience, nor always frank.'

In the talk which Bute had with Pitt on the night of 25 October 1760, after the death of George II, he told Pitt that 'had he given him that meeting ['ask'd by Mr. Elliot's means'] he would have inform'd him that he had laid aside thoughts of being First Lord of the Treasury' ; [4] but judging by the letter which the Prince of Wales wrote to Bute on 4 May 1760 — after having been told the previous day about Pitt's refusal — one can hardly believe Bute to have been wholly sincere and truthful in making that statement.

The late instance in the transaction with Mr. P[itt] [wrote the Prince], is perhaps the strongest that ever happened to a man of

---

[1] Here followed the words : 'I am however read[y]', which Gilbert Elliot smudged over — whenever he wanted to delete something he had just written, he seems, instead of drawing a line, to have drawn his finger across it.

[2] It is not clear whether this word is 'new' or 'now'.

[3] In *The Border Elliots* this sentence is made to follow on '. . . dependent on his enemys', but it does not properly hang together with that concluding and summarising sentence of Pitt's harangue, and moreover, in Gilbert Elliot's MS. there is a cross placed before it, obviously meant to connect it with the place where the sentence was to be inserted — but no corresponding mark appears anywhere in the extant text.

[4] See below, p. 120.

your strong sensations; he has shown himself the most ungrateful and in my mind most dishonorable of men, I can never bear to see him in any future Ministry; what I still flatter myself is, that some method may turn up of regulating affairs, which may still make the Treasury not unpalatable to you; if that should not happen, you will for all that be Minister, for all men will find the only method of succeeding in their desires, will be by first acquainting you with what they mean to request before they address themselves to me: in short, all I interest myself in is your health, for whilst my dearest is near me I care not who are the tools he may think necessary to be in Ministry provided the blackest of hearts is not one of them; for I look on the majority of politicians as intent on their own private interests instead of that of the public.

No news about these negotiations seems to have reached Newcastle at the time, but they were mentioned to him by Viry, in a discourse which, on 8 August 1760, he held on the relations between Bute and Pitt. He told Newcastle

that Lord Bute and Mr. Pitt were very ill together; that when Lord B. thought Mr. Pitt was for peace, he always made difficulties. That when Lord B. thought Mr. P. was for the continuance of the war, Lord B. appear'd to be for peace — that Lord B. had made a proposal to meet Mr. P. to talk upon the affairs of the P[rince] of W[ales] — that Mr. P.'s answer was that he was very ready to meet Lord Bute whenever he pleas'd; but not to talk of the affairs of the P[rince] of W[ales] without the King's leave; or at least without the knowledge of his brother-Ministers (meaning the Duke of New-castle) — that Lord B. replied that formerly Mr. P. had not made these difficulties. To which Mr. P. answer'd that *that* was only accidental conversation, but never by formal appointment. And besides, that then he was only Secretary of State in appearance. But that, at present, His Majesty and his brother-Ministers acted towards him in such a manner, that he had reason to be contented, and that he was Secretary of State; and consequently could do nothing without the consent of the King and the knowledge of his colleagues (and nam'd the Duke of Newcastle).

That all this was carried on between Lord B. and Mr. P., by Mr. Elliot. And my friend says, that notwithstanding this, my Ld. B. wishes to be upon a good foot with Mr. P. And my friend thinks, this negotiation will be renew'd, when Mr. Elliot returns from Scotland. That, however, Mr. P. will adhere to his resolution, and will avoid giving any cause of complaint to Lord B. . . . [1]

[1] Add. MSS. 32909, ff. 343-5.

The fact that Viry was the author of this report may account for any number of fanciful embellishments. The lively arguments and repartees here related can hardly be fitted into the framework of the communications recorded by Elliot, and yet it would seem most unlikely that there should have been any further negotiations between Bute and Pitt after the refusal given to Bute's offer in May 1760. Viry's account merely shows once more that he was informed even about the most secret transactions, hardly known to anyone else, and that the way in which he repeated such information, and the use he made of it, were as unreliable and ambiguous as his person.

GEORGE II AND PARLIAMENTARY ELECTIONS

The belief is current that George II took no interest in Parliamentary elections and that he left Newcastle a free hand in the matter. No doubt Newcastle was his party manager and chief whip, the head of the political machine; still, numerous entries and letters prove that George II, so far from being uninterested in elections, actively concerned himself in them, that the names of Government candidates were submitted to him, and that his approval was required for the disbursement of Government money in elections. Contemporaries had no doubt as to the King's share in the business. Here are a few illustrations, culled from the correspondence relating to the general election of 1754.

On 18 July 1753 Lord Northumberland wrote to the Duke of Newcastle : 'I am truly happy in finding that the King approves of our candidates for Northumberland and I must entreat your Grace's favour to express to His Majesty the most dutifull and gratefull sense. . . .'[1] On 25 August Lord Dumfries sent the King the names of three candidates who had offered themselves for his county: '. . . if Your Majesty would be pleased to mark with a cross the name of the person [who] would be the most agreeable, I should use my best endeavours that he might be chosen. . . .'[2] When Lord Rockingham had made satisfactory arrangements at York,

---

[1] Add. MSS. 32732, ff. 305-6.   [2] *Ibid.* f. 532.

Newcastle wrote to him (6 December 1753): 'I did not fail to let the King know it this day; and His Majesty was most extremely pleased with it; and approv'd your very prudent conduct upon the occasion'.[1]   Nor did in this matter the great democratic bodyguard of the Whigs, the Dissenters, think and act differently from their aristocratic managers; in July 1754, when a by-election was on at Taunton, the following paper was signed by fifty-one leading Taunton Dissenters:

Tis the resolution of the body of Dissenters at Taunton to support the candidate fix'd on by the majority, and to desire my Lord Egremont to recommend to us him of the two gentlemen mention'd in his letter to Mr. Manley, the Mayor, that will at the same time be most agreable to His Majesty and most likily readily to go thro' with the necessary expence of securing his election.[2]

Most of the letters announcing the election results of 1754 are missing from the Newcastle Papers, for Newcastle sent them to the King, who kept them unless he wrote his reply on the same sheet of paper.   On 6 April 1754, 10 A.M., Newcastle informed the King in much detail of the exertions and financial sacrifices made by the Whigs at Bristol; the King replied at the bottom of the page: 'I am exceeding glad and oblig'd to the friends of the Government for the great zele and affection they shew upon this occasion'.[3]   Later in the month Newcastle wrote again about the way in which the Bristol Whigs would use their second votes (having put up only one candidate of their own): 'As I find all the Whigs wish to have Sir John Philips, a broken Jacobite, rather than Mr. Beckford [Richard, brother of William], a wild West Indian, I have humbly presumed to say that Your Majesty would not be against it'. The King replied: 'You did very right, my Lord, to declare for Sir John Philipps against Beckford'.[4]   On 14 April 1754, 'past 12 o'clock', Newcastle sent the King a bunch of election results — 'all which are gone in favour of those set up and

---

[1] Add. MSS. 32733, f. 375.   [2] Add. MSS. 32736, f. 25.
[3] Add. MSS. 32735, ff. 48-9.
[4] *Ibid.* f. 50. This letter, dated only '2.10 P.M.', is placed immediately after that of 6 April 1754. But since Newcastle refers in it to the result of the Berwick election (which took place on 23 April), it must have been written after that date.

supported by Your Majesty'. George II replied : 'I am heartyly glad the elections go on in so successful a way. G. R.' [1]

It might perhaps be argued that the King's name was used without the Ministers having really to count with his opinion, but that this was not so, and that his consent was required for the financing of elections, can be seen from some further examples — for though pretence in the matter might possibly have been used towards people not much about Court, this could not have been done to Henry Fox, and least of all to Newcastle himself.

On 10 January 1756 Henry Fox, then Secretary of State, asked Newcastle to finance a candidate at Hindon, in Wiltshire ; [2] Newcastle replied that he was afraid he would 'with great difficulty get powers' to do so.[3] On Fox pressing further, Newcastle fully explained his position :

If I would do what is proposed for any man alive, I would in the present circumstances do it for Mr. Mabbot, least it should be suspected . . . that the candidate so circumstanced is not agreeable to me. I never did thus without order, that is, engaged in such an affair. The sure way to be disavowed, would be to do so. . . . I will certainly speak on Tuesday, and as strongly as I can, I hope, I shall succeed. If I should have a negative, we may find out some way to indemnify Mr. Mabbot. . . .[4]

If we had time we might find out many who would go as far as £1500. I am amaz'd at Barret's [5] behaviour, but that signifies nothing ; I think, I could make good use of it in the closet. . . .[6]

[1] *Ibid.* f. 92. Phrases such as 'those set up and supported by Your Majesty's order' occur again and again ; see, *e.g.*, Newcastle's letter to the King, 19 April 1754 ; *ibid.* f. 102. At Court election results were treated as urgent matter. When on 7 December 1758, Rockingham announced to Newcastle a Whig victory at York — 'I immediately sent your letter to Ned Finch' [Edward Finch, M.P., Master of the Robes], replied Newcastle, 'to communicate the contents of it this evening to the King, and I am sure it will give His Majesty great pleasure' (Add. MSS. 32886, f. 215). 'The King has no cards', answered Finch, 'and the Countess [Lady Yarmouth] is to be at Lady Barrington's. I therefore immediately inclosed your own and Lord Rockingham's letters to her, and the packet will catch her before she leaves the King' (f. 217).
[2] Add. MSS. 32862, f. 61.   [3] *Ibid.* f. 63.
[4] Obviously to give him the financial support in some other form. Mabbot was a late captain in the service of the East India Company, and a Director of the Company, 1742-45, '46-50, '51-54, and in 1756. He was returned for Hindon on 19 January 1756, but did not stand again for Parliament in 1761.   [5] The opposing candidate.
[6] 11 January 1756 ; Add. MSS. 32862, f. 82.

Numerous entries in Newcastle's 'Memorandums for the King' further prove that he did discuss both candidates and election expenses with George II.[1]

Lastly, here is a letter from the Duke of Devonshire to Newcastle, dated 3 July 1757, and relating to Fox's re-election at Windsor on his appointment as Paymaster-General — Newcastle was now no longer on good terms with Fox, to whom Devonshire continued a friend.

> His Majesty this day desired that I would write to your Grace to endeavour to get the Beauclerk interest for Mr. Fox; he imagines if the Duke of Dorset was to speak to Lord Vere, that it might be got, and as the opposition is of a pretty high nature, the King hopes that any personal animosity in that family may not take place on this occasion.[2]

When George II had to work with managers not of his own choosing, his interference became even more marked. On Pitt's assuming office in November 1756, Dr. Hay, a follower of his, was appointed Advocate-General, which necessitated a re-election; but as Fox, who now controlled Stockbridge, refused to return Hay, some other seat had to be found for him. There was a vacancy at Rochester, caused by the execution of Admiral Byng, and Lord Holdernesse, Pitt's colleague as Secretary of State, reported to Newcastle on 15 March 1757 :

> The Rochester election has thrown every thing into fresh confusion, the Admiralty insist upon chusing Dr. Hay, the King will have Admiral Smith brought in there; His Majesty has had a very *lively* conversation with Lord Temple [First Lord of the Admiralty] this morning upon the subject, and there are those at James's who think my new colleagues will break upon this point and resign.[3]

Dr. Hay was not returned for Rochester.

But George II would go even further and, while Newcastle was out of office, discreetly send him advice on election matters. Holdernesse wrote to Newcastle on 9 December 1756 :

> Upon the news of Lord Harrington's death I *was ordered* to give your Grace a private hint that if the Duke of Grafton would bring

---

[1] See, for instance, Add. MSS. 32852, f. 156 (Bewdley); Add. MSS. 32889, f. 417 (Essex); Add. MSS. 32890, f. 35 (Kent); and ff. 251, 413, 438, and 449 (Camelford).

[2] Add. MSS. 32872, f. 47.   [3] Add. MSS. 32870, f. 285.

Lord Euston into Parliament for Bury your Grace would have an opportunity of obliging some other friend at Aldborough. The hint was well meant. . . .[1]

'Lord Holdernesse's hint was certainly from the King, and I don't wonder at it', was Lord Hardwicke's comment on this letter.[2]

Nor was George II indifferent to divisions and majorities in the House of Commons. When towards the end of 1755, in view of Pitt's dismissal, Newcastle was specially active in mustering his supporters, the Duke of Devonshire, then Lord-Lieutenant of Ireland, wrote to him : 'I desire your Grace will ask the King, whether he wou'd chuse that my brother Frederick shou'd come over to Parliament ; if it is His Majesty's pleasure, he will certainly be with you after the Holydays. . . .' [3] Newcastle replied on 17 January 1756 : 'The King was very much oblig'd to your Grace for your design of sending over Lord Frederick, which, His Majesty desires, may be as soon as it can conveniently ; the King always loving to have as great majorities as possible'.[4]

In short, the practice of George III's earlier years was on real innovation ; the difference was merely in emphasis and degree. Even the term of 'King's friends' was known under George II ; e.g., on 3 July 1753, in a letter to Lord Irwin, Newcastle speaks about 'the friends to the King and His Government',[5] and Thomas Herring, Archbishop of Canterbury, when recommending a candidate for Parliament, writes on 24 March 1754 : 'I will become guarantee for his attachment to the King's interest and the King's friends'.[6]

Nor did the Whigs consider the King's interference in the least unconstitutional, while it worked in their favour. They, as a party, had identified themselves with the King, the

[1] Add. MSS. 32869, f. 305. Aldborough, in Yorkshire, was a pocket-borough of Newcastle's, for which he was about to return Lord Euston.

[2] Hardwicke to Newcastle, 12 December 1756 ; Add. MSS. 32869, ff. 347-8.

[3] Add. MSS. 32861, ff. 320-1. He had previously sent over other Members, but there had been special reasons for keeping Lord Frederick Cavendish at Dublin ; see Add. MSS. 32860, ff. 205-6, 340, and 480-1.

[4] Add. MSS. 32862, f. 122.

[5] Add. MSS. 32732, ff. 158-9.   [6] Add. MSS. 32734, f. 328.

Hanoverian dynasty, and the Protestant succession, and they finished by identifying these with their own party. What could therefore be more constitutional in a King than to support the Whigs ? Indeed, could he forsake himself and the throne ? The King was their leader, and whoever was with them, did 'the King's service'; the King's name was used by them to the fullest extent, and for years the nation was taught by their practice that the King had a right to interfere in elections. Even in 1761, when on one occasion the sentiments of Newcastle and Hardwicke coincided with those of George III and Bute — in wishing to keep out Simon Fraser, the son of the notorious Lord Lovat — these were Newcastle's views concerning the respective rights of electors and of the King, expressed in a letter to Hardwicke on 14 May 1761 :

Your Lordship will see that young Lovat is at last chose for the shire of Invernesse.[1] I spoke to Lord Bute about it, who seems very much offended at it; as, indeed, he ought to be, according to his own account. For, he says, the principal electors have wrote to him (Lord Bute) and in their letter they say, they are independent gentlemen, have no places, no employments; and that nothing, but Col. Frazier's own request, which they had not had, could have prevented their chusing him. Nothing, I think, could be more insolent to the King; or more renouncing His Majesty's influence than this letter to his Minister. I hope, Lord Bute, who seems now very angry, will make the proper inference from it. His Lordship told me, Mr. Pitt took part with Col. Frazier, and wonder'd, how the Duke of Newcastle could object to him who had acted meritoriously in N. America.[2]

While George II was still alive, in the summer of 1760, Newcastle started worrying about the forthcoming general election ; he saw dangers and difficulties, and, shuddering at the thought of lists of candidates which might be forced on him, anxiously turned to his friends for advice. All this should be carefully noted with a view to a proper estimate of terrors yet to come.

[1] There had been an idea of electing him in 1754, but Newcastle and Hardwicke had prevented it ; see Add. MSS. 32733, ff. 161-7 and 28-9.

[2] Add. MSS. 32923, ff. 70-1. Simon Fraser, who had been 'out in the '45', and had been attainted but pardoned, in 1757 raised a regiment for service in America, went out with it himself, served with distinction under Wolfe. and was wounded in action.

Lord Kinnoull (the previous Lord Dupplin — he succeeded his father in July 1758) was on an embassy in Portugal. The world at large 'opprobriously and injuriously' thought him 'an absolute fool',[1] but he was to Newcastle one of the pivots of his political system. 'A new Parliament is to be chose . . . I can do nothing well in it without you', wrote Newcastle to Kinnoull on 22 September 1760.[2] And again on September 30 :

> For God's sake, don't stay, fiddle faddling about your visits and audiences; you may soon dispatch them, if you please; and then you may be very well here before the end of October — I shall have every thing ready for you, sums, estimates, taxes, &ca., elections, candidates, persons to be brought in, and to be turned out &ca., in short you shall have business enough.[3]

Still from Lisbon Kinnoull sent Newcastle his advice in a letter covering thirty-four large pages. The general election, he considered, should be carried on with a view to the continuance of the present system of administration.

> With this view it will be necessary that your Grace should have a freindly communication with Mr. Pitt upon the subject, and without any seeming reserve. . . . First then let it be agreed that no person in possession of a seat who has acted heartily with the Administration . . . should be disturbed. This is a fair . . . proposal . . . and at the same time it secures your Grace's influence, and stamps upon the future Parliament the complexion of the present.

Similarly, no opposition even to the Tories 'in possession' should be encouraged, 'unless where the united voice of the Whigs absolutely calls for it and some future firm establishment of that interest makes it necessary'. He finished by pleading for a cheap election, and reminded the Duke 'how much anxiety and uneasiness' was created by the engagements entered into before the last general election, 'and how long time elapsed before some were concluded'[4] (which, incidentally, contradicts once more the fanciful story of the unlimited funds which Newcastle had for elections under George II).

---

[1] Hardwicke to Newcastle, 13 October 1755 ; Add. MSS. 32860, ff. 30-4.
[2] Add. MSS. 32912, ff. 19-20.
[3] *Ibid.* f. 246.
[4] Add. MSS. 32908, ff. 160-77. For the financial accounts of that general election see *The Structure of Politics*, pp. 196-208.

Meantime Newcastle did not feel altogether easy even about George II, and the degree of support he could expect. The following entry occurs in a 'Memorandum' of 12 August 1760 :

The choice of a new Parliament.
The difficulties I shall meet with.
The money it will cost.
The mortification to find the King thinks all my recommendations are in a circle of my own friends.
To compare my recoms. with Mr. Fox's and others.
Not the worse for being my friends.
Without an entire confidence no chusing a Parliament.[1]

And on 5 September 1760 : 'The choice of a Parliament . . . the King's high support necessary.'[2]

On 16 August Newcastle addressed a letter of about thirty pages to the long-suffering Hardwicke, appealing for advice — Pitt and the Tories fill in it exactly the place which Bute and the Tories were to take three months later :

As things now stand, the King supposes I should chuse the Parliament which is now coming on . . . I see difficulties arising, which I own, I did not foresee. The early declaration of two Tories for Worcestershire looks as if the Tories would be stirring *as Tories*. The consequence of that will be bad ; — on two accounts, first, the opposition will be greater ; *secondly*, if Mr. Pitt is not in extreme good humour, he may, and will, hamper me a good deal by desiring to be consulted in the choice of the Parliament, by supporting *Tories* in many places ; and by perhaps having a considerable list of his own, none of which the King will like. Whereas, if Pitt was really in good humour, I am persuaded, he would leave it all to me, and not trouble his head about it, with only perhaps desiring some of his particular friends to be taken care of, which to be sure is reasonable.

He further asked whether Hardwicke thought the measures concerning the choice of the new Parliament

should be *all* concerted with *Mr. Pitt*. I am clearly of another mind, tho' your Lordship will remember that was the point upon which Mr. Fox and I *originally* broke at setting out.[3]

[1] Add. MSS. 32909, f. 439.
[2] Add. MSS. 32911, f. 55.
[3] Add. MSS. 32910, ff. 120-35.

Hardwicke saw objections to consulting Mr. Pitt :

yet, if it should appear to be expected, I do not well see how it can be avoided, considering Mr. Pitt's situation in the House of Commons and in the Ministry, which is very different from what Mr. Fox's was.

But he advised Newcastle to proceed on the lines sketched out by Kinnoull. As to the Tories stirring, he saw no instance of it, and was not inclined to attach much importance to the Worcestershire incident.[1] (It should be added that this second Tory candidate in Worcestershire, who roused Newcastle's fears to such an extent, was no other than William Dowdeswell, subsequently Chancellor of the Exchequer in the Rockingham Government of 1765, and leader of the Rockingham Whigs in the House of Commons.)

Lord Mansfield, similarly appealed to, gave advice which amounted to telling Newcastle that he should acquire mental independence at the age of sixty-seven. For, having in general terms commended Kinnoull's scheme, he wrote :

You will be considered as answerable for the choice of the Parliament, and therefore must make your own plan. Mr. Pelham did not consult even with you as to the general formation of his; this don't exclude joint deliberations in particular cases nor communication.[2]

There is no indication whatsoever of any concerted election campaign by Leicester House in the summer of 1760. In Scotland alone, Lord Bute seems to have done some electioneering ; and as at that time he was on bad terms with his uncle, Archibald, third Duke of Argyll, and disputing with him who was to be appointed Governor of Dumbarton Castle, Argyll tried to join up the conflict in his own family with that between George II and his grandson, as a sure means to gain the King's support. On 28 February 1760 Newcastle wrote to Hardwicke :

My Lord Duke told me he would wait upon the King, and acquaint His Majesty, that Lord Bute had set up the Prince of Wales's standard in Scotland against the King ; which was for the

[1] Hardwicke to Newcastle, 20 August 1760 ; *ibid.* ff. 171-2.
[2] 30 August 1760 ; *ibid.* ff. 427-31. The statement about Pelham is confirmed by a letter from Newcastle to Hardwicke written in Pelham's lifetime, on 17 October 1753 : '. . . of all subjects my brother is the most uneasy, when I talk to him upon that of elections. He will do every thing himself — he consults none of his friends . . .' ; Add. MSS. 32733, ff. 80-1.

next election — that they had already begun in two boroughs; and
that if this Government of Dumbarton Castle was given to Lord
Eglinton, it would be a declaration in favor of that standard; which
should never be done if he, the Duke of Argyll, could prevent it.[1]

Lord Mansfield, in a letter of 29 February, confirmed that Lord
Bute intervened in some Scottish elections.[2]   Still, this was
nothing more than a local affair in which Bute engaged as a
Scottish lord, not as Manager of Leicester House.[3]

At the end of September a new development filled Newcastle's mind with sombre forebodings. Hardwicke heard from
Lincolnshire of 'a concerted scheme', which according to his
informant, 'will probably be pursued in other counties',
namely, 'that some gentlemen of the militia would be set up
for the county on that interest', and that letters had been sent
to gentlemen serving in the Lincolnshire militia 'that as they
were so considerable a body together, and had so large a share
of property, they would do well to consult together about proper
persons to represent the county'.[4] Upon which Hardwicke
remarked that it was

very natural for such a number of gentlemen of the same county,
all of them with estates, greater or less in that county, when call'd
out and confin'd to live and clubb together, to enter into concert
for projects of this sort, tho' foreign to their proper service.[5]

Newcastle, like all good Whigs, loathed the militia, an
invention of Pitt and his Tory country gentlemen. 'This
spirit of dictating from that species of gentlemen will spread',
he replied on October 3 ; 'and we shall soon feel the effects of
this militia in many shapes.'[6] And on October 5, to the Duke

[1] Add. MSS. 32902, ff. 453-6.
[2] Mansfield to Newcastle, 29 February 1760 ; ibid. f. 484.
[3] About the dispute between Argyll and Bute see, besides the letters,
quoted above : Add. MSS. 32902, ff. 478-9 ; 32903, ff. 96-7, 151, 228, 272-3,
and 313 ; and 32911, ff. 35-6, 101-102.
[4] J. Green, Dean of Lincoln, to Hardwicke, 27 September 1760; Add.
MSS. 32912, ff. 301-2.
[5] Hardwicke to Newcastle, 2 October ; ibid. ff. 299-300.
[6] Ibid. ff. 326-7. See also letter from Newcastle to Hardwicke, 20
October 1760; Add. MSS. 32913, ff. 226-7 : '. . . the little sparks of
opposition rising, in counties, singly from the militia, convince me that the
establishment of the militia (and any continuance establishes the principle)
would be, in time, the ruin of our Constitution and the immediate destruction of the Whig Party'.

of Devonshire : 'I see black as to our elections in some places.' [1]
This was in what was considered the full sunshine of his official
life.

On 25 October 1760, at 7 A.M., George II died.   'I have
lost the best King, the best Master, and the best friend that ever
subject had.   God knows what consequences it may have.' [2]

[1] Add. MSS. 32912, f. 363.
[2] Newcastle to Joseph Yorke, 28 October 1760 ; Add. MSS. 32913,
f. 399.

II

OLD BOTTLES, NEW WINE, AND THE GENERAL ELECTION

Newcastle continued at the Treasury

When George II died, Hardwicke (remaining at Wimple) prayed God to preserve Newcastle, and him to take care of his health and keep up his spirits ; [1] his 'poor friend in distress' reproached him for not returning to town immediately ; [2] Goerge III was gracious by a time-table which went all wrong ; and Bute, to avoid the turn things had taken at the death of George I — when Walpole managed to preserve his position — put a declaration into the hands of the King, prepared a long time beforehand (but having bestowed his time on 'the composition of what he should say', had failed to consider 'what measures he should pursue').[3] The necessary formalities were gone through, and the amendments, insisted on by Pitt, were made in the King's Proclamation. 'It was now seven at night', writes Gilbert Elliot in a paper recounting the events of the day of George III's accession,

and Lord Bute whisper'd Mr. Pitt that he wish'd to see him that evening late as it was.

When they met Lord Bute shortly recapitulated the grounds of their misunderstanding, said notwithstanding he had refus'd him a meeting when it [was] ask'd by Mr. Elliot's means, he was now ready to ascribe that conduct to some particular delicacys in his situation, to bury in oblivion all that was past, and for the sake of the publick to enter upon business with the same spirit as if nothing had ever interrupted their friendship, that he would now hold precisely the same discourse as if the meeting formerly propos'd had taken place.

---

[1] Add. MSS. 32913, f. 334.

[2] See Newcastle to Hardwicke, 26 October 1760 ; Add. MSS. 35420, f. 105 ; and Hardwicke's reply, Add. MSS. 32913, f. 382.

[3] See Shelburne's autobiography in Lord Fitzmaurice's *Life of William, Earl of Shelburne*, vol. i. p. 33.

That had h: given him that meeting, he would have inform'd him that he had laid aside thoughts of being First Lord of the Treasury, meant to hold the situation of a private man at the side of the King and give his best support to publick measures, that he approved of his system of the war and offer'd him his cordial and sincere friendship.

Mr. Pitt in his answer exprest his warm sense of the propriety of his conduct, and of the frank offer [of] his friendship, declaring that no one would return that friendship more heartily with regard to every object that could respect the honour, distinction or interest of himself or of his family. But he desir'd to distinguish betwixt publick and private friendship, the latter was a virtue, the former was faction and cabal if [it] led to the adoption or approbation of one measure which even as an enemy an honest Minister would not have acquies'd in. That he must act as an independent Minister or not at all, that his politicks were like his religion which would admit of no accommodation. That if the system of the war was to undergo the least change or even shadow of a change he could no longer be of any service, he even mentioned particularly the direction of it being left in the hands of Prince Ferdinand and the Hereditary Prince. He approved of the Duke of Newcastle's being continued, and even intimated that he would chiefly respect measures, and endeavour on the plan he had followed during the former reign. That he too wished to be [a] private man, if he could once see his country out of the present plunge, the only difference between [them] was that his Lordship would practise his philosophy in a Court, he in a village.[1]

The statement that Bute's thoughts were still the same on 25 October 1760, which they had been six months before, may be readily accepted. In April 1760 his scheme had been to come to an arrangement with Pitt, such as would have enabled him to assume the Treasury on the accession of the Prince of Wales. The time had now come, and Bute made a last attempt to reach such a settlement, but once more was met with a refusal. Pitt did not entertain the least doubt as to the sense and aim of Bute's discourse and, as he told a friend two years later, 'on the day of His Majesty's accession to the Throne . . . in a private conversation with his Lordship, Mr. Pitt told him his advancement to the management of the affairs of this country would not be for His Majesty's service'.[2] For, as Pitt

[1] Minto Papers.
[2] See 'An account given by Mr. [Thomas] Walpole, of what passed with Mr. Pitt, 13 November 1762'; Add. MSS. 32945, ff. 1-2.

put it on another occasion, 'favour and honours might be allowed, but not within the walls of the Treasury'.[1]

Newcastle had therefore to be continued at the Treasury, at least for the time being; on 27 October, Bute opened negotiations with Newcastle, and the next day H. V. Jones was able to report to the Duchess of Newcastle that the Duke 'had an exceeding good night and hopes, he has entirely got the better of his fatigue'.[2]   Bute reminded Newcastle of the 'sentiments and wishes of retreat' which some time ago he had signified through Lord Lincoln 'in case of the unfortunate event which had now happened; desired to know whether the Duke continued in the same way of thinking'; and 'added, that he had the King's orders to ask his Grace, what was his real inclination'.[3]   The Duke replied that his inclinations 'were not in the least chang'd'.

Lord Bute then said the King wish'd that his Grace would continue in the Treasury; that His Majesty thought, no other person could do him the same service there; and that he hoped my Lord Duke would not abandon the service of his country, at so critical a conjuncture. . . .

The King [Lord Bute continued] was very sensible of the difference there would be between serving a Prince, with whom my Lord Duke had, in a manner, been brought up, and had attended for so many years; and entering into the service of a Prince, so young as he was.   But that His Majesty would endeavour to remove that difficulty, as far as depended upon him, as soon as possible; and that addressing himself to him (Lord Bute) the King had said 'My Lord, it is your business to take care of *that*', from which Lord Bute took occasion to declare that he would act with the utmost confidence and cordiality towards my Lord Duke; who said that if he was to continue, he should expect and must insist upon that behaviour.

Thus Newcastle, while asking leave to retire, and describing himself to the King as 'too far advanced in life' for his present

[1] See 'Conversation between Mr. Pitt and Mr. Nuthall, November 5th, 1762.   As related by Mr. Walpole'; Add. MSS. 32944, f. 277.

[2] Add. MSS. 32913, f. 405.

[3] This and all further quotations about the negotiations of 27 and 28 October, unless marked otherwise, are from the account sent by H. V. Jones to the Duchess of Newcastle on Tuesday, 28 October, 'near two o'clock'; Add. MSS. 32913, ff. 405-11.

station, considered the conditions under which he could remain ; whereas the King and Bute, while pressing him to remain, reminded him of his 'sentiments and wishes of retreat'. In view of Pitt's refusal to serve under Bute as First Lord of the Treasury, they wished Newcastle to stay till peace was concluded, but not to settle down comfortably to a new term of office ; politically they wished him dead with his master, and still they desired him actively to support them in his effacement. They wished — they wished too much — and therefore hardly knew what it was they wished. Nor did Newcastle know his own mind, and he turned to his friends for advice.

Their opinions were divided (as our friends' opinions usually are). Hardwicke and Andrew Stone thought it inconsistent 'with his Grace's honour or personal satisfaction to remain on that foot, upon which alone he could expect to remain'. The Duke of Devonshire and Lord Mansfield suggested that Newcastle should 'remain till the end of the session *pour essayer*'. The Archbishop of Canterbury, the Duke of Bedford, Lady Yarmouth, etc., urged that it was his duty to his country to continue.

But the Duke of Bedford said that if his Grace consented to stay, he should insist upon everything being done which would support his authority and influence in such a manner that he might be useful to his friends ; and particularly with regard to the future elections. The Duke of Bedford added, if you are so necessary to them, it is but just that they should do everything to make you easy.

Pitt, when faced by the alternative of Bute, much desired to continue acting with Newcastle, 'upon whom he could depend' ; and let Newcastle know that he had 'most fully and expressly declar'd' to Bute that Newcastle 'was indispensably necessary to be part of . . . Administration'. 'What could Lord B. mean by declaring that he would be a private man ?' Pitt asked of Hardwicke. 'And shadow'd out, tho' he did not say it, that he must mean to be *the* Minister behind the curtain.' [1]

---

[1] Hardwicke to Newcastle, 29 October 1760 ; *Ibid.* ff. 426-429.

The Old Whigs urged Newcastle to remain for the sake of the 'party'; John White, M.P. for Retford — to whom Edmund Burke, in 1769, meant to address his *Thoughts on the Cause of the Present Discontents* because after a lifetime in Parliament he had preserved 'all his old principles and regards still fresh and alive' [1] — wrote to Newcastle on 27 October 1760 :

> Your Grace will I am sure thoroughly consider how much the aproach of a new Parliament, and the state of publick credit calls on you not to quit or seem uneasy in your present station, every one that wishes sincerely well to you will feel the difficulties you must be surrounded with, but a long life spent in the service of this country must not conclude with a too precipitate retreat.[2]

Similarly, the ring of Government financiers in the City, accustomed to deal with Newcastle, pressed him to retain the Treasury ; and so did numerous dependants who, though ready to serve any Minister, did not relish the prospect of a new scramble for favour, under handicaps and against a heightened competition.

Meantime Viry, active as ever, seems to have played a quaint game. This is the account which, on 29 October, he gave Bute of his interview with Newcastle :

> J'ai vu hyer au soir la personne en question. Quoique j'ai passé près de deux heures avec luy, je n'ai cependant pas encore pû le déterminer, à profiter des graces et bontés qu'on veut avoir pour lui : il m'a paru y être cependant très sensible, mais il est toujours retombé sur ce qui se passa il y a quelques années, entre milord Bute, et son neveu [Lord Lincoln], en disant que dès lors, il était, encore, devenu plus vieux et avoir moins de santé. . . . Je repasserai demain matin chez la personne en question pour lui parler de nouveau.[3]

But Newcastle had reported to Hardwicke on 28 October :

> My friend V. has been with me this morning.[4] He tells me B[ute] and P[itt] are agreed. All P⁸ measures are to be supported.[5]

---

[1] Edmund Burke to Lord Rockingham, 30 July 1769, *Correspondence*, ii. (ed. L. S. Sutherland), 52.
[2] Add. MSS. 32913, f. 390.   [3] Bute MSS.
[4] According to Viry 'au soir' ; were there two interviews between them on 28 October, or did Viry's untruthfulness extend even to time ?
[5] Mr. P. C. Yorke, in his *Life of Lord Hardwicke*, vol. iii. p. 305, thus deciphers this sentence : 'All (?) p[ub]l[ic] measures are to be supported.' I read Mr. Yorke's 'p¹' as 'Pˢ', *i.e.* 'Pitt's'. There is no copy of the letter

P. told B., if he would take the Treasury P. would support him. But he advised him against it. B. said he never thought of it. P. said the D. of N. should continue. B. said he never thought otherwise. My friend told me, 'Continue here to do all their business, and the load and perhaps the blame of all miscarriages fall upon you', and my friend repeated to me almost the same words and the same advice that you, my dearest Lord, gave me last night,[1] for which I shall ever be obliged to you and am determined to follow your advice. I put myself in your hands.[2]

'Your friends may suggest their thoughts', replied Hardwicke the same day, 'but as the decision must be yours, so no body can pretend to advise you but your own heart.'[3] He saw that Newcastle would finish by retaining office, and therefore warned him that this should at least be on clearly defined conditions; and in the meantime, according to Elliot, 'began to assure Lord Bute that nothing was so little thought of by them as capitulations for power, but business could not be carried on without some explanation of that kind, and that the choice of Parliament must also be thought of. Bute answer'd in general terms.'[4] Newcastle (as Hardwicke explained to Pitt on 29 October) was 'delicate' upon the matter, and would not 'stipulate' with the King; 'but surely some plan of persons and things should be opened'. The work of the Treasury required 'a reasonable degree of power or credit', and a prospect of stability. Pitt replied that he himself would have spoken about it to Bute, had he not feared to raise jealousies and suspicions of a concert between him and Newcastle; 'but my Lord Bute may be made to feel it, and driven to open himself upon it'. Pitt added that 'for his part he did not desire to have the chusing of a new Parliament, but only to have some of his friends taken care of'.[5]

---

in the Newcastle Papers, only the original in Newcastle's own handwriting in the Hardwicke Papers, and Hardwicke, after having spent a good part of forty-four years in reading Newcastle's innumerable, interminable letters, wrote to him on 3 March 1762: 'I will endeavour to answer . . . to so much of your Grace's letter as I have been able to decypher; for here are some words which still want to be put *en clair*' (Add. MSS. 32935, f. 160).

[1] Which was to refuse office.
[2] Add. MSS. 35420, f. 108.   [3] Add. MSS. 32913, f. 412.
[4] Notes by Gilbert Elliot; Minto Papers.
[5] Add. MSS. 32913, ff. 426-9.

Newcastle, though he had received nothing beyond vague assurances, by 31 October had decided to retain office, and wrote a letter to that effect which, 'after having been entirely approved' by Bute, was delivered to the King; and Newcastle thus announced the event to his friends : [1]

The Duke of Newcastle sends his compliments to . . ., and acquaints him, that tho' he had almost come to a resolution to retire, yet the commands of the King; the representations of the Duke of Cumberland; the pressing instances of the Archbishop of Canterbury, the Duke of Bedford, the Duke of Devonshire, my Lord Bute, my Lord Northumberland, my Lord Egremont, Mr. Pitt, and all the great noblemen now in town — joined to those of the considerable money'd men in the City; who declared that if the Duke of Newcastle continued in employment, they would raise the money for the service of the ensuing year; but fear'd that if that was not the case, there might be great difficulty in doing it — have determined him to give up his own ease and quiet; and to resign himself again to the King and the Publick.

When he came to kiss the King's hands, the King said:

I thank you for remaining in your employment. I know your zeal and abilities. I will not only give you my countenance and support, to enable you to carry on my business, but such as shall be sufficient to make you happy and easy. My friend, my Lord Bute shall be my guarantee. . . .

And on 31 October, Newcastle wrote to Joseph Yorke:

Yesterday my Lord Bute told me that the King intended to give me his countenance and support; and (which was a strong proof of it) to give me the choice of the new Parliament. That is something indeed, and is the greatest security that can be given to our old friends and the Old Corps. All their service and the support of the Whig cause, is one great reason for my entering again into this turbulent galley. [2]

Hardly four days had elapsed after these touching scenes, when Viry came to Newcastle with an extraordinary tale.

My friend was with me this morning [writes Newcastle in his minute of the conversation] and surpris'd me very much. He said,

---

[1] A letter of this kind was sent on 1 November to Thomas Pelham (Add. MSS. 32914, ff. 3-4), to Lord Godolphin (ff. 5-6), to Rose Fuller (ff. 7-8), and probably to others besides.   [2] *Ibid.* ff. 453-4.

he was not well pleas'd — that some ill-dispos'd persons (not low people, valets de chambre etc.) had made some wicked insinuations to my prejudice to the King or my Lord Bute. That they had insinuated that my talking of *duration* and the choice of the next Parliament, was fixing myself Minister during my own will and pleasure, and *Roy d'Angleterre*. And that therefore he (V.) wish'd I would take an occasion to drop in conversation 'that I came in *provisionnellement* and to obey the King's command; and would be ready to go out whenever it should be His Majesty's pleasure, but that the choice of a Parliament necessarily belong'd to the office of the First Lord of the Treasury'. And that *that* would take off the ill impression made by others. My friend said 'he told me that these insinuations had been *made*; but that he did not tell me that these insinuations had *taken place*'.

I told him very plainly 'that what he said had no foundation — that indeed my friends might have flung out something about the choice of the new Parliament to my Lord Bute, as what was a necessary consequence of my being at the head of the Treasury; and that I did in conversation with my Lord Bute (and it was true) tell him 'that the money'd men of the City said that my bare continuing in office would not be sufficient for them to lend such immense sums of money; but that they must see some *duration*'. Upon which my Lord Bute said 'the King intends to give you his countenance and support, and that, as to the choice of the Parliament which your friends have thrown out, the King intends that you should have the choice of the Parliament; and that is a sufficient proof of *duration*'.

I express'd to my friend great surprise and dissatisfaction, and ask'd 'whether it was intended to revoke any of those assurances which had been given relating to the choice of the Parliament; or whether I was to carry things thro' this winter and then to be dismiss'd'.

. . . I told *V.* plainly 'that, if this was to be the case, and these things were to be flung out every day, they had better at once not renew the Commission [of the Treasury] but let me go out now.

And *that* is my opinion and wish; for I can never stand these daily suggestions; which must have daily ill effects and prevent any real confidence: and we shall have difficulties upon every recommendation which I shall make, on that pitiful suggestion, that I shall by them be too great and too permanent.[1]

Newcastle's jealousies and fears were now awake. 'Every day produces something less promising than the former', he wrote to Hardwicke on 7 November.[2] He saw Pitt and Bute

[1] 4 November 1760; *Ibid.* ff. 76-8.   [2] *Ibid.* ff. 171-2.

at Court 'in the outward room', 'in a long, familiar and serious conversation together'. Later on, each of them talked to him about the future Cabinet, and Bute

said this remarkable thing, 'the King would have every thing go on for the present as it was in his grandfather's time, and till the several officers are appointed after the expiration of the six months; but when the new appointments are made the King will then declare whom he would call to his Cabinet Council', so that we are to expect a new one, and new things every day. . . .

For myself, I am the greatest cypher that ever appear'd at Court. The young King is hardly civil to me; talks to me of *nothing*, and scarce answers me upon my own Treasury affairs. . . .

Is this giving me the countenance and support, which is necessary for me to carry on His Majesty's business, much less what is sufficient to make me happy and easy ? — *Bien au contraire*.

The King's Proclamation had been prepared by Bute, the Speech for the opening of Parliament had to be drafted by the responsible Ministers. On 13 November, Newcastle asked Hardwicke : 'When is the Speech to be shew'd to the King and by whom, and by whom to Lord Bute ?' Obviously he was ready to take rank below Bute. Hardwicke replied : 'Surely your Grace, who us'd to shew it to the late King, should shew it to His present Majesty'.[1] On 16 November Bute surprised them both with the King's demand for the insertion of the famous phrase, 'Born and educated in this country, I glory in the name of Britain'. It was not possible to expostulate about it. 'I suppose you will think *Britain* remarkable', wrote Newcastle to Hardwicke ; 'it denotes the author to all the world.'[2] The dislike of Scotsmen was no less strong in Newcastle and Hardwicke than it was in Samuel Johnson the Tory, or John Wilkes, the Radical.

'THE MINISTER' OF THE NEW REIGN

The game which, in November 1760, started between Bute and Newcastle, provides material for an exquisite comedy. But historical comedy is never written. Authors of historical novels

---

[1] Query and answer on the same sheet of paper ; 13 November 1760; Add. MSS. 32914, f. 277.   [2] *Ibid.* f. 367.

have merely to imagine the past as the readers like to see it. Writers of serious biography have critically to examine records of fact as handed down by the actors or their contemporaries, and then, without smile or grin, adopt what Meredith describes as an ironical habit of mind — 'to believe that the wishes of men . . . are expressed in their utterances'. Historical farce is largely based on the cheap device of conscious anachronisms, and therefore does not count. But historical comedy would require the most accurate and most detailed knowledge and understanding of men and circumstances ; for it would have to ascertain and recognise the deeper irrelevancies and incoherence of human actions, which are not so much directed by reason, as invested by it *ex post facto* with the appearances of logic and rationality. It is more difficult to grasp and fix the irrational and irrelevant than to construe and uphold a reasonable but wrong explanation, and this is the greatest difficulty both in dealing with contemporaries and in writing history.[1]

Conflicts between individuals are almost invariably duels fought in the dark ; isolated, each side develops an overweaning self-consciousness ; unable to see, the combatants listen to the ominous reverberations of every sound ; unable to place the opponent, each side suspects him everywhere ; unable to judge, both act by preconceived ideas ; and — this puts the final seal of humour on the situation — each invariably forgets that the other is in exactly the same predicament.

At an astronomical distance, and provided the stars are taken for granted, historic events acquire some sense, and present movements impressive and monotonous. But when watched at close quarters, the actions of men are in no way correlated in weight and value to the results they produce. The same men have to decide things big and small, and their decisions are reached by the same processes and reactions. The greater a man's power, the less can he gauge the outcome of his own

[1] Besides overrating the importance of the conscious will and purpose in individuals, most people seem to ascribe a co-ordination or 'integration' to historic transactions such as distinguishes the phenomena of life alone ; whereas the joint life and purpose of humanity is, to say the very least, 'unproven'.

actions ; and it is only a truly humble recognition of his own limitations that lifts the great, sincere, religious man beyond the realm of historic comedy. At a moment of acute international crisis, Lord Salisbury had been entertaining guests at Hatfield who were most kindly condoling with him upon the burden of his responsibility. He was relieved when they left — 'I didn't understand what they were talking about'. He was standing at the open door, about to start for a walk and looking out upon the threatening clouds of an autumn afternoon. '. . . I should understand if they spoke of the burden of decision — I feel it now, trying to make up my mind whether or no to take a greatcoat with me. I feel it in exactly the same way, but no more, when I am writing a despatch upon which peace or war may depend. Its degree depends upon the materials for decision that are available and not in the least upon the magnitude of the results which may follow.' Then, after a moment's pause and in a lower tone, he added, 'With the results I have nothing to do'.[1]

History is made up of juggernauts, revolting to human feeling in their blindness, supremely humorous in their stupidity. One of the greatest caricaturists that ever lived, Francesco Goya y Lucientes, reached the highest level of historical humour in his picture of a military execution of Spanish rebels. A bundle of feeling, suffering humanity is huddled together in the last stages of agony, despair, or defiance, and facing them stands a row of the most perfectly trained Napoleonic soldiers, with their hats and rifles all cocked at the same angle. One knows that the next moment the rebels will be at peace, inanimate matter, and the firing squad will dissolve into a number of very ordinary, dull human beings. Similarly, in Brueghel's 'Fall of Icarus' the true humour of the tragedy is not so much the pair of naked legs sticking out of the water, as the complete unconcern of all the potential onlookers ; not even the fisherman who sits on the shore notices what has happened.

History of infinite weight was to be made in the absurd beginnings of a reign which was to witness the elimination of

[1] Lady Gwendolen Cecil, *Life of Robert, Marquis of Salisbury*, vol. i. pp. 118-19.

those who had hitherto governed England, the speedy and irretrievable disgrace of him who brought about their downfall, the lunacy of the man who meant to be King, the ruin of the life and achievements of the greatest statesman of the age, the break-up of an Empire such as the world had not seen since the disruption of the Roman Empire — history was to be started in ridiculous beginnings, while small men did things both infinitely smaller and infinitely greater than they knew. For purposes of historical comedy, and with a view to destroying some beautiful and very rational legends, it will pay to follow up in some detail the duel between these two reputed leaders and statesmen, Newcastle and Bute.

What was the character of Bute ? The witnesses can be called again whose value was tested and proved in the case of Newcastle. Shelburne writes in his autobiography : [1]

As to the Earl of Bute . . . it's not so easy a matter to give a just idea of his character. . . . His bottom was that of any Scotch nobleman, proud, aristocratical, pompous, imposing, with a great deal of superficial knowledge such as is commonly to be met with in France and Scotland . . . and a very false taste in everything. Added to this he had a gloomy sort of madness which made him affect living alone, particularly in Scotland, where he resided some years in the Isle of Bute, with as much pomp and as much uncomfortableness . . . as if he had been King of the Island. . . . He read a great deal, but it was chiefly out of the way books of science and pompous poetry. . . . He excell'd most in writing, of which he appear'd to have a great habit. He was insolent and cowardly, at least the greatest political coward I ever knew. He was rash and timid, accustom'd to ask advice of different persons, but had not sense and sagacity to distinguish and digest, with a perpetual apprehension of being govern'd, which made him, when he follow'd any advice, always add something of his own in point of matter or manner, which sometimes took away the little good which was in it or changed the whole nature of it. He was always upon stilts. . . . He felt all the pleasure of power to consist either in punishing or astonishing. He was ready to abandon his nearest friend if attacked, or to throw any blame off his own shoulders. He . . . did not [want ?] for some good points, so much as for resolution and knowledge of the world to bring them into action. . . . He excell'd as far as I could observe

[1] Lord Fitzmaurice, *Life of Shelburne*, vol. i. pp. 110-11 ; corrected from the original MSS. at Bowood.

in managing the interior of a Court, and had an abundant share of art and hipocrisy. . . .

.   .   .   .

He panted for the Treasury, he had a notion that the K — and he understood it from what they had read about revenue and funds while they were at Kew. He had likewise an idea of great reformations, which all men who read the theory of things, and especially men who look up at being Ministers, and want to remove and lower those that are, make a great part of their conversation. He had likewise a confus'd notion of rivalling the D. de Sully, all which notions presently vanish'd when he came to experience the difficultys of it, and to find that dealing with mankind was the first thing necessary, of which he began to find himself utterly incapable.

On the death of George II, writes Chesterfield in his *Characters*,

Lord Bute arrived from the greatest favour to the highest power and took no care to dissemble or soften either, in the eyes of the public. . . . He interfered in every thing, disposed of every thing, and undertook every thing, much too soon for his inexperience in business and for at best his systematic notions of it, which are seldom or never reducible to practice. . . . Every man who is new in business, is at first either too rash or too timorous; but he was both. He undertook what he feared to execute, and what consequently he executed ill.

.   .   .   .

He was too impatient to shine in the full meridian of his power. . . . He placed and displaced whom he pleased; gave peerages without number, and pensions without bounds; . . . but unfortunately for him, he had made no personal friends: this was partly owing to his natural temper, which was dry, unconciliatory, and sullen, with great mixture of pride. . . .[1] No man living had his entire confidence; and no man thinks himself bound by a half-confidence.

[1] Hardwicke, discussing a letter written by Bute to Newcastle on 12 February 1761 (Add. MSS. 32918, ff. 465-6), and which, to say the least, was unpleasant in tone, gives the following description of Bute's style (*ibid.* ff. 513-14):

As to the manner of his letter, it is certainly particular, and not unctious, and yet I think his Lordship meant some parts of it to be so. I do not think he intended it to be *offensive*; for it is extremely like his conversation; sometimes throwing in an expression or a turn, that seems harsh, in the midst of a civil discourse. . . . But the stile is often dry and awkward."

When the popular run started against him,

Lord Bute, who had hitherto appeared a presumptuous, now appeared to be a very timorous Minister, characters by no means inconsistent. . . .

He had honour, honesty, and good intentions. He was too proud to be respectable or respected; too cold and silent to be amiable; too cunning to have great abilities; and his inexperience made him too precipitately undertake what it disabled him from executing.

Whatever evidence there is of Bute's thinking and actions bears out the testimony of these two contemporaries. The theatricals which had originally introduced him to Leicester House, were his proper element; sense of reality he had none. While craving for power, he emphatically disclaimed all thought of it, and while working hard to establish his sole authority, he had his eyes fixed all the time on the grand, moving scene of his future resignation.[1] 'O quando licebit — procul negotiis, &c., &c. . . .' he wrote on 14 January 1759 while still with the Prince at Kew:

Why am I doomed to climb ambition's steep and rocky height, who, early in life, had the meanest opinion of politicians — opinions that maturer age and dear bought experience too well confirm?[2]

In May 1761, a few weeks after having taken office, he wrote to Sir Francis Dashwood that he was 'not very sollicitous about the world's opinion', that he thought he had 'allready been hardly dealt with', and had suffered 'many instances of perfidy and ingratitude, the necessary tribute paid by people in my situation'.[3] When faced with the first serious difficulties, he saw 'nothing but rocks and quicksands' and felt that every wish of his heart was thwarted;

however, I must go on, while I see the smallest prospect of serving my Prince; but that over, my only care will be to leave Court with the same unblemished character I came into it, and then comfort myself with the testimony of my own conscience.[4]

[1] See also Bute's letter to H. Fox, 2 March 1763, in Ilchester, *Letters to Henry Fox*, p. 172:

Indeed, my dear Sir, the end of my labors was solemnly determin'd, even before I undertook them.

[2] To William Mure; *Caldwell Papers*, Part ii. vol. i. p. 119.
[3] No date, but docketed 'May 1761'; Eg. MSS. 2136, f. 20.
[4] To George Grenville, 25 September 1761; *Grenville Papers*, vol. i. p. 388.

And in May 1763 Edward Weston, who had worked under Bute, wrote about his resignation that 'it was always kept in view from the first' but had been hastened by ill-health 'and a more than ordinary sensibility to unmerited reproach and abuse'.[1]

First Bute had felt the sentimental charm of dying ahead, but when he was dead, he would not believe it, or accept it for a fact ; and throughout, in the semi-reality of his existence, his part resolved itself into fitful, disconnected, haphazard intervention, and sententious, haughty, futile pronouncements. He was disturbing and ineffective ; but what he said and did was sufficient to frighten, upset, and confuse the anxious, despairing Duke of Newcastle, with whom Lord Bute had only one thing in common : unfitness for a place of responsibility.

PREPARATIONS FOR THE GENERAL ELECTION

On 26 November Newcastle wrote to Hardwicke that he had 'appointed Mr. Roberts to begin about settling our elections, and it is high time that should be done'.[2] And on 29 November, to Chesterfield : 'The securing a good Parliament is my great and first object. I am afraid I shall meet with more difficulties *in carrying that thro'* than are imagined. However, I will do my part.'[3]

Incidents accumulated which were of grave portent to Newcastle. The King promised Lord Bath the Lieutenancy of Shropshire held by Lord Powis, the chief of the Shropshire Whigs ; it was given out that no Government money would be spent on the forthcoming general election ; in a few elections old preferences or feuds were revived by Bute and the King, who at St. James's continued the puny methods and politics of Leicester House. But to Newcastle every petty, vindictive, whimsical humour of Bute's ('he felt all the pleasure of power

[1] To Andrew Mitchell, 17 May 1763 ; Add. MSS. 6823, f. 185.
[2] Add. MSS. 35420, f. 118. John Roberts, Henry Pelham's secretary, had assisted Newcastle in the general election of 1754, had been in charge of the secret service money under him, 1754-56, and continued to manage for Newcastle the two Treasury boroughs of Harwich and Orford. About him see *The Structure of Politics*.
[3] Add. MSS. 32915, f. 168.

to consist either in punishing or astonishing') was evidence of far-reaching political schemes, while to the new Court every anxious suspicion of Newcastle's that he was shelved and neglected, was proof of his planning to make himself '*Roy d'Angleterre*'.

By the beginning of December, Newcastle was once more in the trough of despair. On 5 December he wrote to Joseph Yorke :

I shall soon know whether I can be of service by remaining where I am or not.

A most extraordinary phaenomenon appear'd yesterday of which I had the first notice by an accidental information from Ned Finch at my Lady Yarmouth's. Five Tory lords and commoners added to the Lords and Grooms of the Bedchamber. *Lord Oxford*, Lord Bruce, Mr. Geo. Pitt, Mr. Norbonne Berkeley, and Mr. Northey.

I have told my mind very freely and very strongly to my Lord Bute and Mr. Pitt (who concerted together upon it). This has put me upon requiring such explanations as shall determine my continuance in employment or not.[1]

On 7 December, in a letter to Lord Hardwicke, he apprehended there was a resolve that he 'should have nothing, or as little to do as possible, in the choice of the Parliament'. Bute and Pitt

both equally dread my having anything to do in the choice of the Parliament. My Lord Bute thinks his power may be circumscribed by it. Mr. Pitt wishes to have a Parliament of Great Britain as like the Common Council of London as possible ; and then he thinks, *he* shall be master of them ; and in this view, both of them agreed but very lately upon this measure of introducing Tories, to be a succedaneum to the Whig Parliament which would be better inclined to me and my friends than to them. . . . I own the principal, if not the single inducement to me, for continuing in this galley, was the securing a Parliament. That seems out of the question with regard to myself ; but what then will be the consequence with regard to our friends, and the Whigs in the several counties ? They will be given up at once. An inundation of Tories, or Stuarts etc. will be pour'd into every county ; and how is it possible for us to be of any use to the publick, when that once comes to be the case ?

[1] *Ibid.* f. 308.

Newcastle, faced by these imaginary terrors, once more considered resigning, but hesitated what reason to give ; should he name 'the want of *power* to chuse a Parliament', or 'the introduction of Tories', or merely say that he had secured the money for the coming year, and, as his remaining in office was disagreeable to him and not desired by others,

and as the Treasury had always, ever since the Restoration, a great hand in the choice of the new Parliament, the Duke of Newcastle would be liable to so many solicitations and vexations upon that account that he chose to have nothing to do with it.

Still, if he resigned, should he not, for the sake of his friends, first carry through the appointments to the Commissionerships of Customs, Excise, etc., which 'depend upon the Treasury *only*, without intervention of the King' ?

I remained in for the service of the Whigs ; I shall go out because I find, I can do them no real service. I have been injuriously and falsely treated by my Lord Bute and Mr. Pitt . . . with regard to the choice of the Parliament. God forbid that I should ever think of opposing or embarrassing the King's Government ! It ever was the farthest from my thoughts. But I don't intend to go out like a criminal and to hide my head. I see what we are to expect, a Parliament of 1710 — men of no business, no talents, to conduct it under Mr. Pitt. A Commission of Accounts to keep me in awe. But God be praised, I despise it all.[1]

Lord Hardwicke replied the same night, 7 December, at 11 P.M. He advised Newcastle not to speak to Lord Bute about the Tories in the Bedchamber ; 'above all things, avoid saying any thing about employing any of the King's money to chuse a new Parliament'. But if he wanted to resign without going into opposition,

whoever has gone out with such a resolution, has, I think, allways been desirous to leave as many of their friends in Court or in place, as they could. Otherwise they will look upon it as lying down and dying without any hopes of a resurrection.[2]

Newcastle's and Hardwicke's ideas about resigning without going into opposition, and about securing one's return through

---

[1] Newcastle to Hardwicke, 7 December 1760 ; Add MSS 32915, ff. 332-7.
[2] *Ibid.* ff. 339-40.

friends left behind in office — so utterly foreign to modern ideas of party government — should be carefully noted, as they help to explain later developments in a Parliament 'chosen' by Newcastle.

On 9 December, Viry came to see Newcastle and suggested that he should form a close junction with Bute and propose drawing up the list of the new Parliament together. 'Le Roi veut le Parlement à lui, mais qu'il soit fait par vous et de concert avec My Lord Bute.' [1] Newcastle replied that he and his friends were in favour of a close understanding with Bute — 'de lui offrir une confiance réciproque independamment de tout autre'; the King and Bute should give him the names of the men they wanted in Parliament, and he would take care of them; he would fix the list of the new Parliament with his friends and show it to Bute, and, having discussed it with him, to the King. Viry approved of the scheme. But even while they were still talking, Newcastle seems to have felt that he had gone too far, and expressed the wish to preserve 'une union convenable et respectueuse avec Mr. Pitt'; and by the time he sent the minutes of the conversation to Hardwicke, he was overcome by the fear of Pitt: 'I am so embarrassed that I don't well know what to do'.[2]

Nor was Hardwicke pleased with the proposal of an 'absolute league, offensive and defensive'. 'Your Grace may find yourself obliged to come into all sorts of Scotch jobbs . . . or else be liable to be reproach'd with breach of faith.' He should be explicit with Bute in the matter of the choice of Parliament, but take care not to rouse Pitt, who 'would undoubtedly fly out in the most violent manner; and what man has either your Grace or Lord B. to oppose to him in the House of Commons?' The alliance had much better be 'confin'd to the choice of a Parliament, the list whereof must, I suppose, *at last* be communicated to him [Pitt] too. . . .' [3]

By Sunday, 14 December, Newcastle had prepared elaborate 'Heads for my Conference with my Lord Bute'.

---

[1] *Ibid.* ff. 358-60.
[2] *Ibid.* 35420, f. 140.
[3] *Ibid.* ff. 372-3.

To know His Majesty's in-
tentions upon the following
points :

First.

As to the choice of the Parliament and the conduct of the
elections.

First.

My Lord Bute having told me
that the King would leave the
choice of the Parliament to me,
I must know in what sense that
is to be understood ; whether
His Majesty would give me the
names of such persons as he
would have chose ? My Lord
Bute having told me, that the
King might wish three or four
persons to be chose in certain
places, when I receive the names,
I would then place them in
proper places ; and in that case
I should hope His Majesty would
leave the rest to me. And I
should propose that after I had
digested the whole list, I should
shew it to my Lord Bute, before
I shew'd it to the King.[1]

NB.

The expence of several places I
know already will be so very
great, that it will be difficult to
find private persons, able to be
at it ; and therefore we shall not
have great choice.

Q.

Whether in the conversation with
my Lord Bute any mention
should be made about money ?
Or whether I should proceed
upon the supposition that none
is to be given.[2]

[1] Hardwicke, in correcting the above paragraph, made Newcastle cross
out the sentence, 'and in that case I should hope His Majesty would leave
the rest to me'; '. . . after Lord B. has talk'd of three or four persons',
wrote Hardwicke, 'I would rather take the rest for granted' (Add. MSS.
32916, ff. 79-80).

[2] Hardwicke's reply (this and the following replies are in H. V. Jones's
handwriting) : 'No harm just gently to touch it, as it may be necessary to
know the King's resolution'.

Q.

As to the Scotch election — and
whether I should shew the D. of
Argyll's paper, concerted with
me, to my Lord Bute ? [1]

Secondly.	*Secondly.*
To know whether there is any intention to introduce any more Tories and where.[2]	This will be absolutely necessary for the satisfaction of our friends. And under this head, I would endeavour to learn, if any Tories are to be assisted in their elections and where.

The remaining six 'heads' deal with appointments to
various places, and how they should be made ; with the new
Cabinet ; the choice of Secretary at War, etc.

I shall have some general discourse with my Lord Bute about the
method of conducting business in general, by which perhaps I may
make some useful discoveries. The great point will be to manage
this conference and the consequences from it, in such manner, as to
give no jealousy to Mr. Pitt. . . .[3]

As Newcastle himself put it on record in the above notes,
Bute had told him that 'the King might wish three or four
persons to be chose in certain places' — which clearly did not
point to wholesale interference in the elections.

But the conference, for which Newcastle prepared with so
much care, never came off. On 19 December, Newcastle wrote
to the Duke of Devonshire [4] that Bute had seemed 'very indifferent about it for some time. . . . Next Tuesday [23
December] seem'd to be *awkwardly* agreed to. My Lord Bute
said in the beginning of our discourse *that he had nothing to say
to me* but was ready to receive my commands.' He seemed

---

[1] Hardwicke's reply : 'Cannot foresee it can do any hurt unless engag'd
by promise not to communicate it.' — The paper is among the Newcastle
MSS. 32999, ff. 15-17 ; it is dated 27 June 1760 and marked : 'Memorandums with the Duke of Argyll. The whole list of Members gone thro'
with his Grace.'

[2] Hardwicke's reply : 'Very necessary.'

[3] For the original draft, with marginal remarks by Lord Hardwicke, see
Add. MSS. 32916, ff. 49-55 ; for a corrected draft, embodying Hardwicke's
suggestions, ff. 105-8.

[4] Add. MSS. 32916, ff. 207-13.

offended at the support which Newcastle gave to Powis, and accused him of making difficulties

upon every thing that the King proposed, meaning, I suppose, the election in Wales for my Lord Carnarvon ; which (by-the-by) I have accommodated for him, if he pleases ; and the very dirty, shameful part which they have acted in ordering my Lord Anson to direct the docks to be neuter :—That is, to be for whom they please in the Hampshire election : even against the Chancellor of the Exchequer.

When I found his Lordship in this temper ; and that I was to have the King's name put upon me in every Tory election they pleased to favor, I took up a spirit also, and told him very plainly that I could be of no use to the King, if I had it not in my power to serve my friends. . . .

. . . in going to the Council Room, I told him, that I thought it was unnecessary to give ourselves the trouble of a meeting ; and so the whole is dropt.[1]

The same day (19 December) Newcastle had a talk with Richard Rigby, the political agent of the Duke of Bedford, and Rigby's report of it, published in the *Bedford Correspondence*,[2] is one of the 'texts' from which the course of the general election of 1761 has been divined by many historians. The Duke of Newcastle complained

of the very little weight he had in the closet and of the daily means used to let him have as little in the ensuing Parliament. That the Whigs were given up in many parts of England. . . . He named three instances to prove this assertion. The first was the order for the dock at Portsmouth to be permitted to vote as they pleased, to which a private order is annexed for them all to vote for Stewart ; the second was the turning out Lord Powis from his lieutenancy of Shropshire to make way for Lord Bath ; and the third was the removing certain persons in South Wales who have long had the management of elections in that part of the world : I conjecture his Grace meant Mr. Gwynne, who is now member for Radnor, while Lord Carnarvon is sent down with pretty large powers ; and Sir M. [should be J.] Philips's support in Pembrokeshire against Sir Wm. Owen.

Two very petty 'great men', Lord Bath and Lord Carnarvon, had previously been defeated by Lord Powis and his group in Shropshire and Radnorshire, and, as Newcastle

[1] Add. MSS. 32916, ff. 207-13.   [2] Vol. ii. pp. 423-4.

could not renounce the 'Shropshire Whigs', however much he wished to accommodate the two noble lords, these joined Leicester House, and now claimed their reward.[1] Also the Hampshire affair had been originally engineered by Carnarvon. As for Pembrokeshire, this was a purely local matter, and there is no evidence of Bute having interfered in it. Anyhow, none of these cases had the political significance ascribed to them by Newcastle and by historians who accept his expressions of fear for statements of fact ; while before a year was out, Powis and Gwynne, whom Newcastle identified with the Whig cause, were to abandon Newcastle for Bute.

In reality even now no concerted plan for the general election can be traced with the *quondam* Leicester House connexion. There naturally were individual moves by old political wire-pullers and new courtiers, in pursuit of feuds or in the hope of gains. There were these few men, worsted in the past, who now resumed the fight with better chances of success (Lord Carnarvon, Sir John Phillips, Simeon Stuart) ; a few patrons of boroughs, who previously would have offered them to Newcastle, hastened to pay that compliment to Bute (Lord Falmouth, Bubb Dodington, Sir William Irby, G. A. Selwyn) ; a few candidates, either because not accommodated by Newcastle or because of previous personal connexions with Bute, offered to assume, or begged permission to wear, his 'livery' (T. O. Hunter at Winchelsea,[2] William Mayne at Canterbury,[3] William Hamilton — subsequently the husband of Nelson's Emma—at Midhurst,[4] Sir Edmund Thomas in Glamorganshire,

---

[1] For a detailed account of these transactions, see the chapter on 'Shropshire Politics and Men' in *The Structure of Politics*.

[2] See 'Register' of Bute's correspondence, Add. MSS. 36796, f. 59 ; T. O. Hunter to the Earl of Bute, 10 December 1760 : 'As to Winchelsea Election. Desires the King's protection.'

[3] See Add. MSS. 36796, f. 83 ; 32917, f. 16 ; *Hist. MSS. Comm. Stopford-Sackville MSS.*, vol. i. pp. 45-6 ; and *An Address to the Electors of the City of Canterbury*, by Thomas Roch (1761).

[4] Sir H. Erskine wrote to Bute that 'Mr. Hamilton, a friend of Mr. Henry Fox's, desires to come into Parliament, and to attach himself to Lord Bute, and would give £2,000 for that purpose'; Add. MSS. 36796, f. 70 ; on the Midhurst election, see Add. MSS. 32920, ff. 74, 76, 115-16, 137, 274-5, 291, 293, and 315; further information about it is contained in the Shelburne Papers, in the possession of the Marquess of Lansdowne, at Bowood.

etc.).   Various offers were made to Bute, but there is no evidence
whatsoever to show that any were sought for by him.   Occasionally he would discourse on the King's right to nominate 'to his
own boroughs'; but at no time did a formed scheme appear.

Bute seems to have been sincere when he professed to
'abhor all election business';[1] such work did not suit his
temperament.   Even had he wished to manage the general
election, he could not have done it except through Newcastle,
or by first removing him.   In 1760 the only permanent election
organisation on an extensive scale centred in the Treasury,
with certain supplementary resources in the Admiralty and in
some minor offices;   so long as Newcastle remained at the
Treasury, and Hardwicke's son-in-law, Lord Anson, at the
Admiralty, their various local agents clearly could not be used
in a systematic and yet secret manner against them.   As for
independent action, so infinite was the diversity of conditions,
so staggering the complexity — where thousands of men with
individual interests had to be satisfied, and where there were
no masses with a uniform political mentality and training to
appeal to — that it would have required very considerable experience and skill to tackle the problem on a large scale.   But
most of those who had worked general elections for Frederick,
Prince of Wales, were dead or gone, and the Leicester House
group had not the men to undertake it now.   Bute was a
stranger to English politics and a hated Scot;   George Grenville had not yet detached himself from Temple and Pitt;   and
the situation was not sufficiently clear for Henry Fox, the most
experienced political manager who could have been put in
competition to Newcastle.   Though Fox was anxious to re-
enter active politics and made tentative advances with a view
to new connexions, he was too clever and too cautious to drop
his patron, the Duke of Cumberland, without sufficient assurances from his new associates;   his activities were limited to
securing the return of some friends of his own, and to negotiating
a few seats for friends whom he was prepared to share with
Bute (two at Ludgershall, one at Hindon, and one at Midhurst).

[1] In a letter to W. Mure, 20 November 1759; *Caldwell Papers*, Part ii.
vol. i. p. 123.

There were two men who seem to have pressed Bute to engage actively in the general election — Bubb Dodington and Lord Fitzmaurice, better known as Shelburne, to which title he succeeded half a year later. Dodington wrote to Bute on 26 November 1760 :

In consequence of what we last talk'd about,[1] I send you a list of the burroughs, and the Members now serving for them, where the Crown by virtue of its offices, has either the absolute nomination or very much the superior influence. I believe it is very far from being correct ; for I have so long, and with so much success, endeavoured to forget these things (which brought me nothing in return, but dissatisfaction) that they are all out of the way, both in my drawers and in my head : but my zeal for the Kings service, and independency, would I believe recall some of them, if you should think it necessary.

It is not my wish that His Majesty should interfere directly, or indirectly, in any election, where the interest is in any private gentleman as such : but during the two last reigns, a sett of undertakers have farm'd the power of the Crown, at a price certain, and under colour of making themselves responsible for the whole have taken the sole direction of the Royal interest into their own hands, and apply'd it to their own creatures, without consulting the Crown, or leaving any room for the Royal nomination, or direction.

This only, I think, should be prevented, and prevented before they can pretend that it is settled, and the persons promis'd. These gentlemen should not in my opinion be suffer'd to engage the interest of the Crown without previous taking His Majestys pleasure, as to the nomination where he has the power, and the recommendation and support, where he has the influence, of such of His Majesty's friends, and servants as he, not they, shall approve of.[2]

And on 15 December, Dodington again wrote to Bute : [3]

I am exerting all my endeavours to get as many members as I possibly can. For God's sake do not suffer all the King's interest to be employed against his power. If it be not thought proper to raise an army, let us at least secure a phalanx to oppose the malice and faction which are everywhere at work.

[1] This seems to refer to the conversation noted in Dodington's *Diary* under date of 22 November ; nothing, however, is said about the general election in the short summary which Dodington gives of it.
[2] The letter is among the Bute MSS. ; part of it was published by J. Adolphus in his *History of England from the Accession of George III* (1805), p. 24.
[3] See *Hist. MSS. Comm., Various Collections*, vol. vi. p. 47, MSS. of Miss M. Eyre Matcham.

It is not clear where Dodington 'exerted all his endeavours' — judging by results they were limited to the boroughs in which he had been engaged for a long time, Weymouth and Melcombe Regis and Bridgwater.

Lord Fitzmaurice, a young man of twenty-three, who had only just entered politics and had Henry Fox for his friend and mentor, found pleasure in election activities, and, as appears from his letters to Bute, pressed him to engage in them. While Dodington tried to set Bute against Newcastle, Fitzmaurice seems to have been at work to supply Bute with material for effectively meeting Newcastle in an argument on the general election. A list is preserved among his papers at Bowood of the Parliamentary representation of England and Wales at the end of 1760, with remarks placed against the various constituencies in Fitzmaurice's own handwriting, indicating what influences were dominant in them, who were the candidates, what were their chances, etc. ; and among George III's papers at Windsor, there is a list of the House of Commons torn out of an almanac for 1760 and interleaved with blank pages, on which the remarks from Fitzmaurice's manuscript are copied in the King's own hand. They bear as heading — 'List of those for the next Parliament with remarks. London, Dec. 20, 1760.'[1] The date seems to suggest that the list was compiled and transmitted with a view to the conference which was to have been held between Bute and Newcastle, but which was now abandoned.

With whom lay the responsibility for this apparent impasse, which arose at such an inconvenient moment ? Lord Mansfield reported to Newcastle on 24 December that Bute thought New-

---

[1] Though some of the information may have come from Dodington, this list cannot be identical with the one he sent to Bute on 26 November. Dodington's list covered only the boroughs under Government influence, while that of Fitzmaurice covers the entire country ; moreover, the note which appears against Co. Durham in Fitzmaurice's list proves that it must have been compiled after 14 December. It runs as follows : 'Clavering has given up — Shaftoe.' This refers to the by-election caused by the death of George Bowes, Member for the county ; on 12 December 1760, while the poll was proceeding, Lord Darlington wrote to Newcastle : 'This day at noon Sir Thomas Clavering found himself under an absolute necessity of resigning, notwithstanding which Mr. Shafto carries on the poll' (Add. MSS. 32916, ff. 12-13).

castle had 'put an end to the intended conference pretty strongly', that in reality Bute wanted Newcastle to continue in office, that the affair of Lord Powis embarrassed him, 'it having been rashly promised'; and he added: 'It is thought you mean to be absolute and to force &c. and to hallow the Whigs upon the incident of Lord Powys'.[1] Newcastle, on the other hand, feared that the scheme of co-operation with Bute was proving impracticable, 'because he must hope some time or other, to be the *sole Minister*; the dispenser of favors he is at present, and I suppose will soon become the author or adviser of measures'.[2]

As 'dispenser of favors' Bute was superseding Newcastle, as 'author or adviser of measures' he was bound to come into conflict with Pitt; and this prospect once more made him treat Newcastle with more regard and circumspection.[3] Moreover, they were temporarily drawn together by Pitt's support of an application from the City of London that the Commission of Lieutenancy for the militia be vested in the Common Council, a democratic measure equally repugnant to Bute, Newcastle, and Hardwicke. Where common sense and true statesmanship were so signally absent, any trifling question of this kind was sufficient to affect the political barometer, and thus, on 24 December, Newcastle found Bute 'prodigiously gracious and in high good humour. . . . His Majesty . . . rather in better humour than usual.'[4]

---

[1] Add. MSS. 32916, ff. 296-7.

[2] Newcastle to Devonshire, 19 December; *ibid.* ff. 207-13.

[3] An excellent sketch of the situation was given on 16 January 1761 in a letter to Andrew Mitchell, M.P. (at that time British Minister at Berlin), by his political agent in London, Robert Symmer: 'The great lines which I endeavoured to mark you out, with regard to the two personages in the former Administration, the Peer and the great Commoner, and the K. and L[d] Bute endeavouring to hold the reins, and keep the balance even between them, still go on . . . it cannot but prove a difficult task. The P[r] who hitherto had been accustomed to give every thing away, and who is passionately fond and jealous of that power cannot but feel mortified upon seeing employments given away, without going through his hands, and persons let in, that are not agreeable to him and his friends: on the other hand, the C[r] whose power is founded in popularity, and whose passion is to act without controll, will not *easily* descend from the height to which his atchievements have raised him, and enter into concert with others in relation to measures which he has hitherto had all the glory of. In short, it is said he will enter into no explination, and of consequence into no terms with Bute, but with regard to him, will be all or nothing'. (Add. MSS. 6839, ff. 205-6).

[4] Add. MSS. 32916, ff. 298-9.

None the less, negotiations concerning the general election were not resumed for some time. On 16 January 1761 Bute told Dodington 'that he must see the Duke of Newcastle, to settle with him, about the elections, shortly'.[1] And on 19 January, Newcastle wrote to Hardwicke:[2]

The Duke of Devonshire told me that he had seen Viry, that he told him . . . that my Lord Bute thought it was high time that I should speak to him about the Parliament and the changes, that were to be made in the several employments. . . .

I am to be with my Lord Bute to-morrow at St. James's whilst the King is at the House. I told his Lordship that I should come to talk to him about the Parliament, and that I had but just got my papers and lists. He said, it was high time, and I think (though in very good humour) talked in such a manner, that I expect more lists from him than I shall carry to him. He said, Lord Falmouth had offered the King three members, but he did not tell me the King's answer.[3] His Lordship told my Lord Anson that my Lord Parker had been with him and he thought my Lord Parker should be brought into Parliament and asked whether that could not be in some Admiralty burrough.[4] *In short his Lordship seems to have had*

[1] See Dodington's *Diary*, p. 429.

[2] Add. MSS. 35420 ff. 166-7.

[3] The three seats offered by Lord Falmouth to the King must have been one each at Tregony, St. Mawes, and Penryn. The only nomination by the King, which I can actually trace in these boroughs, is of Sir Edward Turner at Penryn; see chapter on Penryn under 'Cornish Boroughs' in *The Structure of Politics*.

[4] Cf. in Dodington's *Diary* under 2 February, the account of that talk given him by Lord Bute: 'That he had told Lord Anson that room must be made for Lord Parker, who replied that all was engaged: and that he (Bute) said, What, my Lord, the King's Admiralty boroughs full, and the King not acquainted with it! That Anson seemed quite disconcerted and knew not what to say.'

The following letter from Newcastle to Hardwicke is referred in Albemarle's *Life of Rockingham* (vol. i. p. 63) to the general election of 1761:

I have received the enclosed list from Mr. Legge. I beg you would communicate it to the Duke of Devonshire, and my Lord Kinnoul, who, I hope, have told you what intelligence I had relating to Mr. Fox and his list. I see Legge proposes to make a complete list at present, and to alter it when he shall see the Court list. . . . I am promised that, as soon as it is settled; but Mr. Fox said this day, that *they* were to meet about it. I doubt whether we shall have time to let our friends know what to do.

As reproduced by Lord Albemarle the letter is undated except 'Monday, 5 o'clock', and I have failed to find it either among the Newcastle or the Hardwicke Papers. But neither Legge nor Devonshire helped Newcastle in managing the general election of 1761, and the letter cannot be fitted

a good deal of transactions with burroughs. I shall speak to him (if I have time) upon all the points that were agreed upon the other night. And I do not promise myself any very good success, either as to the Parliament, or to the changes in employment.

Lord Hardwicke replied the same day :

It is very probable that Lord B. has had a good deal of transaction with boroughs. Those who have the command of some of them, would be ready to make their court to the rising sun and probably your cosin Falmouth not one of the last. Your Grace will form a more certain judgment when you come to talk upon the list.[1]

About the same time Bute made Viry suggest to Newcastle, as an idea of his own, that the best way to strengthen the Government would be by making Bute Secretary of State. To this Newcastle would have readily agreed, for he 'was not a person to make more difficulties than were necessary', but he feared Pitt, who openly declared 'the impossibility of a *favorite* . . . to be *Minister*'.[2] 'I repeated again to Viry', wrote Newcastle in a minute on 21 January, 'that, in all events, Mr. Pitt must not be displeas'd, and that nothing must be done in which he does not readily concur.'[3]

On 20 January, the day fixed for the conference, Newcastle received the following note from Bute :

Oppressed with a violent cold I have found it necessary to take something that prevents my going out this morning; I must therefore take another opportunity of attending your Grace. . . .[4]

Newcastle in reply expressed the hope of seeing Bute soon, 'for indeed the business presses'.[5] But the father of Lady Bute, Edward Wortley Montagu, sen., died on 22 January,

---

into the extant correspondence of any of the three most probable Mondays (19 and 26 January, and 2 February). In reality the lists mentioned in it have nothing to do with the general election of 1761, but refer to the Committee of Accounts, set up in 1763. The following note from Legge to Newcastle, dated 25 February 1763 (Add. MSS. 32947, f. 94) clearly places the letter (and destroys it as evidence of there having been a Court list in 1761) :

A sight of the Court List will be decisive as to our conduct, and will probably shew us how far any list on our side may be necessary.

In the mean while we will put together the names which for various reasons we think most adviseable.

[1] Add. MSS. 32917, ff. 398-400. [2] *Ibid.* f. 435.
[3] *Ibid.* ff. 461-4. [4] *Ibid.* f. 425. [5] *Ibid.* f. 427.

and Lord Bute went into decorous retirement, to consider the vast fortune his wife had inherited, and the ways to break through some inconvenient clauses in the will. He 'is now loaded with an immense fortune', wrote Newcastle to Hardwicke on 24 January. '. . . I have heard that the will gives to Lord Bute's family in land and money upwards of £400,000. . . . This immense fortune will add (I suppose) considerably to the weight and consequence of our great man.' [1] 'This will probably make him hold his head higher', replied Hardwicke, 'and consider himself as upon a different foot in this country.   I suppose Mr. P. feels this and is piqued at it. . . .' [2]

On 27 January, Viry informed Newcastle that he, Viry, had given up 'his' idea of Bute for Secretary of State :

That he had a great honor for Mr. Pitt; and that he would not engage in any thing, that might be disagreable to him.   That what he calls his idea was meant for Mr. Pitt's service; and he (C. V.) still thought, it was so; but fearing that Mr. Pitt might not think so, he (C. V.) would drop it entirely.   That my Lord Bute had nothing to do with the idea. [3]

Obviously Bute, not meeting with sufficient response from Newcastle and his friends, preferred not to press his scheme for the present.

I then insisted [Newcastle continues in his minutes of the conversation] upon my Lord Bute's having so often put me off that it was necessary for me to see him upon the elections; the changes (if any) in the administration etc. . . .

When I pressed him about my seeing Lord Bute and settling things with him; he told me, to my great surprise, that my Lord Bute did nothing and would do nothing; that he never talk'd of business (that is, foreign affairs) to him; and would have it thought

---

[1] Add. MSS. 32918, ff. 45-6.

[2] *Ibid.* ff. 63-4. Wortley's fortune seems to have been even larger than at first reported. 'It is said the personal estate amounts to 7 or 800,000£', wrote R. Symmer to Andrew Mitchell on 30 January 1761 'and the landed estate, coal mines included, to 20,000£ p.ann. Lady Bute, after payment of legacies, has the whole during life . . .' (Add. MSS. 6839, f. 209).

[3] 'Secret Memorandums', 27 January 1761 ; Add. MSS. 32918, ff. 82-6. In the 'Register of Correspondence of the Earl of Bute' the entry appears under the same date : 'Count Viry to the Earl of Bute. He has received a letter from the Duke of Newcastle respecting the Secretaryship' (Add. MSS. 36796, f. 71). There is no copy of such a letter among the Newcastle Papers, and it does not seem likely that it was ever written.

that Lord Bute was no Minister, and would be none, and that the carrying on the public business was the affair of others, and not his.

This 'shyness' on the part of Bute, Newcastle ascribed to 'a jealousy that we have more management for Mr. Pitt than he wishes or designs we should have'.

On 1 February, Hardwicke, seeing Newcastle's 'inclination' that he should meet Bute, asked for an appointment ; whereupon 'his Lordship was so polite as to call at my house'.

I believe he had a mind to talk with me a little about Mr. Wortley's will, for that subject made a great part of his conversation. . . . According to his account the will is odd and dark like the testator; and I find they have hopes of finding openings to break the entail. . . .

After this point dispatch'd, I endeavour'd to put him upon more public ones. I told his Lordship that both your Grace and I had much lamented his necessary confinement. That I was very glad to see him deliver'd from it, for that I thought it high time that you should meet. In this he agreed, and said he had sent your Grace a note this morning. . . . I told him that, tho' I had nothing to do with it, I was sure it was time to settle what related to the new Parliament and the affair of places, and I knew perfectly well that your Grace was desirous to act in concert with his Lordship, and that you might thoroughly understand one another, which I thought would be most useful to the service of the King and the public, and that he would find in your Grace the best disposition. In this he agreed very handsomely in general, but gave me no opening to enter into particulars.[1]

On Monday, 2 February, 'at night', Newcastle wrote to Hardwicke :

My conference is now fixed for Wensday. . . . I am apt to think, it will be a very superficial one, and give us little light into the intended plan of administration, except that it is all to centre in one person. . . . My Lord Bute seem'd very civil, and good humoured, but there was no appearance of confidence, of any stress laid upon our meeting, or the necessity for it. His Lordship only said, confining our meeting singly to the affair of the elections, *that he had little to do in it.* I will go thro' the elections, as well as I can, and endeavour to see what they really intend; I trust it is too late for them to do any great mischief. They may be disagreable, defeat

---

[1] Hardwicke to Newcastle, 1 February 1761, 'Sunday night'; Add. MSS. 32918, ff. 176-7.

some of our friends, and act directly contrary to what was promised, but they can't now alter the tone and complexion of the new Parliament. That is too well settled, and so far my staying in to this time has been of use. . . .

Should I acquaint Mr. Pitt to-morrow of my being too see Lord Bute on Wensday about elections, his Lordship comes to my house at one o'clock that day.[1]

Lord Hardwicke replied the same night :

I think your Grace is very much in the right in your plan of not only going thro' the affair of the elections, but also the several points of business necessary now to be settled. . . .

I think your Grace will be much in the right to tell Mr. Pitt to-morrow, unaffectedly that you are to see my Lord Bute the next day about elections.[2]

The next morning, 3 February, Newcastle received a visit from Count de Viry :

My friend said the King has towns where he names, particularly the places belonging to the Admiralty, and therefore my friend wishes that I would leave the places, where the King names *to them* ; and not put upon the King or my Lord Bute, the difficulty of refusing those who may be propos'd. Lord Bute said, the King has some whom he would have — Lord Bute has but few ; and desires, if he can't make friends by the elections, he may not make enemies.

I put my friend in mind of the promise which was made me about the choice of the Parliament. He own'd it to be true ; but said, What can one say ?

I said, my Lord Bute had told me, that the King had three or four whom His Majesty might wish to have in Parliament; and, in that case, they ought to give me the names. My friend replied, The King has a number ; and he should give their names to you.

NB.—I find by C. V., that they expect a great many. He once said, Suppose the King thinks there are fifty places, which depend on His Majesty.

.   .   .   .

And, upon the whole, I apprehend a disagreeable meeting to-morrow ; that I shall find numbers propos'd for elections who cannot be provided for — and that I shall get little or no light into their future intentions.[3]

---

[1] Add. MSS. 35420, ff. 174-5. No copy of this letter is preserved in the Newcastle MSS.   [2] Add. MSS. 32918, f. 190.
[3] C. V. 'The Parliament'. Newcastle House, 3 February 1761 ; Add. MSS. 32918 f. 235.

These minutes, together with a 'Memorandum for my Lord Bute', Newcastle sent to Hardwicke in a letter dated 3 February 1761, 'near 4 o'clock'. The memorandum starts thus :

To shew my Lord Bute the list of the boroughs.
The probable vacancies and the persons proposed.

'As my conference tomorrow must be ticklish and delicate', wrote Newcastle in the covering letter, 'I wish your Lordship would correct the method I propose to put it in, or add any thing to it which I may have left out, as you may think proper ; as these are the papers I am to shew my Lord Bute to morrow, I must beg to have them back this night.' [1] He further reported that Viry was pressing again his idea about Bute, 'which he says is the only remedy for everything'.

Hardwicke replied the same night :

As to the Secret Memorandums from C. V., I think little new arises upon them, except the extent of their notion as to the number of places to which the King may name. His Majesty and those who advis'd him, must know very little of such matters, if they talk of *fifty* places. But I rather fancy that was thrown out by C. V. at random. The worst symptom seems to be that he talked of the King's having some persons and Lord Bute others to name, for by thus dividing them, they may take a pretence to swell the number. As to their expectation that a list of the places should be given to them, with blanks to fill up with the persons, I think the best answer will be what your Grace once mention'd, 'That a great progress had been made, and engagements taken with many persons before his late Majesty's death'.[2]

Accordingly the second line in the 'Memorandum for Lord Bute' was now redrafted :

The probable vacancies and the persons who have been thought of for them — most of them before the late King died.[3]

As a matter of fact, there is evidence of Bute having talked during those days of extensive election activities, but none of his having formed any definite plan ; Dodington relates in his Diary under date of 2 February :

I asked if he had settled the Parliament with the Duke ? He replied, he had not seen his Grace for some days but supposed he

---

[1] 3 February 1761 ; 'near 4 o'clock' ; Add. MSS. 35420, f. 179.
[2] Add. MSS. 32918, f. 228.   [3] *Ibid.* f. 252.

should soon, and he would then bring his list with him. That what were absolutely the King's boroughs, the King would name to; but where the crown had only an influence as by the customs, excise, etc., he [the Duke of Newcastle] could not be refused the disposition of it while he stayed in.

Bute evidently imagined that there were some uninfluenced 'by the customs, excise, etc.', which could be clearly distinguished as 'the King's boroughs' !

Among the Shelburne papers at Bowood there is a list of 'Ministerial boroughs' extracted from the survey of English and Welsh constituencies which Fitzmaurice made in December. It contains the names of forty boroughs — eleven of them in Cornwall, six in Devonshire, four in Sussex and seven Cinque Ports. Five are marked as Admiralty boroughs, while most show such combinations of interest and influence that a glance even at this much simplified and not altogether accurate chart [1] must have convinced Bute that there were very few indeed which could be described as 'absolutely the King's boroughs'. It seems highly probable that Fitzmaurice compiled that list for Bute in preparation for his talk with Newcastle, but that when Bute spoke to Dodington on 2 February he had not seen it yet ; for on 30 January he had written as follows : 'Lord Bute presents his compliments to Lord Fitzmaurice, and desires he would not hurry himself for he can't meet the great man till next week'.[2]

In the morning of that fatal day, Wednesday, 4 February, Newcastle received a last hint in a letter from Viry :

. . . si vous agissez avec ouverture et une entière confiance, et d'une façon, qui aille au devant de tous soupçons, que plusieurs personnes ont cherché d'insinuer, que votre but était, de vous emparer insensiblement du même pouvoir que vous avés sous le feu Roi ; vous serez content et satisfait, mylord ; . . .

---

[1] *E.g.* Westminster is included among Ministerial boroughs, while Orford is omitted ! The one seat which Thomas Pitt controlled at Okehampton is included but his borough of Old Sarum, equally placed at the disposal of the Government is omitted ; Poole, Hull, Grimsby, East Retford, Christchurch, Sudbury, Arundel, Bramber, Steyning, and Chichester appear in the list, though there is no more reason to include them among Government boroughs than a good many other boroughs which are not mentioned.

[2] Shelburne MSS.

... j'ai lieu de penser que l'on ne veut point avoir de premier ministre, mais qu'en même tems, je ne puis que croire que l'on sent bien, qu'il est convenable, que chaque ministre ait, dans son département, le pouvoir et l'autorité nécessaires, et que l'on me paroît même être pleinement de cet avis.[1]

This Newcastle sent to Hardwicke with the following remarks :

I thank you for your kind and most judicious letter of last night, and shall conform myself to every point. I send your Lordship a copy of an extraordinary paper, sent me this morning by C. V. It does not promise me a very agreable meeting; the fear of a First Minister, is to justify all sort of behaviour, all want of confidence, of communication, and to be a pretence to take from me, even the common right of every Minister, to lay recommendations before the King. But, however, I will reason no more, a few hours will put us more *au fait*. As your Lordship is so good, as to say you would be at leisure this evening for me to make my material report . . . I beg your Lordship would be at my Lord Kinnoull's at eight o'clock this evening, where I will meet you. I hope you will not fail, for you never fail your most grateful, etc.[2]

Hardwicke did not fail him, and waited to receive his report directly he emerged from the terrible ordeal ; and therefore, while Newcastle's forebodings and fears are on record, no graphic account of what happened at that conference is to be found in his letters to Hardwicke. In consequence astonishing conclusions about the share which George III and Bute had in nominating candidates at the general election of 1761 have been reached by writers who prefer to guess the course of events from a few 'texts', rather than work their way through volumes of manuscripts.[3] 'In the deep discovery of the sub-

[1] Viry to Newcastle, 4 February 1761 ; Add. MSS. 35420, ff. 183-4.
[2] *Ibid.* f. 181.
[3] The following 'texts' published in well-known works, are copied, quoted, or paraphrased in most history books dealing with the general election of 1761 : (*a*) Two passages in Bubb Dodington's *Diary* : under 16 January and under 2 February 1761, both quoted above. (*b*) The above-quoted letter from Rigby to the Duke of Bedford, *Bedford Correspondence*, vol. ii. pp. 423-4. (*c*) Excerpts from the Newcastle-Hardwicke correspondence in Lord Albemarle's *Life of Rockingham*, vol. i. pp. 62-4, undated, misdated, and misquoted. (*d*) A passage in John Adolphus' *History of England from the Accession of George III* (1805), p. 24, which, if carefully read, might have saved even historians with a very slender knowledge of the subject from some rash assertions. (*e*) A passage in the 'Memoir on the

terranean world', writes Sir Thomas Browne in his *Hydrio-taphia*, 'a shallow part would satisfie some enquirers ; who, if two or three yards were open about the surface, would not care to rake the bowels of Potosi, and regions towards the centre.'

Actually there is no need for guessing what happened between Newcastle and Bute on 4 February 1761. The facts are clearly stated in a letter from Newcastle to his friend John Page, M.P., of 7 February 1761 :

> I have seen the Great Man and am in general extremely satisfied with my conference, which was long, and very confidential. He brought me the names only of three persons from the King, to be brought into Parliament, who are all very unexceptionable.[1]

This statement is confirmed and supplemented by entries in Newcastle's 'Memorandums'. On 6 February, pleased and reassured, he put down the three names given to him by Bute :

> Elections. — Lord Parker.
>   Mr. Britten [Breton].
>   Mr. Worsley.

> I will certainly take care of them, on very easy and certain conditions.[2]

Travail of mountains, terrors of cowards, legends of historians, and what a ridiculous mouse ! Lord Parker, so far from being a Tory, had been one of the Whig heroes in the famous Oxfordshire election of 1754 ; Breton, after various negotiations, was not returned to Parliament ;[3] and for the

---

Events attending the Death of George II and the Accession of George III', by Henry Fox, 1st Lord Holland, published in the *Life and Letters of Lady Sarah Lennox* (1901), p. 41. (*f*) Some passages in Horace Walpole's letters and in his *Memoirs of the Reign of King George III* which do not add anything material to those quoted above. — The Newcastle Papers are noted in most recent works on the period as cargo on board ; but some authors would do well to add the formula customary in eighteenth-century bills of lading : 'Contents unknown'.

[1] Add. MSS. 32918, ff. 332-3. Similarly in a letter to Lady Katherine Pelham, 5 February 1761 : 'I had a long conference yesterday with my Lord Bute ; which, almost in every point, pass'd entirely to my satisfaction . . .' (*Ibid.* f. 279).   [2] *Ibid.* ff. 310-11 ; see also f. 362.

[3] He was to have been chosen for Old Sarum, but its owner, Thomas Pitt, who had pledged the borough to the Government, begged to be allowed to return himself for the time till he had arranged his affairs with his creditors (see *The Structure of Politics*, pp. 59-60). 'Every thing is settled with Mr. Thos. Pitt', wrote Newcastle to Bute on 22 March 1761 ; 'and Mr.

Tory legion billeted by Bute on the Treasury lists we are left with Worsley alone, a harmless gentleman of over fifty who never made any mark in politics either before or after.[1] Nowadays new Cabinets and policies result from changes in the personnel of the House of Commons, effected at general elections, but the very essence of the scene which opened in 1761 was that this was produced practically without any deliberate change in the composition of the House; and that in the absence of organised parties and clearly defined programmes, most of the struggles and contests which are now carried on in the constituencies took place in the House. There was very much more than a nucleus of a Court party in the new Parliament, but most of them were not new men, nor of a new political faith, nor were they bound by a new pledge as is sometimes alleged. They were mainly those ever 'zealous in the King's service' for fear or favour, or for conscience' sake; and some from habit.

On 14 May 1754 the Duke of Newcastle had written to Horatio Walpole (the brother of Sir Robert): 'The Parliament is good, beyond my expectations. . . .'[2] And on 2 April 1761 he wrote to the Duke of Devonshire that there was 'the almost

---

Britton is very easy in not coming in for Old Sarum till the Parliament meets . . .' (Add. MSS. 32920, f. 452). But when Thomas Pitt died in July 1761, his son repudiated the arrangement; while Breton seems to have been so indifferent to a seat in the House (in which he had sat in 1746–7 as a nominee of Frederick, Prince of Wales) that, although he lived till 1773, and remained one of George III's favourites, he never re-entered Parliament. He was knighted in September 1761, previous to the Coronation at which he represented the Duke of Aquitaine, and became a Groom of the Bedchamber and 'Privy-Purse Bearer' to the King.

[1] His first recorded vote (before Parliament met) was for 'asses' milk'. Here is a letter which he wrote in July 1761:

MY LORD — I think it my duty to acquaint your Lordship that I have been at St. James's this afternoon: and to my great surprize and concern found the King walking about the new painted and white washed rooms, the windows all open, and he having taken a doze of physick this morning. I observed too he coughed two or three times during the short space I was with him; I could not help saying afterwards to Mr. Hawkins I wished he had prevented the King's going about in new rooms at that time, but he said he could not prevent him.

I submit it to you my dear Lord, whether, against another day you will not put in your word upon this subject, as also to vote for asses' milk afterwards, to guard against that cough. I did venture, to beg His Majesty would ride very gently to morrow, as the weather was so excessive hot.   [2] Add. MSS. 32735, ff. 268–72.

certainty of as good, if not a better, Parliament than the last'.[1] But Lord Bute had said : 'the new Parliament would be the King's let who will chuse it' ; and Lord Bath had written, through his penman Douglas : 'the overgrown Minister . . . will soon find that his supposed friends were only the friends of his power, and will continue firm to him no longer than while he has possession of the means of gratifying them'. On the letter from the Duke of Newcastle, dated 2 February 1761, in which he said that the 'tone and complexion of the new Parliament' could not be changed any more, the 2nd Lord Hardwicke, years later, placed the marginal remark : 'Notwithstanding the choice of Parliament, which the D. of N. piques himself upon, they forsook him for Ld. B. — when his *standard* was set up'.

BUTE ASSUMES OFFICE

The question of office for Bute was merely shelved for a short time when Viry announced to Newcastle, about the end of January, that he would drop 'what he calls his idea' ; [1] a fortnight later, he was declaring again 'that . . . *tout ira mal*, if his idea did not take place'.[2]   George III was determined to have Bute for his Minister, Pitt was opposed to it, and Bute consequently hesitated.   The difference between the attitude of Pitt and that of Newcastle towards his assumption of office was not merely personal ; such an appointment was bound to affect differently the two sides of government with which they were concerned, the disposal of places and favours and the direction of measures.   The power of the 'disposing Minister' could to a very high degree be exercised 'from behind the curtain', and Newcastle usually conformed to Bute's wishes even while the latter held no office which would have entitled him to a share in Government patronage.   The work of the 'Minister of measures', on the other hand, required constant and regular application to business ; and though Bute, as 'favourite', could influence the King's ultimate decisions, he

---

[1] Add. MSS. 32921, ff. 272-3.
[2] See above, p. 148.
[3] Newcastle's Memorandum of 12 February 1761 ; 32918, f. 468.

could not truly direct policy. It was therefore only by taking office that he could seriously interfere with Pitt, who told Bute in the conversation on the night of George III's accession that 'his advancement to the management of the affairs of this country would not be for His Majesty's service'.[1]

George III had unlimited confidence in Bute's character and abilities, and saw in him the providential man, destined to carry through the great work of reformation ; and there was nothing unconstitutional in the King entrusting whomsoever he thought fit with the government of the country. The limitation of the power of the Crown in this matter was fundamentally the same in 1760 as it is now — the Minister required a majority in the House of Commons for carrying on the Government. The real difference was in the structure of the House of Commons, and in certain ideas developed in a long practice on that different basis. There were no organised parties in 1760 to reduce the choice of the Crown within very narrow bounds, or even to deprive it of all choice, and, moreover, the Crown could direct a large, though varying, number of votes in the House. To this influence of the Crown no single set of politicians had a 'divine right' (though Burke, in a carefully masked form, came very near claiming it for the men whose livery he happened to have taken), and the King had a perfect right to assign it to anyone whom he thought the proper person to conduct his business.

None the less he could not permanently impose on the nation a Minister who was displeasing to it ; the majority in Parliament would crumble, many Members preferring to forfeit their places than share in the Minister's unpopularity ; or sometimes the paralysing atmosphere of hostility, and the Minister's own consciousness of his inability to carry on, would make him withdraw, though still assured of a majority. Revolutions often succeed merely because the men in power despair of themselves, and at the decisive moment dare not order the troops to fire ; and it repeatedly happened in the eighteenth century that a Minister, while retaining the full confidence of the Crown and a comfortable majority in Parliament, no longer

[1] See above, p. 121.

dared to avail himself of either. It was thus that Newcastle resigned in 1756, Bute in 1763, and that North, in 1778, begged to be allowed to resign. In the last case the King was able to retain a Minister whose resignation was overdue ; but cannot a party in office do so even now ? Can it not outstay its time after it has secured a majority at a general election, be it even on a minority vote and over irrelevant issues ? And cannot a Prime Minister retain his place against the better judgment of his own party, merely because it will not face the risk of an internal crisis ? We have merely substituted party organisations for the Court ; as direct rule by the people is impossible, there must always be a condominium between some fixed political organisation and the electorate.

It would have been entirely in accordance with the theory and practice of the time if in 1760 George III had replaced Newcastle by Bute ; Pitt's refusal to serve under him, and Bute's hesitation to shoulder the full responsibility for war and peace, prevented that change. What then was to happen ? Was he from the very outset to assume the part which, later on, he was accused of acting, and become 'that invidious thing, a Minister behind the curtain' ? Could the King, an active and independent factor in government, be forbidden to seek the advice of the man whose character and judgment he trusted most ? There was good ground for protesting against interference from Bute after he had had his innings, and had left the field, no matter for what reason. Looking, however, at the situation of 1760–61 in the light of the theory and practice of that time, and not of 1930, it seems to have been only right that the man who was the King's choice should be given a fair chance — indeed, a fairer chance than he ultimately received.[1]

---

[1] As late as 1834, William IV still thought himself free, without any cogent reason, to dismiss the Melbourne Ministry, and to entrust the Conservatives with the formation of a new Government ; and Peel, in his Tamworth Manifesto, expressed 'the firm belief that the people of this country will so far maintain the prerogative of the King as to give to the Ministers of his choice not an implicit confidence but a fair trial' (see G. Kitson Clark, *Peel and the Conservative Party*, 1929, pp. 211-12). No less significant was the attitude of the Whigs. 'In the first moments after the Ministry's dismissal neither Melbourne nor Grey had utterly condemned what had taken place' (*ibid.* p. 229), and though other Whig leaders were inclined 'rather . . . to comment on the danger of the King's

But Pitt objected to Bute, and Pitt was the idol of the whole Empire. Ezra Stiles, on 27 February 1767, wrote from Newport, Rhode Island, to Hart, another New England divine : '. . . a Pitt, if such a star be not too great, too rare a blessing to shine in every age — there are stars τῶν αἰώνων'.[1] Still, the nation had to pay a price for that blessing. It was his intractable, incalculable nature, his genius tinged with madness, which, at least as much as the immature, unbalanced, passionate obstinacy of George III, produced the chaos of the first ten years of the new reign, and during the next fatal ten years placed the Government in incompetent hands. He would take no account of other people, nor pay any regard to their wishes or feelings ; he objected to Bute taking office but when Bute declared that 'he would be a private man' Pitt objected to his being 'the Minister behind the curtain'. Even now a leader has to put up with colleagues whom he might prefer to do without, if they happen to be popular with this or that section of the party, or have a prescriptive claim to office ; and the statesman who said 'I will not serve under that banner', ploughed his lonely furrow. In 1760 the King, with his 'friends' or servants, filled the place of the party organisation, and had a clear right to be represented in the Cabinet ; but Pitt would not have it. This produced the first difficulties ;

action than to acquiesce in it', even after having won the ensuing general election, the Whigs did not move a direct vote of censure on those who had supplanted them, but made a show of a fair trial. The idea of the King's right in that matter still lingered on, after its foundations had disappeared.

[1] Stiles MSS. in Yale College Library. See also the letter which Stiles wrote to Benjamin Franklin, on 30 December 1761 ; a copy of it is preserved among the Bancroft Transcripts, in the New York Public Library, 'Connecticut Papers', p. 42 :

> . . . never was a Minister of State treated with so much honor and affection by us in New England. We almost idolize him. His being in the Privy Council and in the House of Commons has given us the *greatest confidence* as well as spirit and alacrity. We know not how to confide in any one personage below the Crown. We have such an idea of the universal corruption and of the national jockeying, that we fail to feel assured with respect to any of the illustrious personages in public administration . . I say, we have confidence in Mr. Pitt, which I do think I may do him the honor to resemble to that confidence which, with infinitely greater justice, ought to be and is exercised . . . in Him . . . with whom is the guidance and administration and guardianship of the Universe.

after that, he would not lead the Opposition, though they were ready to follow him, and in critical moments he would make the proscription of those who had had any share in the Peace Treaty, or the obtaining of office for Lord Temple or of the Great Seal for Pratt, into a cardinal point. Next it was he, more than the King, who destroyed the Rockinghams by his unreasonable refusal to co-operate with them — he withheld from them the strength they required. And after everyone had surrendered to him, and he got an even freer and fuller chance than in 1757, he found himself deprived by his previous actions of colleagues far preferable to the shifty Charles Townshend or the inexperienced Duke of Grafton. In the end his nerves broke down, and the Government and country were thrown into confusion.

Burke, unable openly to deny the King's right to give his confidence, and therefore also the support he could muster in the House of Commons, to whomever he chose — had either been the due of any set of politicians, they would have been 'kings' — constructed the theory that it was George III's deliberate policy and established practice to withhold his support from Ministers, that he meant to form a party which should be 'in favour of the court and against the ministry' and should 'intercept the favour, protection, and confidence of the crown in the passage to its ministers ; . . . come between them and their importance in Parliament ; . . . intended as the control, not the support, of administration'.[1] The truth is that in 1760–61 George III most ardently desired to see the man in office to whom he would have given the fullest confidence that any monarch has ever given to a Prime Minister ; that in 1763 Grenville — at one time called 'George' by the King and Bute — assumed Bute's inheritance, but, with doubtful loyalty and characteristic lack of tact, in order to free himself of the odium which attached to his predecessor, immediately and opprobriously disclaimed his 'maker'; that George III was loyal to the Rockinghams until, in January 1766, they themselves practically admitted that they could not carry on unless reinforced ; that there is no evidence whatso-

[1] See *Thoughts on the Cause of the present Discontents* (1770).

ever of his having intrigued against Pitt and Grafton in 1766–8, but that, on the contrary, he patiently waited for Pitt's recovery and active resumption of office ; and that after he had found his Newcastle in Lord North (in that very year 1770 in which Burke published the pamphlet containing the above passages) he supported him loyally, and with better grace than George II had supported the Pelhams.   There never was a deliberate system of 'double cabinets' as sketched by Burke in a polemical pamphlet, to which he himself might possibly have applied the phrase used by him on a different occasion : 'By Gad, Madam, does any one swear to the truth of a song ?' — but which has been often treated as if it were an impartial verdict on George III.

In 1760–61 there were only two logical lines to adopt : either to say that the Court and the Treasury should have no influence in the House of Commons — but for that a thorough-going reform both of Parliament and of the national services would have been required, for so long as boroughs were controlled by single individuals or Members were returned by narrow Corporations, and so long as appointments were made at pleasure, the Court could clearly influence the House of Commons, even without Treasury boroughs and secret service money ; or to give the King a fair share in the forming of the Cabinet, so that he could own it as truly his Government.   No one could have been more averse to the first idea than Newcastle was in 1760, and Burke in 1793 ; while Pitt negatived the second.   If at the very outset of George III's reign a double Government seemed to emerge, it was because Sir Robert Walpole, Henry Pelham, and Newcastle had provided the King with the effective means for managing the House of Commons, and Pitt prevented him from using these means in the natural manner.

Among Bute's own friends, opinions were divided as to whether he should take office or remain the influence behind the Throne.   Bute's uncle, the Duke of Argyll, seems to have advised him against coming out into the open ; on 12 September 1763 Alexander Forrester, a Bedford Whig, who, as a Scotsman, had also had connexions with the Duke of Argyll and Bute,[1] looking back at the events of 1760–61, wrote to Sir Andrew Mitchell :

Had his Lordship [Bute] taken the sound advice given him, to my knowledge, by one who was a sort of parent, and who knew men and things much better than he, of *keeping behind the curtain whereby he might make and unmake ministers*, much of the mischief would have been prevented. . . .[2]

Others gave him similar advice — Patrick Craufurd, who in 1761, with the help of Bute, was returned for Renfrewshire, wrote to a friend on 17 November 1760 :

I hope he does not aim att being Minister or to have any high station in the English Ministry but that [he] will be content to be the King's friend and to assist him to make and unmake Ministers and to have something to say here [in Scotland] where his power will be less envy'd and more secure in all struggles and changes, besides the power of doeing more good to his country and friends, which last motive will, I hope, weigh greatly with his Lordship.[3]

And Symmer, Andrew Mitchell's political agent, wrote to him on 17 March 1761, after Bute's appointment to office had become known :

Many of Ld. B.'s friends think he has acted rather a bold, and a generous, than a prudent part, in quitting a safe harbour, where he rode secure, to take his chance with others on a turbulent and tempestuous sea.[4]

But Gilbert Elliot, a man of superior character and with a much finer understanding of political decencies and of the con-

---

[1] Alexander Forrester (1705–87) was a distinguished lawyer and sat in Parliament for Dunwich 1758–61, for Okehampton (on the interest of the Duke of Bedford) 1761–8, and for Newcastle-under-Lyme (on the interest of Lord Gower, Bedford's brother-in-law) 1768–74. Newcastle wrote about him in his 'Memorandums' for the King, 8 April 1759 (Add. MSS. 32889, ff. 417-18) : 'Mr. Forrester belongs to the Duke of Bedford and the Duke of Argyll'. At the general election of 1761 Argyll and Bute unsuccessfully tried to have Forrester returned for Edinburgh, and at the end of the year the Duke of Bedford, equally without success, tried to have Forrester appointed Solicitor-General.

[2] Add. MSS. 30999, ff. 16-17. The person referred to seems clearly indicated by the further sentence : 'Indeed, he [Bute] told me himself the very night of the Duke of Argyll's death, that he had by that event lost more than any man in Britain'.

[3] Bute MSS.   [4] Add. MSS. 6839, f. 215.

stitutional system, wrote to Bute, when congratulating him on his appointment to the Secretaryship of State :

A just responsability to the publick ought ever in this country to be the inseparable concomitant of power and favour. It was for that reason that I ever heard you, with real satisfaction, reject the maxims of that false wisdom which I know has often been busy in painting to you the advantages of enjoying the latter, unexposed to the hazards of the former.[1]

And Newcastle thus, rightly, summed up the situation in a letter to his friend John White, M.P., on 25 March 1761 :

. . . we all thought, that, considering his [Bute's] known weight and influence, it was better for the publick, and for us, that he should be in a responsible office, than to do everything, and answer for nothing.[2]

The idea of office for Bute was revived at the first apparent sign of complaisance on the part of Pitt. Bute, when offering the Lord-Lieutenancy of Ireland to Lord Temple at the end of February 1761, is reported by Viry to have said :

I suppose, your Lordship does not mean to look upon me as a bare Groom of the Stole — the King will have it otherwise. To which Lord Temple replied, Certainly so, I look upon you as a Minister ; and desire to act with you as such.[3]

This seemed to hold out some hope of Pitt's acquiescing in his appointment to office ; still, the question remained who was to bell the cat — in other words, to convey the decision to Pitt. George III and Bute were loath to assume the undivided responsibility for the appointment and wanted it to be formally proposed by Newcastle, at least to them, even if he was not to own it in public ; possibly they feared that otherwise, in case of Pitt's resignation, he might declare, as he had done before, that he could not go on without him. On 3 March 1761 Viry sent a note to the Duke of Devonshire about 'his idea',[4] and suggested to Newcastle that he should propose the appointment to the King, who thereupon would send Devonshire to Pitt ; as the man who in 1756 had stood by Pitt, Devonshire was obviously considered the most suitable envoy. The same day,

[1] Bute MSS.   [2] Add. MSS. 32921, f. 60.
[3] Add. MSS. 32919, f. 287.   [4] *Ibid.* f. 406.

'upon full consideration of the note', it was decided by Newcastle, Devonshire, and Hardwicke that Newcastle should talk
to the King 'upon the situation of his Administration, and of
the necessity of making some arrangement for the dispatch and
execution of business'.　Still, he

should not name the particular method of doing it; but make such a
description of it, as His Majesty cannot fail to understand; and that
then, the King should be pleas'd to direct the Duke of Devonshire, to
mention this affair to Mr. Pitt, the Duke of Newcastle, and my Lord
Hardwicke; and that His Majesty would be glad to know their
thoughts upon it.[1]

In short, Newcastle and his friends, while fully agreeing to the
appointment, feared to assume responsibility for it.

The next day Viry again urged Newcastle to take the
initiative and name Bute, but Newcastle still tried to avoid
doing so in an explicit manner.

I talk'd very seriously to my friend [Viry], of the danger of giving
jealousy to Mr. Pitt, and particularly if I was to be the person, who
was first to mention this affair; and that Mr. Pitt might charge me
with having set on foot a measure, which laid him under great
difficulties, without previously communicating it to him: and
indeed, I am afraid, this will be the case.

My friend told me, that if I insisted too much upon the danger of
disobliging Mr. Pitt; it would fling them more into Mr. Pitt's hands
than I would wish. . . . In short, I found that if I did not speak to
the King, the whole was over; or possibly might be put into another
channel.[2]

When, on 6 March, after long preparations, Newcastle was
at last brought to the point of broaching this novel idea to the
King, he did so with involved verbosity, natural in a man who
tries to avoid saying a very simple thing.　He discoursed on
the present state of the Administration and on future dangers,
and concluded:

That the best thing, that could be done at present, was for His
Majesty to have a settled, firm, well-connected, and well-united Administration; compos'd of those, who by their stations, and the confidence His Majesty honour'd them with, were known to speak and
act, according to His Majesty's opinion; that, when measures were

[1] Add. MSS. 32919, ff. 400-1.　　　　　[2] Ibid. ff. 422-3.

agreed, they would be supported, as known to be His Majesty's measures; whereas, without it, one man would vote, according to what he imagin'd to be the sense, and inclination, of one man, or one part of the Administration; and the other, to that of another man, or another part of the Administration. That nothing is so likely to prevent this mischief, as the method above propos'd.

The King prodded him to go on, and Newcastle resumed his speech, came nearer to the point, but still avoided it.

His Majesty said, these are very material points; and seem'd to enter into them; but said, what would you propose ? — and there stop'd.

I then said, Nothing, but my duty to Your Majesty, should have made me go so far; and I fully intended when I came into the closet to go no farther; but, Sir, you have a right to know all I think, upon such a subject.

If Your Majesty should think proper (I only fling it out), to make my Lord Bute Secretary of State, it would have a very good effect.

The King thereupon 'very obligingly' thanked Newcastle, and added that he himself had 'proposed it . . . to my Lord Bute the day the late King died', but that Bute

did not like to fling himself into so much business; and that besides, he (Lord Bute) did not know, what *His Majesty's Ministers might think of it.*

Newcastle resumed his speech, the King listening more placidly now that the fateful words had been spoken; and Newcastle repeated a warning which he had given before :

That, in all events, Mr. Pitt must not be offended; that I had no reason to be partial to him; but that I must tell His Majesty (as I had often done his grandfather), that it was absolutely necessary for the carrying on his service.[1]

He finished by emphasising once more that Devonshire, and not himself, had to be employed in communicating the decision to Pitt.

On March 10 Newcastle had a conversation with Bute, and they arranged how and in what order the news of his assumption

[1] *Ibid.* ff. 481-7.

of office was to be ostensibly broken to Newcastle and his friends. Relations with Pitt were repeatedly discussed :

That he (Lord Bute) very well knew, what difficulties he must go thro' ; but *that* did not discourage him. . . . That the only thing he apprehended was, the temper, and the manner of Mr. Pitt. That therefore, before he would engage, he must know from me, whether, in case Mr. Pitt from his manner, and he should differ, he (Lord Bute) might depend upon the support of the Duke of Newcastle, and his friends.

I assur'd him of it in all our names. He then made me many very civil acknowledgments of what he ow'd me, for the kind and hand-some manner, in which I had spoke to the King, upon his subject.

. . . .

We had a great deal of intermediate discourse, relating to Mr. Pitt : and, tho' Lord Bute assur'd me, that he would do his part, to go on with Mr. Pitt, with the utmost good humour, and desire to agree ; yet he often insinuated, that it was because I, and my friends, advis'd it. I enter'd into the necessity of Mr. Pitt's service. He seem'd not to agree to that ; and said, his credit and popularity, were much sunk. And, when I mention'd that, considering the situation of our affairs, Mr. Pitt might revive that popularity, whenever he pleas'd, and make it impracticable to go on ; he constantly objected to it ; and remarkably said, he knew, Mr. Pitt would never go into opposition ; but, in all events, would retire, with some honorable provision.

Lord Bute talk'd much of the difficulty, and indeed the impossi-bility, of Mr. Pitt's gaining the King. That he thought, Mr. Pitt had not the way to gain the affection of a Prince ; and that, in the present case, if he (Mr. Pitt) was so dispos'd, he would have a great deal of *lee-way* to fetch up ; but that he (Ld Bute) would do his part.

But he seem'd perfectly convinc'd, that Mr. Pitt would acquiesce in this new disposition. What answer can he make me, said Lord Bute. Will he say that I am an exceptionable man ? *He won't say that, my Lord.*[1]

As the Duke of Devonshire was ill and out of town, in the end Bute himself talked to Pitt about his appointment. Pitt coldly acquiesced :

'The thing is done ; and I have all duty and submission to the King, and regard for your Lordship ; but pray, my Lord, what say

[1] 'Substance of what pass'd in my conversation with Lord Bute this day', Newcastle House, 10 March 1761 ; Add. MSS. 32920, ff. 64-8.

the King's other Ministers to it?' . . . You see by this [was New-castle's comment] that Mr. Pitt was pumping; but our friend fended off extremely well; and from the beginning treated it as a measure of the King's.[1]

Next Pitt

went into all his grievances; and said, he would speak out. He began, by his old complaint of going directly to the King, and expecting to have some share in the recommendations in his province; to both which, Lord Bute gave the most ample assent, with an observation, that if he chose that method, and thought it the most likely to succeed, to be sure, he was in the right. The next topick was peace and war, expressing great doubts as to His Majesty's real wish, and intention, &c. To which my Lord B. very prudently answer'd, that the King would adhere to the declaration in his Speech, at the opening of the Sessions.

On 25 March 1761 Lord Bute officially succeeded Lord Holdernesse (who was richly compensated) as Secretary of State for the Northern Department. There is a letter from him to the King, dated 24 March, and docketed 'The night before I received the Seals'.[2] The whole man appears in it with his good and bad qualities, loyal to George III, truly devoted to him, stilted, superficial, verbose, honourable, but wholly ignorant of what public business really meant, thinking of it in vague, personal, and rather romantic, literary terms, and desirous to insure for himself a retreat to his former place next to the person of the King should he fail as Minister. The letter, though exceedingly long, has to be reproduced in full; for its contents are meagre, and it is the form which gives its peculiar flavour:

March 24th, 1761.

I take up the pen at a very serious minute of my life, I have just took off the gold key [3] and taken my farewel of it, and with it of ease, comfort, and (what to a mind like mine the world cannot make up) of having part of my time at least in my own disposal; this is an

---

[1] Newcastle to Devonshire, 13 March 1761; *ibid.* ff. 167-9. — In the talk with Thomas Walpole, on 14 November 1762, Pitt gave a different, though not incompatible, account of their conversation: 'Upon Lord B. taking the Seals, . . . his Lordship came to acquaint Mr. Pitt with his promotion; and received the same opinion as before, that Mr. Pitt did not think it for His Majesty's service' (Add. MSS. 32945, ff. 1-2).

[2] Add. MSS. 36797, ff. 47-50.   [3] Of Groom of the Stole.

aweful change and tho' I have passed the Rubicon and left no retreat a few reflections may not be improper to lay before my dear
Prince and to impress into my own breast. I have had the honor of
being nearest to your Person many years and to instil into your
Royal mind, whatever virtue, honor or public spirit could suggest to
me; ever looking up to your glory and happiness, my every thought
has been pointed to that alone; nor can I accuse myself of having
once entertained a selfish view; one interested thought since the
Princess first entreated me to apply my life to your education, far
from souring your youthful temper or riper age against those who
were to be and now are your subjects, I ever placed mankind before
you in the most honourable light; and when obliged to put you
on your guard against approaching danger, you my Prince will do
me the justice I'm sure to own that I chose to attack vice itself,
and left you to make the application to the person who practiced it,
this enabled you on your accession to bury in oblivion a multitude of
faults, to forget little errors formerly committed and to employ all
the abilitys you found for the public good, in the most critical minute
that ever any Prince mounted the Throne; what you so wisely begun
you have as wisely continued unto this hour; with what success, let
the united prayers, praises and benedictions cf this great kingdom
prove, where (unless cloaked with the deepest hypocricy) there is not
a face that does not carry smiles and happiness, when your Royal
name is mentioned; some few excepted, whose views are far beyond
your power to satisfy, and whose gloomy ideas, will not suffer even
your gentle temper to make them happy; in this universal satisfaction I meet with a little flattery that I do not blush to own, I am
sensible to; while they justly praise my King; some think I have a
little merit in his education, and that I enjoy his friendship and his
favor, these have been acquired by honest noble means and not the
wretched arts thro' which minions have too often fascinated their
Prince; and rendered the very name of favorite odious to every
worthy man, far from being ashamed to hear these insinuations, they
are my pride and glory; I look back my Prince, with joy and secret
satisfaction on all the time that has elapsed since I was first honored
with your confidence; I may want talents for business, faction may
overwhelm me, and Court intrigues destroy me; but all the power
of man cannot take this heartfelt satisfaction, this comfortable retrospect from me; for I know and feel I have in serving you, done my
duty to my God, my Country and my King; and that without
permitting self or selfish considerations to mix an instant in the plan
I followed; so much for what is past, let us now look forwards; the
honorable station, which I have hitherto made subservient to your
Royal interest, I now resign; to tread an unknown path I sacrifice

peace, quiet, and all my little happiness to your commands, to your service, I take the office that of all others my mind has the most repugnance to, and I am torn from one that I have reason to doat on; from the success that the Divine Providence has given me in it, each fond wish of my heart crys out against this important change, but duty and gratitude condemns me to the trial; I make it then, but not without violent emotion and unpleasant forebodings; how fares it with my Prince? Does his heart feel no repugnance at parting with an old faithful servant, no I hope better things; let me think without vanity that we have been too long intimately acquainted to part thus without a mutual pang, these will appear proud words to the generality of the world when addressed to a King, but they are the words of friendship, that my King will never blush to own; here then let me lay the basis of future comfort (for some is necessary) you Sir can alone cement and strengthen it, let me be certain beyond the power of doubt to cross me, that I shall continue in every thought and idea of your heart, still in your family, still next your Person, still nearest your friendship, firm and unshaken, proof to all that malice, faction or intrigue can forge for to supplant me; and as I now launch out into a stormy sea in hopes that I may in some measure answer your expectations that I may do some little good, here suffer me, Sir, to desire in the most solemn manner that I may have your Royal promise to ensure me a safe retreat again near your person, in case I find myself unable to do what I wish, let it proceed from what honest cause it may; whether from the storm of faction bearing me down, from my talents not being calculated for the business I enter on, from the independency of my mind not being able to undergo the drudgery of public business, or lastly from finding my health and constitution impaired by it, or events of private life rendering it insupportable to me, in any of these cases suffer me once more to entreat you Sir as my King, my Master and my Friend, to retire again next your person, or if that suit not your convenience, remember I this day enter my protest that you must not be displeased if I at a sudden warning retire from courts and business at one and the same minute; you may observe my dear Sir that in the cases abovementioned, no notice is taken of your confidence, your friendship and affection to me changing; indeed I purposely omitted this reason; the stating it would hurt me, besides in that event my line would be plain and easy, without having recourse to your solemn promise I now presume to ask, 'tis no trifling boon Sir, that I here request, you may judge of it by the many pages that have introduced it. There then let me finish a very serious letter writ from the bottom of a heart that loves your honour, glóry and happiness, better than you do yourself; may this uneasy alteration in *my* life prove beneficial, to these great points, or if otherwise, the experiment fairly tried, releive me from the heavy burthen, and change a scene at best of eternal anxiety, into one of peace and quiet, and which ever way Providence shall dispose of it, may your character, my dearest Prince, be more and more established, may you be adored by a happy, free and generous people, this the constant prayer, the fondest wish of one you have so long honored with your friendship, and trusted with your most intimate confidence, who is proud enough to think he is not undeserving of it.

III

THE PARLIAMENT OF 1761

I. Its Politics

Forecasts

THE Parliament elected in 1754 was dissolved on 20 March 1761, and the first new returns were made on the 25th. Newcastle had, after all, 'the choice of the Parliament', arranged and managed elections in almost as many boroughs as in 1754, and was well satisfied with the results. That there was no secret service money to spend or waste, made little if any difference : in 1754 the Treasury helped to finance the election of twenty-four members in twenty-one English constituencies,[1] and the Members who in 1761 were returned for these constituencies would have been approved of by Newcastle (with perhaps two exceptions [2]) even in the 'plenitude' of his power. As for Lord Bute's acquisitions of new Members — men who had not sat in Parliament before and whose election can be ascribed directly to his intervention — I put their number in England and Wales at eleven or twelve : Thomas Worsley,

---

[1] See *The Structure of Politics*, pp. 196-204.
[2] I am thinking of two Tories, Sir James Dashwood, M.P. for Oxfordshire, and Eliab Harvey, M.P. for Dunwich ; but in their case it would have made no difference had George II been alive. After £40,000 had been spent on the Oxfordshire election in 1754, it was certain that the representation of the county would be 'compromised' in 1761 ; nor would Dunwich, Sir Jacob Downing's borough, have been any longer at Newcastle's disposal. Newcastle had, in 1754, purchased from him a seat for Soame Jenyns, but when in 1758 it was proposed to choose Jenyns at Cambridge, Lord Royston wrote to his father (on 20 August, Add. MSS. 35352, f. 34) that there might 'be an objection in giving Sir Jacob an opportunity of a new choice at Dunwich'. Hardwicke replied on 27 August (*ibid.* ff. 36-7) : '. . . as Sir Jacob has given him [Jenyns] the exclusion at Dunwich, it may be worth his while to establish himself at Cambridge against a general election'. Jenyns was consequently transferred to Cambridge; and Downing already in 1758 chose the successor without any reference to Newcastle.

returned by Newcastle for Orford at George III's behest; Simeon Stuart, now admitted to the representation of Hampshire; Thomas Whately (subsequently, under Grenville, Secretary to the Treasury) and John Paterson, a member of the Common Council of London, provided for by George Selwyn at Ludgershall; [1] the famous William Blackstone, author of the *Commentaries*, for whom Fox and Shelburne secured a seat at Hindon; [2] W. Hamilton, whose seat at Midhurst was negotiated for him by Bute, Fox, and Newcastle; John Parker, elected on Sir William Irby's interest at Bodmin; [3] Richard Glover, the poet and merchant, put up by Dodington at Weymouth and Melcombe Regis; Charles Jenkinson, Bute's secretary, returned for Cockermouth by Sir James Lowther, who, in September 1761, married Bute's daughter; J. R. Webb, whom Bute returned for Bossiney, a borough he had inherited from his father-in-law, Edward Wortley Montagu, senior; and possibly Sir Edmund Thomas, chosen for Glamorganshire, though it is by no means certain that he would not have carried his election without the countenance of Bute. This is not a formidable host. As for Charles Townshend, Lord Carnarvon, Sir Edward Turner, and Lord Parker, who

[1] Their seats were negotiated through Fitzmaurice. On 7 April 1761, after the election, Whately wrote to Bute that he knew he was indebted to Bute's recommendation for his seat, and would endeavour to justify it by his conduct in Parliament; while Paterson concluded his letter of thanks to Bute by expressing the hope 'that your Lordship will from time to time instruct me how I may do most service to my King and country' (Bute MSS.).

[2] Fitzmaurice, in a letter to Bute docketed February 1761, suggested that Bute should bring in a Member of his own at Hindon, and added: 'Blackstone is a man much devoted to you'. And again, on 7 March, when discussing the choice of candidates for the seat at Hindon: 'Blackstone is a man of business, and may be more so. . . .' (Bute MSS.)

[3] The following letter dated 'Monday' and docketed 'April 1761' is preserved among the Shelburne Papers at Bowood:

> Lord Bute's compliments attend Lord Fitzmaurice; he has mention'd Mr. Parker to Sir Will: Irby, as a person the King recommends; and referr'd him to Lord Fitzmaurice for further particulars; he seem'd extrem'ly pleas'd with the choice. . . .

The date given in the docket cannot be correct, as George Hunt and John Parker were returned for Bodmin on 30 March 1761. — When a year later Sir William Courtenay, bart., M.P. for Devonshire, was created a peer, Parker became a candidate for the county and was again supported by Bute, as can be seen from Bute's letter to Shelburne, dated 28 April 1762 (Shelburne Papers).

were helped by the new Court, they had been in the previous Parliament, and were sufficiently well-connected or rich to find seats without such help.

Very different was the position in Scotland : there Bute had become the acknowledged leader, but not as a result of the general election ; that had been arranged and partly carried through by his uncle Archibald, 3rd Duke of Argyll (whom Newcastle described as 'the absolute Governor of one of His Majesty's Kingdoms'),[1] while Bute interfered only in three or four constituencies. The death of Argyll-on 15 April 1761 gave to Bute the management of Scottish affairs, as the death of George II had secured to him the favour and patronage of the Crown, and the death of his father-in-law, Wortley Montagu, had loaded him with a vast fortune. 'How much death has favour'd the latter [Bute] !'[2] wrote Hardwicke ; and New-castle promptly acknowledged Bute as Argyll's successor, and, as he reported to Hardwicke on 17 April, desired to know Bute's thoughts,

that I might cooperate, in every thing, with him upon the plan, which was to be establish'd for Scotland; and particularly, as to the employments which were in the disposal of the Treasury. He answer'd drily: That, as his uncle's friends would now fling themselves upon him, and were all, or most, chose Members of Parliament, he hoped, I would support them in their boroughs, etc.[3]

The general election of 1761 was concluded early in May, and Newcastle started to tabulate the results, to ponder over them, classify them, and scatter his queries in the margins, till each page became a record of his thoughts, hopes, doubts, and of his monumental ignorance and naivety in matters on which he had laboured so many years. There is a list, in his own illegible handwriting, dated Claremont, 23 May 1761, and marked 'Friends, or others in the present Parliament. New Members.'[4] Altogether 148 men were returned at the general election of 1761 who had not sat in the House at the dissolution ; in drawing up a list of them Newcastle omitted

[1] Add. MSS. 32922, f. 5.
[2] Hardwicke to Newcastle, 16 April 1761 ; *ibid*. f. 4.
[3] *Ibid*. f. 15.   [4] Add. MSS. 32923, ff. 226-8.

four,[1] added five out of ten seats which were vacant,[2] inserted the name of a man who had sat in Parliament since 1715 (merely because he was yoked in a double return with a new man), and having made three mistakes in addition, finished under the impression that he had 149 entries, though in reality there are 150 entries containing 144 valid names.

What did the old election manager think of these 144 men, and how much did he know about them ? He ended by placing 101 as 'friends' and 43 as 'others'; but of the friends 40 are queried, and of the others 9. In short, at the end of a general election which he had managed himself, and to his own satisfaction, he admittedly did not know what to expect from more than one-third of the new Members. In reality his information about at least another third was equally exiguous or unreliable. Can a basis be discerned for his classifications ? Of the 43 'others', 29 were declared Tories, and the rest undevout men, reputed to worship with them; but as some were likely to wish for promotion (lawyers such as Blackstone and Eliab Harvey), or for contracts (*e.g.* Peregrine Cust and Sir Alexander Grant, both merchants), their opposition character was queried. The rest were entered as friends, but the 'friendship' of men known to be closely associated with Bute, Fox, or Pitt was qualified by a query, though even this was not done systematically or with adequate knowledge.

Let us apply one test to Newcastle's classification, that of the vote on General Warrants, taken during the night of 17-18 February 1764. Of the 101 'friends', 34 voted with the Opposition, *i.e.* on Newcastle's side, of the 43 'others', 15 — that is, of either group something over one-third:[3] thus before

[1] Sir James Grant, John Murray, James Stuart, and Robert Waller; the first three were Scottish Members, about whom Newcastle knew little, Scotland having been the province of the Duke of Argyll.

[2] Seven Members had been returned simultaneously for two constituencies, and three Members had died by 23 May 1761.

[3] This does not mean that two-thirds voted with the Government; of the original 144, 11 no longer sat in Parliament, and 15 can be proved to have been absent. Moreover, as in a total of 558 Members 18 remain unaccounted for (see *The Structure of Politics*, pp. 151-2), we can, on a *pro rata* calculation count that the remaining 133 new Members contributed four to that number; which would leave 64 voting with the Government, against 50 on the side of the Opposition.

three years had passed, the original distinction between 'friends' and 'others' was completely obliterated. Taking the subdivisions, one finds that of Newcastle's 61 safe 'friends' 24 (40 per cent) voted with the new Opposition, of the 40 queried 'friends' 10 (25 per cent), of the 34 determined 'opponents' 12 (35 per cent), of the 9 queried opponents 3 (33·3 per cent). The numbers are, of course, too small to yield reliable averages, but (as was to be expected) in the group which included Newcastle's relatives and personal dependants, there was a slight divergence from the average in his favour, and in the group including the original dependants of Bute and Fox, a similar divergence against him.

Some time between 25 May and 26 June 1761 Newcastle drew up a complete list of English and Welsh Members.[1] In this they are classified as 'Friends', 'Doubtful', and 'Others', and their numbers are 292, 113, and 108 ; men with whom Newcastle had worked before make up almost four-fifths of the total — did he know any more about them than about the new Members ? Of the 292 'friends', apparently 219 voted in the division on General Warrants, 121 with the Government, and only 98 with the Opposition ;[2] of the 113 'doubtful', 76 voted, 35 with the Government and 41 against ; and of the 108 'others', 81 voted, 41 for and 40 against the Government. Thus Newcastle's 'friends' gave a majority of 23 to his opponents, while the 'doubtful' and 'others' gave him a majority of five. Even in the vote on the preliminaries of peace, on 9 and 10 December, the difference between the three divisions in

---

[1] 'List of the present Parliament. English Members' ; Newcastle's own draft, Add. MSS. 32999, ff. 182-7 ; Hurdis's copy, ibid. ff. 323-9. The paper bears no date, but the latest vacancy noted in it is that caused by the death of Henry Finch, on May 25, while Henry Lambton, who died on June 26, still appears in the list. In calling the list complete, I disregard the vacancies which are all classified, and also one mistake — John Morton, M.P. for Abingdon, a Tory, is omitted from the list, but the full number of Members is obtained by Newcastle including, in the case of Radnor, both the candidates whose names were given in a double return.

[2] Of the 292 'friends', 27 no longer sat in the House, 34 are known to have been absent, and 10 of the total of 18 'unaccounted for' (see The Structure of Politics, pp. 151-2) are deducted on the pro rata basis. This leaves a total of 221 voting, and as 100 of these can be traced in the list of the minority, I assume that 121 voted with the majority, of which no list has been preserved. The figures of the 'doubtful' and 'others' who voted in the majority are calculated in a similar manner.

Newcastle's list was slight — of his 'friends', only one in five voted against the Government, and of the 'doubtful' and 'others', one in seven.[1]   The path which various Members were to choose in the first years of George III's reign could hardly be gauged from their previous activities or connexions, and certainly not by anyone who went by the labels used in 1761.

Did Bute and his friends see any clearer into the future ? There is an analysis of the Parliament of 1761 — covering England and Wales, but not Scotland — which was compiled for Bute about the middle of December, and was used by him, his assistants, and his successors for almost two years, up to the opening of the autumn session in November 1763.[2] The margins are much scribbled over, and it is impossible to date all the remarks concerning the politics of the Members, or ascertain when various corrections and changes were made ; only a rough estimate can therefore be formed of what Bute and his friends expected from the Members of the new Parliament in December 1761.

[1] For a discussion of the list of the minority on those two days, see below, pp. 397-398.

[2] Add. MSS. 38333, ff. 74-106. — All the Members elected previous to 16 December 1761 were entered when the list was first compiled, while those elected after 18 December had to be added ; but the name of Nathaniel Lister, returned for Clitheroe on 18 December, still appears in the original draft, while that of Thomas Pitt jun., returned for Old Sarum on 17 December, was added subsequently.   The time when the list ceased to be used ·an similarly be ascertained through the corrections.   The names of Members who died during the recess of the summer of 1763 are crossed out, but those elected in their places after the House had met on 15 November are not inserted any more.   On 5 November 1763 Lord Sandwich, then Secretary of State, wrote to Charles Jenkinson, Secretary to the Treasury (Add. MSS. 38201, f. 222) :

> You promised to return my list of the House of Commons with such alterations in it as had come to your knowledge, be so good as to send it me, if you can, by the bearer.

And again on 8 November (*ibid.* f. 232) :

> I wish you would send me a list of all the vacant seats in Parliament at this time, as I cannot compleat my number without it, I make out but 553 Members.   You may put Conolly and Mackworth both present and friends.

Jenkinson had ceased to use the list by 22 November, the date of the Honiton by-election ;   for the entry under Honiton reads : 'Sir Geo. Yonge or Bacon'.

A register of groups docketed 'State of the English Members of the House of Commons' [1] is probably based on that analysis, but seems to have been compiled at a somewhat later date. The figures given for the groups marked 'Bute' and 'Government' are slightly higher, and for 'Newcastle' and 'Newcastle and Government jointly' lower, than those which I obtain from what I take to be the original entries in the list. Such changes would correspond to the trend of the time, but as it is impossible to fix the exact date of the various corrections, and moreover, the question here is what view Bute and his associates took of the situation at the outset, I adhere to the computation which I myself have made from the list; this must not, however, be treated as anything more than a rough approximation, in which the margin of uncertainty is still further widened by more than one allegiance being ascribed to many Members, leaving it uncertain how the original compilers of the list would have classified them.

In Bute's group, which, on the basis of the list, I put at 73, 14 out of those 16 Members are included whom he had provided with, or helped to, seats [2] (only John Parker [3] and Charles Townshend are omitted — 'which last', Bute told Dodington on 16 January 1761, 'had sworn allegiance to him, *for a time*') ; [4] it further includes members of the old Leicester House connexion — Sir Francis Dashwood, Samuel Martin, Sir John Cust, etc. ; George Grenville, at this time 'George' in the correspondence between the King and Bute ; men who had proved eager to make 'their court to the rising sun', *e.g.* George and John Boscawen, Simon Lutterel, Sir Matthew Lamb, Sir John Turner, F. Vernon, T. O. Hunter, Abraham and Alexander Hume, etc. ; and some Tories, either because of their old feuds with the Pelhams, or because of favours already received from Bute : Sir John Phillips, E. Kynaston, Sir A. Wodehouse, A. Parker, N. Berkeley, etc.[5]   On the

---

[1] Add. MSS. 38334, ff. 269-70 ; reproduced here on p. 209.
[2] See above, pp. 171-2.
[3] John Parker is marked 'Government'.
[4] Dodington, *Diary*, p. 429.
[5] Once more I wish to remind the reader that the Scottish followers of Bute are omitted from this list.

whole, Bute had better means of gauging who was likely to join him, than Newcastle of foreseeing who would desert him in case of a break between them ; for in that case Bute, possessed of the 'attractive influence' of power, could expect to fix to his orbit those who were already re-insuring themselves with him against the future, while Newcastle, still at the head of the Treasury, had not the same means of spotting the future 'rats'. None the less, in the division on General Warrants, in which 52 of these original adherents of Bute are likely to have taken part, 13 are known to have voted with the Opposition, *i.e.* one-fourth were to prove unreliable as 'King's friends'. Seeing that, on an average, of any 67 English and Welsh Members [1] drawn by lot, 25 should have voted with the Government, the fact that Bute and his assistants should not have been able to gauge accurately the character and future attitude of more than 39 of the 52 who are likely to have taken part in the division proves that their knowledge of their men was not remarkable.

The groups marked 'Newcastle', 'Newcastle and the Government jointly', and 'Government' necessarily shade into each other, and it would have required a very thorough acquaintance with the men and their circumstances to know how to divide them. The principles of the classification seem to have been these : men who were, or were thought to be personal friends or dependants of Newcastle's, with only a secondary interest in places, pensions, or contracts, were marked 'Newcastle'; men holding important Government posts, or presumed to be primarily attached to their places, were put into the second category ; and men in official positions, not known to have any personal connexions with Newcastle, in the third.

How do these three groups stand the test of the division over General Warrants ?   (See table on page 179.)

Bute did not, any more than Newcastle, foresee how great the 'attractive influence' of Government would prove even for Newcastle's personal friends and dependants, to say nothing

---

[1] I have here to deduct from the original 73 Members, included in Bute's list, 6 who were no longer in the House of Commons.

of the 'Treasury Whigs'. The future opposition to Ministerial encroachments was to come in a large measure from those who had refrained from courting Newcastle as First Lord of the

	Total of Members according to my computation from the list	Likely to have voted on 17-18 February 1764	Voted with the Opposition	Presumably voted with the Government
Newcastle .	61	47	28 (59·5 p.c.)	19 (40·5 p.c.)
Newcastle and Government jointly .	45	38	16 (42 p.c.)	22 (58 p.c.)
Government .	34	26	13 (50 p.c.)	13 (50 p.c.)
	140	111	57 (51 p.c.)	54 (49 p.c.)

Treasury, and had remained independent, by whatever description they went, of Whigs or Tories ; and before we proceed any further with an inquiry into the various groups in the House, we have to examine what was the real nature and meaning of those two traditional party denominations, which to Horace Walpole stood for 'harmless people, that are content with worrying one another for a hundred and fifty years together'.[1]

Whigs and Tories

In the absence of distinct, definable programmes, it was becoming increasingly difficult to say who, from the angle of practical politics, should be considered a Tory and who a Whig — which must not, however, be taken to mean that either the types or the connexions had disappeared which formed the bases of these parties ; and parties at all times rest on types and on connexions rather than on intellectual tenets. Convictions and diseases do not befall human beings but are names given to certain mental or physical conditions of their organisms, while mass movements and epidemics have a joint social, or even a cosmic, basis — there is more sense in astrology which assumes a periodicity 'under the influence of the stars' than in a demonology which deals with personified diseases and

[1] Letter to H. S. Conway, 26 October 1761.

ideas. The division between Whigs and Tories existed in 1761, as before, and as it still exists in the body politic of England ; it was latent in temperament and outlook, in social types, in old connexions and traditions. But it was not focused on particular problems, and did not therefore supply clear lines of division in politics ; the old issues were worn out, while personal politics, which in the course of the last twenty years increasingly replaced party politics, were thrown into confusion by the accession of George III.

About 1761 the political nation of Great Britain can be roughly divided into five groups : the territorial magnates, the country gentry, the official class, the trading community, and the lower classes in the towns ; a rural democracy was practically non-existent — the yeomen-freeholders were declining in numbers and importance, the tenant-farmers at elections owed suit to their landlords, while village labourers had neither votes nor facilities for effective rioting.

The territorial magnates are usually described as an oligarchy, or a nobility, which are misleading names, as they suggest exclusiveness based on inherited rank, whereas one should much rather think of inclusiveness based on wealth, and usually finding in titles its ultimate, formal recognition. The Crown being the source of honours, and Government that of political power, the Court was the proper place for these men ; in fact, they were the Court. They had the longest and most intimate experience of government in State and Church, and therefore were in both unromantic latitudinarians, tinged with a tolerant liberalism, such as most sensible men acquire in the practice of government. Monarchy itself was to them a practical proposition to be worked in a reasonable manner ; they had made the Revolution of 1688, which might fittingly be described as the 'rationalisation' of royalty. From the very nature of their position, they could never keep away from Court for long, and whatever line their families had taken in 1641, 1660, 1688, or 1714, by 1750 they were all 'Whigs' (obdurate 'Tories' were as rare among them, and as picturesque, as members of the Labour Party now are among the peers and the millionaires). Nor is it true that under George III they forsook 'the Whig cause'; they had been, and they remained, the Court Party, while the meaning of 'Whig' underwent a change. They could not enter into a permanent opposition to the King, who was still a real factor in British politics, but had to work in partnership with him.

The territorial magnates were the nucleus of that governing class, whose claims even now are based on rank, wealth, experience, and a tradition of social and political pre-eminence (or, according to George Meredith, are 'comically built on birth, acres, tailoring, style, and an air'). But not even in the eighteenth century did they monopolise government, nor could they have done so under the Parliamentary system, which forced them into a condominium with political and administrative ability, wherever it was found. The age of the so-called Whig oligarchy was dominated by the personalities of Sir Robert Walpole, Henry Pelham, William Pitt, and Henry Fox, none of whom, except Pelham, was connected by family with territorial magnates, or can be called an aristocrat.[1] The men who did most of the work in Parliament and in the Administration can best be described as 'the official class', if we join under that description professional politicians with officers in the army and navy, and civil servants of every rank. They were not drawn from any one social class, but included younger sons of peers, sons of country gentlemen and of the clergy, members of the intelligentsia, and families which had a hereditary connexion with the fighting services or the civil service; and in the lower ranks, they were largely drawn from voters in Parliamentary boroughs and their relatives, and various dependants of influential men. In Parliament and Administration, and at elections, they were the labour army of the Court; and in their double capacity of politicians and placemen under the Crown, they could not enter into a permanent opposition against the Government, in which the King was still the

[1] Even Henry Pelham, the brother of Newcastle, was not quite so ducal as he may seem. Their paternal grandfather was a country gentleman of old lineage, but it was only their father who was made a baron in 1706; while Newcastle, on the strength of estates inherited from his maternal uncle (whose own peerage at his death was only a hundred years old), traversed the entire gamut from baron to duke in 1714-15, the year after he came of age.

supreme magistrate. They were therefore Whigs under the first two Georges, and ceased to be it when the term of Whig changed its meaning. The class extended from ambitious politicians at Westminster to tide-waiters or surveyors of window lights in some distant county.

The big merchants and financiers, and foremost among them the Government contractors, were another group with an immediate interest in government, conceived in terms of administration rather than of politics. They too were Whigs *de par le roi*, Treasury Whigs. If they went into Parliament, it was to share in the spoils of power rather than to indulge in playing the opposition critics.

The point cannot be emphasised too strongly : that so long as the King was a real factor in Government, the actual head of the Executive, and so long as there was therefore a permanent element in Government which did not change with the personnel on the Treasury Bench, there were bound to be powerful political groups constituting a Court or Treasury Party which could not have been fitted into a strict party system ; and so long as there were no disciplined, organised parties, the King was bound to count for a great deal in politics. With the growth of party organisation and discipline the King's freedom in choosing Ministers was reduced to vanishing point, and those in search of advancement or profits had henceforth to adhere to the organised teams, whose leaders alone could satisfy their claims and ambitions. The elimination of the Crown from Parliamentary politics, and the placing of Government on a strict party basis (which finally did away with the idea that a certain Parliamentary allegiance was due to every Government as representing the King and the State), was logically followed by a neutralisation of the national Services, which in time were divorced from the House of Commons as much as the King himself.

The typical country gentlemen in the eighteenth century were largely Tories, and it has been frequently pointed out in what a difficult position they were placed on the accession of the Hanoverians, when they, the most convinced and most romantic of monarchists, found themselves in opposition to the ruling dynasty. No doubt the position was trying, but it was not due to the dynastic conflict alone. The Tory gentlemen worshipped the Throne and loathed the Court, believed in authority and disliked Government — and what better way could there be of expressing these contradictory feelings than in harmless fancies about the 'King over the water', a royalty uncontaminated by administration ? But, even as a dream or pose, Jacobitism was completely worn out by 1760, and its shadow had survived so long only because it suited the Whigs as a bogy, and because in the absence of any other distinguishing principle the Tories occasionally indulged in demonstrations such as the famous *Redeat*, three times repeated by Dr. King at the opening of the Radcliffe Camera at Oxford in 1749 ; which belated Jacobitism may be compared with the premature Jacobinism in the south-west, where during bread riots in 1753 'there were some odd speeches . . . *that the French w'd be here soon*, and menaces of that nature',[1] though this was one of the few years when England was not at war with France. In both cases opposition to the existing system was translated into professions of hope for an external visitation, which very few seriously desired. Where the person of the King cannot be separated from Administration and where there is no way for the governed to imagine themselves part of the Government through a Cabinet superimposed on administration, opposition, unless it counts on the heir to the throne, will run to the length of anti-dynastic professions. Toryism about 1750 was primarily the opposition of the local rulers to central authority and vanished wherever members of that class entered the orbit of Government. The short outburst of Tory enthusiasm for George III, which finally proved the hollowness of whatever still seemed to survive of the Jacobite pretence, was not due to his having been born in England nor to his glorying 'in the name of Britain', but to the expectation that he would dismiss the men against whom these country gentlemen had so long contended and to the naive hope that he would do without a 'Court'. It was the perennial delusion

[1] Lord Poulett to the Duke of Newcastle, Hinton, 23 July 1753 ; Add. MSS. 32732, f. 343.

that there can be a Government not oligarchic in nature, nor based on a bureaucracy.

The smaller business men who could not aspire to honours or contracts formed the urban counterpart to the country gentlemen. They too were in opposition to Government, and the City of London was Tory under the first two Hanoverians and Radical under George III. Lastly, there was what the eighteenth century called the 'mobility'. Dissatisfaction among the working classes, which were as yet unorganised and voted in comparatively few constituencies, found its political expression not in elections but in riots ; their grievances were essentially economic but their inchoate movements were exploited, as they usually are, by a political opposition which at bottom had nothing to offer them. When real labour problems were raised by the seamen's strike in 1768 the Radicals and the Rockingham Whigs attacked Lord North and the Government for their hesitancy in repression.

Naturally no general survey can account for the detail of political groupments and developments. There was a Whig and a Tory mentality ; each was expressed in certain conceptions of State and Church, had its own ideology and idealism, and responded to certain sentimental appeals and traditional watchwords ; the same types are with us even now. But in practical politics the Tory mentality is capable of two widely different interpretations, and to this day there are affinities between the Tory and the Radical, temperamental qualities common to both, which can be satisfied by either creed but run counter to the well-balanced and inconclusive compromise of the Whig ; which again, according to circumstances and without any essential change, can assume a conservative or a reforming character. In the absence of clearly defined issues, these types, which, like everything organic, fail to reproduce the straight (imaginary) lines of human thought, cannot yield clear divisions. Moreover, the disturbing element of personal connexions is always present in politics ; the game is played by groups, and human ties continually cross and confound the logic of social and political alinements.

At the accession of George III, Lord Hardwicke, who under-

stood the interplay of generations and had four sons engaged
in politics and desirous to work with the young King as he
himself had worked with George III's grandfather, was in
favour of the old generation withdrawing. Had this been done,
had Newcastle absolved his friends from their group allegiance,
had the Court Party been handed over in a bulk to George III,
an opposition would still have arisen ; one wonders, however,
by what name it would have gone. But Newcastle, who had
no children, tried to outlast his own generation ; he ended as a
lonely old man among 'boys' whom he did not understand —
'my very zealous young friends' — but to whom he bequeathed
the name of a connexion radically different in character from
that which they themselves were to develop. He did not leave
them a legacy of political methods — his methods were taken
over and continued by George III and Lord North ; nor a
party organisation — this he had discouraged as long as he
could and it was ultimately formed without his assistance ; nor
of ideas — he himself had none and was suspicious of those
who had.

Newcastle laboured in the service of his friends, tried to
attach them to his own person but did not wish to see them
form a party with a mind, a will, and an organisation of its
own. He was in no way the spiritual forerunner of the Whig
opposition, and few of those who were to form it had been
closely associated with him in the days of his so-called power.
Rockingham, it is true, had been connected with Newcastle
since 1754 ; but as for Sir George Savile, in 1762 Bute and his
friends still thought of him as a possible recruit for their party.[1]
Dowdeswell (subsequently leader of the Rockingham Whigs in
the House of Commons), Beckford, and Meredith were in 1761
returned as Tories, and Lord Verney neither before nor after

[1] In November 1761 George Grenville suggested him for the place of
Comptroller of the Household, and Newcastle wrote to Rockingham on
3 November : 'It is certainly a very honorable offer to him, and comes
in an honorable manner. I conclude they wish to get some of our considerable friends over to them. . . .' (Add. MSS. 32930, ff. 299-300) ; and
on 28 November 1762 Bute wrote to Thomas Worsley, a Yorkshireman :
'You tell me you have seen S.G.S. but cannot discover his ideas concerning
the present situation of things' (Add. MSS. 36797, f. 24). S.G.S., I take it,
stands for Sir George Savile.

1761 had any connexion with Newcastle ; while Shelburne, Richmond, Grafton, and Portland were young men who only entered politics in 1760 ; similarly Barré and the two Burkes were newcomers in politics, and of the latter two the future course was, to say the least, still unclear in 1763.[1]

The typical collaborator of the Pelhams in office was Kinnoull, to Newcastle an invaluable and indispensable assistant, but by the rest of the world considered 'opprobriously and injuriously . . . an absolute fool'.[2] He was the real Treasury politician, absolutely unfit for opposition ; on 17 May 1762 George III wrote to Bute :

Lord Egremont . . . acquainted me with Lord Kinnoull's having told him this morning that he would ever support my Government and consequently whom ever I meant to place in the D. of Newcastle's office ; and he farther added that he had many things to say personally to my dear friend [Bute] from that Lord.[3]

When Newcastle entered opposition, Kinnoull withdrew from politics ; and although on the dismissal of the Duke of Devonshire he resigned office, he declared that this

was a single act of his own, to make himself easy in acting a part he owed to the Duke of Devonshire ; that he had the highest regard for the King ; and said, what my Lord Egremont will interpret, had no design to oppose his measures.[4]

[1] William Burke, who preceded Edmund in English politics, had worked for Bute and Fox during the session 1762–3, and on 12 November 1763 Henry Fox wrote to Lord Sandwich (the letter is among the Sandwich MSS. at Hinchingbrooke) :

Pray give Mr. Burke a hearing. He is a very clever fellow, and I believe a very honest one. He has as great a sway with Lord Verney, as I ever knew one man to have with another. Lord Verney has another vote besides his own. I owed them both to Mr. Burke last sessions, and they were never absent. . . . In all this I meddle no farther than to introduce Burke to you, whom I wish extremely well to, and who will lay the whole before your Lordship. And I think you'll like him.

Also a previous application to Grenville from 'Mr. Burke' (presumably William) is recorded in the 'List of Recommendations', 20 April–7 July 1763 preserved among T. Astle's *Historical Collections* at the British Museum (Add. MSS. 34713). The following entry appears under date of 22 April 1763 (f. 117) : 'Mr. Burke desires to be appointed Governor to one of the Colonies'.

[2] Hardwicke to Newcastle, 13 October 1755 ; Add. MSS. 32860, ff. 30–4.
[3] Bute MSS.
[4] Newcastle to Hardwicke, 13 November 1762 ; Add. MSS. 32944, ff. 352–3.

The view which Kinnoull took of the Whig 'party', while he still helped Newcastle to manage it, expresses the political philosophy of that set. It is explained in a letter to Newcastle,[1] reviewing the situation which in the spring of 1760 had arisen over the Qualification Bill and the Scottish Militia Bill ; these measures had been concerted by Pitt with the Tories, and some bolder spirits among the Whigs, whom he neglected, went further in opposing them than was altogether pleasing to Newcastle, who, however much he was averse to those measures, had to manage Pitt.

However numerous, able, and powerfull that respectable corps of your Grace's . . . old friends may be [wrote Kinnoull], nothing but a general good humour and national union could enable the Administration to do what they do. . . . Your Grace's support of your old friends upon proper occasions enables you to curb them, when their spirits are raised too high, and whenever the more lively, or those who secretly harbour inclinations unfavourable to the present system of Administration would carry things too far and produce reall mischeif. . . . I cannot call men of this disposition, friends either to your Grace or to the publick. . . . That division in the House of Lords was promoted . . . by a noble band, who have a great deal of vivacity and some of them very good parts. Inconsiderable as their number may be, if they should take more frequent opportunities of shewing their secret inclinations in publick, they would merit and require attention. But I am in hopes that they do not intend to form a regular body ; . . . this puts me in mind of a flying squadron, which I hear is formed in the House of Commons of young men of ability and parts, and, I really beleive, honest dispositions. But as these separate corps are not only troublesome but dangerous in the House of Commons, especially if supported by abilities, and as the best inclinations, if directed by a vain love of singularity, by refined speculations, and an excess of righteousness which measures every proposition abstractedly by the exact rules of what such minds form in their own ideas to be right and wrong, will render any Government impracticable ; I cannot help expressing my wishes to your Grace, that some prudent measures should be taken to break this knot, before it be tied too fast. I have a great partiality and affection for these young men, but I am persuaded that they already have no mean opinion of their own abilities, and their parts, which by accustoming themselves to speak in the House

[1] Add. MSS. 32908, ff. 160-77 ; the letter was written on 10 July 1760 from Lisbon where Kinnoull had been sent as special envoy.

of Commons, and by application will become more considerable, and they will every day be more sensible of their own importance. I really think they are such men as would do credit to Government, but I wish to see them act as individuals, and that they may be separated, for experience has taught me to be very apprehensive of these combinations.

It may be that Kinnoull's newly discovered Scottish attachments ('for my friend', wrote Newcastle to Hardwicke on 21 August 1760 'never was a Scotchman till very few years ago') [1] accentuated his distrust of the young men in opposition to the Scottish Militia Bill ; still, this distrust of coherent groups, even when moved by Whig principles, was typical of Newcastle and his associates. The mid-eighteenth-century Parliament was pulverised, and its managers wished it to continue in that condition ; but in reality, in the absence of proper party ties, even casual associations were apt to produce curious agglomerations. An interesting example is supplied by Hardwicke, in the letter to Newcastle dealing with the election activities among the officers of the Lincolnshire militia : [2]

It is very natural for such a number of gentlemen of the same county . . . confin'd to live and clubb together, to enter into concert for projects of this sort, tho' foreign to their proper service. It puts me in mind of the Gaol-Committee, which your Grace perfectly remembers, who, from being appointed and united to enquire into the abuses of gaols, became banded together for factious purposes, and were a flying squadron upon most questions during the remainder of that Parliament.

The Committee referred to by Hardwicke was appointed, on the initiative of Oglethorpe on 25 February 1729 — and that Parliament was not dissolved till 1734.

By 1760 the inner coherence of political parties in Parliament had become still weaker, and places and profits were the cement which Walpole and the Pelhams applied to the Whig party. The political nomenclature of Newcastle and his associates was roughly this : men who held office under their Administration or derived profits from it, and further such as

---

[1] Add. MSS. 32910, ff. 195-7. Kinnoull lost the estate of Whetham in Wiltshire through the death of his wife in 1753, and succeeded to Scottish estates on the death of his father in 1759.

[2] See above, pp. 118-19.

applied to them for either, were 'well-affected Whigs', 'zealous
friends to the King and his Government'; those who were
ready to embark in the existing system, but asked for more than
the King and his Government chose to offer them, who, in
short, were candidates for office but were not easily 'accommodated', were the 'disaffected', 'factious' Whigs; those who
never asked for favours and did not attend Court or the levees
of the Minister were suspects, and were called Tories. There
were still in 1760 a few Whigs with a distinctive party outlook
— elderly men born round 1700 and about to withdraw from
politics,[1] and country gentlemen with Whig traditions, sometimes described as 'country Whigs';[2] and there were young
men of about twenty-five to thirty, with the spirit of enterprise
not yet destroyed in them, the Parliamentary boy-scouts of the
new Whig Party. But the generation now between forty and
fifty, who had entered Parliament about 1745 and had been
nurtured in it by the Pelhams, knew no politics except in terms
of office; men such as Charles Yorke, Charles Townshend,
Granby, or Barrington, though each of them representing a
different type, were all alike unfitted for the work of opposition.

The condition of the Whig Party about 1760 can be summed
up in the terms in which the Balkans correspondent of *The
Times* described the Serb Radical Party, on 20 November 1928
— there is a logic in the development of institutions which

[1] *E.g.* John Page, M.P. for Chichester, born in 1697 and first returned
to Parliament in 1727, whom Pelham in 1754 and Newcastle in 1761 had
great difficulty in persuading to stand again, and who finally withdrew from
the House in 1768; John White, M.P. for East Retford, who by 1768 was
so indifferent to continuing in the House that he managed to have himself
defeated in a constituency which he had represented for thirty-six years —
'I don't call Retford lost', wrote Newcastle to Lord George Cavendish on
20 March 1768 'for if my friend Jack White did not care to come into
Parliament, it was mighty easy for him to lose the election' (Add. MSS.
32989, f. 226; see also *ibid.*, letters from Rockingham, f. 189, and John
Offley, f. 218); Robert More, who voluntarily withdrew from Parliament
in 1761 (see his letter to Lord Bath dated 19 June 1759 and published in
The Structure of Politics, pp. 258-9 — it may serve as an example of the old
Whig spirit such as survived in some parts of the country, away from the
Court and Newcastle).

[2] Thus, *e.g.*, Newcastle wrote to John White, on 10 October 1761, about
the choice of a new Speaker (Add. MSS. 32929, f. 172): 'I also named our
friend Mr. Hewet, Mr. Whichcotte, &c., as countrey Whigs. . . .' Hewett
and Whichcote were both knights of the shire.

surmounts differences of nationality, social organisation, and traditions.

The formation of a Government [in Yugoslavia] is not a question of programme or policy, but of the distribution of portfolios between the political parties concerned. A party justifies itself to its adherents not by its legislative record while in office, but by being able to staff the Ministries and departments under its control with its own members, who can then look after the interests of other members of the corporation.

This system, in which officials are chosen on account of their political opinions rather than of their technical qualifications, is responsible for the appalling inefficiency of many Government departments in this country. . . . With the reduction of the number of posts at their disposal much of the currency of present-day Serbian politics will be withdrawn from circulation and the basis on which the power of the governing parties has been built up will be destroyed.

This applies particularly to the Radicals who have been the dominating force in Serbia for twenty-five years. In all professions and grades of society to join the Radical Party is recognised as a useful and sometimes indispensable aid to advancement. Its ranks are consequently full of men who have joined it for material advantages alone. The party has long ceased to represent any idea or policy other than that of self-preservation. But what will be the point of being inscribed a member if the bestowal of contracts, permits, and administrative facilities of all sorts is no longer in the hands of Radical Ministers and Radical officials ?

A long term in the wilderness was required to purify the Whig Party of 1760 by changing most of the personnel covered by its name. When twenty years later the new Whig opposition made 'economical reform', *i.e.* the suppression of sinecures and unnecessary offices, a cardinal point in their programme, they were out to destroy the edifice which the Pelhams had built for their party and which George III had taken over with most of its residents. With the change of owners the building changed its name, and the Government party was now called 'Tory' by its opponents and still continues to be described as such by some historians ; but nothing can be more confusing than the application of the same name to bodies so widely differing in character and principles as the Tories of 1760 and the so-called Tories of 1780. Shelburne, who spent the best years of his life in opposition to the so-called Tories, thus describes in his autobiography the Tories of George II's reign :

They were the landed interest of England who desired to see an honourable, dignified government conducted with order and due economy and due subordination, in opposition to the Whigs, who courted the mob in the first instance, and in the next the commercial interest. The Tories, being men of property and precluded from all degree of Court favour since Queen Anne's time, lived upon their estates, never went to London but to attend Parliament, and that for a short time, while the Whigs surrounded the Court, governed the two Kingdoms, knew confidentially all that passed at home and abroad, were in the secret of everything, and provided for younger brothers, cousins, nephews and dependents, whose wits were sharpened by their advancement.[1]

As for the Tories, when at last Pitt 'brought forward the most producible into administration, and about the Court as grooms etc.', there were not many to be found fit for office — 'it is wonderful how those that are long out of employment or business of any kind, fall off in talent and knowledge of mankind'.[2] Not even in George II's reign were the Old Tories to supply the personnel for the political 'labour army'.

Whether before 1760 they kept away from Court and Government because they were Tories or whether it would be more correct to say that those remained Tories who were not at Court and in office, their disinterestedness made them the most independent and most dignified body in Parliament and in the country. But although they had certain principles in common there was no uniformity of views among them — Sir John Phillips, the reactionary Jacobite who was in future to adhere to Bute, and William Beckford who was to lead the City Radicals, about 1754 closely co-operated in politics and in elections under the common denomination of 'Tory' ; and although there were Tory clubs and associations in various towns and counties, there was no Tory programme (except opposition to paying taxes for other men's 'provision from office') and no Tory party-organisation on a national scale. Indeed, by 1760 they had no acknowledged leader in Parliament

[1] See Fitzmaurice, *Life of William, Earl of Shelburne*, vol. i. p. 38.
[2] *Ibid.* vol. i. p. 70.

and would have been at a loss where to find one. 'I had
[at Oxford] a *tête à tête* for six hours with old Doctor King',
wrote General Robert Clerk to Lord Fitzmaurice on 15 September 1759. 'He says the Tories have not one man amongst
them at present capable to be put at their head.'[1]   The only
political attachment of many among them towards the end of
George II's reign was for Pitt ; disinterested and independent,
they expressed the feelings of the country, and the bulk of them
were neither Jacobites before 1760, nor Court sycophants under
George III.   Lord Barrington, a Treasury Whig, wrote to
Andrew Mitchell on 28 December 1756 :[2]

> Mr. Pitt is the idol of the Tories. . . . I verily beleive the said
> Tories have neither made conditions for their party nor for themselves,
> that they are willing to support Government in this time of need and to
> support it for nothing ; a disposition very unusual in this country,
> which cannot long subsist, but which (to speak impartially) does
> honour to the persons who act this disinterested part even for a day.

How many Old Tories were there in the Parliament elected
in 1761 ?   How were they distributed, regionally and as between
the different types of constituencies?   What groups or tendencies
can be discerned among them ?

Not even before 1760 was it always easy to decide who
should, and who should not, be counted as a Tory.   The
talk about the 'extinction of parties' did not originate with
George III or Bute ; pronouncements to that effect were current towards the end of George II's reign, especially after the
co-operation between the Tories and Pitt, now leader of the
House of Commons, had established national unity in Parliament and even in many constituencies.   Kinnoull himself,
although an old party hack, urged in July 1760 that the Tories
should not be unnecessarily attacked at the forthcoming
general election in their *status possidendi*.   Lord Ducie apologised
in a letter to Newcastle, on 13 September 1758, for speaking in
terms of parties — 'tho' all party is now happily at an end . . .
that I may be intelligible, must make use of the old terms of
distinction'.[3]   When, in October 1759, Simeon Stuart was put

---

[1] Shelburne MSS. at Bowood.   [2] Add. MSS. 6834, f. 7.
[3] Add. MSS. 32883, f. 442.

up for Hampshire by Lord Carnarvon, Lord Clanricarde complained of such being 'the present doctrine of politicks that
Whiges are no longer Whiges'.[1] Nor were Tories of Stuart's
type any longer Tories — he offered to the Duke of Bolton 'to
take any part, join any part of Administration' as price for his
support.[2] Only Hans Stanley, who was soon to become a
regular 'King's friend', warmly protested to Newcastle against

the false tho' popular doctrines, so often repeated in Parliament, that
there no longer remains any difference of politicall opinion among
His Majesty's subjects, an error which will ever appear in reall
practise on these occasions [in elections], however plausible the
contrary theory may sound.[3]

But in reality the practice of the time by no means beais
out Stanley's contention. In many counties in the east and
north, where the Whig magnates had a very considerable or
even preponderant influence, they tried none the less to placate
the rank and file of the Tory gentry ; Whig candidates would
seek the support and concurrence of the Tories, while, on other
occasions, Tory gentlemen would be accepted for candidates
on declaring their allegiance to the ruling dynasty and a general
adherence to the Government.

Here are a few examples of both types of compromise :

The Dukes of Rutland and Bedford stood in the front rank
of the 'Revolution families'. But in 1753 Rutland's son, Lord
Granby, having engaged with the Cambridgeshire Tories that
'he would not stand for the county upon a particular interest,
nor be set up by a club',[4] took little 'notice of the Whig gentlemen in the county' ('his civility' having 'all gone to the other
side'),[5] and, to 'avoid giving the most distant handle of complaint to the Tories that he had not acted strictly conformable
to his declaration even in the minutest article',[6] refused to
become joint candidate with Philip Yorke till both had been

---

[1] To Newcastle, 3 November 1759 ; Add. MSS. 32898, ff. 73-4.
[2] Bolton to Newcastle, 4 November 1759 ; *ibid.* ff. 84-5.
[3] 24 November 1759 ; Add. MSS. 32899, ff. 83-4.
[4] Philip Yorke to Hardwicke, 8 July 1753 ; Add. MSS. 35351, ff. 233-5.
[5] Same to same, 27 July ; *ibid.* ff. 243-4.
[6] Lord Montfort to Lord Hardwicke, 19 August 1753 ; Add. MSS.
35592, f. 131.

formally approved by the general meeting of the county. The Duke of Bedford, the same year, concluded a compromise with the Bedford Corporation for the general election. 'The Duke brings in Mr. Ongley, and the Corporation Mr. Herne [a Tory], his Grace is also to chuse Alderman Dickenson (who is reckoned a moderate Tory) for one of his boroughs.' [1] Meanwhile the Tory gentlemen joined the Duke in nominating Lord Upper Ossory at a by-election for the county, after which 'the gentlemen all dined together . . . and the Duke was very civil and gracious to every body.'

The Duke of Bedford's entertainment at Bedford is much talk'd of in town [wrote Hardwicke to his son on 22 August] and I find it is generally thought that his Grace has made an odd bargain with the Tories for the town, and that he has really no Member of his own for that place. It is strongly affirm'd here that your neighbour, Mr. Ongley, is a determin'd Tory, but I thought you had told me otherwise.[2]

In 1761 Robert Ongley was returned for the county (together with Lord Tavistock), Francis Herne once more for Bedford, and Marshe Dickinson for Brackley, and all three were reckoned 'Tories' and 'Bedfords' at the same time.

When George Delaval, of a *quondam* Jacobite family,[3] offered himself in 1757 as candidate for Northumberland, he applied for Newcastle's support, and was accepted by him. 'My constant attachment to His Majesty and his family', he wrote to the Duke on 9 October 1757, 'may, I hope, entitle me to the favour of those that have the honour to serve the Government in this county.' [4] In Parliament he was sometimes reckoned a Tory and sometimes a Whig, and it is difficult to say which he was. Similarly, Robert Shafto, though of a Tory family, was returned to Parliament for the county of Durham as a semi-convert to Whiggism, under the auspices of Lord

---

[1] Philip Yorke to Hardwicke, 5 August 1753 ; Add. MSS. 35351, ff. 248-251.   [2] *Ibid.* ff. 265-6.

[3] He was a son of Edward Shafto, whose elder brother, William, had forfeited the family estate of Bavington by complicity in the Jacobite rising of 1715 ; but Admiral George Delaval, whose sister was married to Edward Shafto, purchased the estate and settled it on his nephew, who took the name of Delaval.   [4] Add. MSS. 32874, f. 499.

Darlington and the Bishop of Durham. The Bishop wrote to Newcastle on 7 October 1760 : 'Shaftoe has been with me to declare his attachments to the Government, in which I believe him sincere ; but the Tories are certainly pleased with his standing and glad to join him'.[1] Thus the Durham Tories, so far from resenting Shafto's candidature under Whig auspices, were glad of it, personal connexions and considerations being all that, in this case, was left of parties.

Again, when a vacancy occurred in the representation of Essex in 1759, and none of the Whig gentlemen could be persuaded to stand because of the expense which, it was said, 'will be near £10,000', a meeting of the leading Essex Whigs at Lord Rochford's, who was Lord Lieutenant of the county, 'sent to Sir William Maynard to offer him their support and assistance if he would stand upon that interest' ;[2] 'as Sir William Maynard is a very moderate man', explained Rochford to Newcastle on 11 April, 'I find it is the opinion of the Whigs to support him, especially as it will entirely divide the Tory interest'.[3] To which Newcastle replied the same day :

> I am extremely glad to find that Sir William Maynard has been prevail'd upon to stand for Essex. I was afraid it would have fallen into absolute Tory hands. Sure the Whigs should give Sir William all the support in their power, and make him the Whig candidate.[4]

It is difficult enough to classify in terms of Whig and Tory such compromise candidates returned during the last years of George II's reign ; but still more difficult is it in the case of men who first entered Parliament in 1761, when the extinction of parties had been officially proclaimed, when even the Old Tories had gone to Court, and there was no longer a premium on being a Whig. Unless the political character of the Member's family or constituency is clearly marked, one cannot venture to guess what his politics would have been before 1761 ; and one must not mix up the adherents of the new Court, the so-called Tories of Whig pamphlets and of pseudo-history, with the late Tory Opposition. To give again a few examples :

[1] Add. MSS. 32912, ff. 455-6.
[2] See letter from James West to Newcastle, 7 April 1759 ; Add. MSS 32889, f. 394.   [3] Add. MSS. 32890, f. 23.   [4] *Ibid.* f. 25.

Francis Buller entered the House of Commons in 1761 as Member for West Looe, a borough which his brother John managed for the Government; his eldest brother, James, a knight of the shire for Cornwall, had ranked as a Tory under George II, John, a borough manager, as a Whig.[1] John Buller, because of personal connexions with Legge, in 1762 adhered to the Opposition; James generally went with the new Court, but, *e.g.*, over General Warrants voted with the Opposition; while Francis, in December 1763, accepted the place of Groom-Porter, and even on General Warrants did not vote against the Government. Before 1760 he would probably have been a Treasury Whig, and in 1761 certainly cannot be reckoned among the Old Tories.—John Duke, Member for Honiton, was returned on his own interest, did not belong to an established political family or connexion, in Bute's list was classified as a Tory, but was counted by Newcastle in May 1761 as a 'friend', and in November received the Duke's circular letter, to which he replied that had he received it in time he would have attended the opening of the session, and that he would now come up as soon as possible; in these circumstances it would seem unsafe to count him among the Tories.—Peregrine Cust, first returned to Parliament in 1761, is usually described as a 'Tory' because he generally adhered to the new Court. Still, his brother, Sir John Cust, the Speaker, with whom he remained on the closest and most friendly terms, had never ranked as such under George II, but at the utmost as a Leicester House Whig; and Peregrine Cust, a merchant and Government contractor, would most certainly have adhered to the Treasury before, as he did after, the death of George II.— The case of Sir Francis Knollys, Member for Reading, is specially instructive; he sat 'on his own interest', was counted by Newcastle in May 1761 among the 'others' (the presumed opponents), did not receive the circular letter in November, and in Lord Bute's list was first put down as a 'Tory'; this mark was subsequently crossed out, and 'Old Whig' put in its place, to which Bute added in his own handwriting 'rather a

[1] About him see the essay on 'East and West Looe' in *The Structure of Politics*, pp. 321-35.

Walpolian', a curious recognition of the fact that even opposite types, if inherited from an age of which the issues are worn out, come closely to resemble each other. Still, I do not include Knollys among the Tories.—And here is another difficult case : the seats of Edward Morant and Richard Pennant, who first entered Parliament in 1761, were secured for them by William Beckford. Both he and their cousin, Henry Dawkins, had hitherto ranked as Tories ; but how can Morant and Pennant be classified as such for the first time in 1761, when the Tories were supposed to incline to the new Court, and Beckford's connexion was with Pitt and the City Radicals ? —Lastly, how should Simeon Stuart be classified, after he had offered in 1758 to adhere to any 'part of the Administration' which the Duke of Bolton would wish him to join ? [1] As his offer was refused, his past connexions must be allowed to stand, and he has to be counted as a Tory, even though this may be an indignity to the men who for forty-six years had patiently persevered in a disinterested opposition. In Bute's own list he does not appear as a Tory, but then Bute never applied that description to men who were closely connected with him. One wonders how much of the outcry about 'Toryism', both in the case of Bute and of the new Member for Hampshire, was due to their being 'Stuarts'.[2]

Omitting doubtful cases, the list which I have compiled of the Old Tories [3] comprises 104 English and 9 Welsh Members (in Scotland, where Toryism had retained a Jacobite character, practically all Members before 1761 were Whigs, while after 1761 most of them followed Bute for national and personal reasons). Thus in England the Old Tories held, in 1761, 21·5 per cent of the seats, and in Wales more than one-third. Of the Welsh Tories, four represented counties and five boroughs,

[1] See above, p. 193.

[2] 'An inundation of Tories, or Stuarts, etc. will be pour'd into every county', wrote Newcastle to Hardwicke on 7 December 1760 (Add. MSS. 32915, ff. 332-7). Lord Albemarle, in his *Life of Rockingham*, describes Simeon Stuart as 'a cousin of Lord Bute' (see vol. i. p. 64). In reality his family had settled in England in the fifteenth century, had intermarried with English families ever since, had several times represented Hampshire constituencies in Parliament, and was no more Scottish than, *e.g.*, the Napiers of Dorset, whom no one ever described as such.

[3] See Appendix A, pp. 419-21.

but as in Wales counties and boroughs alike had numerous electorates and were dominated by the landowners, the distinction between them is immaterial.   In England, on the other hand, it is essential.   Here, even after having ceded to the Whigs semi-Tories such as George Delaval, Robert Shafto, and Sir William Maynard, we find that 40 knights of the shire, *i.e.* exactly half, were Tories.[1]   Of the 46 Members returned by English boroughs with an electorate of over 1000,[2] in 1761, 18, *i.e.* 39 per cent, were Tories.   Of the two Universities, the Tories held Oxford, and the Whigs Cambridge.   Thus of the 130 Members representing the most independent English constituencies, in 1761 no less than 60 (46 per cent) were Tories of the old school, which means primarily independents. Elaborate research has yielded an obvious, tautological result, and yet it had to be done where there is so much confusion between names and realities.

Of the 66 Members returned by English boroughs with an electorate of about 500 or 500-1000 voters, in 1761, 12 (18 per cent) were Tories ;   while of the 293 Members returned by boroughs with less than 500 voters, only 33, *i.e.* slightly more than 11 per cent, were Tories.   Adding the smaller boroughs to the narrow, or even nominal, constituencies, we obtain a total of 45 Tories among 359 Members, *i.e.* an average of only 12½ per cent.   An independent seat for a county or a large borough conferred an honour on its holder ;   but few families would have for generations cultivated an interest in a small borough (which was bound to be inordinately expensive to those who had no claim to official patronage), and still fewer individuals would have paid a heavy sum for a seat in a rotten or a pocket borough, merely to carry on in the House of Commons 'the nonsense of a nonsensical opposition'.

What was the geographical distribution of the Tory seats ?

[1] Among the 40 Tory knights of the shire, there was only one son of an English peer, among the 40 Whigs, 15 sons of English peers, one son of a Scottish peer, and one Irish peer — which numbers well illustrate the difference between the 'Country' and the 'Court Party'.   Of the 40 Tories, 24 had been educated at Oxford and 6 at Cambridge ;   of the 40 Whigs 8 at Oxford and 19 at Cambridge — which distribution was determined by proximity as well as by preferences.

[2] See *The Structure of Politics*, pp. 80-1.

Politically England in 1760 can be divided into four districts.
The first, in the south-east, round the Thames estuary, consists
of the five counties adjoining London (Middlesex, Herts.,
Essex, Kent, and Surrey) and the two coastal counties of
Suffolk and Sussex. From here to the north and west extend
three zones, each including eleven counties. The south-
western district comprises 'Wessex' and the counties on the
Lower Severn, round Bristol.[1] This is the country of the
Elizabethan Protestants and the Western Puritans, of 'Squire
Western' and 'Roger de Coverley', the classical home of the
independent country gentry. Next comes the region which,
for lack of a better name, may be called the 'midland' district,
extending from Oxford to Lancaster and comprising the
strongholds of the Papist recusants and the Laudians, of the
Cavaliers and the English Jacobites.[2] The rest of England,
which can best be described as the north-eastern district,[3] is
the home of the Eastern Puritans, of the Whig squirearchy,
and of the great territorial houses.

The south-west returned, in 1761, 19 Tory and 3 Whig
knights of the shire (two of these sat for Monmouthshire, and
one for Hampshire) ; in the four most westerly counties —
Cornwall, Devon, Dorset, and Somerset — the Tories had
held both seats ever since 1715, without a single election
contest. In the 'midland' district also, the Tories formed a
majority among the knights of the shire, though in five counties
one seat was conceded to the leading Whig family (to the
Stanleys in Lancashire, to the Cavendishes in Derbyshire, to
the Spencer-Churchills in Oxfordshire, to the Leveson-Gowers
in Staffordshire, and to the Russells in Bedfordshire), and in
Buckinghamshire, too, the county representation was divided
between Whigs and Tories ; thus, in 1761, 16 of 22 shire representatives in the midland district were Tories. Of the seven
counties round London, the three south of the Thames returned

---

[1] Hants, Berks., Wilts., Dorset, Somerset, Devon, Cornwall, Glos.,
Worcs., Herefordshire, and Monmouth.

[2] Lancs., Cheshire, Salop, Staffs., Derbyshire, Warwickshire, Leicestershire, Northants, Oxon., Bucks., and Beds.

[3] Norfolk, Cambridgeshire, Hunts., Rutland, Lincs., Notts., Yorks.,
Durham, Northumberland, Cumberland, and Westmorland.

a solid Whig representation, while in the four north of the Thames the representation was divided, yielding a total of 10 Whigs and 4 Tories. The eleven counties of the north-eastern district returned, in 1761, 21 Whigs and only one Tory (in Norfolk).

The county representation supplies the best indication of political tendencies in these four zones, as with regard to boroughs the differences are partly obliterated in the west and the south by the great number of boroughs which were managed, or usually purchased, by the Government ; still, even in the borough representation the essential Toryism of the midland district and the Whiggism of the north-east were quite clearly marked. The south-eastern division returned 84 borough Members, including 11 Tories ; the south-western 183, including 26 Tories — which yields for the entire south an average of one Tory to seven or eight borough Members. The midland district returned 66 borough Members, including 20 Tories, *i.e.* about one in three ; and the north-east 72 and 6, *i.e.* one in twelve.

The total of Whigs and Tories returned in these four divisions in 1761 is (adding the Members for the two Universities) as follows :

	Whigs	Tories
In the south-eastern district . .	83	15 (15·3 per cent)
„ south-western „ . .	160	45 (22 per cent)
„ midland „ .	52	38 (42·2 per cent)
„ north-eastern „ .	89	7 (7·3 per cent)
	384	105 (21·5 per cent) [1]

The division here made into districts is not primarily based on the relative strength of the Tory connexion in them, but rather on the striking differences which there were in the character of their Toryism. The midland Tories were genuine reactionaries, heirs to the Counter-Reformation, to the authoritarian High Church, and the Jacobites ; and in the eastern and northern counties, the half-submerged Tories were of a

---

[1] I know of no lists of Tories in previous Parliaments, but there are computations of the Government side and the Opposition, which latter includes of course both Tories and Opposition Whigs. Thus there is a computation for 1741 in the Hardwicke Papers (Add. MSS. 35876, ff: 138-9)

similarly intransigent type.   In the south-west, the Tories
were independent country gentlemen, who left most of the
very numerous small boroughs to Whig politicians, while they
themselves enjoyed an undisturbed sway in the counties and
held their own in the larger towns (Exeter, Bristol, Gloucester
and Hereford) ;   in sentiment and traditions they stood nearest
to William Pitt, himself from the west country.   The London
Tories were City Radicals, while those of the surrounding
counties were rather mixed in character.   The difference
between these groups is well brought out by their vote on
General Warrants : [1]

and for 1747 in the Newcastle Papers (Add. MSS. 33002, ff. 440-46).
Grouping the returns into the same districts as I have drawn for 1761, I
obtain the following results :

	1741		1747	
	For the Government	*Against the Government*	*For the Government*	*Against the Government*
South-eastern district . .	62	36	73	25
South-western ,, . .	107	98	116	89
Midland ,, . .	24	66	40	50
North-eastern ,, . .	60	36	66	30
	253	236	295	194

Thus in these two Parliaments also one can clearly discern the opposition
character of the midland districts where the country gentry were Tory and
only comparatively few boroughs were marketable. Of the sixteen gains
which the Government made in that district in 1747 as against 1741, six
were in Staffordshire, where the Leveson-Gowers had changed sides, and
four in Bedfordshire, owing to the Bedfords having joined the Government ; while in the south-west eight of the nine net gains were in Cornwall,
where the borough-mongering of the Prince of Wales was less successful
in 1747 than in 1741.

[1] I do not here take into account men chosen at by-elections since
1761, even if returned in the place of Old Tories, for with regard to these
new men the difficulty of determining whether they should be counted as
such becomes even greater. This explains why among the Tories the
proportion of those voting in the division appears lower than in the whole
House. Further, it should be noted that the number of Tories who voted
with the Government is slightly exaggerated in my table, as, barring those
who are known to have been absent, it includes all who did not vote with
the Opposition, and no deduction is made for Tories among the 18 Members
unaccounted for on that occasion. On a *pro rata* division there ought to
have been at least four Tories among them, which would reduce the percentage of Tories voting with the Government to 43.5.

	Total Number of Members	Tories	Voted with the Opposition	Likely to have voted with the Government
South-eastern district .	98	15 (15·3 p.c.)	9 (75 p.c.)	3 (25 p.c.)
South-western district .	205	45 (22 p.c.)	26 (76·5 p.c.)	8 (23·5 p.c.)
Midland district . .	90	38 (42·2 p.c.)	7 (25 p.c.)	21 (75 p.c.)
North-eastern district .	96	7 (7·3 p.c.)	1 (16·6 p.c.)	5 (83·4 p.c.)
	489	105 (21·5 p.c.)	43 (54 p.c.)	37 (46 p.c.)

Thus in the division on General Warrants a majority of the Tories voted with the Opposition — in fact, a higher proportion than of those who in 1761 had been classed as Whigs. But whereas of the southern Tories voting in that division three in four joined the Opposition, from the midland district the same proportion voted with the Government; and of the seven 'midland' Tories who voted against it, four were from Cheshire and Leicestershire, the only two counties in England which returned a solid Tory representation,[1] and one was a Member for Liverpool connected with the City Radicals.

It would seem by my last accounts from England [wrote Thomas Prowse, a typical west-country Tory, from France on 8 March 1764] that some people must have begun to recover their senses, for I see parties balancing. It is a strange infatuation that for the sake of punishing one impudent worthless fellow, persons that have a grain of understanding or honesty left, should be desirous of throwing down all the fences of their liberties which the wisdom and courage of their ancestors had provided.[2]

Those who went with the Court were to him 'renegado Tories'; but then he was from Somerset.

[1] Politics in various parts of England were as yet strongly provincial in character, and where, as in these two counties, the representation was uncontested and undivided, the Members seem to have been more strongly conscious of representing the whole county, and were therefore less partisan.

[2] Thomas Prowse to H. B. Legge; among the Legge Papers in the John Rylands Library, Manchester. Prowse represented Somerset from 1740 till his death in 1767; he was absent from the division on General Warrants, being at that time abroad.

Groups and Factions

A forecast concerning the Parliament of 1761 made under the headings of Bute, Newcastle, and the Government, a retrospect under the denominations of Whigs and Tories, or a survey in any other terms we may choose, opens up certain vistas, but cannot supply safe guidance with regard to the further political action of the Members thus classified. There were no parties or groups with an exclusive, registered membership, and the same men have to be classified in various ways, according to the nature and purpose of the survey; each Member was bound by different, and often conflicting, loyalties, and was directed by various, frequently contrary, interests; his political action was the resultant of a number of factors, among which in most cases none so far predominated as party allegiance does at present. But even surveys based on the same principles and the same information cannot be expected to yield identical results where so much depends on the interpretation given to terms and on individual opinion. It has been explained to me by a President of the Liverpool Cotton Exchange that the grading of cotton is an art and not a science, and that even the length of its staple, measurable as it might seem, is always open to dispute, as 'no two men pull the fibre alike'. What degree of consensus can we then expect from attempts to 'grade' an eighteenth-century Parliament?

The groupings made above, first under Bute, Newcastle, the Government, and next under the name of Tories, have this much in common, that few of the Members comprised in them owed a primary allegiance to minor political patrons or group leaders; [1] and it is in the region intervening between the 'Ministerialists' and the Tories that we must expect to find whatever Whig factions and groups directed by oligarchs existed in 1761. To those groups we now must direct our attention.

---

[1] But even this statement has to be made in the guarded and qualified form which I have given it above: among the Tories there were a few who were not altogether independent, e.g. R. H. Ongley, M.P. for Beds., and F. Herne, M.P. for Bedford, who were reckoned 'Bedfords'; and similarly among the followers of Bute and Newcastle there were men who were to some extent 'determined' by intermediary patrons.

A survey of the House of Commons — incomplete, determined by a pragmatic purpose, but none the less useful — can be obtained from lists which Newcastle drew up in preparation for the Parliamentary session of November 1761. It was the custom at that time to send circular letters to the friends of Administration inviting their attendance at the House at the opening of the session, and also at the preliminary meeting of followers of the Government held at the Cockpit the night before.[1] A general list dated Claremont, 16 October 1761, and marked 'Members to be wrote to, to attend the first day of the Session, and by whom',[2] contains the names of 342 Members of Parliament,[3] and against each Member there is a mark through whom his attendance was to be secured. Personal letters were to be written by Newcastle to the more prominent or independent Members, and to his own friends, while other Members were to be summoned through their group leaders, patrons, official chiefs, through powerful relatives, or through friends who were supposed to have influence with them ; and in a large number of cases, to ensure the desired result, both methods were to be employed. A further paper, dated 26 October,[4] gives thirty-six lists sent to such deputy-conveners ; they contain 194 names.[5] I place them in the order which seems

[1] See my article on 'The Circular Letters : An 18th-Century Whip to Members of Parliament' in *The English Historical Review* for October 1929.

[2] Add. MSS. 32929, ff. 303-11.

[3] Of the 216 who were not summoned, 103 were Tories ; some were connected with Pitt and Temple (not more than ten, unless some of the Tories are included) ; some 20 were omitted because unavoidably absent (*e.g.* naval and military officers on active service, and diplomats employed abroad), and a few seats were vacant ; a few Members were new-comers of no particular political colour, but with whom Newcastle had no previous acquaintance or connexion ; lastly, there were those whom Newcastle left to Bute — personal friends and dependants of Bute, some late Leicester House men, about three-fourths of the Scottish Members whom in the past the Duke of Argyll used to convene, George and Charles Townshend and the Sackvilles, who were estranged from Newcastle, etc.

[4] Add. MSS. 32930, ff. 37-42.

[5] Twelve of the 36 persons to whom these lists were sent were themselves Members of Parliament ; I mark them as such in the list below but do not include them in the numbers placed against their names. Moreover, I deduct from the total four names which appear twice in these lists : Captain W. Trelawny, R.N., M.P. for West Looe, appears in the list of Anson, the First Lord of the Admiralty, and of Gashry, the Treasury agent for the two Looes ; W. Osbaldeston, a Yorkshireman, in those of Rockingham and of Wilkinson ; Thomas Miller, Lord Advocate of Scotland, in

most convenient for the purpose of further analysis (the arrangement in Newcastle's paper is purely fortuitous) : [1]

(1)	Duke of Bedford	10	(19)	Lord Bateman, M.P.	5
(2)	Duke of Devonshire	12	(20)	George Onslow, M.P.	6
(3)	Lord Rockingham	10	(21)	Lord Rochford	2
(4)	Lord Powis	11	(22)	Lord Albemarle	4
(5)	Lord Anson	15	(23)	Lord Kinnoull	5
(6)	Lord Hardwicke	14	(24)	Andrew Stone	4
(7)	H. Fox, M.P.	12	(25)	James West, M.P.	4
(8)	Lord Barrington, M.P.	11	(26)	F. Gashry, M.P.	3
(9)	Lord Sandwich	5	(27)	A. Wilkinson, M.P.	3
(10)	Lord Northumberland	5	(28)	Lord Lincoln	7
(11)	Duke of Rutland	4	(29)	Duchess of Newcastle	4
(12)	Lord Buckinghamshire	4	(30)	Lord Mansfield	4
(13)	Lord Darlington	4	(31)	Lord Grantham	4
(14)	Duke of Bolton	4	(32)	E. Eliot, M.P.	2
(15)	Lord Exeter	4	(33)	Thomas Pelham, M.P.	2
(16)	Lord Archer	4	(34)	Lord Ashburnham	2
(17)	Duke of Ancaster	3	(35)	Lord Robert Bertie, M.P.	1
(18)	James Brudenell, M.P.	3	(36)	John Page, M.P.	1

These lists, the resultants of different and disparate factors, show the influence in the House of Commons with which various friends of the Government were credited by Newcastle. There is some value in such a survey of totals, irrespective of the various elements, permanent or transitory, which entered into their composition ; still, the mixed character of these groups calls for the greatest caution in comparing them with each other. The degree to which various deputy-conveners could influence those entrusted to their care was very uneven, and, *e.g.*, against Lord Barrington, who had neither electoral influence nor a political following, there appears a higher figure than against the Duke of Bedford, merely because Newcastle chose to saddle Barrington with a number of Members whom he did not know how else to approach. It must further be remembered that there were other patrons and leaders who are not mentioned in this register, because Newcastle did not

Hardwicke's and Kinnoull's ; and G. B. Brudenell, M.P. for Stamford, in that of its patron, Lord Exeter, and of his friend, Lord Lincoln.

[1] Newcastle went through the register of the House of Commons, and started each list whenever he came across the first Member to be included in it.

feel in a position to invite their co-operation ; and that various Members placed in the lists of his friends may have been more intimately connected with such leaders, or more closely dependent on such patrons, omitted from this register. The figures given in it must therefore be treated as maxima ; for whereas Newcastle, in many cases, tentatively included in the lists of his friends the names of Members with whom these were only distantly connected, he naturally, both in his own interest and in order not to belittle his friends, was very careful not to omit any of those over whom they had a decisive influence. Lastly, it must always be borne in mind that these were lists compiled for one specific purpose, and not theoretical exercises undertaken in pursuit of knowledge ; their register is given here not as an impartial index of the House of Commons, but merely for the general picture which it supplies.

That picture is one of many small, loosely knitted, shifting groups of which hardly any is of a uniform character, but most show some predominant characteristic, and can be described accordingly as bearing an oligarchic, territorial, professional, political, or a family character. This is the analysis of the eight longest lists given in my article on 'The Circular Letters' in *The English Historical Review* for October 1929 :

Seven of the ten men whose attendance the Duke of Bedford was asked to secure largely or entirely owed to him their seats in Parliament ; two others were distant relatives and close associates of the Duke's. Of the twelve Members in the list of the Duke of Devonshire, four were Cavendishes, one was his nominee at Derby, and two were men returned through his mediation ; another one was a Derbyshire man. These two lists represent the type of aristocratic, oligarchic groups.

Of the eleven Members on Lord Powis's list, seven were Shropshire and three Welsh Members, and one lately a Member for a Welsh constituency.[1] Of the ten on Lord Rockingham's list, eight sat for Yorkshire constituencies and the other two were Yorkshire men. These two lists represent groups under territorial managers.

Of the fifteen men on the list sent to Lord Anson, First Lord of the Admiralty, two were Admiralty officials (John Clevland and

---

[1] For a description of Lord Powis's group see the essay on 'Shropshire Politics and Men at the Accession of George III' in *The Structure of Politics*.

Philip Stephens, the secretaries) and nine naval officers; [1] two were near relatives of Anson's, returned by him to Parliament, and two civilian Members for boroughs under Admiralty influence. This can be described as a professional group. Lord Hardwicke's list is more of a family character, though the legal profession still appears in it, a reminiscence of his Chancellorship. The fourteen names in the list include four sons of Hardwicke and one son-in-law, and two nephews of his wife, and four lawyers: John Hervey, a Welsh Judge; Dr. Simpson, Dean of the Arches and Judge of the Cinque Ports; P. C. Webb, Solicitor to the Treasury; and Thomas Miller, Lord Advocate of Scotland.

The twelve Members in Henry Fox's list were almost all personal friends, political associates, or dependants of his, for whom he had negotiated seats; he owned no pocket boroughs in which to accommodate his men, but he had his political 'pack' which he provided for, both in Parliament and in offices. This is not an oligarchic, territorial, professional, or family group, but a Parliamentary 'faction', *i.e.* political in the eighteenth-century sense of the term.

Lord Barrington's list is a mere jumble, and, as likely as not, contains men with whom he had little acquaintance or influence. When Newcastle did not exactly know what to do about certain Members, he assigned them to one of his political or official drudges, Barrington or Kinnoull, James West or Andrew Stone.

Of the smaller groups, Nos. 9–18 [2] can be described as predominantly oligarchical, that of Lord Bateman is of a mixed character,[3] Nos. 20 and 21 are territorial (Surrey and Essex), No. 22 can be reckoned as quasi-professional (Albemarle, the political secretary of the Duke of Cumberland, was asked to summon four officers, of whom three belonged to the Duke's household), Nos. 23–5 were those of Newcastle's 'drudges'; Gashry (No. 26) was the intermediary between the Treasury and John Buller, the manager of East and West Looe; Wilkinson (No. 27), Newcastle's chief steward and political agent in Yorkshire; while lists Nos. 28–36 were of people asked to exercise their personal powers of persuasion with relatives or friends over whom they had little, if any, enforceable influence.

---

[1] The summoning of the naval officers through the First Lord of the Admiralty had the additional advantage of providing them automatically with leave of absence, if required.   [2] See p. 205.

[3] Two of the Members in it were dependent on the Duke of Marlborough, Bateman's cousin and patron, and the other three sat for constituencies in which Bateman had dealings.

Even the old Duchess of Newcastle had to write letters inviting the attendance of four Members of Parliament, one nephew and three cousins.

With Newcastle's survey we may compare the 'State of the English Members of the House of Commons', preserved among the Liverpool Papers. Totals only are given in that register, and not the names of the Members included in them, and the calculations were probably made on the basis of the annotated list of English and Welsh Members drawn up for Bute about 15 December 1761.[1] This paper may possibly have been prepared at the time of Newcastle's resignation, to gauge the chances of carrying on the Government without, or even against, him. In these circumstances the bedrock basis would be sought of each man's politics, and mere friendships would be disregarded. The knowledge and judgment of the man, or men, by whom the paper was compiled are, however, in many cases open to criticism and doubt, and I do not put forward this register, any more than that of Newcastle, as an authoritative statement from which single entries could be safely quoted. Still, here too, the general picture is correct : the large groups in Parliament were of a political or official, and not of an oligarchic, private, character, and the groups directed by territorial magnates or borough patrons were but tiny clusters in the Parliamentary sands. I preserve here the order adopted in the original.[2] (See facing page.)

The lists of Newcastle and Bute agree in putting the following of the Duke of Bedford at ten Members and that of the Duke of Cumberland at three or four, and in knowing as yet no 'Grenvilles'; but these groups are sometimes credited with considerable importance even in 1761.[3] The reason seems obvious : as the negotiations of 1767, for a coalition between the Rockinghams, the Bedfords, and the Grenvilles, happen to be known, and more relevant data are lacking, the politics

---

[1] See above, pp. 175-8.   [2] Add. MSS. 38334, ff. 269-70.
[3] See, e.g., C. W. Alvord, *The Mississippi Valley in British Politics* (1917), vol. i. pp. 31-2 : 'The principal Whig offshoots in 1760, besides that of the Old Whigs, were the followers of the Duke of Cumberland, the Bedfordites, the George Grenville faction, and the adherents of William Pitt'.

Government . . .	44	Lowther 3
Newcastle and Government jointly	43	Lord Egmont . . . 4
		Lord Egremont . . . 1
Bute	76	Duke of Bolton . . . 1
Newcastle	59	Lord Gower 2
Tory [1]	67	Duke of Rutland . . . 4
Fox	22	Lord Sandwich . . . 3
Pitt [2]	19	Lord Weymouth . . . 4
Bedford . . .	10	Lord Exeter 3
Hardwicke	11	Duke of Marlborough . . 3
Admiralty	15	Lord Halifax . . . 2
Rockingham	6	Lord Melcombe . . . 1
Devonshire	5	Lord Bathurst . . . 2
Duke of Cumberland . .	3	C. Townshend . . . 2
Duke of Dorset [3] . . .	9	Lord Suffolk . . . 1
Lord Powis	7	Lord Northumberland . 1
Lord Archer	4	Lord Bristol 1
Lord Bruce [4]	4	K. Clayton 2
Lord Shelburne . . .	2	Lord Orford 1
Mr. Legge [5]	4	Lord Pembroke . . . 2
Lord Buckinghamshire .	3	Lord Feversham . . . 1
Mr. Nugent	4	Lord Oxford 1
Lord Darlington . . .	4	Lord Foley 1

[1] The Tories who had any connexion with Bute, Pitt, Fox, or Bedford are obviously included in their groups.

[2] This figure obviously includes a number of Tories.

[3] The figure here given is a vast exaggeration; even if to the two Members for Dorset's pocket borough of East Grinstead we add two Members for Hythe and one for Dover, where he had a certain influence as Warden of the Cinque Ports (though it is very doubtful in how far Glanville and Simpson can be counted as his men), we are still short of this estimate.

[4] This list corresponds to that of James Brudenell in Newcastle's register.

[5] This probably corresponds to 'Gashry' in Newcastle's register; Legge had no seats or boroughs of his own, but had the greatest influence with John Buller, the manager of East and West Looe. If this register was compiled about the time of Newcastle's resignation (which took place on 26 May), the change would be natural, as Gashry died on 19 May after having, for a few weeks, been given up by the doctors.

of 1761 are often discussed in terms of later years, which is wholly inadmissible.

In 1754 there was a Cumberland party, in 1761 there was practically none ; in 1765 there was one again, but resting on quite a different basis. In 1754 *The* Duke was Captain-General of the British Army and was looked up to by those intent on military promotion ; Fox was Secretary at War and Cumberland's political agent, and they pooled their influence, military and political ; Sandwich and Bedford were friends and political associates of Cumberland's ; and in case of the King's death, Cumberland, though not Regent, would have played an important part in the Council. When after Klosterzeven (September 1757) he resigned his command, he forfeited, with the military patronage, his own influence in Parliament ; when, on the accession of George III, Fox turned to Bute, Cumberland lost his able Parliamentary manager ; and when in the autumn of 1762 both Fox and Sandwich definitely abandoned him, his group in the House of Commons was reduced to two members of his household, Lord Ancram and General Fitzwilliam.[1] And when at the end of 1762 Fox wished that Cumberland's disapproval of the Peace Treaty should not be openly declared by members of his 'family' voting against it in the House of Commons, he conceived the idea of doing away altogether with the remnant of the Cumberland group. Lord Ancram was paid £4000 for withdrawing from Parliament, and on 30 November 1762 Fox wrote to Shelburne : 'Pray get Lord Ancram's seat vacated. It is the affair of a quarter of an hour and if not done before 'tis known may be prevented . . .' ; and added in a postscript : 'When Ancram's is done, should not Fitzwilliam ask leave to do the same ?'[2] In 1765 Cumber-

---

[1] In October 1761 Lord Albemarle, Cumberland's political secretary, was requested by Newcastle to secure the attendance of four officers connected with the Duke : Lord Ancram, John Fitzwilliam, John Boscawen, and Sir John Mordaunt. As a matter of fact Boscawen, together with the rest of his family, had already entered the political orbit of Bute, and Mordaunt held Court office.

[2] Shelburne Papers at Bowood. The deal was not carried through immediately, and on 9 December 1762 both Ancram and Fitzwilliam voted against the preliminaries of the Peace Treaty ; but on 23 December Newcastle wrote to Devonshire : 'There is one circumstance which shews how desirous they are . . . not to have any of the Duke's family against them.

land once more stood in the forefront of politics, as the dynastic leader of the Opposition, but his following now bore no resemblance whatsoever to that of 1754.

Whoever in the eighteenth century had the 'attractive power' of office, received an accession of followers, and whoever retained it for some time, was able to form a party; such parties, barring cases of exceptional mismanagement, would not break up at once on the loss of office: it was natural for those who had held and lost their places together to remain united, bound as they were by common friendships and hostilities. But while some remained true to their friends from disinterested motives, and others because they believed in collective bargaining and expected to do better by going in and out as a group, there were always some who could not, or would not, wait, and made, therefore, their individual agreements. Thus every single group in opposition was bound to melt, even if Opposition as a whole was on the increase: for the basis of the various groups was eminently personal.

It was when Grenville was at the head of the Treasury that he, who in October 1761 had told Newcastle that he had 'no friends',[1] acquired a following; and similarly it was in office that the Duke of Bedford welded together his group of peers, most of them his relatives. An analysis of the Bedfords and Grenvilles in 1766–67 shows how those groups were built up, and, although such a study carries us beyond the period covered by this volume, it is included here because it illustrates the nature of its politics. There are two lists among the Newcastle Papers giving the names of those who voted in the minority in February 1766, both in the handwriting of Sir William Meredith: the first, containing 134 names, relates to the 'Division on Mr. Grenville's motion for an address to the Crown, to enforce the Stamp Act'[2] (7 February); the second, containing 168 names, to the 'Division on the Repeal of the

His Royal Highness told me, that my Lord Ancram had accepted four thousand pounds to vacate his seat in Parliament' (Add. MSS. 32945, f. 345). Ancram had since 1747 represented Richmond (Yorks.), the pocket borough of his brother-in-law the 4th Earl of Holdernesse; Richmond was now sold to Laurence Dundas, 'the Nabob of the North', a late army contractor.

[1] See below, pp. 218-19.   [2] Add. MSS. 32974, f. 167.

Stamp Act being read the first time' [1] (22 February). Each time the Opposition is grouped under the headings of Bute, Grenville, Bedford, and Tories, though — and this is an important point — these two lists, drawn up by Sir William Meredith at a fortnight's interval and sent to Newcastle together,[2] do not invariably place a Member in the same group ; in many cases it was indeed difficult to say how a man should be classified whom the Grenville-Bedford Government had inherited from Bute, and who now voted against the Repeal of the Stamp Act, to which all three groups were opposed. Next there are two lists, also in Meredith's handwriting, which classify the Members who voted in the division of 27 February 1767 on the reduction of the land tax. The majority list contains the names of the Bedfords, Grenvilles, Tories, and Rockinghams ; that of the minority, of the 'King's Friends', and of the followers of Bute and Chatham. Lastly, there is a paper marked 'Parliamentary Lists, March 2, 1767', in the handwriting of Newcastle's secretary, which classifies 547 out of 558 Members.

The two division lists of 1766 yield the following figures :

	7 February	22 February
Bute . . .	37	43
Grenville . .	37	43
Bedford . .	34	41
Tories . .	27	41

Taking the list of February 22 for basis, and adding to it the names which appear on 7 February only, we obtain this table :

Bute	44	
Grenville . . .	47	89
Bedford . . .	42	
Tories . . .	43	

The division list of 27 February 1767 gives the following results :

Grenvilles . . .	44	66
Bedfords . . .	22	

[1] Add. MSS. 32974, f. 169.
[2] See letter from Meredith to Newcastle, 10 March 1766, *ibid*. f. 165.

Tories   .   .   . 73
Rockinghams   .   . 67
King's Friends .   . 73⎫
Bute .   .   .   . 43⎬ 188
Chatham   .   .   . 72⎭

Lastly, Newcastle's list of March 1767, which is only eleven
short of the full House, divides it as follows:

For the Administration   232
Tories   91
Friends to last Administration [the Rockinghams] 101
Bedfords and Grenvilles 54
Doubtful or absent 69
                                                 ———
                                                 547

The differences between the lists of Meredith and that of
Newcastle are even greater than mere numbers would suggest,
for in no case is the smaller figure completely included in the
larger; of the 66 Grenvilles and Bedfords of Meredith's list
and of the 54 of Newcastle's, only 44 are identical.[1] Were
we to accept as a follower of Bedford or Grenville every
Member named as such in either list, we should still, in 1767,
obtain a total of only 75, or 14 short of the number mentioned
in the necessarily less complete division lists of February
1766. The groups were melting, as they always did when out
of office.

Who were the 75 men still classified in 1767 as Bedfords
or Grenvilles? Half of them, and three-fourths of those who
are classed as Bedfords and Grenvilles both by Meredith and
Newcastle, were nominees and friends of the Duke of Bedford
and of the noblemen allied to him, or were men who had
served under Grenville during the years 1763–65. In the first
category there are seven Members returned entirely or largely
on the influence of the Duke of Bedford;[2] two, returned by

[1] Of the 21 added by Meredith, eleven are classed by Newcastle as
'Administration', three as Tories, three as Rockinghams, three as 'doubtful
or absent', and one is omitted altogether. Of the ten added by Newcastle,
five are omitted by Meredith, two are classed by him as Tories, two as
'Butes', and one as a follower of Rockingham.

[2] His son, Lord Tavistock, and R. H. Ongley, M.P.'s for Beds.;
F. Herne and R. Vernon, for Bedford; R. Rigby and R. A. Neville, for
Tavistock; and Alexander Forrester, M.P. for Okehampton.

his brother-in-law, Lord Gower; [1] two, by his nephew, the
Duke of Bridgwater; [2] two, by the Duke of Marlborough, [3]
who was Bedford's son-in-law; and one by Lord Bolingbroke, [4] Marlborough's brother-in-law; four Members returned
on the interest of Lord Sandwich, [5] and three on that of Lord
Weymouth; [6] lastly, four friends returned for boroughs not
controlled by those peers: [7] together 25 Members. Of those
who had held places of responsibility and business in the
Grenville Administration and were now out of office, and who
are not included in the previous groups, there were 12: Grenville himself, and Sir John Turner, T. O. Hunter, and James
Harris, who had been Lords of the Treasury; Dr. Hay and
Thomas Pitt, who had sat at the Board of Admiralty; [8] Lord
Orwell, Edward Bacon, and Bamber Gascoyne, late Commissioners for Trade and Plantations; Fletcher Norton, Grenville's Attorney-General; Whately, his Secretary to the
Treasury; and W. G. Hamilton, Chancellor of the Exchequer in Ireland. None of the eleven here associated with
Grenville had been connected with him in 1761; and all of
them now appear both in Meredith's and in Newcastle's list
as his adherents, being united to him by the bond of a clearly
political connexion.

The remaining 37 include some friends of Grenville and of
Lord Temple, and two of the late Lord Egremont; a few men
whom Grenville had returned on the Government interest
when at the Treasury; four nominees of peers connected with

---

[1] L. Dundas and T. Gilbert, M.P.'s for Newcastle-under-Lyme.

[2] R. Wood and Lord Hinchingbrooke, M.P.'s for Brackley.

[3] His brother, Lord Charles Spencer, M.P. for Oxfordshire, and
Anthony Keck, M.P. for Woodstock.

[4] H. St. John, M.P. for Wootton Basset.

[5] Lord Carysfort, M.P. for Hunts.; E. Montagu and R. Jones, for
Huntingdon; and J. Stephenson, returned for Mitchell on the interest of
Charles Courtenay, a nephew of Lord Sandwich.

[6] H. F. Thynne and W. Lynch, M.P.'s for Weobley; and E. Thurlow,
M.P. for Tamworth.

[7] T. Brand, a friend of Bedford; Henry Seymour, a half-brother
of Sandwich; T. Caswall, who seems to have been connected with Bridgwater, and had a secret service pension from Grenville; and Colonel
Mackay.

[8] Thomas Pitt remained for a few months at the Admiralty under the
Rockingham Administration, but passed into Opposition before the end of
1765.

Grenville ; etc., etc. On the whole, they are a motley collection, and few of them appear both in Newcastle's list and in
Meredith's list.

It seems that the reliable part of the Bedford-Grenville
group in March 1767 should not be placed at more than 50 :
the two years 1763–65 were sufficient to create a Parliamentary
army where there had been practically none in 1761, and two
further years, 1765–67, to reduce it to a size at which only
the peculiar circumstances of the time could make it count.
It is mistaking the structure of politics at that time to talk
about various Members as if they had been returned in
1761 on a party-ticket by which they could be described
throughout that Parliament.

II. THE PERSONNEL

Charles James Fox entered Parliament at the age of nineteen, and the younger Pitt became First Lord of the Treasury
at twenty-four. Facts like these seem to have fostered the
idea that the House of Commons consisted largely of immature youths, a belief which apparently prevailed even at that
time. In 1776, a careful observer, Samuel Curwen — a Judge
of the Admiralty at Boston who had come to England as a
loyalist refugee — referred to the House of Commons as 'that
assembly of untutored, inexperienced youths, (for half, I
believe, have not seen thirty,) called the Parliament of Great
Britain, or the great council of the nation'.[1] When he wrote
these words, men under thirty formed in reality about one-
eighth, not one-half, of the House — more or less the same
proportion as men over sixty.

Horace Walpole, George Selwyn, and Edward Gibbon have
left an inexhaustible fund of anecdote about 'the world at
large' (which Gibbon once accurately defined as 'the few
people I happen to converse with'), and in descriptions based
on those sources the House of Commons appears as an assembly
of macaronis, gamblers, wits, and butts, of placemen and

---

[1] *Journal and Letters of the late Samuel Curwen*, ed. by George Atkinson
Ward (1842), p. 87.

parasites. But again, how big a proportion of the House can the circles of those three men have formed?

What, then, was the real character and composition of the Parliament which had to deal with America? What was the age and standing of its Members, the duration of their membership, and what was their professional character, if any? Statistical data are the biographical facts of an assembly.

Age, and Tenure of Seats

In this volume I deal with the Parliament of 1761 only, and synchronism being essential in a statistical survey, I base mine on the names which appear in the returns made at that general election. I include therefore the six Members who died before Parliament met on 3 November 1761,[1] and the three who had succeeded to peerages;[2] also one who was subsequently unseated on petition.[3] A difficulty arises from seven Members having been returned simultaneously for two constituencies:[4] if the seats which they gave up were treated as vacant, there would not be the full complement; while by counting their holders twice over, we might land ourselves in absurdities. In this case I have therefore to deviate from the strict 'unity of time' and to treat the men returned in their place[5] as if they had been elected at the general election of 1761.

I have been able to ascertain the exact or approximate date

[1] Henry Cornwallis, who died in April on his way back from the army in Germany; Sir William P. Williams, killed in action on 27 April; Sir James Colebrooke (died on 10 May); Henry Finch (25 May); Henry Lambton (26 June 1761); and Thomas Pitt (17 July). George Treby died on 5 November 1761, and Thomas Lister on 3 December, so that they, too, probably did not take their seats.

[2] Lord Fitzmaurice, now Earl of Shelburne (Ir.) and Baron Wycombe in England; George Edgcumbe, 2nd Lord Edgcumbe; and John Campbell, who had succeeded to the dukedom of Argyll a day before his election, but the news of it had not reached the constituency in time.

[3] John Levett, M.P. for Lichfield. In the case of the double return for Radnor Borough, I take Edward Lewis, who retained the seat.

[4] Sir James Lowther (Cumberland and Westmorland), Lord Egmont (Bridgwater and Ilchester), Lord Thomond (Minehead and Winchelsea), Andrew Archer (Coventry and Bramber), Lord George Sackville (Hythe and East Grinstead), Lord Frederick Campbell (Dumbarton and Ayr Burghs), and Archibald Montgomery (Co. Ayr and Wigtown Burghs).

[5] Sir Wilfred Lawson, William Wilson, Thomas Sewell, Lord Winterton, Sir Thomas Hales, Alexander Wedderburn, and Keith Stewart.

of birth of 533 of the 558 Members returned at the general election of 1761 :

Born before	1701	. . 65
,, between	1701–10	. . 110
,, ,,	1711–20	. . 125
,, ,,	1721–30	. . 149
,, ,,	1731–40	. . 84
		533

Although a large proportion of the remaining 25 were elderly self-made men (whose age it is often difficult to ascertain), and therefore the above figures probably make the House appear slightly younger than it was, none the less the first three groups, of men above forty, comprise 300 Members, *i.e.* more than 56 per cent of those whose age is known to me. The group between thirty and forty is the most numerous of all and accounts for 28 per cent; and only 84 Members, *i.e.* 16 per cent, were below thirty [1] (one of them was under age when elected).[2] Seeing that men ripened quicker in the eighteenth century than they do now, the composition of the House of 1761 was eminently respectable as to age.

What previous political experience had the Members returned at that general election ? What was the date of their *first* entry into Parliament ?

142 had entered it before Walpole resigned at the end of January 1742.

122 between the fall of Walpole and the death of Henry Pelham on 6 March 1754.

162 between the death of Pelham and that of George II on 25 October 1760.

1 in January 1761.

126 at the general election of 1761.

5 replaced Members returned simultaneously for two constituencies at that general election.[3]

---

[1] It is stated above that about one-eighth of the Members in 1776 were below thirty, while 16 per cent in 1761 makes about one-seventh; but 1776 was two years after the general election, whereas in 1761 I take Parliament in the very year of the general election.

[2] Henry Cornwallis, born on 10 September 1740; he never entered Parliament, as he died in April 1761 on his way back from Germany, where he had been on active service as a captain in the 24th Regiment of Foot.

[3] The other two returned for seats thus vacated, Thomas Sewell and Sir Thomas Hales, had sat in the House before.

Thus, roughly speaking, one-fourth of the Members of 1761 had served under Walpole, one-half under Pelham, three-fourths under Newcastle as George II's Minister, and only one-fourth were new Members, their number being about the same as at the two preceding general elections.[1] That the change on those occasions was almost a constant, speaks of its nature : it did not result from a party 'sweeping' the country, but represented the sum-total of individual cases arising from personal or local circumstances ; it was like the seasonal moulting of birds.

The sum-total of the change which came over the House during the lifetime of the Parliament of 1761 was greater than that wrought by the general election ; during the eighty-two months of its existence

101 of the original Members died.
 29 entered the House of Lords (17 by inheritance, 10 by new creations, 2 by being given peerages which had been in abeyance).
 24 vacated their seats.
  1 was unseated.
  1 (John Wilkes) was expelled from the House.
___
156, *i.e.* 28 per cent of the Members returned in 1761, left the House of Commons before its dissolution.

The mortality in that Parliament is remarkable, but then it was an old House ; and in spite of the extensive renewal of its personnel during the years 1761–68, an exceptional number of men who had never sat in Parliament before, entered it in 1768 — obviously many of the old men came to feel that they could not readjust themselves to the new conditions. It was during the seven years following on the accession of George III, and not during the first year of his reign, that the great change occurred both in the governing circles [2] and in the House of Commons. Here is a computation of men elected in 1768 who had never served in Parliament under George II :

¹ See *The Structure of Politics*, p. 159.
² See above, pp. 60-63.

Of the 132 Members first re-turned in 1761 . . .	64 were re-elected in 1768.
Of the 138 Members first re-turned at by-elections, 1761–1768	102 were re-elected in 1768.
At the general election of 1768 .	164 Members were returned who had never sat in the House before.

330

Thus by the time of Newcastle's death, in November 1768, the men returned before George III's accession formed only about two-fifths of the House.

The average term in Parliament of the 558 Members returned in 1761 — even though the term of many was shortened by the changed circumstances — amounts to twenty-two years, which would seem very high when judged by present-day standards. But as a good many seats in the eighteenth century were of a proprietary character, men were able to acquire them at an age at which they could hardly have secured the confidence of a real electorate ; and as seats of that type called for pecuniary sacrifices rather than for personal exertions, many Members continued to hold them to an age at which few would have undergone the bustle of contested popular elections. Lastly, as the majority of Members 'sat on their own interest', and not *qua* representatives of organised parties, changes in personnel were seldom of a political character, and consequently there was a much greater permanency of tenure. At the general election of 1929 only four Members were returned who had sat in the House for thirty continuous years, including two in the very front rank of politics and one for a constituency of a unique character ; [1] at that of 1761 there were no less than 19,[2] presenting a picture of Parliamentary still-life rather than of great political achievement. There was Phillips Gybbon, the Father of the House, M.P. for Rye from 1707 till his death in

---

[1] Mr. T. P. O'Connor, Mr. Lloyd George, Sir Austen Chamberlain, and Col. W. G. Nicholson.

[2] Besides, there were four Members who had been in Parliament 30 years or more but whose tenure was not uninterrupted.

1762 ' [1] Benjamin Bathurst, first returned in 1713, and the father, not of the House but, by two wives, of thirty-six children ; Sir John Rushout, who, having sat in Parliament 1713–68, withdrew from it at the age of eighty-three, much improved in mind and temper — in his youth he had been 'choleric', but Nash, who visited him about 1775, found 'his memory, good humour, and politeness . . . in their full bloom' ; [2] William Aislabie, who represented Ripon 1721–81, and about whom his only biographer records that 'the contemplation of the beauties of nature, and rural occupations, formed his chief and unceasing delight' ; [3] Henry Finch, whose father thought that he would 'never be able to live', but who, as Member for Malton from 1724 till May 1761, secured for himself 'a provision out of Parliament' ; [4] etc., etc.

Social and Professional Standing

What was the social composition of the House elected in 1761 ? Eighty-one Members were sons of English peers and 10 of Scottish peers ; of these 91,[5] 35 were courtesy lords. Further, 23 Members of the House were Irish peers, and 5 sons of Irish peers. This makes a total of 119, *i.e.* 21 per cent of the House. (I have left out of account more distant relatives of peers, even if heirs-apparent to their peerages ; [6] classifica-

[1] About him see 'Historical Anecdotes of the Family of Gibbon', by Sir Egerton Brydges, in *The Gentleman's Magazine*, 1788, vol. ii. p. 699, and 'Memoirs of the Family of Mr. Gibbon', *ibid.*, 1797, vol. ii. p. 1109.

[2] See *History of Worcestershire*, vol. i. p. 99. In the days of Sir Robert Walpole, both Gybbon and Rushout had been Opposition Whigs ; subsequently they became regular Pelhamites.

[3] John Richard Walbran, in the *Genealogical and Biographical Memoir of the Lords of Studley, in Yorkshire* (1814), p. 21, a book so rare that the British Museum has only a typewritten copy of it ; Aislabie deserves, however, to be remembered for having purchased Fountains Abbey and preserved it from further decay.   [4] See *The Structure of Politics*, pp. 19-20.

[5] In *The Structure of Politics*, p. 355, I put their number at 93 ; but I now exclude Charles Fitzroy and N. Berkeley, whom I had previously counted — about them see the following two footnotes. I have not included in either figure two illegitimate sons of peers, Ph. Stanhope and Charles Fitzroy Scudamore.

[6] I have even to omit Charles Fitzroy, brother of the 3rd Duke of Grafton, as their father, Lord Augustus Fitzroy, died *vivente patre*. Were I to count Charles Fitzroy, I should have to count him as a courtesy lord, whereas he was never given that standing.

tion is much more difficult than those who have never tried their hand at it would suppose,[1] and rigid lines must be drawn.) Further, there were 70 baronets in the House, and 28 sons of baronets. Of the remaining 341 Members, at the utmost 40 had 'no pretence to arms'. But even the men 'of no family' were less 'self-made' than contemporaries tried to make out ; the story of a man's rise usually comes to be embroidered, to prove his mean standing or to extol his perseverance and achievements.[2]

The House of Commons returned in 1761 included 59 army officers,[3] 21 naval officers,[4] 7 regular civil servants, 5 diplomats,

---

[1] Should, *e.g.*, N. Berkeley, who subsequently came into a peerage which had been in abeyance, be counted as the son of a peer ? Even though his claim was derived through his father, I do not include him. Again, should Simon Fraser be included whose father forfeited the peerage through attainder ? I think on the whole, yes, as he was born the son of a peer. (The estates were restored to him in 1774 ; whereas for the title, the attainder was reversed only in 1857.) None the less this inclusion results in a bad anomaly : for, had not Lord Lovat been attainted, Simon Fraser would have been in 1761 either a Scottish peer and not eligible anywhere, or the eldest son of a Scottish peer, and as such not eligible in Scotland. And here is another curious case : Archibald, 3rd Duke of Argyll, died on 16 April 1761 ; his cousin and heir, Lieut.-Gen. John Campbell, was elected for Dumbartonshire on 17 April, the news not having reached Scotland. His eldest son was to have stood for Glasgow Burghs, but as the death of the 3rd Duke of Argyll had become known before that election, John Campbell, jun. — now Lord Lorne — had to be replaced by his younger brother, Lord Frederick Campbell, whom I naturally include among the sons of peers, while his father appears in the same list as a commoner, and the son of a commoner.

[2] Here is an example : *The City Biography*, published in 1800, alleges about Sir Samuel Fludyer, 1st bart., that 'his origin was so low, as to be employed in attending the pack-horses, which were formerly used to bring cloth from the west country to London' (p. 82). In reality his father was a well-to-do London clothier, his mother a daughter of Francis de Monsallier, a Huguenot, and young Samuel was educated at Westminster School.

[3] In *The Structure of Politics*, p. 25, I put their number at 64 ; but since I computed that list I have found that four Members whom I had originally included in it, had by 1761 given up their commissions (Lord George Manners, Spencer Compton, Jenison Shafto, and Sir George Warren), and that the statement about Lord Mandeville in *The Complete Peerage*, that he 'entered the army in 1757', is not correct — at that time he held a commission in the militia only. Neither my original nor the revised figure includes Joseph Yorke, who was still on the army list, but who, since 1748, had been in the Diplomatic Service.

[4] I ought perhaps to put the number of naval officers at 22, but there are two doubtful cases : (*a*) At the general election of 1761, Wigtownshire was contested between John Hamilton of Bargeny, a friend of Lord Bute, and John Murray of Broughtoun, a friend of Lord Rockingham ; Hamilton was returned, but Murray petitioned and was likely to succeed, when

some 40 practising lawyers,[1] and 50 merchants ; thus 182, *i.e.* almost one-third of the Members, were actually engaged in professions, while a good many of the older men had practised them but had retired. Moreover, there were the professional politicians, the country squires, etc. The picture so often drawn of the House as mainly composed of idle youths is not borne out by statistics.

With the character of the various professional groups in the House I have dealt at some length in *The Structure of Politics at the Accession of George III* ; here I limit myself to the bare statistics of the House of 1761.

The army officers, as might be expected, formed the most aristocratic professional group in the House : 29 of the 59 were sons of peers, and 2 were Irish peers, 21 held Court office, and a large proportion served in the Guards ; 14 army officers sat for Scottish constituencies (naturally all Scotsmen), comprising almost one-third of the Scottish representation, whereas the remaining 45 formed only about one-eleventh of that of England, and there was not a single army officer among the Welsh Members in 1761. Moreover, of the 45 army officers representing English constituencies, 2 were Scotsmen (Lord Ancram, M.P. for Richmond, and John Craufurd, M.P. for Berwick) ; in other words, Scotsmen formed more than

through the intermediary of Bute, Newcastle, and Rockingham, a compromise was concluded. Wigtown Burghs were vacant, as at the general election Archibald Montgomery had been returned simultaneously for Ayrshire and Wigtown Burghs, and chose to sit for the county. It seems that in his place Lord Galloway, who controlled Wigtown Burghs, intended to return his second son, Captain Keith Stewart, R.N. But on 11 February, Rockingham sent to Galloway asking him to delay the election and to agree to 'Mr. Murray's being Member for the county and Capt. Stewart having a post ship, for which he is to bring Mr. Hamilton in for the boroughs' (Add. MSS. 32934, ff. 279-80) ; and on 12 February, the Lord Advocate sent a note to Newcastle that 'he could not find Lord Garlies yesterday', and that 'the day for the election of the Galloway Burrows stands fixed for the 19th instant' (*ibid.* f. 305). That day Stewart was returned, but almost immediately vacated his seat in favour of Hamilton. (*b*) The other case is that of Vice-Admiral Frankland, who had practically withdrawn from the Service, and who, although he still continued on the flag list, after about 1756 'appeared no more in the character of a naval commander' (see Charnock, *Biographia Navalis* (1797), vol. v. p. 20). I am therefore doubtful whether, strictly speaking, he should still rank among the naval officers, and on a rough compromise I put their number at 21.

[1] See *The Structure of Politics*, p. 44.

one-fourth among the army officers, but less than one-tenth of the whole House. Of the English army Members, only 3 represented counties, of the Scottish, 12; the Scottish nobility and gentry were poor and filled the Services. Of the English army Members, about half sat for boroughs owned or controlled by their own families, and only one partly on the Government interest.[1]

Although among the army officers there was naturally a good sprinkling of young men, exceeding their average in the House, even here the young did not form any very considerable proportion. Only of 11 was the age thirty or less, of 42 it was between thirty and sixty, and 6 were more than sixty years old. Nor were there many 'young subaltern puppys', whom Pitt and Chesterfield would have liked to exclude from the House; [2] there was one field-marshal, one full general, 16 lieutenant-generals, 9 major-generals,[3] and 22 colonels and lieutenant-colonels; and only 2 majors and 8 captains. As Pitt's proposal had been to bar army officers below the rank of lieut.-colonel, it would, if carried, have excluded only 10 of the 59 returned in 1761.

Of the 21 naval officers, two were admirals, four vice-admirals, and two rear-admirals; [4] five were sons of peers,[5] and one an Irish peer. Nine of the naval officers sat on the Government interest, mainly for Admiralty boroughs.[6]

Among the 50 merchants returned in 1761, two only, Sir Ellis Cunliffe, M.P. for Liverpool, and George Lind, Lord Provost of Edinburgh and its Member, were not 'London merchants'. Besides these, the four Members for the City and the two for Southwark were practically the only *bona fide* representatives of the commercial communities which returned them to Parliament; perhaps Sir Samuel Fludyer, M.P. for Chippenham, and William Willy, M.P. for Devizes, should be added, as they, though settled in London, continued in the cloth trade of their boroughs; and possibly also Joseph

---

[1] See *The Structure of Politics*, p. 25.   [2] *Ibid.* p. 26.
[3] Besides Joseph Yorke, who still appeared among them.
[4] See *The Structure of Politics*, pp. 29-31.
[5] Keith Stewart is not included.
[6] See *The Structure of Politics*, p. 31-2.

Gulston, M.P. for Poole, who had some connexion with the Newfoundland trade of which Poole was the centre. Certainly not one of the remaining 39 merchant Members had any genuine professional connexion with the borough he represented, and, in fact, practically all sat for corrupt or pocket boroughs, chiefly in the southern counties. The merchants, as one would expect, formed the oldest group in the House : the age of at least three-fifths of them was above forty-five ; while the youngest, such as Francis Child, John Thomlinson, and Philip Fonnereau, were sons of rich merchants, brought up at public schools and Universities, and not behind the counter.

'Placemen'

Of the 558 Members returned in 1761, about 300 seem to have held no place, office, contract, or pension from the Government. Although in compiling my list of the House of Commons I put down whatever I was able to trace about every single Member, I prefer not to commit myself to specific figures ; they are sure to contain a 'margin of error'. Here or there I may have marked against a Member a place which he held no longer, and I am certain to have omitted others. It is especially difficult to trace places held 'in trust' for Members, or fixed payments received by them from office-holders on whom they were billeted,[1] as these things naturally do not appear in any contemporary Registers or Calendars ; nor is it easy to classify various business transactions — e.g., is a regular underwriter of Government loans to be considered a contractor ?

In saying that 300 Members had nothing from the Government for their own persons, I do not mean that they received

[1] Thus, e.g., John Butler, M.P. for Sussex, was in receipt of £700 a year from Thomas Steele, of Chichester, who held in trust for him the place of Comptroller of the Excise, incompatible with a seat in Parliament (see Add. MSS. 38335, f. 51, and 32946, f. 179). In the summer of 1761 the sinecure of Searcher of the Customs at Chester, Liverpool, etc., worth £700 p.a., became vacant — 'one of the most valuable sinecures in the gift of the Treasury' — and Newcastle offered his friend John Page, M.P. for Chichester (as the place was inconsistent with a seat in the House of Commons), that he should choose some one upon whom he could 'depend' ; Robert Bull was appointed on Page's recommendation (see Add. MSS. 32924, ff. 203 and 267, and 32925, f. 79).

no favours or that they were really independent, nor do I mean to draw a sharp distinction between them and the other 260.[1] Many of those 300 were indebted for their seats to Government support, had their relatives, friends, or constituents provided for, were brothers, sons, or dependants of men closely connected with the Government, etc. On the other hand, the 260 'marked' Members include men who had their places for life and therefore irrespective of their political conduct, a number of officers in the army or navy who held nothing except their commissions, and lastly, men to whom their places were of very minor importance and who were ready to give them up at any time.

At the general election of 1761, four chiefs of Government departments were returned to the House of Commons : William Pitt, Secretary of State in the Southern Department ; Lord Barrington, Chancellor of the Exchequer ;[2] Charles Townshend, Secretary at War ; and Lord Ligonier, Commander-in-Chief in Great Britain and Master-General of the Ordnance ; moreover, Charles Pratt, the Attorney-General, and Charles Yorke, the Solicitor-General. The Treasury, the second Secretaryship of State, the Admiralty, and the Board of Trade were, in April 1761, held by peers (Newcastle, Bute, Anson, and Sandys).

Next there were the members of the three Boards, of the Treasury, Admiralty, and of Trade and Plantations, at which the seats were by no means sinecures. The three Commoners who sat with Newcastle and Barrington at the Board of the Treasury — Lord North, James Oswald, and Gilbert Elliot — were hard-working men, and the latter two, first-class financial experts. The five Commoners at the Admiralty, George Hay, T. O. Hunter, Hans Stanley, Thomas Pelham, and Lord Villiers, were perhaps not the best possible selections, but at least the first four were undoubtedly men of business. At the Board of Trade, there were six Members of the House of

[1] There were only 558, and not 560, Members, but I want to speak in round, and not in specific, figures.

[2] It might be questioned whether the Chancellor of the Exchequer should in 1761 rank as 'chief' of a department, seeing that the First Lord of the Treasury still presided at its Board ; but having stated the doubt and limitation, I leave him among the 'chiefs'.

Commons in April 1761. Together, there were 14 of these ministerial juniors, filling to some extent the place now held by Parliamentary Under-Secretaries, etc.

Of regular civil servants, doing full-time office work, seven, to my knowledge, were returned at the general election of 1761 : the two Secretaries to the Treasury (James West and Samuel Martin), the two Secretaries to the Admiralty (John Cleveland and Philip Stephens), the Surveyor of the Ordnance (Sir Charles Frederick),[1] and two Under-Secretaries of State (Robert Wood and Charles Jenkinson). There were further five diplomats : Andrew Mitchell, Minister at Berlin ; Sir Joseph Yorke, at the Hague ; James Stuart-Mackenzie, at Turin ; Philip Stanhope, at Hamburg ; and Henry Grenville, at Constantinople. Moreover, the following judicial or legal officers should, I think, be included among the civil servants : Thomas Morgan, Advocate-General of the Forces ; Thomas Miller, Lord Advocate of Scotland ; James Hayes and John Hervey, Welsh judges ; Edward Simpson, Judge of the Cinque Ports ; P. C. Webb, Solicitor to the Treasury ; Richard Hussey, Counsel to the Admiralty ; and Sir Matthew Lamb, Counsel to the Board of Trade.

Lastly, there were the Paymasters : Henry Fox, Paymaster of the Forces ; George Grenville, Treasurer of the Navy ; and Francis Gashry, Treasurer and Paymaster of the Ordnance.

Adding all the office-holders hitherto mentioned, we obtain a total of 43 whose places cannot be treated as sinecures.

Next came some 45 holders of 'cushy' jobs or of downright sinecures — I do not include among them any of the preceding 43 who held such places together with posts of real work and responsibility, nor holders of Court office and of sinecures of a naval or military character ; but Tellers of the Exchequer, Comptrollers of the Imprest, of the Pipe, etc., Rangers and Verdurers of various Parks and Forests, officials of the Duchies of Cornwall, Lancaster, etc.

---

[1] I am not certain in how far the place of Principal Storekeeper of the Ordnance, held by A. Wilkinson, M.P., and that of Clerk of Deliveries, held by Chs. Cocks, M.P., were posts of business ; I rather think they were sinecures — anyhow their holders were not ordnance experts like Sir Charles Frederick.

As my list is unlikely to be complete under either heading, we shall probably not be far out if we round off the figures and say that there were about 50 Members actively engaged in the Administration — as ministers or regular civil servants — and about 50 holders of civilian sinecures or semi-sinecures.

Next there were some 42 holders of Court offices, Grooms of the Bedchamber, Equerries or Aides-de-Camp to the King, Clerks of the Board of Green Cloth, of the Wardrobe, etc., Masters of the Household, of the Tennis Courts, of the Foxhounds, the Buckhounds, etc., etc. ; and at least twelve holders of places in the households of other members of the Royal Family.

Of the 59 army officers returned to Parliament in 1761, only about one-third, mostly young men, held no places of profit. Senior men in the service were almost all colonels of regiments — there were 29 of them in Parliament (not including Joseph Yorke, who remained colonel of the 8th Dragoons, though now in the diplomatic service). Eight of these colonels of regiments held, moreover, the military sinecures of governorships or lieut.-governorships of certain islands or castles in Great Britain or Ireland, and 21 of the 59 Army Members held Court office. Deducting the Master-General of the Ordnance and 21 officers holding places at Court who have been included above, the Army adds some 37 servants of the Crown, though only 15 of these remaining 37 can be said to have held places of profit (regiments or governorships), the other 22 holding nothing besides their commissions.

The places of profit in the Navy tenable with seats in Parliament were few : Admiral Isaac Townsend was Governor of Greenwich Hospital ; Charles Saunders, its Treasurer, and Lieut.-General of the Marines ; Sir Piercy Brett, Lord Howe, and Augustus Keppel were Colonels of the Marines (Keppel was, moreover, Groom of the Bedchamber to the King). The main chance of profits for naval officers was in prizes.

Of the 50 merchants returned in 1761, I reckon 37 to have been Government contractors.[1]

[1] See *The Structure of Politics*, p. 48-9.

Lastly, there were, in 1761, 10 Members in receipt of secret service pensions who held no places or sinecures.[1]

Thus, speaking very roughly, I calculate that there were in the House 50 ministers and civil servants, 50 holders of civilian sinecures, another 50 Court officials, 57 officers of the Army and Navy not included under previous headings, 37 Government contractors, and 10 holders of bare secret service pensions. This, I repeat again, is nothing more than a rough estimate, and it would hardly pay to go deeper into the matter ; anyhow, these figures do not represent the voting strength of the Government. Not every one who held a place, office, commission, or pension was truly dependent on the Government, while among those who do not appear in this list, there were many men bound to it by the strongest ties and ever ready to serve it.

[1] A. A'Court, R. Bull, R. Cavendish, J. Dodd, R. Fairfax, H. Finch, A. T. Keck, T. Medlycott, Sir F. Poole, and T. Watson held secret service pensions only ; George and James Brudenell, J. Jeffreys, Sir T. Hales, J. Offley, Lord Parker, and J. Stuart-Mackenzie combined them with places of profit. I include here Bull, Cavendish, and Stuart-Mackenzie, even though the pensions may have been settled on them slightly later ; but they were made to run as from Lady Day 1761

IV

THE HOUSE OF COMMONS AND AMERICA

WHAT acquaintance with the American Colonies had the House in which the Stamp Act was passed and repealed, and in which the Townshend Duties were enacted ? How many of its Members had been to the American Colonies, had connexions with them, or had an intimate knowledge of American affairs ? Were any of them American-born ?

By 1768, when that Parliament was dissolved, nearly all those who during the next fifteen critical years were to rank as the foremost experts on America had entered the House, but they had come in at by-elections and not at the general election of 1761. Whatever other considerations may have contributed to their being chosen, with patrons and leaders their knowledge of American affairs must have counted when these were becoming a major problem in politics and administration, and to those men themselves their interest in America must have been an additional incentive for entering Parliament. Lieut.-Col. Isaac Barré, who had served in America, was returned to Parliament on 5 December 1761 ; the 'omniscient' Richard Jackson, agent for Connecticut and assistant-agent for Massachusetts, on 1 December 1762 ; John Huske, a native of New Hampshire, on 26 April 1763 ; Charles Garth, agent for South Carolina, on 5 January 1765 ; Edmund Burke (agent for New York, 1770–75), on 13 December 1765 ; and Thomas Pownall, who had been Lieut.-Governor of New Jersey, 1755–1757, and Governor of Massachusetts, 1757–60, and whose brother, John Pownall, was Secretary to the Board of Trade and Plantations, on 11 February 1767. Besides these, a few others were returned, less prominent as experts on America, but not unimportant : Anthony Bacon, a merchant who had spent a number of years in Maryland and continued to trade with the southern colonies (and whose brother Thomas was the well-known compiler of the *Laws of Maryland*), was elected on 25 January 1764 ;[1] John Sargent, another merchant, to whom the New York Assembly 'voted a piece of plate for his services in connexion with the Repeal of the Stamp Act'[2] (and to whose care Benjamin Franklin, on the eve of the Revolution, confided his financial affairs in England),[3] on 19 January 1765 ; Admiral Sir Charles Hardy, who had been Governor of New York, 1755–57, on 23 March 1764 ; William Harvey and William Amherst, who had served in America during the Seven Years' War, on 24 February 1763, and 17 November 1766.[4]

Not a single American had been returned at the general election of 1761, though five were to sit in the House between 1763 and 1783 : John Huske, M.P. for Maldon, 1763–73 ; Barlow Trecothick, for the City of London, 1768–74 ; Henry Cruger, for Bristol, 1774–80 (and 1784–90) ; Staats Long Morris, for Elgin Burghs, 1774–84 ; and Paul Wentworth for Saltash, July–September 1780.[5] John Huske had come over to England as a merchant ; Barlow Trecothick and Henry

[1] About him see my essay in the *Journal of Economic and Business History* (Boston, Mass.), November 1929.

[2] See letter from Dennis Deberdt to Stephen Sayre, London, 29 July 1766, *Publications of the Colonial Society of Massachusetts*, vol. xiii. p. 318. Sargent had sat in Parliament, 1757–61, but was left out in the cold in 1761.

[3] See letter from Franklin to Sargent, Philadelphia, 27 June 1775, *Writings*, edited by A. H. Smyth, vol. vi. pp. 406-7.

[4] Among *The Papers of Sir William Johnson* (ed. by A. C. Flick), vol. v. (1927), pp. 116-17, there is a letter from Johnson to John Watts, dated Johnson Hall (N.Y.), 27 March 1766, and dealing with the subject of some new Members of Parliament, unfortunately unnamed ; the letter itself is badly damaged.

> The new Members in the House of [Commons?] may be of service to America with regard to the Stamp Act, but if it is [repealed?] there is a likelihood they will adopt something else to answer their purpose [to which?] we cannot with justice make a like opposition. At all events our late conduct here [　　　] known at home may [　　　] more restrictions and a stricter eye upon this country than [　　　] have met with. . . .

John Watts' *Letter Book*, published by the N.Y. Hist. Soc. (vol. lxi), extends only till 22 December 1765 — the letter to which that of Johnson is the reply, might otherwise have supplied the missing names. As it is, the reader must make his own choice from among those given above.

[5] I refrain from giving here biographical sketches of these American Members, as, with the exception of Huske, none of them sat in the Parliament of 1761 ; I may deal with them in separate essays, or in future volumes, if I resume this work.

Cruger were American merchants settled in London and Bristol; S. L. Morris, a brother of Gouverneur Morris, was an army officer, had married the widow of the 3rd Duke of Gordon, and was returned to Parliament on the Gordon interest; Paul Wentworth was a loyalist and a Government agent. All five were Northerners: Huske and Wentworth from New Hampshire, Trecothick from Boston, Cruger and Morris from New York. It is remarkable that during these years not one Southern planter entered Parliament; [1] and that the slogan that the American Colonies, because of their remote situation, could not be represented in the British Parliament, was started in Virginia and South Carolina, and not in Massachusetts.[2] But with the Southern planters the refusal to entertain the idea of a 'British Union' was not due to differences in outlook, such as might have been alleged in the case of New England Puritans; they were Episcopalians, most of

---

[1] In 1774 William Lee, a Virginian, a brother of Arthur and Richard Henry Lee, unsuccessfully contested Southwark in the Whig interest. He was a London merchant and agent for Virginia.

[2] The earliest official denial that I have found of the possibility of Colonial representation in the British Parliament is in a 'Memorial' which, in December 1764, the General Assembly of Virginia addressed to the House of Lords, and in their 'Remonstrance' to the House of Commons; see *Journals of the House of Burgesses of Virginia, 1761–1765*, ed. by J. P. Kennedy (Richmond, Va., 1907), pp. liv-lviii. No such denial appears in the 'Petition' from the Council and House of Representatives of Massachusetts, of 3 November 1764, nor in the instructions given by the town of Boston to its representatives in the General Council in May 1764, and in September 1765. But James Otis, at that time the leader of the Massachusetts Assembly, indeed favoured the idea of Colonial representation at Westminster — he pleaded 'that the Colonies . . . should . . . be represented in some proportion to their number and estates in the grand legislation of the nation : that this would firmly unite all parts of the British empire in the greatest peace and prosperity; and render it invulnerable and perpetual' (see *The Rights of the British Colonies*, etc., Boston, 1764, p. 99). The instructions which, in September 1765, the House of Representatives of Massachusetts gave to its delegates to the Stamp Act Congress show that meantime the opponents to Colonial representation had gained the upper hand — 'the House think that such a representation of the Colonies as British subjects are to enjoy, would be attended with the greatest difficulty, if it is not absolutely impracticable, and therefore, you are not to urge or consent to any proposal for any representation, if such be made in the Congress'. But the 4th Resolution of the Stamp Act Congress, voted on 19 October 1765 — 'That the people of these Colonies are not, and from their local circumstances, cannot be, represented in the House of Commons in Great Britain' — did not originate with the Massachusetts delegation; as almost all the resolutions of that Congress, it follows closely those voted in September 1764 by the Assembly of South Carolina.

them were educated at English schools, Universities, or at the Inns of Court,[1] and they resembled the English gentry. But probably the very fact that they were squires rooted in their own land, made them averse to entering the territorial assembly of another country. Meantime, whereas a good many merchants from the northern Colonies were settled in trade in Great Britain, there was nothing here for the planters to do, and without that their fortunes were not sufficient to support permanent residence in England, still less to finance British Parliamentary elections. The author of the pamphlet *Remarks on the Letter Addressed to Two Great Men* wrote in 1760 : [2]

With regard to the estates in North America spent in England, I may affirm that from Nova Scotia to Maryland and Virginia there are absolutely none ; . . . even to the southward of this line there are few estates either in number or value spent in England.

. . . The truth is tho' their estates supply them with plenty to live at home, they do not furnish money enough to send them abroad. Excepting Proprietaries,[3] I do not remember that this vast Continent supplies our House of Commons with one single Member.

[1] Joseph Johnson, in the introduction to his *Traditions and Reminiscences chiefly of the American Revolution in the South* (1851), writes that all the Colonials 'who could afford it sent their sons *home* to England for their education, . . . many sent their daughters also'. This was true of the South only, and especially of his own State, South Carolina ; *e.g.*, of the four men who signed the Declaration of Independence on behalf of South Carolina, E. Rutledge had been educated at the Inner Temple ; Th. Lynch at Eton, Gonville and Caius College, Cambridge, and the Inner Temple ; Arthur Middleton at Hackney, Westminster, and possibly also St. John's College, Cambridge (see Barker and Stenning, *The Record of Old Westminsters*, vol. ii. p. 644) ; Th. Hayward at the Middle Temple. The Dissenters were barred by the Test Act from the English Universities, and even the leading Northern Episcopalian families, for financial reasons, do not seem to have found it easy to educate their sons in England ; see, *e.g.*, *The Letter Book of John Watts* (*Collections of the New York Histor. Soc.*, vol. lxi.) for the difficulties caused by the cost of educating Peter Delancey, jun., in England. On 4 October 1765 Watts wrote from New York to Sir William Baker (*ibid.* p. 390) : 'I must own from the samples I had seen, I never expected any good from his stay in England, it seems to me to be the most ready way to bring the branch of one of our north American family's, with the moderate fortunes they possess and the industry that is of course required to being [bring:] them into life, to destruction'.   [2] Pp. 48-9.

[3] This remark refers to the Calverts of Maryland — Charles Calvert, 5th Lord Baltimore (Ir.), Governor of Maryland, 1732–33, sat in the British Parliament from 1734 till his death in 1751. The Penns of Pennsylvania did not sit in the House between 1661 and 1784, and the author can hardly be supposed to refer to a few 'Proprietaries' of South Carolina who had sat in it round about 1700 — *e.g.*, Sir Peter Colleton, who was returned in 1681, 1689, and 1690.

Thus America at first lacked even that measure of quasi-representation which would have been supplied by Americans returned for British constituencies; only after the conflict had become acute, did two of the three great English cities trading with America, London and Bristol, return Americans to the House of Commons, a choice which — whatever accidental circumstances may have contributed to it — proved their good-will toward the Colonies.[1]

Still, there were always Members with a personal knowledge of America. There were, in the first place, the West Indians, themselves in a sense Colonials, and in close touch with North America. Next there were a good many British merchants trading with America, and though only very few of them ever crossed the Atlantic, their knowledge of Colonial affairs, and interest in them, were by no means negligible; moreover, these men, as a rule, entertained personal friendships and connexions with Americans. Further, most naval officers in the course of their professional duties visited America, though more often Newfoundland, Nova Scotia, and the West Indian Islands than the intervening Continental Provinces; and in the Seven Years' War a certain number of army officers acquired personal knowledge of America, as during that time at least one-fifth of all the British infantry regiments crossed the Atlantic. Lastly, there was a miscellaneous group of men interested in America, some of whom acted as agents, *i.e.* as quasi-representatives, for the American Colonies.

[1] Trecothick had thought of standing for the City of London in 1761, but had to give up the idea. *Read's Weekly Journal* reported on 7 March 1761 that at the meeting at the Guildhall, 'Barlow Trecothick, Esq., was proposed, but not being free of the City, was not put in nomination'; and the *British Chronicle* for 20-23 March 1761 stated that on 20 March he 'was admitted to the Livery of the worshipful company of Clothiers, or Drapers, and, it is said, still intends to stand a candidate for this city'. When he did stand in 1768 he was described by his opponents as 'unfit to represent his fellow-citizens, because he received his education at Boston, and has, upon many occasions, warmly espoused the interests of the Colonies' (W. S. Johnson to Governor Pitkin, 12 March 1768, Trumbull Papers, *Collections of the Mass. Hist. Soc.*, 5th Series, vol. ix. p. 267). The fact that he was elected after his American extraction had been made an issue, renders the fact even more significant. — Henry Cruger's election at Bristol was helped by his being the son-in-law of Samuel Peach, a leading Bristol merchant.

The West Indians

In 1775 Alexander Elmsly, a London merchant who had resided in North Carolina and been a member of its Assembly, arguing in favour of Parliamentary union between Great Britain and the American Colonies wrote to an American friend : '. . . against this you object that you cannot get Members to represent you, to this I answer that there are more Jamaica men alone in England than will be sufficient for all America' (but, obviously remembering the misgivings with which the Americans regarded the West Indians, he added : 'and if you dont like to trust your concerns in their hands, pay your Members well and send them from your own Colonies').[1] Elmsly's statement was hardly an exaggeration ; the West Indian was a familiar figure in London society about 1770.

The inhabitants of the West Indian Islands never consider them-selves as at home there; they send their children to the Mother Country for education; they themselves make many trips to the Mother Country to recover their health or enjoy their fortunes; if they have ambition, 'tis hither they come to gratify it. I need not, I suppose, observe to you, how many gentlemen of the West Indies have seats in the British House of Commons. I might I believe venture to say, there are very few who have inherited plantations in any of our Islands, who have not had a European education, or at least have not spent some time in this Kingdom. Many who have plantations receive and spend the whole profits of them here, without ever having even seen the West Indies.[2]

'If I am not mis-informed,' wrote an anonymous author in the *Gentleman's Magazine* in 1766, 'there are now in Parlia-ment upwards of forty Members who are either West Indian planters themselves, descended from such, or have concerns there that entitle them to this pre-eminence.'[3] This very wide definition of a 'West Indian' seems justified so long as it is used with a view to gauging the voting strength of that 'interest'

[1] *Colonial Records of North Carolina*, vol. ix. p. 1094.
[2] *Remarks on the Letter*, etc., pp. 46-7.
[3] 'A short Sketch on the Transactions that led to the new Regulations of Commerce that have lately been agitated in Favour of the Colonies', *Gent. Mag.*, vol. xxxvi. p. 229.

in Parliament, say, on questions affecting the price of sugar. But as a rule the statement that there were forty 'West Indians' in the House, was repeated without the explanatory definition, and it came to be believed, even at that time, that there were so many real West Indians in the House. As such, however, only those should be counted who were born in the West Indies, had spent there part of their lives, had been members of a West Indian Assembly or Council, or had held office in one of the islands; and of these I find only thirteen in the House of Commons elected in 1761 : William and Julines Beckford, Henry Dawkins, Thomas Foster, Rose Fuller, Sir Alexander Grant, and Edward Morant from Jamaica; James Edward Colleton and Sir John Gibbons from Barbados; Samuel Martin from Antigua; William Matthew Burt and Charles Barrow from St. Kitt's; and William Woodley from Nevis.

Even counting those who might be described as the 'outer ring' of the West Indian group, it is doubtful whether the figure of forty can be reached — I know of only eight or nine Members in 1761 whose connexions with, or interests in, the West Indies qualify them for being placed in that 'outer ring'. There was Richard Pennant, a grandson of a Chief Justice of Jamaica, and owner of a plantation in the island, who does not seem ever to have resided in the West Indies; Thomas Erle Drax and Sir William Codrington, who owned plantations in Barbados, and whose families had played a great part in its history; the three Lascelles (Edwin, Daniel, and Edward), whose parents had resided, and whose heirs still own plantations, in the West Indies; John Thomlinson, whose father was of West Indian origin, and jointly with Barlow Trecothick (a partner also in his London house) owned a plantation in Grenada;[1] Sir James Lowther, who owned estates in Barbados and whose father had been its governor 1711–20; and Fane William Sharpe, whose father had been agent for various West Indian islands and whose maternal grandfather, George Newport, a London merchant and Barbados planter, left the residue of his fortune 'towards building a ship or man-of-war for the service of His Majesty and the nation', desiring her to 'be

[1] About the Thomlinsons see below, pp. 246-50.

named Barbadoes'.[1] Arnold Nesbitt, a London merchant of
Irish extraction, owned a sugar plantation in Jamaica and an
estate in Grenada,[2] but I am not certain that he should be
included even in the 'outer ring' of West Indians. It is quite
likely that some of the other merchants, too, owned property
or had interests in the Sugar Islands, but I do not know of any
with whom these were sufficiently prominent or permanent, to
make me place them even on a level with Nesbitt.

Of the thirteen Members who were genuine West Indians,
seven were from Jamaica, only two from Barbados, and four
from the Leeward Islands, although in 1761 the white population of either exceeded that of Jamaica.[3] Possibly the exhaustion
of the old Sugar Islands was already affecting the financial
resources of their planters ; [4] also the percentage of 'absentees'
in the second or third generation, placed here in the 'outer
ring' of the West Indians, was higher among the owners of
plantations in Barbados and the Leeward Islands (of the eight
mentioned above, Richard Pennant alone was from Jamaica).

[1] See F. C. Cass, *The Parish of East Barnet*, pp. 110-14. Horatio
Sharpe, the Governor of Maryland, was a brother of John Sharpe.

[2] About him see Alexander and Cecilia Nesbitt, *History of the Family
of Nisbet or Nesbitt in Scotland and Ireland* (1898).

[3] In the Long Papers, Add. MSS. 12438, f. 22, there is a computation
of the white population of the West Indian Islands, the first for 1734, the
second for 1773 :

1734. The whites in our Islands thus stated by the Lords of Trade :

Jamaica	7,644
Barbadoes	18,295
The Leeward Islands . .	10,262
Total . .	36,201

I think the white people in our Islands may at this time (1773) be
computed

Jamaica	16,000
Barbadoes	20,000
St. Christopher's . . .	6,000
Antigua	6,000
Nevis	3,000
Montserrat . . .	3,000
Other islands	4,000
Total . .	58,000

[4] See *Remarks on the Letter etc.*, p. 31 : 'You know that another Island,
I mean Barbadoes, formerly one of our best, is at present much exhausted ;
so that the produce, and the profit made on that produce, diminishes
daily. . . .'

To some extent, however, the disproportion may also be due to the coming in of one powerful 'cousinship' ; in the eighteenth century the success of a pioneer in Parliamentary adventure was frequently followed by an inrush of relations or friends, hitherto without Parliamentary ambitions. All the Jamaicans, with the exception of Sir Alexander Grant (who was not a West Indian by birth, but had spent many years in Jamaica, and had made his fortune there), were intermarried, and the chief figure among them was William Beckford, the biggest landowner in the island.[1] Pennant, Morant, and Dawkins were cousins, being grandsons of Edward Pennant, Chief Justice of Jamaica. Pennant's mother was a first cousin of William Beckford ; Ithamar Vassal, a cousin of hers and of Beckford was the first wife of Rose Fuller. Her brother, Florentius Vassal, married a sister of Thomas Foster[2] (and W. M. Burt of St. Kitt's, who owned also a plantation in Jamaica, married another sister of Foster).

The Jamaica cousinhood established its Parliamentary strongholds in Hampshire and Wiltshire. In 1761 Julines Beckford was returned for Salisbury, E. Morant for Hindon, a borough in the immediate neighbourhood of William Beckford's estate of Fonthill and under his control, and Henry Dawkins for Southampton, where the West Indian group had gained a footing. In the first half of the eighteenth century the representatives of Southampton had been natives of the town, or at least of Hampshire, but in 1747 A. L. Swymmer, a

[1] There is in the Long Papers (Add. MSS. 12436) 'A List of the Land-holders in Jamaica with the quantity of acres of land each one possesses', drawn up about 1750. It appears from it that there were at that date in Jamaica 47 estates of 5-10,000 acres each, 8 of 10-20,000 acres, and one only above 20,000, namely that of William Beckford, which amounted to 22,022 acres. His two brothers, Richard and Julines, owned 9242½ and 8198 acres. The estate of John Morant, father of Edward Morant, comprised 1859 acres, and of James Dawkins, M.P. (who died in 1757), 14,295, of his younger brother Henry, the Member of 1761, 5761 acres, of Anthony Langley Swymmer, M.P. (who died in 1760), 7272, and of John Pennant, father of Richard, 2956 (another member of the family, Edward Pennant, owned 8365 acres). In fact, the families of Price, Gale, and Hals were the only ones among the chief planters of which no members ever sat in the British Parliament, and which did not leave the island.

[2] See genealogical tables vii. and viii. in John Britton's *Graphical and Literary Illustrations of Fonthill Abbey* (1823).

Jamaica planter, established himself in the borough, which he continued to represent till his death in 1760. Hans Stanley, a cousin of Swymmer's,[1] became his colleague at Southampton in 1754, and on Swymmer's death, Henry Dawkins was returned with the support of the Fullers ;[2] he was re-elected in 1761. On the death of Hans Stanley, in 1780, his cousin, John Fuller (a nephew of Rose Fuller), succeeded to Stanley's seat, which he retained till 1784 ; while from 1780 till 1784, the other seat was held by Hans Sloane, a grand-nephew of Sir Hans Sloane, married to a niece of Rose Fuller. After 1784, at South-ampton, as in several other boroughs, nabobs replaced the West Indians.

What was the attitude and what the influence of the West Indian Members of Parliament with regard to the American Colonies ? Their commercial interests clashed, as the West Indians aspired to a monopoly in sugar and molasses for the entire British Empire, while to New England it was essential to be able to import them also from the French and Dutch islands. When forbidden by law, such imports were continued by illicit trade, and rum was distilled at Boston from smuggled molasses — the bootleggers can claim a more distinguished ancestry than the prohibition agents, for the British Customs officials were singularly tame and inefficient, and naturally were not on the side of 'liberty'. But as far as the letter of the law was concerned, the West Indians were successful, and the Americans, exasperated by restrictive Acts, imagined themselves defeated by the superior Parliamentary influence of those 'pampered Creoles'. What in reality helped the West Indians much more

[1] Jane (Langley) Swymmer, the mother of A. L. Swymmer, was a sister of Elizabeth Langley who married Fulke Rose of Jamaica (and was by him the grandmother of Rose Fuller), and next in 1695 married the distinguished physician and scientist, Sir Hans Sloane, of British Museum and Chelsea fame. By that marriage she had two daughters, of whom one married George Stanley of Paultons, and the other Charles, first Lord Cadogan (which is the origin of the Cadogan connexion with Chelsea). Hans Stanley, M.P. for Southampton, was a son of George Stanley.

[2] R. Rideout wrote to Newcastle, from Lewes, on 22 March 1760 (Add. MSS. 32903, f. 465) : 'I have this morning received two letters from Mr. Rose Fuller and his brother to desire my vote at Southampton for one Mr. Dawkins who intends to offer himself there in the room of Mr. Swymmer. . . .'

han some twenty votes in a House of 558, was that their commercial demands were in accordance with the mercantilist
doctrines of trade, which at that time were universally accepted
and punctiliously adhered to in Great Britain.

In 1764 the Boston merchants wrote in a 'Statement of the
Trade and Fisheries of Massachusetts':

This Act [concerning sugar and molasses] was procured by the
interest of the West India planters, with no other view than to enrich
themselves, by obliging the northern Colonies to take their whole
supply from them; and they still endeavour the continuance of it
under a pretence, that they can supply Great Britain and all her
Colonies with West India goods, which is perfectly chimerical.[1]

And in a letter to the merchants of New London, dated Boston,
9 January 1764, they spoke of their own 'endeavours to defeat
the iniquitous schemes of these overgrown West Indians'.[2]

The idea of the great power wielded by the West Indians
in Great Britain was firmly rooted in the minds of the Americans
and their friends. The contributor to the *Gentleman's Magazine*
who put the West Indian interest at 'upwards of forty Members',
asserted that

in almost every contest between the West-Indians and North-
Americans, the West-Indians gained their point: In a very few
instances national justice and good sense, defeated the combined
power of the West-Indian aristocracy; for, in short, they considered
themselves entitled to double influence, as members of the H—— of
C——, and people of large property both at home and abroad.

To recite the different struggles between these contending interests, to shew by what means the West-Indians maintained their
ground, and advanced in oppressing the Americans, would require a
volume.[3]

When in 1765 Sir Harry Moore, a West Indian, was appointed
Governor of New York, the wisdom of the appointment was
questioned, as 'the northern colonies have always considered
the planters of the southern their enemies from self-interest',[4]

---

[1] See *Collections of the Conn. Hist. Soc.*, vol. xviii., *Fitch Papers*, vol. ii.
(1920), pp. 271-2.   [2] *Ibid.* p. 261.   [3] Vol. xxxvi. p. 230.
[4] See letter from John Watts to General Robert Monckton, New York,
24 September 1765; *Collections of the Mass. Hist. Soc.*, Fourth Series,
vol. x., *The Aspinwall Papers*, vol. ii. pp. 575-6.

and the only thing which seems to have secured for him a tolerable reception was that he replaced a Scotsman.

But on constitutional questions, which were soon to loom so large in Parliamentary debates, West Indians were prominent among the few Members who from the very outset upheld the American thesis. The Stamp Act came before the House of Commons on 6 February 1765 and as Charles Garth, M.P., agent for South Carolina, wrote to its Committee of Correspondence, 'the power of Parliament was asserted and was universally agreed to. . . .'

The advocates for the Colonies therefore chose to take the sense of the House upon the question for adjourning, Mr. Alderman Beckford moved it, seconded by Colonel Barré, and to which Sir William Meredith, Mr. Jackson and myself assisted, we divided the Committee about midnight, but they carry'd it against us by 245 to 49.[1]

To the speakers mentioned above, Jackson adds the name of Rose Fuller.[2] Of these six champions of American rights, Garth and Jackson were agents for American Colonies in Great Britain, Meredith was a Member for Liverpool, Barré had personal knowledge of America, while Beckford and Fuller, who were to play a most important part as active leaders of the pro-American side, were West Indians. No list is preserved of the 49 who voted in the minority on 8 February 1765, but Jared Ingersoll, an American then in London, states that they were 'West Indian gentlemen and a few others connected with America'.[3] When before the general election of 1774 an anonymous writer in the *Gentleman's Magazine* warned the public against the various types of unsuitable candidate who in newspaper advertisements offered themselves 'as proper persons for Parliament', he placed among them the

West Indians, who publicly deny the legislative power of Great Britain over our American colonies, and for that reason chiefly want

[1] Correspondence between Garth and the Assembly of South Carolina published by J. W. Barnwell and T. D. Jervey in *South Carolina Historical and Genealogical Magazine*, vols. 26, 28-31, and 33.
[2] In his letter to Thomas Fitch, Governor of Connecticut, 9 February 1765 ; *Fitch Papers*, vol. ii. p. 360
[3] See his letter to the General Assembly of Connecticut, 19 September 1765.

to be in the ensuing Parliament, that they may there declare their opinion.[1]

The exertions of the West Indians on behalf of the constitutional claims of America, to some extent mitigated American hostility against them, but did not altogether extinguish it ; the difference in outlook, habits, and morals was too great. 'As for the West Indies,' wrote Ezra Stiles on 5 March 1769, 'they will die in their iniquities. . . . Assuredly I account the West Indies, both priests and people, most amazingly debauched.' [2]

THE MERCHANTS

Of the merchants returned to Parliament at the general election of 1761, at least ten had connexions with the American Colonies : Sir William Baker, Sir James Colebrooke and his brother George, Sir Ellis Cunliffe, Adam Drummond, Sir Samuel Fludyer, Joseph Gulston, Arnold Nesbitt, John Thomlinson, and Chauncy Townsend. None of them, except Drummond and Gulston, seem ever to have crossed the Atlantic, but all knew a great deal about the North American Colonies, and carried on an extensive correspondence with them.

Alderman Sir William Baker, 'a strong thinker and often a very free speaker',[3] stood in high repute both in the City and in the House of Commons. His trade was chiefly with America, where it covered perhaps a wider radius than that of any contemporary of his. During the War of the Austrian Succession and the Seven Years' War, he held important contracts for victualling both British and provincial troops in North America [4] (e.g. that with the Treasury, signed on 26 March 1756, was for 12,000 men at 6d. a day, and thus represented a yearly turn-over of about £110,000) ; still, Government contracts were not the main part of his American trade,

---

[1] *Gentleman's Magazine*, vol. xliv. pp. 404-5.

[2] To the Rev. Charles Chauncy, of Boston ; Stiles MSS., in the Yale College Library, New Haven, Conn.

[3] Newcastle to Hardwicke, 16 July 1762 ; Add. MSS. 32940, f. 372.

[4] For his British army contracts, see Minute Books of the Treasury Board at the Record Office ; for a contract for the provincial troops, see the *Northcliffe Collection* (Ottawa), 1926, pp. 82-3.

and, towards 1760, he seems to have voluntarily withdrawn from most of them.   Like most London merchants trading with America, he worked in conjunction with an American partner (Christopher Kilby).   He never held any place under the Government, though on one occasion, in 1758, he applied to Newcastle for the office of Postmaster-General.[1]   A fairly frequent speaker in the House, especially on financial and Colonial matters, he was one of Newcastle's chief advisers on American affairs, and his advice seems to have been invariably of a liberal and pro-American character.   In 1760–62 Baker was repeatedly consulted by Newcastle on the peace terms in so far as America was concerned,[2] and in 1765–66, by Rockingham on the Repeal of the Stamp Act.   Thus on 31 December 1765 Rockingham wrote to Newcastle that he had 'company to dinner which consisted of Sir William Baker and Dowdeswell and Tregothick, Ld. Dartmouth etc. upon American topicks'.[3] The son of Sir William Baker, bearing the same names, married in 1771 Juliana, a granddaughter of William Penn, and was a leading pro-American.

The two Colebrookes, James and George, and Arnold Nesbitt, held victualling contracts in America and worked them in partnership with Moses Franks, of a prominent Jewish family at Philadelphia ; the Colebrookes and Nesbitt, together with Thomlinson and Hanbury, had also the remitting of Government money to America, often of large sums at exorbitant rates. James Colebrooke died in 1761 ; and George Colebrooke and Nesbitt, because they adhered to Newcastle, were deprived in 1763 of their Government contracts for America.   These were now granted to Sir Samuel Fludyer and Adam Drummond, who continued the partnership with Moses Franks.   Fludyer, who was born a Nonconformist, seems to have been well known in America, but apparently was not popular with the American Dissenters, as his baronetcy and his marriage with 'a Church of England lady' had made him forsake the re-

[1] Add. MSS. 32885, f. 478.
[2] See Add. MSS. 32913, f. 128, and 32925, ff. 9-10, 26-9 ; also below, pp. 274 and 280.
[3] Add. MSS. 32972, f. 384.   Tregothick stands for Barlow Trecothick.

ligion of his parents ; [1] so did his younger and poorer brother Thomas.[2]

Adam Drummond had been to America, not as a merchant, but as an officer in the Seven Years' War. John Watts, of New York, who was connected with Moses Franks in business (and also by intermarriages with the Delanceys), wrote to him on 9 June 1764 :

> Mr. Drummond was my old friend and acquaintance and an extremely well disposed man to all appearance, he would laugh till he set the whole company laughing, and was very jolly in the bargain, but I own when he left us in the King's livery, I little thought of having a connection with him of this kind.[3]

The two Fludyers and Drummond were partners of Anthony Bacon in a contract for coal mines at Cape Breton,

[1] See letter from Ezra Stiles to Dr. Alison, 5 September 1766 ; Stiles MSS.

[2] The two Fludyers are buried in the old cemetery, in St. Margaret's Church, at Lee, Blackheath. The monument bears on one side the inscription :

> To the memory of Sir Samuel Fludyer | Late of this Parish. Baronet. Died 21st January, 1768 | To the Memory of Jane, first wife of Sir Samuel Fludyer | died the 15th March 1757 | To the memory of Caroline, daughter of the Hon. James | Brudenell, second wife of Sir Samuel Fludyer, died October, 1808.

And on the other side :

> To the memory of | Sir Thomas Fludyer | late of this Parish, Knight | brother of Sir Samuel Fludyer | Baronet | Died March 1769.

The name of the father of poor Jane, the wife of Samuel Fludyer's humble Nonconformist days, is not mentioned, while Thomas Fludyer remains in death, as he was known all his life, the 'brother of Sir Samuel Fludyer, Bart.' Lysons, in his *Environs of London*, vol. iv. (1795), p. 505, *n.*, quotes a long and florid inscription in honour of Sir Samuel, presumably placed on a memorial tablet in the church — this was rebuilt in the nineteenth century, and I have not been able to find the tablet. The inscription recorded how Sir Samuel Fludyer 'by indefatigable industry and uncommon abilities for business . . . carried the woollen manufacture of this Kingdom to the greatest height', and how he 'acted in every public capacity upon principles of a strict loyalty and firm attachment to the Protestant succession of the House of Hanover, and a steady adherence to the liberties of the English Constitution'.

In 1762 he abandoned Newcastle for Bute, and became a Government contractor ; he died reputed worth £900,000.

[3] *Letterbook of John Watts, Collections of the N.Y. Hist. Soc.*, vol. lxi. p. 263. Drummond married in 1755 Catherine, daughter of Henry, 4th Duke of Bolton, and sat on the Bolton interest for Lymington, 1761–68 and for St. Ives, 1768–78. In 1775 he joined Thomas Coutts as a partner in his bank (see letter from Coutts to Sir Charles [Hotham] Thompson, 4 September 1775 ; Stirling, *The Hothams*, vol. ii. pp. 168–9).

which they obtained from the Government in 1764 ; [1] but in that enterprise Bacon was presumably the leading figure — since his youth he had been conversant with the coal trade, and subsequently became a prominent mine-owner in Cumberland and Glamorgan.

Sir Ellis Cunliffe, a leading Liverpool merchant, carried on an extensive trade in the southern provinces, especially in Maryland, but held no Government contracts.[2]

Joseph Gulston traded chiefly with Portugal, Brazil, and the Mediterranean, but apparently through the fisheries, which supplied one of the British staple exports to those countries, became connected with Newfoundland ; and in Parliament he represented Poole, which at that time was so closely connected with Newfoundland that it could almost have ranked as a Newfoundland colony in England. The Members for Poole acted as its quasi-representatives in the British Parliament. Gulston had also close commercial connexions with New Hampshire.[3]

Chauncy Townsend, on his father's side, was descended from a family of brewers ; [4] his maternal grandfather, Richard Chauncy, was a prominent mining adventurer ; [5] his uncle, Richard Chauncy, jun., to whom he was apprenticed,[6] was a linen draper, and in the *Complete Guide* for 1740 (a commercial directory) Chauncy Townsend himself appears as such. Later in life he worked lead mines in Cardiganshire,[7] established the

---

[1] For that contract, see my essay on Bacon in the *Journal of Economic and Business History*, November 1929.

[2] About Cunliffe's trade in Maryland, see L. C. Wroth, 'A Maryland Merchant and his Friends in 1750', in *The Maryland Historical Magazine*, September 1911.

[3] In the 'Thomlinson Correspondence', *Provincial Papers of New Hampshire*, vol. iv. p. 842, workmen are mentioned employed by Gulston in New Hampshire in cutting trees. In a letter from Benning Wentworth to Thomlinson, dated 21 October 1743, ships belonging to Gulston are stated to have come up to New Hampshire from Casco (see R. M. Howard, *The Longs of Jamaica*, vol. i. p. 207).

[4] For the pedigree of the Townsend family, see *Miscellanea Genealogica et Heraldica*, N.S., vol. iv. pp. 125-9.

[5] For the pedigree of the Chauncys of Edgcote, see Baker, *Northamptonshire*, vol. i. p. 494. For Richard Chauncy as a mining adventurer, see *List of Adventurers in the Mine-Adventure*, 1 May 1700, and *Gentleman's Magazine*, 1731, p. 497.

[6] See *Notes and Queries*, Series XI. vol. v. pp. 2-4.

[7] *E.g.*, about the lead mine of Esgair-y-Mwyn, see Add. MSS. 32735, f. 573, 32737, f. 279, and 32885, ff. 405-8 ; and at the P.R.O., T. 29/32-29/34.

'Middle Bank Copper Works' near Swansea,[1] and opened up
large collieries near Gwernllwynwyth and at Llansamlet; [2] his
grandson, Henry Smith, in evidence given before the Coal
Committee of 1810, mentioned the pits which Townsend had
sunk at Llansamlet, and the great sums of money they had
swallowed up — 'the amount I cannot speak to otherwise than
by guess, but I am certain that my grandfather had expended
his whole fortune in it, for he died without any other property
but that'.[3]

Between his beginnings as a linen draper and the concluding
stages of his career in the coal and metal trades, Townsend was
engaged in extensive business with New England, Newfoundland, and what are now the maritime provinces of Canada.
The nature of that trade, except for the victualling contracts
which, between 1744 and 1770, he held for British troops in
Nova Scotia, Newfoundland, and also in the island of Ruatan
(off Honduras), is not known to me, but the following letter
addressed by Townsend to Newcastle on 28 March 1741,
shows the interest he took in the affairs of New England, and
the connexion he had with those provinces :

I know I need no apoligy for laying before your Grace any thing
that is for the service of the present happy establishment.

I correspond, and am conversant with the most considerable
persons of New England which has given me a perticuler knowlege
of that Government from whence I am fully perswaded the design of
raising men there, can not be done under the influence of the present
Governor.[4] . . .

The former Governors generally musterd the Militia four times
a year, when attendance and great respect was shown to them, this
gentleman can not make a tollerable muster. . . .

I am allmost afraid of the success of the attemp at the best, on the

---

[1] See 'An Act for confirming a lease made by the Hon. Louisa Barbara
Mansell . . . to Chauncy Townsend, Esq. . . .', 7 George III, cap. 58 (the
original lease of 1756 is described as 'for the purpose of building and erecting
divers works for carrying on the business of smelting, refining, and making
copper ore and copper') ; and Grant Francis, *The Smelting of Copper in the
Swansea District* (1867), pp. 84-5.
[2] See *ibid.* ; and also Charles Wilkins, *The South Wales Coal Trade and
its Allied Industries* (1888), pp. 48-9.
[3] See *Report from the Committee on the Petition of the Owners of Collieries
in South Wales*, p. 2 ; ordered by the House of Commons to be printed,
7 June 1810.   [4] Jonathan Belcher.

present footing of inlisting, but was such a man as Mr. Sherly,[1] whom
that country has expected would be appointed over them and whom
they all adore it would have a much better prospect of success, and
I have been assured and by some of the old caballers they would give
up their favourite point and come into the settlement of the sallery
agreeable to his Majestys instructions. I speak not this as my own
sentiments alone but that of every single New England gentleman
now here. . . .[2]

In later years, New England ceases to take a prominent
place in Townsend's interests and correspondence.

John Thomlinson, jun., M.P., the last of the merchant-
Members enumerated above, was in 1761 a young man of
thirty ; he had been educated at Christ's College, Cambridge,
where he 'incurred the displeasure of the Master of his College
as well as that of his father, apparently on account of extravag-
ance',[3] was admitted to Lincoln's Inn in 1752, and subsequently
joined his father's firm in the City. At the general election of
1761 he was put up for Steyning by his father-in-law, Thomas
Sergison, M.P. for Lewes,[4] and was returned with Newcastle's
approval.[5] His rise in the world was entirely due to his father ;
it was him that the young man primarily represented in Parliament, and it is owing to his father's close connexion with
America that he appears in this chapter.

John Thomlinson, sen., was a son of Major John Thomlinson of Antigua,[6] 'one of the best planters . . . in these

---

[1] William Shirley, subsequently Governor of Massachusetts.

[2] Add. MSS. 32693, f. 121.

[3] See R. M. Howard, *The Longs of Jamaica*, vol. i. pp. 222-7.

[4] John Thomlinson, jun., although at his death in 1767 only thirty-five
years old, seems to have been married three times. F. C. Cass, in his
history of the *Parish of East Barnet* (pp. 40-4), and R. M. Howard, *op. cit.*
vol. i. pp. 226-7, mention only two wives : Mary, daughter of T. Sergison,
M.P., who died in 1762 ; and Margaret, daughter of Martin Blake, of
Antigua, whom he married on 16 June 1763 ; she survived him, and by
her he left an only child, Mary, who married E. B. Long, of Jamaica. The
famous Arthur Young mentions, however, in his *Autobiography*, that he
was to have entered the firm of his brother-in-law, Thomlinson, but that
owing to the death of his sister, that plan was dropped. As the City address
of the Thomlinsons mentioned by Young — Bucklersbury — was that of
John Thomlinson, unless Young's sister was the second wife of John
Thomlinson, sen., she must have been the first wife of his son.

[5] See Add. MSS. 32909, f. 34, and 32910, ff. 228, 344, 389, and 391.

[6] Major (subsequently Colonel) Thomlinson was appointed a Member
of the Council of Antigua in 1746 (*Acts of the Privy Council (Colonial)*,

parts'.[1] In the 'thirties he is usually referred to as Captain
Thomlinson, and, according to Belknap, he had frequently been
to New Hampshire 'in quality of a sea commander'.[2] It is not
certain what year he settled as a merchant in London, but when,
in 1733, Rindge, who had been sent to England as special agent
to represent New Hampshire in their frontier dispute with
Massachusetts, was returning home, he 'committed the case of
his agency to Capt. John Thomlinson, merchant in London, a
gentleman of known ability and integrity'. On 10 January
1734 the House of Representatives, 'assured of this gentleman's
good disposition to serve this Province', confirmed the appointment.[3] As, however, the dispute was not with Massachusetts
alone, but also with Governor Belcher, who at that time
presided over both these provinces,[4] Thomlinson's appointment was vetoed by the Council ; [5] 'we are worried to distrac-
tion with this Governor and the Lord send us a deliverance',
wrote a Member of the New Hampshire Assembly on 10
December 1734.[6] Thomlinson had now to contest in Whitehall
the edicts and works of a colonial potentate, and he had to do
so at his own expense, receiving from New Hampshire nothing
except votes of thanks for his 'extraordinary care and diligence'

1745–66, p. 781). He died on 20 September 1753 as Deputy-Governor of
the island (see *Gentleman's Magazine*, vol. xxiii. p. 445).
  [1] Jonas Langford to Abraham Redwood, March 1731 ; *Commerce of
Rhode Island*, 1726–1800 ; *Collections of the Mass. Hist. Soc.*, Seventh Series,
vol. ix. (1914) p. 13.
  [2] See *Provincial Papers of New Hampshire*, vol. iv. p. 677, footnote.
  [3] See *ibid.* pp. 612, 650, 653, and 655.
  [4] 'We apprehend,' wrote the Committee of Correspondence of the
House of Representatives to John Thomlinson in a letter marked 1735, 'as
he is a resident in the Massachusetts and his principall support arising
from thence and his estate and interest in that Government and not so
much as a freehold in this Province, he has not bin so impartiall as a Governor
ought to have bin, but has bin much attached to the interest of that province
in the affair of the lines.' See 'Thomlinson Correspondence', *Provincial
Papers of New Hampshire*, vol. iv. p. 844 ; this correspondence is copied
from a MS. volume in the library of the N.H. Historical Society at Concord,
N.H.—For Belcher's side of the case, see *Belcher Papers, Collections of the
Mass. Hist. Soc.*, Sixth Series, vols. i., ii., and vi.
  [5] *Ibid.* p. 709 ; the Council's action, according to the vote of the House
of Representatives of 8 May 1736, was 'by reason as we conceive of the
great and undue influence his Excellency hath over a majority of the Council,
most of whom have been imployed and put into posts of profit and honour
by his Excellency.'
  [6] *Ibid.* p. 841.

and his 'great prudence and industry', and requests 'to continue their agent'.   At last, in 1741, New Hampshire got rid of its enemy, and the new Governor, Benning Wentworth, a native of the province, in his speech of 14 January 1742 reminded the Assembly that 'the faithful services' of their agent called for a reward.[1]   They acknowledged thereupon their 'great obligations' to Thomlinson 'for his fidelity and indefatigable industry and labours',[2] and voted him — apparently the first payment after eight years — the sum of £100 until they would be able to make him 'a more ample reward'.

When, during the War of the Austrian Succession, New Hampshire was in need of munitions, John Thomlinson procured them from England, but, in spite of repeated reminders, could not obtain payment from the Province for what the British Government did not supply free.[3]

As for the gunpowder [wrote Thomlinson on 21 December 1745], . . . I think the Province has used me very ill, for . . . I had obtained as many guns etc. as cost five or six thousand pounds, on condition that I would pay for gun powder for those guns, which is never allowed to any colony, and now I have been obliged to pay for it. . . .[4]

He asked them to hand back to him either the powder or the money.   On 17 May 1746 the House of Representatives decided that the powder should be paid for 'if a proper method can be agreed upon by the General Assembly',[5] on 25 September the Governor still described it as 'Mr. Thomlinson's property',[6] and on 9 December the Assembly voted to draw up the accounts of the Louisbourg expedition, send them to Thomlinson with a view to obtaining payment from the British Government, and to 'return him the thanks of this House for all his past services'.[7]   On 20 May 1747 it was voted unanimously by the Assembly

that John Thomlinson, Esq., Agent for this province at the Court of Great Britain be and hereby is intitled to all the priviledges, immunities and advantages that any of the subjects or inhabitants of

---

[1] *N.H. Provincial Papers*, vol. v. p. 137.   [2] *Ibid.* p. 140.
[3] See Governor Wentworth's speech to the Assembly, 6 May 1746, *ibid.* pp. 798-9.   [4] *Ibid.* p. 799.   [5] *Ibid.* p. 419.   [6] *Ibid.* p. 462.
[7] *Ibid.* p. 471.

this Province are or as tho' he the said John Thomlinson did actually reside within the limits of this Province for and during the continuance of the said John Thomlinson's agency as aforesaid.[1]

There is rich material for a monograph on Thomlinson's relations with New Hampshire,[2] and on his Government contracts,[3] but I cannot pursue the subject here any further.

In 1763 John Thomlinson jun., M.P., was appointed by New Hampshire joint agent with his father, and was henceforth active on behalf of the Province. He wrote to his father on 26 March 1764 while duties to be paid in the Colonies on molasses and Madeira wine were under discussion :

> I have been a good deal engaged this week in attending upon the House and in meetings with the North American agents upon the present duty proposed to be raised in the provinces. . . . We agents have adjourned our further meeting till too morrow when we shall after this days proceeding be better able to draw up our joint memorial to the Treasury.[4]

The Thomlinsons had two Americans for partners in business, Trecothick and Apthorp, and on 8 June 1758 John Thomlinson, sen., wrote to Newcastle asking him to support East Apthorp [5] for a Fellowship at Jesus College, Cambridge :

> My Lord Duke,—How I come to be so far interested in this affair, as to presume to give your Grace so much trouble is this ; this Mr. East Apthorp is the son of my worthy friend, Charles Apthorp, Esq., of Boston in New England, who is one of the most considerable men in North America ; and I think one of the most servicable men in those parts to this Government. This son of his was sent very young to me here, to be under my care, to have him fitted for, and bred at the University ; all which I have with the greatest pleasure

---

[1] *Ibid.* p. 497.

[2] Besides the sources quoted above, see *Collections of the New Hampshire Hist. Soc.*, vol. x., *Calendar of New Hampshire Papers in English Archives.*

[3] In the Treasury Papers at the P.R.O.

[4] See R. M. Howard, *The Longs of Jamaica*, vol. i. p. 226.

[5] A daughter of Charles, and sister of East Apthorp, was the first wife of Barlow Trecothick ; see 'Boston Marriages' in the *Reports of the Record Commissioners of Boston*, p. 336. Trecothick, Thomlinson, and Apthorp were all three members of the Church of England, and Thomlinson was occasionally active on behalf of the New England Episcopalians (see, *e.g.*, article by T. Alden, 'An Account of the several Religious Societies in Portsmouth, New Hampshire', *Collections of the Mass. Hist. Soc.*, First Series, vol. x. pp. 37-72; 1801). This apparently did not spoil his good relations with the Dissenters of that Province.

performed. . . . I love him next to my own and firmly hope that your Grace will prevent the disapointment we are affraid of.[1]

John Thomlinson jun., M.P., had grown up together with this young American in a house which had strong American connexions ; and he was engaged in American business and on American affairs till his death in 1767.[2]

What were, in broad outlines, the relations between the British merchants and the American Colonies ? These relations counted for a great deal, seeing that about 1760 trade was considered the foundation and the purpose of the Empire, and that, consequently, in Colonial matters the views and wishes of the merchants carried very considerable weight with Parliament and the Government. In one way, their influence worked in favour of the Colonies, as they were naturally interested in the productive capacity and the buying power of their customers, and were anxious to cultivate their good-will. On the other hand, these merchants had an interest in the strict enforcement of the navigation laws and of certain irksome mercantilist restrictions, which, by limiting most of the foreign trade of the Colonies to Great Britain, secured for her merchants the commissions of middlemen, and for her manufacturers a monopoly in the Colonial markets. Still, it required only a reasonable measure of 'give and take' between the two sides to reach a compromise — mostly at the expense of the British taxpayer ; and between the British merchants and the agents in charge of

---

[1] Add. MSS. 32880, f. 363.—East Apthorp was elected to the Fellowship (see Venn, *Alumni Cantabrigienses*), was an S.P.G. missionary at Cambridge, Mass., 1759–64, and a loyalist in the Revolution ; he died in England, in 1816, as a Prebendary of St. Paul's.

[2] No agent for an American Colony was returned to Parliament in 1761. But James Abercromby, M.P. for Clackmannanshire 1761–68, had lived in South Carolina 1730–44, been a member of its Assembly, served as Judge-Advocate to James St. Clair's American expedition in 1746, been agent for North Carolina 1748–58, for Virginia 1753–61, and also private agent to Gov. Glen of South Carolina ; 'his total emoluments from salaries, incidentals, and commissions were probably £2000 yearly' (see R. A. Brock, *Dinwiddie Records, 1753–1758*, pp. 37–8). He remained agent for the Governor and Council of Virginia, 1758–74, and was regimental agent of the Royal Americans 1758–59, while they were commanded by his relative, General James Abercromby, with whom he is often confused. On 7 February 1766 Abercromby voted against the Repeal of the Stamp Act.

Colonial interests in Great Britain a system of co-operation was established so close that at certain junctures the London merchants trading to America came even to form quasi-constituencies for these quasi-representatives of the Colonies. In the City, the coffee houses frequented by those merchants — *e.g.* the New York or the Carolina Coffee House — were clubs to which the Colonial agents resorted, to discuss and arrange matters big and small ; while in the House of Commons the merchants and the Members representing the trading cities actively co-operated with the Colonial agents in promoting, amending, or defeating Bills which vitally affected the Colonies, provided, of course, that their interests were not deemed contrary to those of British trade.

It was my original intention to enter more fully into the subject of the Colonial agents in Great Britain, and of their co-operation with the merchants, but circumstances have prevented me from fully carrying out my design.[1] All I can do now is to give a few examples of that co-operation, and I take them from an essay of mine on Charles Garth, agent for South Carolina (which I still hope to finish some day).

The first example is the case of a trade bounty to be paid to the Colonies by the British Exchequer. The British merchants had not the least objection to such expenditure, and, therefore, when in the autumn of 1763 Charles Garth, together with other Colonial agents, petitioned the Treasury and the Board of Trade for a bounty on hemp grown in the Colonies, each of them approached the merchants trading to the Colony he represented.

I . . . have prepar'd a Memorial accordingly [wrote Charles Garth to the Committee of Correspondence of South Carolina on 20 November], which has been approv'd by the Agents, and we have

---

[1] Pious Jews in Eastern Europe, when building a new house, leave one place unfinished ; it is called in Hebrew '*zekher lekhurban*' ('the memorial of destruction'), and commemorates the destruction of the Temple. I had concluded my researches for the rest of this book, but not on the complex subject of the Colonial agents, when the Arab attack in Palestine, in August 1929, compelled me to relinquish my historical studies earlier than I had planned, and to take up work in the Jewish Agency for Palestine. After that I could do no more than complete the parts for which the material was ready ; this unfinished chapter has to be the *zekher lekhurban* of my book.

got it signed as you will see by almost all the merchants trading to America, except those who have seats in Parliament, and who, as being to be judges, could not with propriety or decency make themselves parties by signing it.

The Memorial bore the signatures of 102 firms, among them David Barclay & Sons, Trecothick & Thomlinson, Sargent, Aufrere & Co., and Anthony Bacon ; [1] and Government and Parliament acceded to the request.

Next I choose an example in which the interests of the Colonies clashed with those of the merchants — the case of Colonial paper money, which, by depreciating the currencies, effected unfair reductions in the claims of British creditors. Naturally, in a case of that kind, the agents could not expect whole-hearted support from the merchants, but even so, while some of those who were more directly concerned were instrumental in bringing the subject before the House of Commons, others helped to arrange a compromise acceptable to the Colonies.

I have reason to believe [wrote Charles Garth to his American constituents in March 1764], we should have heard no more of it this year had it not been for a Mr. Anthony Bacon (a North Carolina merchant) who had mooted that point with us before the Board of Trade ; since that time he has procured himself to be elected for Aylesbury, and on 29th March started the question in the House.

On 4 April, Bacon moved for permission to bring in a Bill, and Mr. Rice, a Commissioner of Trade, seconded ; Peregrine Cust, a London merchant, and Sir William Meredith, M.P. for Liverpool, opposed the motion, Charles Garth supplying Members on that side with arguments and material.

After a debate for some time [wrote Garth to his constituents] the Commissioners for Trade propos'd to Sir William Meredith and our friends that the present Bill should be confin'd to the single point of preventing the Colonies for the future from passing acts issuing

---

[1] The Memorial is published in the *Acts of the Privy Council* (*Colonial*), *1745-1766*, pp. 646-8. John Thomlinson, jun., was in Parliament, but the firm, and not he in his individual capacity, signed the Memorial. Sargent and Bacon shortly afterwards entered Parliament at by-elections, and Trecothick and Aufrere at the general election of 1768.

paper bills with the clause of legal tender, but not to affect or set a period to any at present subsisting: Sir William Meredith came to me in the gallery to acquaint me with the proposition made and as the sense of the House was strong in favour of restraining the provinces of this power, we [Garth and some other Colonial agents] thought it better to close with the proposition.

The scene supplies a remarkable example of Colonial quasi-representation in Great Britain: a proposal for compromise was made by the Board of Trade to the Member for Liverpool, was communicated by him to the agents in the gallery, and accepted by them on behalf of the Colonies.

As a third example of the working of this quasi-representation by agents, merchants, and Members connected with the trading centres in Great Britain, I take the case of the Mutiny Bill of 1765 which contained provisions for the billeting of soldiers on private houses in America. This was deemed an infraction of the civil rights of the Colonists, and the case was of a political, not a commercial, character. The Mutiny Bill, wrote Charles Garth to South Carolina on 5 April 1765,

I think of so much importance and so interesting to everything a subject can hold dear and valuable; that I have taken every opper-tunity of giving it all the opposition in my power.[1] It has been twice the subject of four or five hours debate already. . . . I have sent to the merchants to acquaint them with the purport of it, leaving it to their discretion what steps they will choose to take but not without a hint what I think their friends in America have a right to expect from them upon this occasion.

When finally the Bill was passed, it was 'of a very different nature' from what had originally been proposed.

In consequence of the intimation I mentioned in my last to have given to the merchants, I received a polite message requesting me to give them a meeting which I obeyed with pleasure, and explained to them the purport of the Bill offer'd, with such reflections as occurr'd to me thereupon. The result of that meeting was, the body of mer-chants trading to America appointed a Select Committee to meet every evening to consider of the most effectual method to avoid a measure so oppressive in its tendency, and Mr. Glover, a very

[1] By this time Charles Garth was himself a Member of Parliament, having been returned for Devizes on 15 January 1765.

respectable Member of Parliament,[1] and myself were requested to attend as often as we should have it in our power.[2]

The Committee agreed that Garth and Glover should wait upon Grenville — 'Mr. Grenville gave us an audience of two hours' (wrote Garth), and gave the assurance that he 'would talk with the Secretary at War upon it and endeavour that the bill should be altered to our satisfaction'. This he did, and Shelburne, writing to Chatham a few years later, remarked that the Mutiny Bill had been 'altered by the merchants and agents'.[3]

When the Stamp Act produced the first great political crisis in British-American relations, the merchants in the House of Commons were naturally foremost among the advocates of the Repeal, and six only, out of some fifty-two who sat in Parliament in February 1766,[4] voted against it.[5] Outside Parliament, too, the merchants were extremely active on the side of the Colonies.

Some ten years later, on the eve of the American Revolution, the interest of British merchants in American affairs, and the pressure exercised by them in favour of America, had become much weaker; new developments in trade — the coming of the 'Industrial Revolution' — were reducing the importance of America for British trade. 'It is a capital mistake of our American friends to expect insurrections

---

[1] Richard Glover, M.P. for Weymouth and Melcombe Regis, a London merchant; about him, see *D.N.B.*

[2] Charles Garth to the Committee of South Carolina, 25 May 1765.

[3] See Fitzmaurice, *Life of William, Earl of Shelburne*, vol. i. p. 311.

[4] Of the fifty merchants returned to Parliament at the general election of 1761, seven had died by February 1766 (F. Child, Sir James Colebrooke, M. Dickenson, F. Honywood, G. Lind, J. T. Lockyer, and W. Willy); but at least nine new merchant-Members had been meantime returned to the House (A. Bacon, G. Clive, J. Coutts, J. Darker, W. Ewer, Richard Fuller, J. Sargent, J. Sutton, and B. Way).

[5] The only two merchants representing Scottish constituencies, James Coutts, the banker, M.P. for Edinburgh, and Sir Alexander Grant, M.P. for Inverness Burghs, voted against the Repeal; so did Robert Jones and John Stephenson, who were followers of Lord Sandwich and connected with the East India Company, but had no interests in America; George Prescott, originally a Leghorn merchant-banker, helped to a seat in Parliament by Henry Fox; and Henry Shiffner — he was connected with the Grenvilles, in 1760 had become very nearly bankrupt, and was given a secret service pension of £500 p.a. by Newcastle's successors in 1763 or 1764 (this appears from a secret service list preserved among the papers of George III in the Royal Archives at Windsor Castle).

here . . .' wrote Samuel Curwen from London on 8 August 1775. 'The manufactories are in full employ, and one of the warmest of the friends of America told me that letters from Manchester expressed joy that no American orders had been sent, otherwise there must have been disappointment somewhere." [1]

Another loyalist refugee, Samuel Quincy of Braintree, wrote on 18 August 1775 that people in Great Britain were 'at peace and contented, immersed in wealth and commerce, and caring little what passed beyond them'. And Colonel John Maunsell, on 5 July 1775 :

England was never in a more flourishing state — new doors opened to commerce ; manufacturers fully employed ; stocks as high as before the dispute. [2]

Some merchants would still petition in favour of the Colonies, but, as William Lee wrote from London on 10 March 1775, [3]

the Ministry knew well enough the merchants, except 2 or 3 of us, were not at all serious ; hence it is, that our petitions are almost all . . . little else than milk and water. The Glasgow merchants played the same game but with less trouble, they sent a strong petition to the H[ouse] of C[ommons] in favour of America, but at the same time gave Lord North to understand by their Member, Lord F. Campbell, that they did not mean any opposition, but to gain credit in America, and thereby more easily collect their debts. This is currently reported here but I cannot vouch it for fact.

There was a certain naïve meanness in the politics of eighteenth-century merchants, but it was not limited to Great Britain ; I conclude with a letter from Henry Cruger, to whom England and America have equal claims — born and educated in America, he represented Bristol in the British Parliament, 1774–80 and 1784–90, but having returned to his native country 'before the expiration of his term, . . . was

[1] See *Journal and Letters* (1842), p. 35.
[2] See H. C. Van Schaack, *Life of Peter Van Schaack*, p. 42 ; about Maunsell, see article by W. Hall in the *Magazine of American History*, vol. xii. pp. 558-63, and by M. Van Rensselaer, *ibid.* vol. xxvii. pp. 519-30.
[3] See 'Letters to Thomas Adams' in *The Virginia Magazine of History and Biography*, vol. vi. (1898–99), pp. 30-1.

elected to the New York State Senate while a Member of the House of Commons'.[1] On 5 March 1783 he wrote from Bristol to John Hancock, the Boston revolutionary leader :

It is with heartfelt joy that I felicitate you on the channels of our intercourse being again open'd, by the accomplishment of our most sanguine wishes — the liberty and independency of America — an event on which I do most sincerely congratulate my countrymen. I embrace the earliest opportunity to inform my old friends and correspondents that I shall continue in this city in the American business, where I hope, by receiving fresh marks of their favor, and by redoubled industry, to redeem the time lost in the late accursed war, and to repair the ravages which its influence has made on my fortune, because of the steady principles which so strongly attach'd me to the just cause of America and mankind.[2]

For the mutual convenience of myself and correspondents, I have also made a *connection in London* with two gentlemen, whose attachment to the American cause and whose open exertions in it, have at times brought upon them the most furious persecutions of the enemies of liberty. As we have long been united in one political principle, which at length is happily triumphant, we are encouraged to form a commercial connection that we hope may be equally successful.[3]

THE ARMY OFFICERS

In 1754 Sir William Baker submitted to Newcastle 'Some Thoughts on the Expediency and Manner of supporting a Regular military Force on the Continent of North America'.[4] He proposed that four regiments, forming part of the British establishment, should be stationed there, that one regiment should change every year, and 'that no dispensation be granted to any of the officers for absence from their regiments on any pretence whatsoever'.

The residence of the officers in America will give them a knowledge of the country, the people, and the different forms of the several governments in the plantations ; these particulars, however

---

[1] See note by J. W. Dean in *The New-England Historical and Genealogical Register*, vol. xxviii. (1874), p. 51.

[2] Despite this, he was in receipt of a secret service pension of £500 per annum when he left Parliament in 1780. See Laprade, *Parliamentary Papers of John Robinson*, 50.

[3] *The New-England Historical and Genealogical Register*, vol. xxviii (1874) pp. 51-2.   [4] Add. MSS. 32737, ff. 16-20.

usefull, are very little known by gentlemen; the particular accounts
of seafaring people, and the altercations of the different parts of the
several legislatures before the Board of Trade, is all our present
information. How fortunate it would be at this time if some gentlemen could on their own knowledge contradict the false or at least
suspected assertions of those who assume to themselves the sole
discretion of matters relative to the American settlements !

Although in the Seven Years' War at least one in five of
all the British infantry regiments crossed the Atlantic, only
six of the fifty-nine army officers returned to Parliament at
the general election of 1761 had been to, or were actually in,
America. Of the senior officers very few went there ; the
Guards, which naturally comprised the greatest number of
young men of Parliamentary rank, had not been out ; and
in the Royal Americans, the most numerous corps in America,
foreigners formed a high proportion among the officers —
there were some fifty of them, including the well-known
Colonels Haldimand and Bouquet. The following are the six
army Members who had personal acquaintance with America :
Lieut.-General Edward Cornwallis, who, from 1749 till 1752,
had been Governor of Nova Scotia (a post, at that time, always
filled by a general) ; Major-General John Stanwix, who in
1756 volunteered for service in America, and, as a Brigadier-
General in the Royal Americans, was still there in 1761 ; Maj.-
Gen. George Townshend, who, when Wolfe was killed and
Monckton wounded, took over the command at Quebec ; and
Simon Fraser, William Howe, and Archibald Montgomery,
who, in the spring of 1761, commanded regiments of Foot in
America.

Army officers had undoubtedly better opportunities for
becoming acquainted with the American Continent than
sailors or merchants, as their task carried them far beyond the
tide-water country, into the backwoods and on to the 'frontier' ;
and their relations with the Americans were not necessarily
warped by that antagonism which prevailed between the royal
officials standing on their dignity,[1] and the colonists who,

---

[1] In England 'personages of the greatest importance affect not that
distance and magisterial reserve, which is so common among those who
can only preserve their dignity by the mysterious appendages of greatness',

under a system that gave them 'representative institutions but
not responsible government', sat 'permanently upon the opposition bench'.[1] Still, in view of differences in outlook, anteced-
ents, and training, even operations carried out in common by
the British regulars and the Colonial militias did not invariably
result in a good understanding. Christopher Gadsden, of
South Carolina (born the son of a purser in the Royal Navy,
educated in England, and yet one of the bitterest enemies of
England in the Revolution), for years 'carefully preserved the
correspondence relating to a controversy between Colonel
James Grant of the regulars in the Cherokee War of 1761, and
his friend Middleton'.[2] Moreover, the British officers in
America naturally consorted with the British officials, who were
not slow in poisoning their minds against the Colonials and
infecting them with their own 'hubris' ('Imperialism', wrote
a boy in an Oxford scholarship examination in 1912, 'is the
pleasure of living with one's inferiors'). But even when British
officers entered Colonial society, it was almost invariably that
of the well-to-do Episcopalians, who did not differ much from
Englishmen [3] and, on the whole, were inclined to support

wrote J. Vardill from London on 5 April 1774 (see H. C. Van Schaack,
The Life of Peter Van Schaack (1842), p. 26). And John Watts wrote
from New York on 9 November 1765 : 'For my own part I allways go to
the fountainhead, the waters generally grow muddyer as they go down,
there we are sure to meet with civility and candor . . .' (*Letter Book of
John Watts, Collections of the New York Hist. Soc.*, vol. 61, pp. 398-9).

[1] For a brilliant and eminently fair sketch of the system, see chapter
on 'The Machinery of Empire' in James Truslow Adams, *Revolutionary
New England* (1923), from which these quotations are taken.

[2] See E. I. Renick, 'Christopher Gadsden', in the *Publications of the
Southern Historical Association*, July 1898, pp. 242-55. The controversy
arose over the vexed question of the relative value of rank in the regulars
and the militia. Grant's attitude towards the American militia seems to
have changed in the course of the campaign, but the harm he had done
was not to be undone. William Bull, Lieut.-Gov. of South Carolina, wrote
to C. Colden, Lieut.-Gov. of New York, on 15 July 1761 :

> Colonel Grant informs me that the Provincial Regiment has behaved
> well as he always expected, the Rangers have been useful and alert, they
> have never made difficulty and he is as much pleased with them now, as
> he was displeased with them when they took the field (*Collections of the
> New York Hist. Soc.*, 1923, vol. 55 ; *Colden Papers*, vol. vi. p. 55).

Grant was Governor of East Florida, 1763-73, and sat in Parliament,
1773-80 and 1787-1802.

[3] Peter Van Schaack, when a refugee in England, noted in his diary
that the manners of the people were in no way materially different from

government as such. Still, that association of officials, officers, and Episcopalians did not endear any of them to the Dissenters of the Northern and Middle Provinces.

The Episcopalians [wrote Ezra Stiles on 27 February 1767] confederate themselves with the Crown officers of every department, procure ecclesiastical revenues, monopoly of all lucrative and honorary employments. . . . As the civil and military and revenue officers will lend all their aid and coincide with the missionaries in episcopizing the Dissenters . . . so it is to be expected that the Church will grow from this quarter.[1]

Nor would the strict Puritans have welcomed the British officers, had these tried to associate with them ; on 24 September 1759 Stiles wrote to his friend Eliot, a Dissenting minister :

From the conduct of the officers of the Army you entertain an expectation favourable to virtue. Far from this I imagine the American morals and religion were never in so much danger as from our commerce with the Europeans in the present war. . . . The religion of the Army is infidelity and gratification of the appetites. . . . [Here] the British officers put on the mask and profession of sobriety and regularity, as they conceived they were among the strict Presbyterians whose public morals were not debauched by the polite national vices, except at New York and a few other places. . . . I look upon it that our officers are in danger of being corrupted with vicious principles, and many of them I doubt not will in the end of the war come home minute philosophers initiated in the polite mysteries and vitiated morals of Deism.[2]

The best among the officers certainly answered Sir William Baker's expectations — they were keen to learn about the vast American Continent, to gauge its future, and to contribute to the upbuilding of the great Empire which they saw arise. In October 1750 James Wolfe wrote to his friend, Captain Rickson, who was going out to Nova Scotia :

In what a state of felicity are our American colonies compared to those of other nations. . . . Within the influence of our happy Government, all nations are in security. The barrier you are to form,

those of the people in America, and that 'an acquaintance with the manners of the principal families at New York, before the present troubles, gives a good idea of those of the *towns* in England' (see H. C. Van Schaack, *op. cit.* p. 162). [1] Stiles MSS.

[2] *Ibid.* He admitted, however, the 'virtue' of some of the Scottish Presbyterian troops.

will, if it takes place, strengthen ourselves, protect and support all our adherents; and as I pretend to have some concern for the general good, and a vast desire to see the propagation of freedom and truth, I am very anxious about the success of this undertaking.

I beg you will tell me at large the condition of your affairs and what kind of order there is in your community; the notions that prevail; the method of administering justice; the distribution of lands, and their cultivation; the nations that composed the colony and who are the most numerous; if under military government, how long that is to continue; and what sect in religious affairs is the most prevailing. If ever you advise upon this last subject, *remember to be moderate.* I suppose the Governor has some sort of council, and should be glad to know what it is composed of. The southern colonies will be concerned in this settlement, and have probably sent some able men to assist you with their advice, and with a proper plan of administration. Tell me likewise what climate you live in, and what soil you have to do with; whether the country is mountainous and woody, or plain; if well watered.[1]

Isaac Barré, an officer of Wolfe's school, while on service in America 'contracted many friendships with American gentlemen, and . . . entertained much more favourable opinions of them than some of his profession have done. . . .'[2] Soon after his return to England, Barré was provided with a seat in Parliament by Lord Shelburne, and in the debate on the Stamp Act on 6 February 1765, spoke against the proposed taxation:

God knows I do not at this time speak from motives of party heat, what I deliver are the genuine sentiments of my heart; however superiour to me in general knowledge and experience the reputable body of this House may be, yet I claim to know more of America than most of you, having seen and been conversant in that country.[3]

But Barré did not rely on his past experience only; he kept in touch with American friends, tried to obtain information from them, and acted as a quasi-representative for the

---

[1] Beckles Willson, *The Life and Letters of James Wolfe* (1909), p. 134. See also Wolfe's forecast of the future of America written from Louisbourg on 11 August 1758: 'Nature has refused them nothing, and there will grow a people out of our little spot, England, that will fill this vast space, and divide this great portion of the globe with the Spaniards, who are possessed of the other half' (*ibid.* p. 395).

[2] Jared Ingersoll to Gov. Thomas Fitch, London, 11 February 1765, *Fitch Papers*, vol. ii. pp. 321-2, *Collections of the Connecticut Hist. Soc.*, vol. 18 (1920).   [3] *Ibid.* p. 323.

Colonies. John Watts, a leading New York merchant (sub-sequently a loyalist), wrote to Barré on 28 February 1762 :

> You have my sincere congratulations on the distinguish'd trust reposed in you by your country, the discharge of it faithfully and ably I can never doubt, while my present impression of Coll. Barré remain, but I very much doubt whether I shall be able to furnish one single mite to it, by any information I can give from America, tho our great Continent as you justly observe, is likely soon to be the subject of much deliberation. It is difficult to ascertain facts, informations are so imperfect and peoples dispositions in general so partial and so unsteady, that ones mind is allways tottering, however I will attempt to stumble over some particulars as well as I can.

After this introduction he proceeded to give Barré his views on the aims to be pursued in the peace treaty, and urged the desirability of retaining Canada.[1]

The correspondence continued during the following years, Barré encouraging the Colonies in their resistance to the Stamp Act, and his friends in America counting on him to plead their cause. On 24 May 1764 Watts noted in his letter book :

> N.B. Wrote to Coll. Barré by the foregoing packet. Thank'd him for his opposition to the oppressive views of Parliament, but imagin'd the Colonys would not avail themselves of his advice by uniting, they were but a rope of sand. . . .[2]

---

[1] *Letter Book of John Watts, Merchant and Councillor of New York*, 1 January 1762–22 December 1765, *Collections of the N.Y. Hist. Soc.*, vol. 61 (1928), pp. 24-7. The letter concludes with a rebuke for the well-known attack against Pitt which Barré delivered in the House of Commons on 10 December 1761 :

> We have a report here that you have address'd Mr. P. rather roughly in the House 'a worthless and a profligate Minister' he has done so much for America, that we dont allow him such epithets.

For the interest and feelings evoked in New England by Pitt's resignation, see *e.g.* 'The Diary of Dr. Nathaniel Ames', published in the *Dedham Historical Register*, vol. i. (1890) :

> December 1761.
> 14. Mr. Pitt resign'd the Seals &c.
> January 1762.
> Mr. Pitt's resignation make a great noise among the people. . . .
> Wagers that Will the Coachman will get upon the box in less than a fortnight.
> February 1762.
> 15. Mr. Pitt reinstated.
> 20. Mr. Pitt not reinstated.

[2] *Letter Book of John Watts*, p. 258.

When, towards the end of 1764, the Assembly of New York became engaged in one of their many conflicts with the highly unpopular Lieut.-Governor, Cadwallader Colden — this time over the question 'whether appeals in fact, from verdicts of juries, as well as appeals in law, on writs of error, lay to the Governor and Council' [1] — Watts wrote to a friend in London : 'Do tell Coll. Barré he must defend us against the old man's invasion of our libertys here, he is making French men of us all, by in a manner taking away the effect of jurys. . . .' [2]   And a month later he thus concluded a long letter to Barré on that matter : 'I am afraid I have trespassd too much on your patience if any thing occurrs farther it must serve for another meal, at present if I could flatter myself you are not surfeited, I am sure you must be satisfyd.' [3]   But Barré seems to have pressed for more and more information about the Colonies — Watts wrote to a common friend in London, on 15 April 1765: 'Sho'd be glad to give Coll. Barré all the assistance in my power, but its a difficult task to form a judgment of such mixt interests as the Colonys are compos'd of'.[4]

Barré was not, however, typical of English officers, and not typical of the best among them either ; in fact, he was not English, either by parentage or birth.   The son of Huguenot refugees, born at Dublin, he was *déclassé* and poor, and did not share in the privileges of the British upper classes ; but men of a stock which has sacrificed honours and wealth to a principle or an idea will not readily put up with the humiliations of a subordinate position.   In the eloquence and enthusiasms of Barré there was an admixture of bitterness and demagogy, which sprang from personal grievances.   Such was the origin of his attack on Pitt, who in 1760 had refused his application for promotion,[5] and also, perhaps unconsciously, of much that was best and worst in his attitude towards the Colonies.   Without roots or assured standing in England, without connexions to promote his interests, only after many years 'rescued from obscurity' by Wolfe and Shelburne, he

[1] See *Letter Book of John Watts*, p. 307, note 155.
[2] To James Napier, New York, 14 December 1764 ;   *ibid.* p. 318.
[3] 19 January 1765 ;   *ibid.* p. 326.   [4] *Ibid.* p. 345.
[5] See *Chatham Correspondence*, vol. ii. pp. 41-3.

watched how the well-connected were promoted far beyond
their merits, and how they inherited the earth without a trace
of meekness ; he hated these men — 'to whom my pride will
not permitt me to allow precedence of class'[1] — and he
sympathised with those who resisted their pretensions ; but
this did not add to his popularity at home, nor render his
influence beneficial in the Colonies.[2]

More representative of the best type of English officers was
General Robert Monckton (M.P. for Pontefract, 1751–54 and
March-September 1774),[3] who served in America during the
Seven Years' War and was Governor of New York 1761–63.
When Monckton was leaving for England, his friend John
Watts wrote, on 13 May 1763, to Sir William Baker : 'Whether
he will return or no is very uncertain, the Province regrets the
loss of him much, his conduct has been so kind, just and
moderate, and at the same time so impartial and independent'.[4]
After Monckton had gone back to England while retaining
his Governorship, Watts kept him constantly informed about
the affairs of his province and its quarrels with his deputy,
Cadwallader Colden, obviously expecting him to intervene on
its behalf with the Government ;[5] and even after Monckton

---

[1] In a letter to Lord Shelburne, date 18 April 1763, and preserved
among the Bowood Papers. 'Harsh usage', he wrote, 'may break my
temper, it shall not affect my spirit. Administration with all the solidity
it is likely in its present shape to procure, may in some important hour
want the assistance of one firm and honest man.'

[2] Still, there was a good deal besides demagogy in Barré's speeches and
letters, and it is rather hard on his memory to be yoked with that of Wilkes
in the name of the town of Wilkesbarre in Pennsylvania. Here is an example
of the extreme 'patriot' cant, culled from a letter which, on 21 September
1770, John Wilkes addressed to Nathaniel Barber of Boston (it was intercepted in the Post Office and is now at the Record Office ; C.O. 5/38):

> I shall expect every thing good and intrinsically valuable from the
> young gentleman [Barber's son] . . . when I consider that he is educated
> under your care, and among the generous sons of freedom in America,
> who remain undebauch'd by the wickedness of European Courts, and
> Parliamentary prostitution. I pray heaven. . . .

And so on in the perfect Wilkesite style.

[3] One seat at Pontefract was controlled by Monckton's brother, William,
2nd Viscount Galway, who himself sat for it, 1747–48 and 1754–72.

[4] *Letter Book of John Watts, Collections of the N.Y. Hist. Soc.*, vol. 61,
pp. 313-14.

[5] Monckton was not on good terms with Colden ; he 'entertain'd some
disgust with me', wrote Colden to John Pownall on 26 November 1761
(see *Colden Letter Books*, vol. i. p. 137, *Collections of the N.Y. Hist Soc.*

had relinquished his Governorship, Watts wrote to him on 22 February 1766 : 'The very great regard the people of this Colony universally profess for you, seems to inspire them almost as generally with an idea of having a filial title to your protection and good offices as if you was still their benevolent Governor'.[1]

Similarly the two Amhersts, General Sir Jeffrey and his brother, Colonel William Amherst, a Member of Parliament 1766–74, were popular in America, if we accept the testimony of John Watts, who seems a reliable and independent witness. When on the conclusion of the war they returned to England, Watts wrote about them on 15 November 1763 :

General Amherst I suppose will be less abroad than the younger part of his family ; they all know of course more of American transactions than any people in it, being at the fountain head, sensible and attentive. Coll. Amherst I have mentioned to you as one of the best disposed men imaginable, there never was a more temperate orderly family than they all are, with hands not only clean but unsuspected.[2]

Wolfe, Monckton, and the Amhersts were of the type of soldier which supplied many of the best and most enlightened colonial administrators ; but the same range of interests and understanding could not be expected from smaller men endowed with what is known as the 'military outlook', and Ingersoll, while praising Barré, clearly hinted at the unfavourable opinion which some of that profession entertained of the Americans. Personal contact with strange and disrespectfus Colonials, especially after violent popular commotions had started in America, no doubt merely confirmed such officers in their 'disciplinarian' principles and in their predilection for dragooning.

---

for 1876). And in the same letter, having explained the difficulties which had arisen between him and Monckton over the 'perquisites' of the Governor's office, he went on to say : 'I went to Mr. Watts, one of the Council, an eminent merchant in this place, and the only person I knew to be intimate with Mr. Monckton, to desire his assistance to reconcile matters between Mr. Monckton and me'.

[1] See *Aspinwall Papers, Collections of the Mass. Hist. Soc.*, 4th Series, vol. x. p. 590.

[2] *Letter Book of John Watts*, p. 194.

Moreover, Scotsmen formed a very high proportion among the British officers and officials in the Colonies,[1] and they were hard, grasping, efficient men, who could fight and conquer, but lacked that spirit of sympathetic toleration and restraint which, even in the eighteenth century, could occasionally be found in Englishmen ; they had a genius for action rather than for compromise, and were much better at building Empires than at preserving them.   At home the rights and interests of the Colonies were hardly ever championed by a Scotsman or Irish-Scot,[2] and they who as Presbyterians might have formed a link between the British Government and the great body of Dissenters on the American Continent, were as unpopular in New England as they were, at that time, in England.   In office they were authoritarians, and showed little understanding for the constitutional refinements and 'the sound doctrine of Mr. Locke', which were of English, and not of Scottish, origin ;

---

[1] Hardwicke wrote to Royston on 23 July 1763 (Add. MSS. 35352, f. 387) :

> I have heard no news, except that Governours are nominated in form for our new conquer'd Colonies ; — General Murray for Canada ; James Grant, Esq., for East-Florida ; George Johnstone, Esq., for West-Florida, and Robert Melvill, Esq., for Grenada, and the Grenadines, St. Vincent's, Dominica and Tobago.   All Scotch !

Similarly John Calcraft wrote to his friend Col. Ralph Burton, on 15 August 1763 (Add. MSS. 17496, f. 12) : 'I had great hopes of carrying the point of Canada for you and try'd my utmost but the Scotch were too powerfull and succeeded'.   And again on 13 April 1764 (*ibid.* f. 34) : 'Lord Malpas is dead.   Colonel Mackay got his regiment.   General Barrington is dead also, Stanwix gets his, and Colonel Greem [Graeme] succeeds Stanwix.   Scotch and all Scotch.'

Samuel Estwicke, Agent for Barbados and subsequently M.P. for Westbury, wrote in his *Letter to the Rev. Josiah Tucker*, in 1776, that 'America . . . became the land of promise to the Scots'.   'I am warranted to say that of these places [in America] three-fourths have been filled by the Scots' ; and 'as a proof in part of this', he proceeded to give a list stating that in Jamaica the Governor, his Secretary, the Clerk of the Court, the Register in Chancery, the Receiver-General, the Naval Officer, the Comptroller, and the Commander of Fort Charles were all Scotsmen ; only the Secretary of the Island and the Collector were Englishmen.   'N.B.   Many other subordinate appointments under these, all Scotch.   There is not in the civil, military or revenue establishment, even a Creole of this country that enjoys any appointment of £20 a year' (*ibid.* pp. 104-5, footnote).

[2] Two exceptions have to be mentioned : Governor George Johnstone championed the Colonies in Parliament, but few men have done more harm than he when with the Conciliatory Mission in America in 1778 ; and Lauchlan Macleane, of Scotch-Irish origin, who was for some years secretary to Lord Shelburne, and sat in Parliament 1768-71.

while as settlers Scotsmen were independent, and, together with their kinsmen from Ulster, formed the vanguard of the American Revolution.[1] It would be unfair to put the chief blame for the catastrophe on the Scots — England supplied her own quota of Bernards and Boones, and of ill-chosen officials who at a distance from home displayed their moral and mental inferiority. But, on the other hand, Scotland never supplied a Thomas Pownall or a Richard Jackson ; no Fraser, Grant, or Gordon seems to have thought or spoken of America in the terms used by a Wolfe ; and no Loudoun, Abercromby, or Colden was ever spoken of by Americans in the terms applied to a Monckton — and this though more Scottish than English officers and officials went out to America, and more Scotsmen belonging to the upper classes had relatives in America, or were intermarried with colonial families.[2]

In the division on the Repeal of the Stamp Act, on 21-22 February 1766, 168 Members (forming 30 per cent of the House of Commons) voted against it ; of the 54 army officers who at that time sat in Parliament, 23 (*i.e.* almost 43 per cent of the total, and probably a majority of those taking part in the

[1] 'The first public voice in America for dissolving all connection with Great Britain, came, not from the Puritans of New England, the Dutch of New York, nor the planters of Virginia, but from the Scotch-Irish Presbyterians' (see George H. Smyth, 'The Scotch and Scotch-Irish in America', *Magazine of American History*, vol. iv., 1880). The only clergyman who signed the Declaration of Independence was Dr. John Witherspoon, a descendant of John Knox ; and there were no less than six Scotch-Irish among the signers, four of them pupils of Dr. Allison, himself Scotch-Irish and educated at Edinburgh.

[2] To quote a few examples : Andrew Elliot, Collector of the Port of New York, was an uncle of Gilbert Elliot, who was one of the closest associates of Bute and a trusted servant of George III ; one daughter of Andrew Elliot married William Cathcart, subsequently 10th Baron Cathcart, and another Sir David Carnegie, 4th Baronet, M.P. But Andrew Elliot, while through Thomas Hollis in close touch with English Dissenters, does not seem to have kept up any correspondence with his Scottish relatives, and in a letter to Hollis even shows a certain dislike of the Scottish officials in America (see *Collections of the Mass. Hist. Soc.*, 4th Series, vol. iv. p. 420). Archibald Kennedy, whose father had been Collector of Customs in New York, was an officer in the Royal Navy, and a cousin of David Kennedy, M.P. for Ayrshire, 1768–74 ; he married first Miss Kath. Schuyler of New Jersey, and, as his second wife, Ann, daughter of John Watts, from whose letter books I have quoted above. Lord William Campbell, Governor of South Carolina, married Sarah Izard, of a leading South Carolinian family ; Richard Maitland, son of the 6th Earl of Lauderdale, an army officer serving in America, married Mary MacAdam of New York ; etc., etc.

division) voted with the minority.[1] This may have been partly
due to the disciplinarian bias of the military mind, but partly
also to the fact that Scotsmen who, in February 1766, formed
less than one-tenth of the House, constituted about one-fifth
of the army group. Of the 54 officers in Parliament, 42 were
English, 11 Scottish, and 1 Welsh ; of the English officers, 15
voted against the Repeal (36 per cent, against an average of
27 per cent for all the English Members), but of the Scotsmen,
8 (73 per cent, against 60 per cent for all the Scottish Members).[2]
Of the 15 English army officers who voted against the Repeal of
the Stamp Act, not one is known to have been in America ;
of the eight Scotsmen, three (Simon Fraser, Lord Adam
Gordon, and Archibald Montgomery). Lord Adam Gordon
had, in fact, been there during the Stamp Act crisis, and had
but recently returned to England.

Note on the American Tour of Lord Adam Gordon

It is much to be regretted that Adam Gordon himself has left
little more than an itinerary of his American tour, mentioning the
places he visited and the names of the persons he met, and that the
editor of his notes, except for one or two remarks reproduced in
the introduction, has omitted even the little there seems to have been
of comment on general topics and events.[3] In April 1764 Gordon
took out to Jamaica the 66th Regiment of Foot, of which he was Colonel, and having touched at Madeira, Antigua, and St. Kitt's, arrived
in Jamaica in June. So far his journey was in discharge of his professional duties ; but in August he proceeded with his friend, Admiral
Sir John Lindsay,[4] to Pensacola, in West Florida ; next he seems to
have planned a visit to New Orleans, but it is not clear whether he
ever got there.[5] In November he visited East Florida, in December

[1] As there is no list of the majority, percentages within special groups
of Members have to be calculated on their total number, and no comparisons
can be made within each group of the votes given on either side.

[2] Of the three Scottish officers who did not vote against the Repeal,
Col. Pringle was absent in America.

[3] The itinerary was published by Mr. Keith W. Murray in *The
Genealogist*, New Series, vol. xiv. (1897–98). My thanks are due to Mr.
J. M. Bullock for having drawn my attention to that itinerary.

[4] Adam Gordon was M.P. for Aberdeenshire, and Sir John Lindsay,
with the help of the Gordons, was returned for Aberdeen Burghs at a by-
election in 1767.

[5] Neither New Orleans nor any of its French officials is mentioned in
Gordon's itinerary ; but see letter from M. Dabbadie, New Orleans,

Georgia and South Carolina — returning to Georgia in February —
and next North Carolina, Virginia, Maryland, Pennsylvania, and New
Jersey ; in May 1765 he reached New York, and from that moment
he steps into the limelight of several well-known collections of correspondence, *e.g.* the papers of Cadwallader Colden, Sir William
Johnson, and John Watts.[1] The journey along the Atlantic coast was
carried out at the time of the commotions produced by the Stamp
Act, and on 1 June 1765 Adam Gordon wrote from New York to a
friend in England : 'This is a good place and sensible people in it,
yet touched with the times, as all North Americans are'.[2] And on
1 June, John Watts wrote to James Napier :

> Lord Adam Gordon is arrivd from the southward and sets out
> next week for Niagara to return to this place thro' Canada and
> New England and to embark in a packet after finishing the
> American tour, wont he be the greatest curiosity in England, by
> the by he seems to be as sanguine about laying it thick upon
> the Colonys, as they are to throw off every thing, an immense
> difference.[3]

Having visited Montreal, Quebec, and Trois Rivières, Gordon
proceeded by way of Connecticut to Massachusetts. About Boston
he wrote in his notebook :

> The better kind of people seem well bred and sensible, they
> lament their present plan of government which throws too much
> weight into the popular scale. . . . After all it would appear as if
> nothing but a thorough alteration of their Charter and form of
> government . . . would operate effectively.[4]

From Boston he returned through Rhode Island to New York
whence he embarked for England, arriving at Falmouth on 11
November 1765. Sir William Johnson wrote to the Lords of Trade
on 28 June 1765 : 'Lord Adam has made an extensive tour thro'
this country, and has made many remarks and observations worthy

---

10 September 1764, to the Minister in Paris ; printed from the Archives
Nationales, Ministère des Colonies, by C. W. Alvord and C. E. Carter in
their book on *The Critical Period, 1763–65* (*Collections of the Illinois State
Historical Library*, vol. x. pp. 311-12).

[1] See *Colden Papers*, vols. ii. and v., and *Letter Book of John Watts*,
both in the *Collections of the N.Y. Hist. Soc.*, and *Documents Relative to
the Colonial History of New York*, vol. vii. ; the *Aspinwall Papers* in the
Collections of the Mass. Hist. Soc., 4th Series, vol. x. ; and the *Papers of Sir
William Johnson*, vol. v.

[2] *Hist. MSS. Comm., Rutland MSS.*, vol. iv. p. 233.

[3] *Letter Book*, pp. 355-6.

[4] See 'Manuscript of Lord Adam Gordon', ed. by Keith W. Murray,
The Genealogist, vol. xiv. p. 12.

of attention'.[1] And C. Colden to Sir Jeffrey Amherst on October 10 :
'Lord Adam Gordon . . . can inform you of every thing you may
desire to know from America. He has perform'd the tour of all the
Colonies, and has been an eye-witness of some extraordinary events
in several of them at this time.' [2] And a relative of Lord Adam,
Harry Gordon, thus described him in a letter to Sir William Johnson
on 4 March 1766 : 'Lord Adam is warm sometimes, whimsical a
little, but of the warmest friendship. . . .' [3] That friendship did
not, however, extend to the American Whigs and their cause, as is
shown by his vote against the Repeal of the Stamp Act.

It would be interesting to know what was the original purpose of
that Imperial 'grand tour' of Lord Adam Gordon. Was curiosity
the chief motive, stimulated no doubt by American connexions —
his sister-in-law, the widow of the 3rd Duke of Gordon, had married,
secundo voto, a New Yorker, Staats Long Morris — or was there also
an admixture of prospecting in that tour ? It seems that at one time
Adam Gordon had meant to return to America as a governor. 'It is
said', wrote Colden to Johnson on 20 February 1766, 'Lord Adam
Gordon is to be appointed Governor of the Massachusetts.' [4] Johnson replied on March 8 that he had a letter from Gordon which said
'nothing of his being appointed for any American government,
neither is there much news in his letter, as nothing could then be
determined upon, and the Ministry were not expected to hold their
places, there is a hint of Lord Butes coming into office. . . .' [5]

Indeed it could hardly be expected that the Rockinghams should
appoint Lord Adam Gordon to a Colonial governorship ; nor did he
revert to the idea, if he had ever seriously entertained it, when it
became once more feasible. The only tangible outcome of his American tour was his entering the ranks of speculators in American land.

In 1766 Lord Adam Gordon received a grant of 20,000 acres in
East Florida,[6] and about the same time he became a member of the
Illinois Company.[7]

---

[1] *Documents Relative to the Colonial History of the State of New York*,
edited by E. B. O'Callaghan, vol. vii. (1856), p. 767.

[2] *Colden Papers*, vol. ii. p. 44, *Collections of the N.Y. Hist. Soc.*, 1877–78.

[3] See C. W. Alvord and C. E. Carter, *The New Régime, 1765–1767*
(1916), p. 162.

[4] *Papers of Sir William Johnson*, ed. by A. C. Flick, vol. v. (1927), p. 33.

[5] *Ibid.* pp. 61-2.

[6] *Acts of the Privy Council (Colonial), 1745–1766*, vol. iv. p. 815.

[7] See letter from Sir William Johnson to William Franklin, 3 May
1766, nominating Gordon for that Company, and also letter from Benjamin
Franklin to the same, London, 12 September 1766, saying that he would
take 'the first opportunity of conferring with him' (Gordon) ; both letters
are published in Alvord and Carter, *The New Régime, 1765–1767*, pp. 224-5
and 376.

THE NAVAL OFFICERS

Of the admirals returned to Parliament in 1761, Rodney had been Governor of Newfoundland, 1749–50 (its Governors, and later those of West Florida, were invariably naval men) ; [1] Francis Holburne had commanded the fleet in the Louisbourg expedition of 1757 ; Charles Saunders had been in command of the Newfoundland station in 1759, and of the fleet operating against Quebec in 1760 ; while Sir James Douglas and Charles Holmes had served under Saunders in that expedition (Holmes never entered the Parliament of 1761, for he died in Jamaica the same year, on 21 November).   Thomas Frankland had seen a considerable amount of service in North America and the West Indies ; Augustus Keppel had commanded, in 1754–1755, the squadron which escorted Braddock's army to America and had supported its operations ; and Sir Edward Hawke had commanded, in 1749, the convoy for the Nova Scotia settlers. Thus at least eight of the 21 naval officers returned to Parliament in 1761 can be proved to have been to North America ; further, Peter Denis and Thomas Cotes had served in the West Indies.   It may be assumed that a majority of the naval officers in the House at some time or other had been in America.

How much they had learnt by visiting it, is another question ;   still, so much is clear, that they, too, appreciated the great future of the Continent of which they visited the seaboard — merchants and officers in the army and navy figure prominently among the applicants for grants of land in America.

LAND SPECULATORS

Speculation in American land on a large scale naturally did not start till after 1763, and the subject lies beyond the scope of this book.   A great deal of historical research is being done about it in America, and here I only wish to call attention to the great number of Members of Parliament who during the

---

[1] Rodney was preceded in the Governorship of Newfoundland by Sir Charles Hardy, the famous admiral, and a Member of Parliament, 1764–1768 and 1771–80 ; and succeeded by Captain F. W. Drake, R.N., M.P. for Beeralston, 1771–74.

years following on the conclusion of peace applied for, and obtained, grants of land in America. It is obvious that the belief in the great future of the American Colonies, universal among their own inhabitants, was shared by these Members ; and having gone through a few lists of the recipients of grants of land in the two Floridas, in Nova Scotia, and especially in the Island of St. John, and at Cape Breton, I feel certain that on close examination the number of Members of Parliament who between 1764 and 1774 engaged in such speculation will be found to have been considerable.

The case of the Island of St. John can be taken as an example. In February 1764 Lord Egmont, 'on behalf of himself and his nine children, and a great number of land and sea officers', applied 'for a grant in fee of the island of St. John's'.[1] His associates included 16 naval officers, 14 army officers, 5 merchants, and 8 Members of Parliament.[2] The Board of Trade was opposed to grants on such a scale, and declared that as a rule not more than 20,000 acres should be granted to one person ; 'we do not see that any advantage whatever can arise to the public, or to the several adventurers, by leaving the parcelling out of the lands to the said Earl. . . .'[3]

There is, in the *Acts of the Privy Council*, a record of another such application — 'a Memorial of Admiral Knowles, Sir Charles Saunders, Sir George Brydges Rodney, and Richard Spry, Esq., in behalf of themselves and other officers and merchants, asking for the grant of the whole Island of St. John to be divided among them in lots of 20,000 acres' ; [4] this too was refused on the same grounds as the application from Lord Egmont.[5] When at last, on 23 July 1767, the Island of St. John was parcelled out, 66 grants were made to private individuals, or groups of individuals, each grant comprising about 20,000 acres. Of these grants 17 were to Members of the House of Commons (in several cases these Members had

[1] *Acts of the Privy Council (Colonial), 1745–1766*, vol. iv. p. 654.
[2] *Ibid.* vol. vi. pp. 361-2.   [3] *Ibid.* vol. iv. p. 656.
[4] *Ibid.* p. 658. There is yet another (undated) 'Memorial' of the same kind from Lord Albemarle, Sir Charles Saunders, and Augustus Keppel; see Add. MSS. 14034, f. 213.
[5] Acts of the Privy Council (Colonial), *1745–1766*, vol. v. p. 56.

partners) ; and seven further grants were to men who at other times sat in Parliament though not in July 1767. Taking these twenty-four together, eight of them are found to have been merchants (Adam Drummond, E. Lewis, Joshua Mauger, A. Nesbitt, John Pringle, Samuel Smith, S. Touchet, and Chauncy Townsend), four naval officers (A. Keppel, Hugh Palliser, Sir G. B. Rodney, and Sir Charles Saunders), and three army officers (Simon Fraser, George Townshend, and Richard Worge). There were also among the recipients of such grants : Philip Stephens, M.P., Secretary to the Admiralty ; John Pownall (M.P. 1775-76), Secretary to the Board of Trade ; James Montgomery, M.P., Lord Advocate of Scotland ; Lauchlin Macleane, in 1759 a doctor in America, a friend of Burke's and Wilkes's, in 1765 Governor of St. Martin's in the West Indies, subsequently secretary to Lord Shelburne, Member of Parliament, 1768-71, and after that agent to Warren Hastings ; [1] General James Murray, Governor of Quebec, and Guy Carleton, its Lieutenant-Governor ; etc.

Of the grants to others than Members of Parliament, at least twenty were wholly or partly to army officers, and ten to merchants ; another feature is the great number of Scotsmen among the recipients of these grants, which is easily explained by the number of Scotsmen among the army officers in America, and also by the mass emigration proceeding at that time from Scotland, especially the Highlands, to the American Colonies. As besides the payment of almost nominal quit-rents, the chief obligation incumbent on the recipients of such grants was the settling of white, Protestant settlers upon the land, Scottish 'adventurers', who could attract emigrants from their own

[1] About that quaint Scotch-Irish adventurer, one of the most interesting figures of the political underworld of his time, see Add. MSS. 21643, ff. 86 and 182-3 ; 21644, ff. 28 and 32 ; and 21647, f. 169 ; *The Gentleman's Magazine*, vol. 94 (1824), part II. pp. 400 and 483 ; Charles Dilke, *Papers of a Critic* (1875), vol. ii. pp. 30-46 ; Alexander Graydon, *Memoirs* (1811), p. 33 ; James Prior, *Life of Oliver Goldsmith* (1837), pp. 149-53 ; Fitzmaurice, *Life of Shelburne* ; Galt, *Life of Benjamin West* ; *Hist. MSS. Comm.*, Fourth Report, *Macaulay MSS.*, Fifth Report, *Lansdowne MSS.*, Tenth Report, *Weston Papers* ; also *Palk Papers* ; and most books on Wilkes and Warren Hastings. His name being fairly common and his person obscure, he is often mixed up with other people, or not rightly identified.

country, were in a specially favourable position for taking up such grants.

CANADA *versus* GUADALOUPE

An analysis of the pamphlet literature on 'Canada *versus* Guadaloupe' was published by Professor W. L. Grant in *The American Historical Review* for July 1912, and an extensive study on the subject, by Professor C. W. Alvord in his book on *The Mississippi Valley in British Politics*, in 1917. Little could be added to their summary of the arguments on either side — the variety was not great, and, as is usual in such controversies, the stock was soon exhausted. But Professor Alvord has gone beyond a mere discussion of arguments, and has attempted a study of the men engaged in that controversy ; to gain a proper comprehension of British policy in America, he ventured into the wilderness of eighteenth-century British politics — 'covered by the dense underbrush of . . . political intrigue, where I found many a path leading only to a *cul-de-sac* and was so frequently misled that I have despaired at times of ever finding my way out of the darkness and gloom'.[1] Professor Alvord has clearly recognised that there was 'no such division of men and measures' as was assumed by writers who thought that these could be classified 'as Whig and Tory' ; none the less, even his own map of that political 'wilderness' is too neat and symmetrical. And this is the caveat which I wish to enter against accepting the conclusions of his otherwise admirable study : he ascribes more permanence and coherence to eighteenth-century Parliamentary groups than they possessed,[2] and he assumes that the question of Canada *versus* Guadaloupe was with them a major issue, on which the members of any one group had to think, or at least to speak and vote, alike.

In reality there is nothing to show that in 1760, or early in 1761, either Newcastle or Bute, or any of the other 'group leaders' in Parliament, held strong settled views on the choice to be made between conquests, still less that they tried to force any such views on their adherents. Peace or no peace was at various times an issue, but not whether preference in

[1] P. 14. [2] See above, pp. 203-15.

the peace treaty should be given to Canada or to Guadaloupe. It was but slowly that opinion matured on this point, and even then it did not become an issue as between Parliamentary groups ; and while I do not mean to enter here into the history of the peace negotiations, or of Pitt's foreign policy — which both lie outside the scope of this book — I propose to illustrate the various angles from which the problem was considered, and the terms in which it was discussed, preferably by using hithero unpublished material.

Sir William Baker, who had considerable influence with Newcastle, from the outset pleaded strongly for retaining Canada ; Newcastle noted in his 'Memorandums for the King'[1] on 14 October 1760 :

Alderman Baker's reasoning. About keeping Canada or the Newfoundland fishery ; and Cape Breton or Guadaloupe. Senegal etc. . . .

The keeping Canada the most necessary for preserving the peace; which cannot be done whilst Canada and those parts are divided between two rival Powers, England and France, as the Indians will always be stir'd up one against the other.

The keeping the others might be more beneficial in point of trade ; but the other for the preservation of the peace.

A full statement of Baker's views is given in a paper sent by him to Newcastle on 13 April 1761.[2] These are its main points — I omit his arguments and explanations :

Canada including the Islands of Cap Breton and those in the Gulph and River of St. Laurence are now compleatly in our possession ; the value of that acquisition as a security to our other dominions in America, and as a means of wealth and power to Great Britain is so universally admitted, nothing

[1] Add. MSS. 32913, f. 128.
[2] Add. MSS. 33030, ff. 1-2. The paper is unsigned, but in William Baker's handwriting.

need be added thereto, and there can be no doubt but that the whole will be clearly and fully ceded to us, if any part of our conquest are to remain to Great Britain.

Louisiana, is less known and seems to have been less attended to, but ought nevertheless to be insisted on to make a part of the British dominions together with all the rivers that the French possessed or occupied in the Gulph of Mexico. . . .

The Newfoundland fishery, as a means of wealth and power is of more worth than both the forementioned provinces, and therefore the exclusion of the French is extreamly to be wished. . . .

   . . . It is well worth while to endeavor at an entire exclusion of them from even a pretence of navigating in North American seas. . . .

Guadaloupe is well worthy to be retained if possible, but not in an equal degree with North America, and if somewhat must be given up this island seems the fittest.

The Neutrall Islands are very differently circumstanced, they are of right belonging to Great Britain, and ought to be ceded as such, and be immediately possest and planted by the English. . . . The English want more sugar land to plant not only to supply foreign markets, but also to encrease the quantity for home consumption, and thereby reduce the price of a commodity now become of general and necessary use. . . .

This paper Newcastle sent to Hardwicke, who replied on 17 April :

I . . . return . . . inclosed Ald. Baker's paper, which is very sensibly and well drawn up. . . . For my own part, I am not for bringing Louisiana upon the carpet.[1]

This was the very time at which Pitt was formulating his demands ; they coincided fairly closely with those of Baker, but Pitt added Senegal and Goree, and Minorca, which were not disclaimed, but merely omitted, in Baker's paper. Still, as there was a very different weight behind Pitt's demands, they alarmed the pacific Newcastle, who, on 16 April, complained to Hardwicke of Pitt having told the King that he expected Great Britain to be 'able to get a peace which should secure us all Canada, Cape Breton, the islands, the harbours, the fisheries, and particularly the exclusive fishery of Newfoundland', and

[1] Add. MSS. 32922, f. 28.

of his having declared that he would not be willing to sign a different peace ; Pitt even wished terms to be declared to the French, 'from which we will not depart'.[1]

At the opposite pole to Pitt stood the Duke of Bedford, a 'Little Englander' who had some objection to any and every conquest, and merely wanted peace. He wrote to Newcastle on 9 May 1761,[2] strongly deprecating the intended demands, which he thought excessive. He was doubtful of the desirability of retaining Canada — 'indeed . . . I do not know whether the neighbourhood of the French to our Northern Colonies was not the greatest security of their dependance on the Mother Country who I fear will be slighted by them when their apprehensions of the French are removed'. Guadaloupe he thought a rich island, but difficult to hold with its French planters. Senegal and Goree were, he admitted, of infinite use to our commerce, but their possession would be an endless source of future quarrels. And as for an exclusive right to the Newfoundland fisheries, this would be resented by every maritime Power, 'as it would be a great step towards gaining the monopoly of a trade which is the great source of all maritime power and might be . . . dangerous for us to grasp at'. Thus by the time Bedford had finished, he had declared against a strengthening of the British position in the 'white man's land' of North America, in the Sugar Islands of the tropics, on the Slave Coast, and in the naval nurseries of Newfoundland, i.e., in every single corner of what was the classical Empire diagram in 1761.

Generally speaking, British opinion, both as recorded in private letters and in the press, inclined to favour the retention of Canada, considerations of security and distrust of the French being foremost in people's minds. Chesterfield wrote to Newcastle on 30 November 1760 : [3]

I think we should keep Quebec and Canada as preventives of future war, and for the rest scramble and negotiate as well as we can. The French I am persuaded would more willingly give up Canada than Guadaloupe, as they have no great notion of that furr trade and

---

[1] Add. MSS. 32922, ff. 5-6. [2] Ibid. ff. 449-51.
[3] Add. MSS. 32915, f. 194.

indeed never received any great returns from it; but Guadaloupe is a much more lucrative possession.

Lord Morton, who took a close interest in American affairs, on 15 January 1760 sent a paper to Newcastle and Hardwicke [1] in which he pleaded for extending the British possessions in North America, not

from a prospect of cultivating so immense a tract of land, but to remove bad neighbours to such a distance, and place such barriers in their way, as that they should not have it in their power to disturb our settlements.

This 'boundary of greatest security' could, he thought, be obtained by keeping Cape Breton, the Island of St. John, Nova Scotia, and the line of the St. Lawrence up to Montreal, further the line of the Great Lakes and of the Mississippi, but in a way which would cut inland communications between Canada and Louisiana.

If the French are to remain upon the Continent of North America the boundary above described . . . might best answer the purposes of our Colonies in general: perhaps better than if the French were entirely to evacuate Canada, because in that case they would undoubtedly draw their whole force to Louisiana. In which they would be much too strong for our Southern Colonies.

Having discussed some of the other 'principal points' with a view to 'accommodating our differences with France in North America', Morton concluded:

But we ought still to keep in view the invariable character of the French nation, and it will be found that . . . that perfidious and restless people have never suffered their neighbours to remain quiet. No ties can bind them where the infraction affords the smallest prospect of a present advantage.

Therefore the most desirable thing for Britain would be to have that Continent entirely evacuated by the French.

The same day (15 January 1760) Morton wrote to Hardwicke:

The idea of driving the French intirely from the Continent of America may appear wild and chimerical and I mention it as a very

[1] Add. MSS. 32901, ff. 290-301.

doubtful proposition; yet the French for many years have had in their view to dispossess the English intirely; tho' their numbers never bore any proportion to ours in that part of the world.[1]

In another letter to Hardwicke, on 15 June 1761, Morton once more urged the need for keeping Canada; but he did not allege, as so many others did, that the conquest of Guadaloupe would hurt the interests of the British Sugar Islands; indeed, his argument runs counter to the current notion of the West Indians having been all united in opposing the retention of Guadaloupe. It would seem from his letter that while the 'saturated' planters of the old Islands, who did not contemplate further extension, were averse to including a competitor in the British commercial system, planters 'on the make', who wished to extend their activities to new islands, favoured conquests. According to Morton, people in the West Indies considered that

if we dont keep Guadaloupe it will be the greatest misfortune that ever attended our Sugar Colonys for we have not only shewed the French what a valuable one it is but also shewed them the way of making it produce more sugar than all our Islands together. . . .

Such is the language of the West Indians but still I should think the peaceable possession of North America a thing of greater consequence.

I dont imagine we should people that immense tract in ten centurys but unless we have the name of the whole we shall never be at rest in those parts that are peopled while the smallest germ of French government subsists from the Gulf of Mexico to Hudsons Bay. . . .

The other objection is that the awe of the French keeps our Colonys in dependance upon the Mother Country. The answer to this is obvious: if our Governments are properly circumscribd and care taken that the new settlements should be formed into new Governments of small extent; the mutual jealousys amongst the several Colonys would always keep them in a state of dependance and it would save a vast expence to Britain in not being obliged to keep up a great number of regular forces which must be maintained if the smallest spot is left with the French upon that Continent.

Thus on the very eve of the decision concerning Canada and Guadaloupe, a man in the counsels of Newcastle and Hardwicke still thought it necessary to argue the point; and when

[1] Add. MSS. 35910, f. 16.

the matter came before the Cabinet Council, on 24 June 1761, Bedford, who a month earlier had declared against all conquests, does not seem to have given any opposition to the claiming of the whole of Canada and of Cape Breton, which demands were voted unanimously.[1]

But that even this Cabinet vote about Canada did not altogether close the subject in the minds of the leading statesmen, can be seen from the letter which Hardwicke wrote to Newcastle on 2 April 1762 ;[2] and as this letter supplies an excellent summary of the arguments used on either side, it is reproduced here almost in full :

. . . As to the retention of conquests, Mr. Pitt made North-America entirely his object. Some of his enemies objected to him that he did this out of partiality to his friend Beckford, and out of condescension to the particular interests of our Sugar Colonies; but in that I suppose they did him wrong; tho' I allways suspected that one reason why he contended so much for the totality of the Fishery, impracticable to be obtain'd, was that he saw the country of Canada was not greatly worth keeping. Your Grace knows what has been debated in pamphlets, whether we should keep Canada or Guadaloupe. It will come now to be a more grave question whether you should restore to France all her Sugar-Colonies, or great part of Canada. The most material argument for retaining Canada has been the delivering your Northern Colonies from such bad neighbours, and from the danger of French encroachments for the future; but some persons have thought that could never be securely attain'd without conquering Louisiana also; and that for this purpose some parts of Canada might serve as well as the whole. The question now may come between Canada, or a great part of Canada, and all the French Sugar Colonies, except St. Domingo.

Canada is a cold northern climate, unfruitful; furnishes no trade to Europe that I know of, but the fur trade, the most inconsiderable of all trades; and therefore never compensated to France the expense of maintaining and defending it. It's products are mostly or nearly of the same kind with those of Great Britain, and consequently will take off not much of our's. Besides, if you remove the French inhabitants, this Kingdom and Ireland cannot furnish, or procure, people enough to settle and inhabit it in centuries to come; and, if you don't remove the French inhabitants, they will never become half subjects, and this country must maintain an army there to keep them in subjection.

[1] Add. MSS. 32924, ff. 311-22.   [2] Add. MSS. 32936, ff. 310-11.

It will be said that none of these objections occur against the *French Sugar-Colonies*. They are fertile countries; may be easily peopled, and, being islands, be easily defended, particularly by your squadrons now in use to be sent annually. They must take all the necessaries of life from the Mother Country, as your own islands now do. The sugar-trade is a most profitable one, and you may engross almost the whole of it, and serve all the European markets. To defend them you will not want troops, or, at the most, a very few.

A great deal of this reasoning has been already retail'd in the pamphlets; but, when it was confin'd to Guadaloupe only, it did not carry so great weight, for France still remain'd in possession of the greater part. But it will come with redoubled force, now you have acquired the possession of *all* the Caribbee Islands, especially if what is said be true *that they are the key of the whole West-Indies*. I am very glad that Rodney did not put this into his public letter.

I have seen no body but my horse all this day, so have not talked to, or heard, any body upon the subject. Nor will I raise one word about it to morrow, nor at all without communication with your Grace and our friends; for I see the delays and difficulties that may arise from your being to form in some measure, a new plan of peace. And yet the national interest must be attended to in so important and decisive a conjuncture, in which new circumstances will give rise to new ways of thinking. I have scribbled this very hastily, that your Grace may turn it in your serious thoughts, and perhaps you may get some lights by talking, *at a proper time*, to your friend Sir William Baker upon the subject. If these Caribbee Islands could be kept it might possibly be worth the while of this country to restore almost any thing, except a greater proportion of the Fishery than was yielded in our last ultimatum.

Don't take this as an opinion, for I have form'd none.

Newcastle replied the same night (2 April):

I have this moment read over, with the greatest attention, your Lordship's most wise and material letter. . . . I own it startles me who never was startled as to the Sugar Islands before.

I have, upon it, sent for Sir William Baker, to be with me to-morrow.

Luckily we shall have no meeting; they are not yet ready.[1]

The letters quoted above will suffice to illustrate the character of the discussion and of the arguments used; I add merely one more letter, from an ordinary 'man on the spot',

---

[1] Add. MSS. 32936, f. 312.

not from a leading politician. It is from Walter Rutherfurd, one of the nineteen children of Sir John of that ilk, and younger brother of John Rutherfurd, jun., M.P. for Roxburghshire, 1734–42, who was married to a sister of Gilbert Elliot. This Walter Rutherfurd 'served in the British Army from the age of 17 and after taking part in the Canadian campaign of Sir Jeffrey Amherst, resigned his commission, married a daughter of James Alexander, and became a citizen of New York'.[1] He wrote to Gilbert Elliot from New York on 14 December 1759 [2] urging that if Canada had to be handed back to the French it should first be 'disabled' from ever hurting the Colonies again :

If at the peace we can retain Cape Breton, Crown Point, Oswego, Niagara, and Pitsburgh we shall secure the frontiers and engross the furr and fish trade. Many are of opinion that occupying this barrier would be of more advantage, than actually possessing all Canada, as the Colonies then would be under no restraint, more difficult to be managed, and might push trades detrimental to G. Britain, while the poorer sort of inhabitants, having nothing to fear, would retire far into the woods, free from Government, rent or taxes, where they would raise and manufacture every thing for their own use, without consuming any thing from Britain, or being the least benefit to that country. Another advantage of a French neighbourhood would be a good pretext to oblige each Colony to support a certain quota of troops, apparently for their defence, but also to keep them in proper subjection to the Mother Country. I formerly mentioned the great importance of attacking Louisiana, the single Colony interfers in the trade of all ours and encreases wonderfully. If the troops were ordered to conclude the campaign with an attack on this country, it would probably succeed to be highly beneficial, it is not the Cherokees we ought to hunt in the woods, but lay the ax to the root and seize New Orleans.

It is to the honour of British statesmen that they did not heed the warnings of those who looked upon the presence of the French in North America as a useful check on the Colonies — although the view was widely canvassed, and ultimately proved correct. For with the removal of the French, the road

[1] See Appleton, *Cyclopaedia of American Biography*. Under John Rutherfurd.
[2] The letter is among the papers of Gilbert Elliot in the possession of the Earl of Minto.

to independence, and even to a French alliance against Great
Britain, was opened for the Colonies.   But at first some Americans appear to have seen the new situation in a very different
light, and to have thought that with the removal of the French
it was they who, with the British Government, had lost in
importance and standing,   John Watts wrote to General
Monckton on 16 May 1764 : [1]

The colonys are extremely incensed at the treatment they have
receivd from the Mother Country, and tho' it has not had its effects
in one sense, it has in another, which I beleive will never be obliterated.   They seem to wish Canada again French, it made them
of some consequence, which consequence they lost when it was
conquerd, if their reasoning be just.   They certainly would not grant
a man for that or any other use was it to be done over again.

[1] Letterbook of John Watts, *Collections of the New York Historical
Society*, vol. lxi. p. 255.

BUTE AND NEWCASTLE

New Systems

By 1761 the war had clearly reached its concluding stage, the most difficult stage of all. The last battles had to be fought and the last word to be said, decisive points of vantage had to be gained and terms of peace to be secured which should consolidate Britain's Imperial achievements and secure the future of her Empire. To steer her course during that fateful period a strong Government was required, enjoying the full confidence of all the political factors — the King, the Parliament, and the nation. The coalition of Bute, Newcastle, and Pitt would have answered the purpose, had it been sincere and spontaneous — which it was not.

Bute had agreed to the continuing of Pitt in office because Newcastle was not willing to go on without him, but had stipulated beforehand for Newcastle's support against Pitt, should difficulties arise between them ; and though stipulating for that support, he could not get himself for any length of time to treat Newcastle with even seeming regard. Newcastle had helped to bring Bute into the Council and had insisted on Pitt remaining in it, because he was afraid to go on without either of the two, but he had not any clear idea of how he could go on with both, or they with each other. And Pitt had agreed, under protest, to Bute's inclusion in the Government, but from now onwards remembered against Newcastle and his friends their having been instrumental in forcing that decision upon him. It was obvious that the patchwork of this Coalition could not reconcile the jealousies which subsisted between Newcastle and Bute, nor make them see the problems of the war and the peace with the eyes of Pitt. Newcastle, who had brought about the juncture of Bute with Pitt, stood between the two, without being the friend of either; his position was pitiful from the outset, and was rendered even more wretched through his sensitiveness and fears, and more ludicrous through the utter lack of judgment he showed in estimating the relative value of things.

When, early in April, Prince Ferdinand met with a reverse in Germany, Pitt laid the burden of the miscarriage 'upon the commissariat, the want of care, oeconomy, and attention in the Treasury; and plainly shew'd his intention to complain of it or to attack the Treasury for it'.[1] In this, Newcastle thought, ill-humour was mixed with the design to intimidate him should he disagree with Pitt in regard to peace terms.

For my part [wrote Newcastle to Devonshire on 19 April] I shall neither repent of my junction (in concert with your Grace and my Lord Hardwicke) with my Lord Bute; or be in the least silenced as to what is, or shall be, my opinion with regard to the terms of peace. I shall depend upon my own innocence; and the friendship, advice and powerful assistance of my friends; especially *those* who, by their credit with me, *engaged me* to continue in employment; and thereby to expose myself to this man's outrageous resentment.[2]

It was Bute himself who very soon made Newcastle repent of the 'junction', by reviving the difficulties over patronage. He was 'very cold and dry', and complained that Newcastle 'would do nothing for his (Lord Bute's) friends, but sent them away constantly with refusals'.

I ask your Grace [wrote Newcastle to Devonshire on 12 June 1761], how is it possible for me to go on in the Treasury, if the not complying immediately with an unreasonable request of a Mr. Doddington to the prejudice of our old friends is to be resented in this manner by Lord Bute? . . .

In publick matters, I mean the great object of peace or war, the making the one, or the measures for carrying on the war, I can do little or nothing. And, if at the head of the Treasury, I can be of no service to my friends, I expose myself for nothing.[3]

A month later Newcastle wrote again to Devonshire about his 'ridiculous situation':

---

[1] Newcastle's minute of a conversation with Count de Viry, 18 April 1761; Add. MSS. 32922, f. 32.   [2] *Ibid.* ff. 65-6.
[3] Add. MSS. 32924, ff. 48-54.

The establishment of the Family of a new Queen, in which the Treasury is something concern'd, and no one word said to me upon it, 'till the day the declaration is made in Council, a Scotch peer to be chose, and I don't yet know who is the person. . . . And above all, the report that the Bishop of Norwich is to be Bishop of London, a man . . . who has acted so ungratefully to me, who made him every thing, that he *ever* was; shews such a disregard to me and to my situation, and to what I owe to myself, that I own, it is with difficulty I swallow it, *even at present*.[1]

When, on 17 July, Newcastle approached Bute about these matters, he was told that the long illness of the Bishop of London had given the King 'ample time to consider of a proper subject for filling that important see', so that the choice was presumably made ; and as for 'the Queen's Family' the King 'had so many applications, and for so many months past', that this, too, was probably settled.[2]

Is this the way [wrote Newcastle to Hardwicke] to engage me to undertake the carrying on an impracticable war, continued purely by our own fault, ambition, and obstinacy ? . . . I must soon take my resolution.[3]

That the war appeared to him 'impracticable' and its continuance a grave mistake, was not a sufficient ground for resigning, but the choice of the Bishop of London and of the Queen's Family was.

The party is taken [Newcastle wrote to Devonshire on 5 August] to have no regard to my situation ; to any recommendations that may come from me ; and to leave me to take such resolutions thereupon, as I may think proper ; either to swallow it ; and thereby make the most contemptible figure, that ever man did ; or to resign my employment ; in which case, my Lord Bute is ready and desirous to undertake it.[4]

---

[1] 11 July 1761 ; Add. MSS. 32925, f. 10. See also Newcastle's 'Memorandums' of 15 July (*ibid.* f. 85) :

My situation. Never consulted — hardly informed.
     Difficulties about common things in my own office.
     A different behaviour to every body else.
     The Duke of Devonshire, Duke of Bedford, etc.

[2] Bute to Newcastle, 17 July 1761 ; *ibid.* f. 133.
[3] 18 July 1761 ; *ibid.* ff. 155-6.
[4] Add. MSS. 32926, ff. 187-93.

He now solemnly appealed to Hardwicke for advice, declaring himself 'determined to follow it' :

> I must call forth all that strength of judgement and cordial affection, with which you consider all questions, that immediately concern me. . . .
>
> . . . You will consider *my duty* (I can't *now* say, *my obligations*) to my King, and my countrey ; and you will consider what I owe to myself, my figure, and reputation in the world, after having sacrificed my time, my fortune etc. for such a number of years for the service of this Royal Family. . . .
>
> You will consider also my safety, which, I am far from being sure, may not be hazarded, perhaps either way, by my resignation at this time ; or by a pursuit in supporting difficult and dangerous measures.[1]

Hardwicke hesitated what advice to give — the time to quit, he wrote to Newcastle on 8 August, had been on the late King's death when 'several plausible, temperate, and decent reasons might have been alledged, which now exist no longer'.

> If your Grace quits now it must be either upon reasons of *personal usage*, or of *public measures*. Forgive me to say that the promotion of the Bp. of Norwich to the See of London, contrary to your opinion and advice, will not be thought a sufficient justification by the public, or by the Whig Party.

But should he resign the Treasury on the ground that he could no longer bear the responsibility for financing the war, this would be decried as lowering the public credit. If, to counter this, Newcastle offered his support

> to carry on the public service in other hands . . . who will go out with him on this foot ? He cannot in that case expect any party or following, for most persons have their views, and those views will carry them into Court or into opposition. The Court has strengthened itself and created many new dependances. The gratification to the Tories ; the new Queen's Family ; must have attach'd many persons. . . . If there is any weight in all this, the conclusion is that your Grace can only quit to be a private man, without any further Court-views ; and, if there shall appear, upon consideration, to be so much danger in the situation, as your Grace suggests, that may finally be the wisest part to take.

[1] 7 August 1761 ; Add. MSS. 32926, ff. 284-5.

As to remaining on conditions, 'they will be things in the air ; blown off and distinguished away upon any particular occasion'.[1]

In reply to this letter, Newcastle, on 10 August, drew up a paper which should be remembered in appraising the actions both of his friends and his opponents in 1762 :

In my present disagreable, difficult, and dangerous situation . . . my friends, perhaps, may desire to know, what are my own thoughts and inclinations ; *that* I cannot tell them, as I shall form *none*, 'till I am fully apprized of theirs ; by which I shall be finally directed.

But I can now tell them, *what they are not*, and never shall be ; viz. to put myself at the head of an *Opposition* in this new reign ; I would as little do that, as I would undertake (if it was offer'd me, and was in my power) *to be at the head of an Administration* in a new reign, under a young King ; this no consideration on earth would make me consent to.

Should it prove necessary to resign,

I should resign my employment without any declared *resentment* to any body, without any wish or desire, *that any one man should follow me* ; the known and declared approbation of my friends in my so doing, *is all I want or expect*.

As I should by no means think of entering into *an Opposition*, I would give no assurance of support ; but be at liberty to act as I should think proper (as my friends would also be) upon such occasions as might arise.

I shall certainly in and out of office oppose *the continuance of the Militia*, in any shape, at least *after the war is ended*.

I shall oppose any alteration, that may be proposed, of any part of the present Constitution, or receiv'd usage and practice, with regard either to *Scotland, Ireland, or our Settlements in America*.

I am far from meaning or desiring to be upon a foot of enmity with the Administration ; I would retain, if the King would permit me, the Lieutenancies, or some of them, which I have now the honor to hold. But, I own, the last conversation with Count Viry has made a deep impression upon me, wherein he gave me an account of his late interview with my Lord Bute ; and repeated that most extraordinary, ridiculous, and offensive proposal, which he had often flung out before, viz. 'that I should declare that it was not my wish or intention to continue in my employment for ever ; or to that purpose'. And added 'that the King had a notion of not being

[1] *Ibid.* ff. 310-12.

governed, led, or to that effect, by his Minister or Ministers, as the late King had been'. I could hardly help *smiling*, when my friend said *that*.

The King and his Minister *extremely* mistake me, if they think, I have a wish *to govern His Majesty*. So far from it, my wish, my desire is (as far as relates to myself) that my Lord Bute should have as much *credit*, *power*, and *influence* as it is reasonable for any one Minister to have; that screens me from those imputations and re-proaches, which, in a former reign, I was often very unjustly forced to submit to. I desire only that share of *regard* and *credit*, which one of my standing and in my situation ought to have, for the support of his own *honor*; and for the service of those *friends*, in whose cause I am, and have ever been, embarked; and for whose sake I have, and would still bear many things, but not every thing.

It may be vanity in me to think, that, when I am out of the Ad-ministration, tho' great and proper *regard* and *countenance* will be undoubtedly shew'd by His Majesty and his Ministers to *individuals*, yet I am afraid, that *the support of the Whigs* as a body, will not come much under their consideration.[1]

Thus Newcastle, while still at the head of the Treasury, emphatically denied being 'at the head of the Administration', and fully accepted Bute's pre-eminence; and in case of resignation, he still repudiated the idea of leading an Opposition, though he meant to give no assurances of support. As for his political programme, the part on home politics is extremely meagre, and its only point, concerning the militia, was directed primarily against Pitt and his country gentlemen; while the part concerning Scotland, Ireland, and the Colonies is exceed-ingly vague — it is not clear what changes he feared, and one must be careful not to read into it, in the light of subsequent events, more than is likely to have been in the thoughts of the writer in August 1761.

When on 17 August Newcastle sent Hardwicke this paper about his intended resignation, he declared that 'the question *an*' was settled with him, and there was 'therefore nothing . . . left, but the *quo modo*'.

I . . . shall assign nothing but a publick cause, and that in no degree *offensive* to any body. I don't arraign the measure. . . . I even offer my own assistance in support of it, *as a private man*;

---

[1] Add. MSS. 32926, ff. 352-4.

perhaps that may be too much. It may be thought *vanity* by *some*; and too strong *an engagement* by others. I put the whole upon my own age. . . . You see by my paper . . . that I detest the thought of *an Opposition*; and that I neither wish nor desire any one man to follow me.[1]

But no sooner had Newcastle decided to resign than he began to consider on what terms he might remain. 'I don't engage again', he wrote to Devonshire on 20 August, '. . . without knowing upon what foot I am to go on, both as to measures and credit. . . . Lord Bute's behaviour must be thoroughly explained.'[2]   Devonshire duly transmitted the message to Bute, who ascribed the misunderstandings to their 'not talking enough together', suggested 'that there might be a day and hour settled in every week to talk over all business', and professed the wish to come to an explanation with him.[3] Newcastle turned also to Mansfield for advice concerning his intended resignation.[4]

The manner may be embarrassing [was Mansfield's reply], it will be very difficult to do it so as to escape publick reproach, . . . retiring now is not the same thing as to have quitted upon the late King's death. . . . Squabbles about places or preferments won't bear discussion and tho' they may very reasonably operate in your own mind, yet you must both to the King and the nation deny your being actuated by any such motive. Publick measures won't do. The answer to France will probably go at last according to your opinion. Unavoidable difficulty is not a reason to desert. . . . The only clear way of getting out is if the King shou'd be induced to wish another system and to part with you in great friendship.

If you are to stay in . . . conditions now wou'd be nothing. They wou'd not be kept. The King might be taught to see the mere mention of them as an indecent bargain to share, or perhaps to engross his power. . . .

Lord Bute I think certainly wishes you to continue . . . it is impossible he shou'd not see and dread the difficultys. It is manifest that he is jealous of your grasping at the disposition of every thing. . . . If you mention terms you fix him in that erroneous belief [that by threatening to resign, Newcastle merely wished to bargain].

[1] Add. MSS. 32927, ff. 69-70.   [2] *Ibid.* f. 133.
[3] *Ibid.* ff. 154-5. On a previous occasion Bute had expressed his surprise to Viry at Newcastle's bad humour — 'all this for a Bishop of London' (Add. MSS. 32926, f. 286).   [4] *Ibid.* ff. 173-4.

What is worse, the mention of terms destroys ev'ry publick ground upon which you can stay in or go out with dignity. Your making or not making bishops won't encrease or lessen the specie and credit of the Kingdom or vary the weight of twenty millions. If the King is taught to wish you to stay in and to believe you seriously desire to retire, they will cajole you by evry douceur to stay.[1]

Meantime the differences between Bute and Pitt over foreign policy had come to a head, but in the discussions of the peace terms, during the last few months, Newcastle had differed even more from Pitt than had Bute, or, barring Bedford, any other member of the Council. The main territorial claims of Great Britain had been settled in the Cabinet Council of 24 June 1761. It was over the article of the Treaty of Utrecht conceding to the French rights of fishery in Newfoundland that opinions differed. Pitt was not prepared to renew it ; Lord Granville argued that the French would not give it up, and that to demand its surrender would set all the maritime Powers against Great Britain ; Hardwicke, Bedford, and Newcastle supported Granville ; while Bute suggested a middle course, namely, to try to obtain the point without making it a *sine qua non* of peace.

When, the next day, Bute argued that 'not making the attempt would set the whole City against us', Newcastle replied : 'It was our duty to speak our opinions, and I should not govern myself by the opinion of the City' ; and when, on 26 June, the King himself repeated that argument, Newcastle answered again that 'if we were to be govern'd or to yield to the reasonings of the Common Council, His Majesty would find what demands they would make in time'.[2] This was not to be his view of the City in September 1762.

Finally Bute's middle course was adopted ; Newcastle thereupon complained to Devonshire :

. . . my dear Lord, what can *we* do ; when one Secretary, who has the pen, has filled his head with such conquests in the air, and the other, *who has the power*, apprehends the loss of his own popularity if he essentially differs with Mr. Pitt. Under these circumstances I have seen more courage and resolution in the rest of the Council in

---

[1] 23 August 1761 ; Add. MSS. 32927, ff. 179-81.
[2] Newcastle to Devonshire, 28 June 1761 ; Add. MSS. 32924, ff. 311-22.

this instance, than I ever expected; and more than, I am afraid, may appear upon future occasions.[1]

Bedford in turn complained to Newcastle :

My spirits are so much sunk with what passed last Friday [26 June], and so much alarmed for the very salvation of this country, which I see (tho' at present in condition to make a peace glorious to herself, and desirable to the rest of Europe) at the brink of ruin thro' the obstinacy and insolence of one man, that I am almost driven to despondency, and determine to absent my self from all Councils.[2]

Newcastle too feared that the chance of peace might be lost, was worried about the vast expense of the war, and planned in future to concert matters with Bute.[3] In preparation for the Cabinet Council of Friday, 24 July, he wrote in his 'Memorandums' : [4]

The unanimity of the Council.
Mr. Pitt's behaviour.
To see how he forms the contre projet.
Our meeting on Friday.
If France does not accept, what is to be done.
The war in the present shape impracticable.
How is it possible to reduce it ?
Abandon the King of Prussia; and give up the King's Hanover dominions and our Allies.

When at the Council meeting Pitt submitted his 'Paper of Points', it contained the demand for all Canada ; for Senegal and Goree ; for the restoration of Minorca ; for a partition of the Neutral Islands ; a refusal to let Louisiana be extended to the Ohio and the confines of Virginia ; and only if the fortifications of Dunkirk were reduced, was he prepared to consider the French claim to fishery rights of Newfoundland. But the language in which Pitt subsequently couched these points caused even more dissatisfaction among his pacifist colleagues than the demands themselves. Hardwicke described his style as 'haughty and dictatorial', such as even Louis XIV never used ; he said that it showed the power of the man 'who holds

[1] *Ibid*. ff. 320-1.   [2] 2 July 1761 ; *ibid*. f. 384.
[3] Newcastle to Devonshire, 4 July ; *ibid*. f. 410.
[4] 22 July ; Add. MSS. 32925, f. 251.

the pen', and that, if after long and full deliberations such liberties could be taken, 'the whole may as well be left to one man'.[1]

Similarly Devonshire wrote to Newcastle on 5 August:

I do not see to what purpose it is for us to come up to town to attend meetings if it is to be in the power of any person to alter them, or render them fruitless by the manner of conveying them.[2]

But when Newcastle raised a similar complaint to the King and Bute, the latter replied 'that the points were read over to us at Council; and then said that, if they were not right, why did *we all* run out of town, and not stay to read the letter and Paper of Points before they went?'[3] The week-end habit was already common among the great about 1760.

The French answer of 5 August was such that Newcastle himself described it as 'very abominable'. Still, when Bute called it a declaration of war, Newcastle deprecated this view and 'beg'd his Lordship, that we might not yet renounce the thoughts of peace'.[4] Most of all Newcastle feared that Spain might now come into the war; he wrote to Hardwicke on 7 August:

I know my Lord Bute and Mr. Pitt despise Spain. The latter carries it so far as to fling out that we shall be better able, by our captures, to carry on the war, with Spain against us, than without it. My Lord Bute depends upon the certain success . . . of stopping their galeons.[5]

But to him 'the great national point' was peace. 'There I hope', he wrote to Hardwicke on 9 August, '*we* (you know whom I mean by *we*) shall act a strong, prudent and uniform part. I have wrote to the Duke of Devonshire upon it, and shall write, this day, to the Duke of Bedford.'[6]

Devonshire was equally keen on peace; he wrote to Newcastle on 10 August:

I wish to God some expedient may be found out, to prevent the continuance of the war. I have answer'd Lord Bute's letter and told

---

[1] Hardwicke to Newcastle, 2 August; Add. MSS. 32926, ff. 140-2.
[2] *Ibid.* f. 185.
[3] Newcastle to Devonshire; *ibid.* ff. 187-93.
[4] Newcastle to Hardwicke, 6 August; *ibid.* ff. 269-70.
[5] *Ibid.* ff. 281-2.   [6] *Ibid.* ff. 326-7.

him so and have added that if the war is to continue I for my part see no day light.[1]

Such was in 1761 the attitude of those who, towards the close of 1762, were to oppose the peace treaty negotiated by Bute. In fact, Newcastle's pacifism went the length of *défaitisme* — he wrote in his 'Memorandums' on 20 August : 'The victories hurt us as they make the peace more difficult'.[2] He forgot these sentiments on the capture of Havana, when he was not in office any longer.

When by the middle of September 1761 every one in the Council had lost hope of peace, and even Devonshire and Hardwicke were for recalling Stanley, the peace envoy, from Paris Newcastle still pleaded for leaving him there, hoping that 'incidents may happen' which would reopen the road to peace. On 18 September he wrote to Sir Joseph Yorke :

We lost l'heure de bergier [*sic*]; and that I thought from the beginning. We had, or pretended to have, such a diffidence of M. Choiseul's sincerity at first, as gave him such doubts of *our sincerity* that he found himself obliged in interest to adopt another system by way of resource.[3]

This new system was the 'family compact' with Spain ; but while Pitt demanded that the full consequences should be drawn from what was seen to be the new trend of the Bourbon policy in the two countries, and that a blow should be struck at Spain immediately, Newcastle was foremost in opposing such an extension of the war ; and this time Bute and all the other members of the Council (except Temple) were of his opinion.

Once more, for a while, Bute courted Newcastle, who wrote to Joseph Yorke in high delight :

My Lord Bute acts with the greatest sincerity and cordiality *towards us* imaginable. It is a proof of it, when Drummond is made Archbishop of Yorke, Yonge Bishop of Norwich, and Green Bishop of Lincoln ; and when your brother James will be Dean of Lincoln. The King, I should have said *first*, is most gracious to us all.[4]

[1] *Ibid.* f. 356.   [2] Add. MSS. 32927, ff. 131-2.
[3] Add. MSS. 32928, ff. 211-12.
[4] *Ibid.* f. 212. See also undated paper in Newcastle's handwriting, Add. MSS. 32927, f. 25, which, I suppose, should be placed in September, rather than in August 1761 (as it is in the Add. MSS.) :
   I wish you would find out, whether your friend is as well satisfied

Pitt resigned, and Newcastle remained to appoint bishops, to provide money for 'an impracticable war', and, above all, to manage Parliament.

Over the very choice of successors to Pitt and Temple, new differences arose between Bute and Newcastle. Bute suggested Fox for Secretary of State, but Newcastle doubted whether Fox would prove acceptable to his friends, and named George Grenville. 'Lord Bute rejected it ; and then said, he had not a manner of speaking, which would do against Mr. Pitt' ; [1] moreover, Grenville 'would not take Pitt's place', and Bute therefore proposed him for Chancellor of the Exchequer. This Newcastle was 'determined never to agree to'.

The moment Mr. Grenville is Chancellor of the Exchequer [he wrote to Hardwicke], it is to him, and to him only, to whom the King and his Minister will apply ; and it is he, who will have singly the King's confidence. . . . I should not pass one easy moment in the Treasury after that was done.[2]

Hardwicke thought it a mistake on Newcastle's part to have named Grenville for any office (he was at that time designated for Speaker in succession to Onslow). Bute, on the other hand, pressed Grenville to accept the seals — 'if he remains Speaker, my Lord', Bute wrote to Newcastle, 'I see no system whatever, proper for this dangerous minute ; or that I can . . . recommend to the King'.[3] As, however, he failed to persuade Grenville, Bute, on 7 October, offered the seals to Egremont ; [4] Grenville was to remain Treasurer of the Navy, but none the

with me, as I am with him, and whether that sort of concert and confidence for the future, is to be understood to be settled between us ; and then things will continue to go right.

As he took down in writing all these ecclesiastical dispositions, I must suppose he intends to do them all.

Find that out from yourself.

This was presumably addressed to Viry.

[1] Newcastle to Hardwicke, 26 September 1761 ; Add. MSS. 32928, ff. 362-3.

[2] *Ibid.* ff. 364-5.   [3] Add. MSS. 32929, f. 74.

[4] Bute to Newcastle, Tuesday, 6 October 1761, *ibid.* f. 76 ; see also account given by George Grenville in a narrative of the crisis, *Grenville Papers*, vol. ii. pp. 410-11 ; he claims that 'the seals were given to Lord Egremont at Mr. Grenville's recommendation'.

less to take the lead in the Commons, and together with Bute, Egremont, and Newcastle, to form the inner Cabinet. 'I mightily approve the narrowing the council', wrote Newcastle to Hardwicke on October 8, 'but I can never think it reasonable, that the first concoction should be confined to us four, when I am sure to have three against one, if ever (which I dare say will very seldom happen) I should differ in opinion from my Lord Bute'.[1]

The next day Newcastle asked Bute that the Privy Seal, vacated by Temple's resignation, be offered to Hardwicke; Bute replied that 'he was rewarded enough by the great things which were done for his family', and reproached Newcastle — 'as usual' — with his friends having everything.

At last his Lordship talked of his danger and responsibility [wrote Newcastle to Devonshire on 9 October], and that he must now provide *for friends of his own*. . . . I suppose Lord Bute has some Tory in view. . . . I told your Grace some time ago that I thought my Lord Bute's view, by confining the concert about business to himself, his two friends, my Lord Egremont and Mr. Grenville and myself, was to get the whole power and disposition of business as well as employments, to himself. I am now fully convinc'd of it. . . . The point indeed is to make me as weak in Council as possible. My Lord Bute has got rid of his rival, Mr. Pitt; who dared to contradict him; and will make everybody else, as insignificant as he can. This is certainly his scheme.

'My resolution is taken', was Newcastle's conclusion, to which the postscript was added: 'I dont mean to quit immediately'.[2]

Devonshire replied with a serious exhortation:

Never was a time when it was more necessary for two persons to agree than it is for you two at present. And therefore for Godsake keep your temper, if this point dont clear up, send to Viry, I am persuaded he will set it right. I do assure [you] when I took my leave of Lord Bute on Thursday [8 October] he seemed to be as well disposed towards you as possible.

. . . It is very hard that I can't be gone four and twenty hours but you must be all quarrelling. *Pray be friends*, for the public will suffer if you are not so.[3]

[1] Add. MSS. 32929, ff. 115-16.   [2] *Ibid.* ff. 139-42.
[3] Chatsworth, 10 October; *ibid.* ff. 155-6.

On 11 October Newcastle, Bute, and Grenville discussed the choice of Speaker ; Grenville

put an absolute negative upon Sir Geo. Saville, and was very positive and determined for Mr. Morton. I objected most strongly to it ; that I could not be for Mr. Morton ; that he was a Tory and besides a very low, inconsiderable man.[1]

This led, two days later, to a further talk between Newcastle and Bute.

His Lordship [wrote Newcastle to Hardwicke on 13 October] with an air of the greatest gravity and discontent began with making most severe reproaches, that he found things could not go on between us, that his friend Mr. G. Grenville, was to be put into the most difficult station and to be mortified, hurt, and not supported ; and this because I had put a negative upon Mr. Morton. . . . He would advise him [Grenville] to return to the Chair etc. . . . I . . . complain'd of my side, of some late discouragements which I had met with ; to which I had the usual answer, that I and my friends had every thing. I asked his Lordship, Have I the Great Seal ? Have I the Secretaries of State ? Have I the War Office, army &c. ?—All he could answer was, I had the Treasury and the First Lord of the Admiralty.—In friendship, yes, but the head of the Admiralty had not always gone as I could have wished.—My Lord Hardwicke can do what he pleases with him.—This sort of stuff hurt me so much that I said shortly but really in good humour, Since it is so, for Godsake let me go out and I will support whomever you put in. His Lordship then took fire and said, No, my Lord, I know your power ; you have all the great men of the Kingdom ; if it was to come to that, that we are incompatible. I would myself retire, and desire the King to put his affairs into your hands. I laughed at that. His Lordship talked of his own situation, He had nothing but his credit with the King ; he had nothing else to support him ; his danger was great ; he had no friends in the administration. . . . To which I answered, you may have all my friends, if you please. I talked pretty home to him on some points, I think him disturbed, and still desirous to talk and act high towards every body.[2]

In a letter to Devonshire, on 14 October, Newcastle developed further the point about his friends :

[1] Newcastle to Devonshire, 14 October, Add. MSS. 32929, f. 252.
[2] Add. MSS. 35421, ff. 112-13. There is no copy of this letter in the Newcastle Papers, only the original in the Hardwicke Papers, and that is in Newcastle's own scrawl ; he remarks in a postscript : 'This letter wrote in a hurry, more than ordinary, I believe you cannot read'.

I told his Lordship, when he talk'd of having no friend, and no
support, that we were all ready to be his friends, if he would let us;
that we wish'd for nothing but to support him; and that as to the
disposal of employments, the person, who was the fittest, and could
do the most service, should have them, without distinction, to whom
they belong'd. . . . His Lordship is always talking of getting
friends, and preferring his own friends.[1]

On the night of that conversation (13 October) Gilbert
Elliot brought Grenville a letter from Bute, with the fullest
assurances of the King's support.

Mr. Elliot shewed him this letter, but said he had orders from
Lord Bute to bring it back again to him, which he did; but Mr.
Grenville made Mrs. Grenville set down the heads of it immediately,
which he repeated to her.[2]

It was 'upon account of the expressions relative to the Duke
of Newcastle' contained in the letter that Bute insisted on
having it returned.[3]

General conduct of the Duke of Newcastle, and reasons to show
the impossibility of him or his friends acting the part that I [Gren-
ville] suspected: immediate punishment, crazy old man. Young
king, young nobility . . . detail of N.'s conduct during the last
reign: odious in his, B.'s, opinion: pusillanimity in the closet,
foreign system, foreign ideas, sole access, power of calling people
rascals and Jacobites: since the accession, B. has no reason to find
fault with his behaviour: great change in his situation in regard to
the King: knew his own power diminished: would insist on
nothing: would press for his friends and acquiesce where it would
not do: had many pledges for the performance of N.'s promises:
to speak more freely, and open himself more fully than he had done
since the accession: his graces not so desultory; had bestowed them
on men of worth and character: had certain information that after
the Peace N. would resign when called upon: thought it therefore
better to let this old man tide over a year or two more of his political
life: saw many among his people who were worthy and fit to be
brought forward in the King's service: opened this plan to remove
my jealousies and any idéa I might have formed of being led into a
situation amongst people hostile to me, and to be dropped in the
middle of it.

[1] Add. MSS. 32929, ff. 253-4.
[2] Grenville's narrative of the transactions, 3 October–9 November
1761, *Grenville Papers*, vol. i. p. 412.
[3] *Ibid.* pp. 395-7. The original is among the Bute MSS.

Meantime Hardwicke warned Newcastle to stop the continuous wrangle with Bute : 'If your Grace means to continue in the Administration, I hope you will avoid these altercations as much as possible. . . . They will end at last, if repeated and continued, in real differences and in alienation.' [1] Similarly Devonshire deprecated 'these bickerings that seem to pass every day' :

I can only be sorry for them, for I am *au bout de mon latin*, having exhausted every argument and motive that I cou'd think of to persuade him steadily to cultivate and promote union with your Grace and your friends, and I have always fancied that I left him in a thorough resolution so to do.[2]

Though it was perfectly true that Devonshire preached union with Newcastle to the King and Bute, his way of doing it can hardly be described as altogether flattering, or even respectful, to his friend. George III wrote to Bute on 18 November 1761 :

The Duke of Devonshire touched upon the situation of things in general, I declaring the necessity of harmony and due spirit being shown on all sides ; he added he did not fear things would go ill, provided you and the Duke of N——e acted cordially together, that the D. of N——e was easily managed for that trifles pleased him ; a little seeming good humour from me and your telling him things before he hears them from others are the sure maxims to keep him in order, for nothing is so hateful to him as the thoughts of retiring.

On 15 October Hardwicke had a long talk with Grenville :

It turned [he wrote to Newcastle] upon three general heads — his own situation ;—measures and transactions in Parliament — and the plan of the Speech. Your Grace knows the manner . . . he was prolix. . . .
Mr. G. gave assurances that he would do his best with all the vigour and exertion possible ; but he must be supported and assisted, and named several of the King's servants for that purpose, and amongst others I observ'd Mr. Fox. He did not imagine that Mr. Pitt would have any great following of the Tories, that Ald. Beckford and Sir John Phillips pretended to answer for them but could not ;

---

[1] Hardwicke to Newcastle, 13 October 1761 ; Add. MSS. 32929, ff. 227-228.   [2] *Ibid*. f. 326.

and that Sir Charles Mordaunt and the soberer part of them were sick of Mr. P.——'s measures of war, more especially continental, and of the immense expence. That Lord Bute had gain'd my Lord Lichfield and Lord Oxford and Lord Bruce who had great credit with the party, and in short had made a great inroad amongst them.

His main dependance seem'd to be on your Grace's friends, the Whig party, which was the sheet anchor; and did not doubt of numbers for right measures.[1]

In reality Grenville was still full of doubts and apprehensions. He feared attacks from Pitt, and he feared almost as much support from Fox, 'lest his superior abilities should eclipse him', the Minister in the House of Commons.

The promise of that support was obtained with some difficulty, as Fox demanded a peerage for his wife as immediate payment for it. 'Yield to Mr. Fox . . .' said Bute to Newcastle on 13 October, 'I shall not do it. He shall comply. I know how to deal with Mr. Fox. His removal would be as popular, as the removal of others may have been otherwise.' [2] Two days later the matter was settled between them.

I, this moment, am come from my Lord Bute [wrote Newcastle to Devonshire on 15 October]; and he tells me, that every thing is agreed between Mr. Fox, and him.

Mr. Fox is to act, speak, or not speak, when, and as my Lord Bute will advise.

My Lord Bute has stuck to his text. He has absolutely refused the peerage for the present; but, as I understand, Lady Caroline is to be made, when others are. In short, Fox is very well satisfied, and I am *extremely* glad of it.[3]

But Grenville was not; on 17 October, Bute told Hard-wicke

that Geo. G. had teaz'd him out of his life for these two days past. That his brother, my Lord Temple, was most hostile and outragious against him; that he had deserted the family; that he would never let him come within his doors, nor see his face more. . . . Lord Bute said that he had now tranquilliz'd Mr. Grenville pretty well. . . . I suspect that G.G. wants to retreat to the Chair himself.[4]

---

[1] *Ibid.* f. 332.
[2] Newcastle to Devonshire, 14 October 1761 ; *ibid.* f. 255.
[3] *Ibid.* f. 258.
[4] Hardwicke to Newcastle, 14 October ; *ibid.* f. 334.

About that time Bute wrote to Gilbert Elliot : [1]

I think George is at last quiet, I omitted nothing in my power to make him so; but he remains inexorable about having any communication with Fox, or even suffering him to take a part in the House ; . . . for Godsake Elliot, see what this amounts to : can I gag a man, who wishes to serve the King, can I prevent his supporting the King's measures; besides, I have in friendship to George talk'd strongly to Fox, as well as to every other man I had any interest with, claiming their assistance on my account; how am I to eat this up, what an opinion must Fox have of me. . . .

'Poor man', wrote Newcastle about Grenville on 28 October, 'he is certainly much frighten'd and alarm'd ; and I don't wonder at him.' [2] Grenville had expressed his confidence in Newcastle and his friends,[3] and indeed Newcastle did his best to bring them all up to town for the first day of the session and to the preliminary meeting of Members of the House of Commons at the Cockpit, which was always held at that time on the night preceding the opening of Parliament — a formal muster of adherents of the Government to whom on this occasion the drafts of the Speech and the Address were read out by the Minister who was to take the lead in the House.[4] But Grenville, though he wished Newcastle's friends to turn to him as leader and complained that none of them 'had been to see him', felt uncomfortable at the thought of having to preside at that meeting, and at the last moment desired Barrington, the Chancellor of the Exchequer, to take his place.

My Lord Bute has been very uneasy [wrote Newcastle to Devonshire on 31 October], and so have I too, at the uncertainty and ballancing of Mr. Grenville, which, for this last week, has been, to such a degree, and from different causes, that the King told me, the day before yesterday, that my Lord Bute had given it over. . . .

I had two most long and tedious conversations with Mr. George Grenville; and, I think, I have contributed a little to quiet him. His proposal was, that Lord Barrington should read the King's Speech at the Cockpit; and then said, that, as to himself, he would rather

---

[1] The letter is in the Minto Papers, 'MSS. vol. vii.' No. 10 ; it is not dated, merely marked '½ past 4'.

[2] To Hardwicke ; Add. MSS. 32930, f. 104.

[3] See above, p. 299.

[4] See my article on 'The Circular Letters : an 18th-Century Whip to Members of Parliament', in *The English Historical Review*, October 1929.

have his part be forced, or put upon him, than seem to assume it himself. I talked very strongly to him; shew'd him that it was too late; that he should have made these difficulties at first; that it was now so late he could not go back; what a figure should I make, who had summon'd all my friends, to meet him at the Cockpit ? . . .

I soon found, that jealousy of Mr. Fox, and want of marks of credit, and power, were his real objections to the taking the lead of the House of Commons upon him; and the assurances, which *his friend* my Lord Bute had given him, of Mr. Fox's acting a thorough part with him, and assisting him upon all occasions, were the great motives of his present uneasiness.

He told me, what a figure shall I make ? Mr. Fox has superiour parliamentary talent to me; Mr. Fox has a great number of friends in the House of Commons, attached strongly to him; Mr. Fox has *great connections*, I have none; I have no friends; I am now unhappily separated from my own family.—True, Mr. Grenville; all these considerations may have weight with them; but the thing is now over. Mr. Fox may have some advantages; but there are circumstances in Mr. Fox's case, which may counterbalance these advantages; he himself is sensible, they are such, which make it impracticable for him, at present, to be the man; and what can you wish more ? Your friend my Lord Bute tells you, Mr. Fox has promised him, to do every thing he is desired, or to be quiet, and do nothing at all.[1]

Finally, 'Lord Bute was forced to promise him [Grenville] that Fox *should be silent*, and not meddle'[2] or, as Bute put it, 'that Mr. Fox, who is ready to assist him, and do any thing, *shall do nothing at all*'.[3] 'I own', remarked Rockingham, 'without being a friend to Mr. F. I could hardly help smiling at the bargain made with him.'[4]

Meantime Newcastle had become once more uneasy about his own position; it hurt him not to be consulted and to feel unimportant, it frightened him to be credited with power, if that implied responsibility.

Every day convinces me more and more [he wrote to Devonshire on 31 October] that my Lord Bute intends to confine the first *concoction* of affairs to himself, Lord Egremont, and Mr. G. Grenville.

[1] Add. MSS. 32930, ff. 225-6.
[2] Newcastle to Rockingham, 3 November 1761 ; *ibid*. ff. 299-300.
[3] Newcastle to Devonshire, 31 October 1761 ; *ibid*. f. 227.
[4] Rockingham to Newcastle, Wentworth, 14 November 1761 : Add. MSS. 32931, ff. 51-3.

With them, he is conferring every moment; and Lord Egremont has already got the *cant* — *he had received the King's orders*. For your Grace knows, it is *the King* who does everything.[1]

While this 'most remarkable reserve' on the part of Bute mortified Newcastle, he was no less upset by the language which his friends in the City reported to him as its 'general discourse or opinion', namely, that he was 'the Minister for peace' and 'the chief person (and consequently the responsible one)'. To this Newcastle replied,

that I was not by any means to be look'd upon as the directing Minister; that I was not, could not, and would not, be so; that I remained in employment to assist and support the King's affairs; that, when I was called upon I should, as I had always done, give my opinion, as an honest man, and then leave it to those who had the execution and were, by their offices, responsible; without insisting, like Mr. Pitt, upon my opinion being taken or quitting if it was not.

Moved by these contradictory feelings, Newcastle grew once more unhappy and found it necessary to talk about his position to Gilbert Elliot, Count de Viry, James Stuart-Mackenzie, etc., which produced a new *éclaircissement* :

When I came yesterday to Court, my Lord Bute had quite a different air, from what I have seen for some time past. My Lord Bute began with me; My Lord, I hear from some persons, (meaning, I suppose, Mr. Elliot) that you are uneasy, that I have said nothing to you, about the vacant employments. I did not deny it. I vow to God, said he, I had formed no resolution about them.[2]

The farcical character of these proceedings has to be appreciated if some of the legends about what happened to the British Constitution at the accession of George III are to be laid to rest at last. In Newcastle, Bute, and Grenville, the King had, indeed, three brave men to govern the nation.

THE GERMAN WAR AND NEWCASTLE'S RESIGNATION

Newcastle, whose thankless task it was to find the money for the war, had for years preached the need of peace to his colleagues ; barring the Duke of Bedford, there was no greater

---

[1] Add. MSS. 32930, f. 221.   [2] *Ibid.* f. 227.

pacifist in the Council. But if peace could not be had — he
thought it could — then at least the scope of operations was to
be reduced to manageable proportions. Pitt's idea 'to meet
the House of Bourbon everywhere' — in every quarter of the
globe — seemed to Newcastle fantastic and impracticable, and
fraught with inevitable ruin to this country ; and George III
and Bute readily agreed with him, as neither they nor any of
their advisers had the boldness of Pitt, or the desire to engage
in vast operations for which he alone would have dared to
shoulder the responsibility. But while they too wished to
'contract' the war, they differed from Newcastle as to where
the restriction was to be effected, and the differences were
passionate and irreconcilable, for they arose from sentiment and
not from sober calculations. Here was a conflict between
generations, a reaction of sons against fathers, here were old
loyalties treated with supercilious contempt, a glorious past
remembered by the old and unknown to the young, a new
glory watched by the young with eager eyes and receptive minds,
but to which the old no longer responded. When Newcastle
was young, Marlborough established the power of England
and the balance of Europe on the battlefields of Flanders and
Germany ; and Newcastle, during forty-five years of his active
political life, had served two Kings whose thoughts and feelings
centred on their original home in Western Germany, a region
which he, too, had learnt to consider of paramount importance.
'Foreign system, foreign ideas', wrote Bute about Newcastle
in October 1761 ; [1] while Bedford remarked that Newcastle
'had been by the late King turned from an Englishman into a
German'.[2] And as Europe rather than the Empire engaged
Newcastle's thoughts, Pitt's colonial expeditions were mere side-
shows to him, as unimportant and as dangerous (in distracting
attention and diverting forces from the main front) as operations
outside France seemed to the Westerners in the Great War.

For George III, Hanover, Germany, and the Continental
war were indissolubly bound up with the person of George II ;
he gloried in the name of 'Britain', primarily because that distinguished him from his grandfather, and he talked of Hanover

---

[1] See above, p. 297.   [2] George III to Bute, 27 May 1762.

as 'that horrid Electorate', because it was his grandfather's home. George II had cherished memories of Dettingen, while George III could only remember his grandfather's refusal to let him join the army. With dislike and apprehension he had followed the campaigns of his uncle, the Duke of Cumberland, whose defeat at Klosterzeven, resulting in his downfall, had been a most welcome event to Leicester House; and after the Battle of Minden their sympathies went out to George Sackville, the man who had failed to do his share in it. If the war was to continue, George III and Bute would carry it on anywhere rather than in Germany.

On which side was the country at large? Questions concerning so-called public opinion can seldom be answered with precision; here, too, only a few generalisations can be attempted. The typical country gentleman had always been opposed to Continental entanglements and wars, 'this execrable, detestable, ruinous, ill advis'd, ill concerted, romantick, quixote, senceless, all consumeing land war',[1] of which the only tangible result was for him 'a double land tax'. The City, on the other hand, flourished on national expenditure; 'though they say', wrote Horace Walpole on 14 November 1761, 'they have ceased to be Jacobites, they have not relinquished principles of privateering, brokerage, insurance, contracts. . . . Merchants thrive by taxes which ruin everybody else.' But even in the City naval and colonial wars, with their prizes and conquests, were preferred to operations in Germany. No doubt Frederick II of Prussia, 'the Protestant hero', enjoyed a certain popularity among all classes, and so did Lord Granby, if we may judge by the number of public-houses called after him. None the less, the younger generation turned towards the Empire rather than Europe, being thoroughly bored with marches and counter-marches in Germany, of which no one could see the aim or term. The dislike for the German war was not limited to George III, and among the younger Members of Parliament there was an active group strongly opposed to the Continental 'system' of the previous generation; it included types other-

---

[1] Lord Tyrconnel to Sir John Cust, 30 April 1748; *Records of the Cust Family*, vol. iii. (1927), ed. by Sir Lionel Cust, p. 129.

wise far apart, such as Lord Shelburne, Charles Bunbury, Peregrine Cust, and George Dempster.

Peace, even on the most modest terms, was, in the autumn of 1761, Newcastle's only objective. He wrote on 11 October :

Tho' it may be right, to have, at present, an appearance of carrying on the war with vigour, yet — *if we think to outwar Mr. Pitt, we shall find ourselves greatly disappointed.* But, if our real view is peace, all our measures [should] tend to that object, which certainly was not Mr. Pitt's. Thus, and by that only shall we get the better of Mr. Pitt, and serve, and please the publick.[1]

And on 15 October :

I am sorry to observe . . . that our new Secretary of State [Lord Egremont] talks war . . . much more than I think . . . he should do. I will repeat it again. *Out war Mr. Pitt*, we cannot. And *we* [*with ?*] *the nation*, have no ground to stand upon, but to get a good peace, as soon as we can ; and God grant it may be soon, or we shall be all undone.[2]

Even Hardwicke's draft of the Speech for the opening of Parliament hardly satisfied Newcastle's pacifism ; 'I admire the Speech extreamly', he wrote to Hardwicke on 21 October. 'It is however full warlike enough.'[3] As for Egremont's draft of the dispatch to Spain demanding the disclosure of the terms of the Family Compact :

I never can, nor will, agree to my Lord Egremont's letter, as it now stands. *They* breath war as much as Mr. Pitt did ; but from this principle for fear of Mr. Pitt's popularity which *they* would endeavour to gain, but will never obtain it : and for that will all our measures be hamper'd ; and this Administration (such as it is) confounded.[4]

What added to Newcastle's exasperation was that, coupled with the readiness to proceed to extremes against Spain, he saw a desire to abandon the Continent :

I see, my Lord Bute (*entre nous*) wants to get rid of the Continent war . . . a too hasty giving up of our Allies, and abandoning the

---

[1] Paper marked 'Points for Consideration' ; Add. MSS. 32929, f. 190.
[2] To the Duke of Devonshire ; *ibid.* ff. 258-9.
[3] *Ibid.* f. 422.
[4] Newcastle to Hardwicke, 23 October ; *ibid.* f. 472.

King's electoral dominions . . . will, with all reasonable men, affect His Majesty's honor, as much as a less advantageous peace would do.[1]

In reality Bute, though not averse to the idea of such a withdrawal, gave as yet no direct encouragement to those who urged it in Parliament; and even George Grenville said 'he was for the war wherever France was vulnerable, and for our supporting the King's engagements so long as it was practicable'[2] — which was, however, a significant and ominous reservation. Pitt, on the other hand, 'declared himself strongly in support of the war in Germany', and 'spoke with contempt' of those who were for 'ending the Continent part of the war'. Thus the men whom Newcastle had joined against Pitt over the Spanish war, were now drifting into it themselves, while Pitt, more firmly than any one of them, supported Newcastle's Continental 'system'. And however little open support the proposal of withdrawing from Germany received at present from anyone in office, Newcastle felt that the trend was in that direction.

. . . the squinting speeches of these young men, Lord Shelburne, Mr. Dempster, Mr. Eliab Harvey [he wrote to Hardwicke on 15 November]; all in the same connection, will not fail to give jealousies, that the measure of abandoning the Continent is not entirely the produce of *these young hot heads*. Besides, that is a doctrine which is greedily run into by my friends, Mr. Legge, Mr. Oswald, etc., as well as by my Lord Bute's, viz. my Lord Melcombe, Lord Shelburne, Sir Francis Dashwood, etc.

Rather than give up Germany, Newcastle would have carried on the war 'in its full extent' — but for that Pitt was required; 'when people see the extensive war we are going into, many people, *even of our own friends*, will wish him back'. So did Newcastle himself.

With all his faults, we shall want Mr. Pitt, if such a complicated, such an extensive war is to be carried on; I know nobody who can

---

[1] Newcastle to Hardwicke, 18 October; Add. MSS. 35421, f. 124 (original), and 32929, f. 357 (copy).
[2] Barrington to Newcastle, 13 November 1761; Add. MSS. 32931, ff. 19-20.

plan, or push the execution of any plan agreed upon, in the manner Mr. Pitt did. . . .[1]

Some satisfaction was vouchsafed to Newcastle when, in December 1761, the 'yelping young speakers' — 'those idle boys who set up to be Ministers' — gave up, at least for a time, their intention 'to move an address to the King for the recall of the British troops from Germany'. But the war with Spain was bound to add weight to their arguments, and on 25 December Newcastle wrote to Hardwicke :

> I suppose, you know the *die* is cast ; Lord Bristol coming away, and the orders sent to Admiral Saunders. What will become of this *poor* countrey, God only knows. What to do, I am sure I am not able to suggest ; but shall attend, whenever I am sent for. . . . I never saw this nation so near its ruin, as at present. What remedy will be proposed, I know not. I see by Mr. Grenville *his inclination* is to withdraw our army in Germany *immediately* and send them to Portugal, or imploy them against Spain. To me, that is the weakest and would expose us more to the contempt of France and Spain, than any other measure, that could be proposed. Peace, my dear Lord, is *the only remedy*.

.   .   .   .

> What is to be done ? To *defend*, or *offend* ? That is the question. And I own, I don't know, *how* to go about either. . . . For Godsake don't let us begin by so disgracefull a step, as recalling our troops from Germany.[2]

While loudly professing his perplexity and bewilderment, Newcastle resented not being consulted, *i.e.* if his jeremiads were dispensed with. He wrote to Devonshire on 26 December :

> His Lordship [Bute] is full of vigour ; *vigour* and *spirit*, are the only words now used at Court. . . .
> . . . As to myself I am every day more a cypher amongst them.
> My advice or opinion, are scarce ever ask'd, but *never* taken. I am kept in, without confidence, and indeed without communication.

[1] *Ibid*. ff. 45-9 ; and Add. MSS. 35421, ff. 141-5. Newcastle knew, however, that the King and Bute did not think they could work with Pitt ; the declaration 'that Mr. Pitt would *direct*, was such as had determined my Lord Bute *never to sit* at a Council Board with Mr. Pitt again' (Newcastle to Devonshire, 18 December 1761 ; Add. MSS. 32932, ff. 235-41). 'But what cannot be forgiven between Ministers', asks Fox in his 'Memoir'.
[2] *Ibid*. ff. 345-51.

This cannot do. I cannot be an *actor* in these very critical times, without being a *party*. And, in part, an adviser. . . .

What will become of this poor country ? Nothing but a peace can save it ; and we are further from it every day.[1]

A paper marked 'Considerations' [2] and a letter to Hardwicke contain Newcastle's budget of grievances. He had not heard a word from Lord Bute on 'the arrival of the account of the rupture with Spain' ; there had been no desire to consult him ; 6000 troops were promised to the Portuguese ambassador without a word said to him, although 'troops are *money*' ; he had offered Bute to come up from Claremont to the Council whenever required, and had received no answer.

Was ever any man in my station, or infinitely less, treated with so much slight and contempt ? . . .

In this situation, I cannot, I *will not*, go on to execute the most burthensome, the most difficult, the most responsible office in the whole kingdom, without original concert, confidence, and communication ; . . . I have my doubts, whether any, the best, instead of the worst, behaviour towards me, could, or should induce me to expose myself any longer in the station I am now in.[3]

The bitterness of neglect was blended with a desire and hope to escape responsibility.

When on 2 January 1762 Newcastle asked Bute where the money for Portugal was to come from — 'His Lordship . . . said, "he would speak out", that the German War could not be supported. To which I observed, that I had always imagined, that that was the *intention*.' [4]   On 6 January the King wrote to Bute about Hanover :

. . . indeed tho' I have subjects who will suffer immensely whenever this Kingdom withdraws its protection from thence, yet so superior is my love to this my native country over any private interest of my own that I cannot help wishing that an end was put to that enormous expence by ordering our troops home. . . .

. . . I think if the D. of N—— will not hear reason concerning the German War that it would be better to let him quit than to go on with that and to have myself and those who differ from him made

---

[1] Add. MSS. 32932, f. 363.
[2] 31 December 1761 ; *ibid.* ff. 419-20.
[3] Add. MSS. 35421, ff. 170-71 (original) ; 32932, ff. 408-9 (copy).
[4] Add. MSS. 32933, f. 34.

unpopular, and perhaps forc'd to put our hands to what we now would start at having only mentioned.

The same day Bute brought the matter before the Council, though he submitted

the great question *for consideration only*, of withdrawing all our troops from Germany, and giving up the German war. His Lordship seemed most strongly for it, and founded his arguments upon my not being able to declare that we could carry on *the whole war*, at this immense expence, another year.

Newcastle and Devonshire opposed a withdrawal, Grenville pleaded for it, while others — Egremont, Anson, and Ligonier — remained silent.[1]

The next day Bute sent Newcastle the draft of a letter to Joseph Yorke, the British Minister at the Hague, which contained the following sentence :

. . . you are to insinuate (tho' in very guarded terms), to Prince Louis, the impossibility, this country is under, of continuing so expensive a war ; against which men's minds seem more and more averse every day.[2]

But the covering letter from Bute was full of unusual complaisance and even deference :

I enclose a very rough draught indeed of a letter I have just scribbled to S[ir] J. Yorke ; to be sent or not as your Grace pleases ; look it over ; make whatever alterations you shall judge proper, or condemn it entirely ; and when sent me back it shall be either flung in the fire, or drawn out more correctly and shown the King. . . .[3]

Newcastle was deeply touched :

Your Lordship does me great honour in sending me the rough draft of your letter to Sir Joseph Yorke ; and, as you desire me to make any observations that occur to me upon it, I would submit, whether the first part may not convey an opinion, that the resolution was actually taken to recall our army, and to have nothing further to do with the war in Germany.

I am very sensible that my own opinion (too strongly possibly taken, tho' very sincerely) may make things appear to me rather

[1] Newcastle to Hardwicke, 10 January 1762 ; *ibid.* ff. 179-82.
[2] *Ibid.* ff. 82-3.
[3] *Ibid.* ff. 80-81.

more liable to such an interpretation, than in reality they are; and therefore I am sure your Lordship will forgive me. . . .[1]

Bute softened the letter 'in the places his Grace objected to', inserted a futile suggestion of Newcastle's, and did not propose to send the letter unless approved by him and the rest of the Cabinet.[2] Newcastle thereupon declared that never in his whole life, had he seen an abler letter, 'or better, and more judiciously turned to answer the purpose'.[3]

A severe cold which Newcastle had contracted insured for a while the continuance of the atmosphere of mutual good-will; Bute showed his solicitude for Newcastle, and encouraged him to stay at home as a sure relief for his cough (and colleagues).

I think your Grace acted prudently in keeping house this bad day; tho' it deprived us of the pleasure of your company; I hope this acquiescence to Dr. Wilmot will entirely remove the illness you complain'd of.[4]

Lord Bute rejoices to hear that the Duke of Newcastle finds himself so much better; and hopes he will not venture out, till the disorder is entir'ly over.[5]

I am very sorry to find the pain and cough return; but I hope keeping at home for a little will banish it entir'ly. I am sure His Majesty, (who asks me dayly, what accounts I have from Newcastle house . . .) will be very unwilling your Grace should think of coming abroad till you are perfectly recovr'd.[6]

Parliament was to meet on 19 January, and on the 16th Newcastle wrote to Hardwicke:

I have, this day, seen the Duke of Bedford again. His Grace was extremely good and kind to me; but more determined in his resolution [to move for the withdrawal of the troops from Germany]; with more invectives against the German war . . . than ever. His Grace also told me, *that the King told him, he was determined to give up the German War.* That was news, and more than Lord Bute will say, or admit I am sure.[7]

---

[1] 7 January; Add. MSS. 32933, ff. 84-5.   [2] *Ibid.* f. 144.
[3] To Bute, 10 January 1762; *ibid.* f. 173.
[4] Bute to Newcastle, 12 January; *ibid.* f. 230.
[5] 14 January; *ibid.* f. 286.
[6] Bute to Newcastle, 15 January; *ibid.* f. 302.
[7] *Ibid.* f. 320. Cf. also letter from H. Fox to Shelburne, 8 January 1762: 'The Duke of Bedford has in form declared his resolution to move,

Bedford's motion, on 5 February, was met by Bute with 'the previous question', for, as Bute explained to Devonshire, Grenville would never have agreed to a direct negative — 'he never was for those measures on the Continent'. Newcastle was exasperated by Bute's behaviour.

To assume to himself the sole direction of the majority of the House of Lords, to assert, contrary to fact, that *that* majority would reject the Duke of Bedford's motion no other way than by a previous question; and, as contrary to fact, to assert, afterwards, that it was his Lordship that had induced that majority to do it, by the previous question. Is it possible for me to go on with this man ? [1]

Was he, disregarded and unconsulted, to follow these new Ministers 'through all their wild and desperate projects', their West Indian expeditions ? — of which the success, a year later, was to supply the excuse for his criticisms of the peace negotiated by Bute. He wrote to Hardwicke on 12 February:

A most *expensive*, hazardous, uncertain expedition to the Havanna when both ships and men are wanted elsewhere, a wild goose chace (as I now understand) afterwards, after Mexico, St. Augustin, and God knows what, and the whimsical plan of expeditions going on faster than ever. Portugal is also to be defended at a vast expence.

God knows from whence or, how ? [2]

The death of the Tsarina, the enemy of Frederick II, raised Newcastle's hopes — 'this must make our peace in Germany; and, I think, with France and Spain also'.[3] But the improved prospects merely encouraged Frederick in his warlike plans,[4]

as soon as the House meets, for the recall of the troops from Germany. Lord Bute is of the same opinion, but as it should seem not in concert with the Duke of Bedford' (Shelburne Papers at Bowood; printed in Fitzmaurice's *Life of Shelburne*, vol. i. p. 103).

[1] Newcastle to Hardwicke, 17 February 1762; Add. MSS. 32934, ff. 393-4 (copy), and 35421, ff. 189-90 (original).

[2] Add. MSS. 32934, f. 292; see also letter of 16 February (*ibid.* f. 379): 'I see things every day worse and worse; . . . this itch after expeditions will exhaust our treasure . . .'

[3] Newcastle to Hardwicke, 28 January; Add. MSS. 32934, f. 45 (copy); and 35421, f. 183.

[4] Frederick's intercepted letter to his Minister in London, that the British Ministers 'ought to be sent *à la petite maison* to Bedlam', was hardly calculated to improve tempers (see Newcastle to Hardwicke, 22 February 1762; Add. MSS. 32935, ff. 9-13). Hardwicke replied, on 23 February, that he was not surprised at the nature of the dispatches from Berlin.

and Bute and Newcastle naturally grew suspicious and desired to know his scheme and ideas before answering the question whether Great Britain would continue his subsidy. In fact, Newcastle himself would have liked to get out of paying the subsidy — Prussia was freed of two enemies, Russia and Sweden, Great Britain was burdened with a new war against Spain, and with the defence of Portugal ; but he feared that stopping the subsidy might 'be interpreted as if the resolution was taken here, to abandon, *entirely* the German war'. This he would not admit, though when asked by Bute whether he could pay and support Prince Ferdinand's army of 70,000 men, he replied that if the expense of Portugal did not exceed what was now expected, he could do so 'for this present year', though he could not answer for anything more.[1]

On 8 March, Newcastle wrote to Hardwicke in high delight that Bute was prepared to conclude peace on moderate terms.

> Count Viry . . . has acquainted me, that Lord Bute had, yesterday, trusted him with his notions upon the terms of peace ; which, in every point but one (in which Lord Bute does not seem determin'd), are exactly the same with mine and must result from his Lordship's resolution to make peace, finding the impossibility to continue the war.

On all points concerning France, Bute was 'as reasonable as I can wish him' ; but Egremont 'was more difficult', and there were, moreover, some difficulties concerning Spain.

> For God's sake, my dear Lord, when things are brought so near, don't let us lose this great object for a mere formality. If my friend is not mistaken Lord B. acts like a man, and is determin'd to conclude forthwith.[2]

'Tho' I own I have long wonder'd that they have ventur'd to write such abusive stuff by the post without considering that we in England can peep into letters and know how to decypher. . . . I have been long convinc'd that this Prince has done himself much more harm by his pen than ever he has done himself good by it, notwithstanding his excessive vanity of writing. Upon this head he himself deserves *la petite maison*' (Add. MSS. 32935, ff. 33-5).
[1] Newcastle to Hardwicke, 25 February ; *Ibid.* ff. 74-5. See also Newcastle's letter to Joseph Yorke, 2 March 1762 (*ibid.* ff. 145-147), about the Prussian subsidy : 'I own, I was once doubtful about it myself. . . .'
[2] *Ibid.* ff. 249-51.

When on 8 April 1762 Newcastle proposed in the Cabinet

to raise the second million upon the vote of credit, in order to supply this expence; Mr. Grenville opposed it with the utmost warmth. . . .

He arraign'd the German War; said, such immense frauds would appear as would surprise every body.

The Duke of Newcastle defy'd him upon every article.[1]

And on 10 April, Newcastle wrote to Hardwicke:

Mr. Grenville, and perhaps others are determined to get rid of the German War *immediately*; he therefore loads it, with all the imputations he can find out; in order to render it so odious, that nobody should be for it. . . . I am not sure, that his view may not be to force me out, and to set himself *at the head of the Treasury*: That, with all my heart; for, if there is not a peace, this summer, (of which I don't see the least appearance) I am determined, not to engage another year. Let Mr. Grenville carry on his Maritime War, as he pleases; and *much good may it do him* ![2]

Two days later dispatches from Russia produced an explanation between Bute and Newcastle and Hardwicke who argued strongly against a withdrawal from Germany.

My Lord Bute said he knew it, that was very bad [wrote Newcastle to Devonshire]; and nothing could justify it, but saving ourselves *from ruin*: We debated that with him, and then his Lordship very candidly own'd to me, that he had got all our Treasury accounts, which proved it. . . . He certainly had them from Mr. Martin,[3] from whom he had the others, some time ago. I told him, . . . that I had never concealed the state of our finances from him, nor the expence of the German War. And your Grace will please to remember, that you often thought I had said too much of it, as it gave them a handle, to declare stronger against the German War.

When Newcastle saw that their arguments 'signified nothing', he asked 'that we might have an opportunity of giving

[1] Newcastle to Barrington, Add. MSS. 32936, f. 440.

[2] Add. MSS. 32937, f. 14.

[3] Samuel Martin, M.P., Joint Secretary to the Treasury. It should be noted that on 12 April, and even 'some time' before, Newcastle knew of Martin supplying Bute with Treasury papers. The earliest trace which I can find both of such dealings and of Newcastle's knowledge of them, is in an entry in the 'Register of Correspondence of the Earl of Bute', Add. MSS. 36796, under date of 18 March 1762: 'Mr. Samuel Martin, to the Earl of Bute. The Duke of Newcastle suspects that he has given his Lordship some hints about the King's extra revenues in the Exchequer: which he will not disown.'

our opinions, in Council, upon these two great points; in order, to justify ourselves, and our consciences'; to which Bute readily assented.

My Lord Bute said to me; 'My Lord, you don't know the thoughts of numbers of your own friends upon this point, who are as strongly of this opinion, as any others can be.' 'My Lord, I don't know, *who are my friends*; as will be the case of every one, when he is in the situation, I am in at present.' Whether my Lord meant any particular *Lord*, or not, I don't pretend to know. His Lordship told me, '*They said*, that we had worked Mr. Pitt out, and were now following his extravagant measures; (meaning the Continent measures;) and that we had better have Mr. Pitt again.' 'And, my Lord,' I replied; 'I will tell your Lordship what *they say*, that Mr. Pitt went out, because we would not declare war against Spain; and as soon as he was out, we did the same thing; and that being the case, Mr. Pitt would carry on his own measures better than any body.' 'That is true,' *says his Lordship*, 'they say *that also*.' And I will add to your Grace, by way of prophecy, *there it will end*, if his Lordship goes on, this way.[1]

Newcastle now once more talked of resigning.

Every day convinces me that I grow more insignificant, and time will make *many* though not *all*, follow power; . . . my remaining in the Treasury, to be baited, and perhaps overruled by Mr. Grenville, would be of no service to the publick and very disagreeable to myself.

He did not want to remain at the Treasury 'only to help those gentlemen to carry on this their ridiculous, popular war, as they think it', but, on the other hand, feared being accused of 'quitting for the German War',[2] which, as he himself came to see, was becoming unpopular.

The next day (13 April) Hardwicke resumed the conversation with Bute, who heard him 'with the appearance of great attention, and . . . answer'd with the greatest civility'. His chief objection was 'what made the subject of G. G.'s speech at Lord Egremont's on Thursday, viz., that the making such a vast expence this year would absolutely disable this countrey

---

[1] Newcastle to Devonshire, 13 April; Add. MSS. 32937, ff. 85-8.
[2] *Ibid.* ff. 92-3. The Duke of Cumberland, when consulted by Newcastle, warned him against 'all hasty measures' and thought that when the time came for resigning 'the subject matter of complaint need not be Germany alone' (*ibid.* f. 128).

from going on with any part of the war the next year, in case
peace should not be made sooner'.   If Bute could be reassured
on this point, it might be possible to win him over ; 'though I
will never affirm nor answer for anything, especially as we
change so from day to day. . . .'¹

But unless the negotiations which were now carried on with
France took a favourable turn, or 'more comfortable ideas'
were received from the Treasury concerning the financial
situation, George III was determined to withdraw the British
troops from Germany.   He wrote to Bute about 15 April :

. . . if this part is taken perhaps the D. of Newcastle will resign, and
what if he does, are not those who now appear attached to him men
of the most mercenary views, men who will ever follow him that pays
them ; in my conscience I don't believe he would have ten followers
if out of place and what is that, therefore for God's sake, let us put
this question to him if the French are not reasonable, or this dear
country is ruined inevitably.

The question whether the vote of credit should be for one
million or for two, now became a personal point between Newcastle and Grenville.   'Mr. Grenville and I cannot *jointly* have
the conduct of the Treasury', wrote Newcastle to Hardwicke
on 17 April 1762 ; ² while Grenville declared to the King that
if a second million was granted, Bute and he 'were beat by the
D. of N——, and that it would be making him master'.   The
King refrained from giving Grenville any definite answer, as he
'is weak enough to think he may succeed the D. of N—— and
therefore wishes to have him out of office'.³   The prospect
of Newcastle's resignation was by no means unpleasant to
George III, but Bute, not Grenville, was to be his successor.

The more I consider the Prussian subsidy [wrote the King to Bute
in the middle of April] the more objections arise in my mind against
it, and as to the German War, I am clear that if France is not willing
for peace, we must instantly nock it in the head and if men will leave
my service because I love this country preferably to any other, it will
be they that will be run at and not me ; the successor I have long
had in my eye to the D. of N. is a man void of his dirty arts who will
think of mine and his country's good, not of jobs ; if my dearest

¹ Hardwicke to Newcastle, Richmond, 14 April 1762 ; *ibid*. ff. 103-4.
² *Ibid*. ff. 183-6.   ³ The King to Bute, 6 May 1762.

friend does not know him by this character, I will add that he now holds the Seals, and lives in S. Audley Street.

The question of the Prussian subsidy and of confining the vote of credit to one million, came up again in the Cabinet Council on 30 April ; Newcastle's view was upheld by Hardwicke and Devonshire, and opposed by Bute, Grenville, Egremont, Henley, Granville, and Ligonier, while Mansfield remained silent. 'Every thing seems to have been determined before our meeting', wrote Newcastle to Hardwicke the same day. If the vote of credit is to be applied to Portugal only, '*my resolution* must take place *next week*, for I will never be overruled by Mr. Grenville, in a point *singly* relating to the Treasury'.[1]   Still, he admitted that he would not 'like to be drove out singly and immediately upon this point'.[2]   On 3 May Newcastle and Barrington presented their case to the King, but failed to make any impression.   George III wrote to Bute :

They both went away much dissatisfied and I verily believe will both in a day or two quit : and with all my heart, for I would rather go through anything than have a man negligent of the public money in that responsible office.

There was little, if any, hope of Newcastle carrying his point in the further discussions, and even his friends now considered that he would have to resign ; some of them, however, and also apparently he himself, thought that Bute 'was not yet prepared for a breach in the Ministry, tho' the appearances are against us'.[3]

Underhand dealings which Bute and Grenville had with Samuel Martin, joint Secretary to the Treasury, are represented usually (and by Newcastle himself), as the immediate cause of his resignation, though in reality he seems to have known for some time past that Martin was supplying Bute with Treasury

[1] Add. MSS. 32937, ff. 451-2. And to the Duke of Devonshire : 'Your Grace knows I have bore a great deal ; but it is now come to a point that all publick measures, even those where the Treasury must have the execution, are determin'd before I know any thing of the matter ; and all our meetings are only to wrangle about things agreed before hand by the King and his Minister' (*ibid.* ff. 452-3).
[2] Add. MSS. 32938, f. 20.
[3] Devonshire to Newcastle, 5 May ; *ibid.* f. 65.

papers and information.[1]   On 5 May, Newcastle wrote to
Devonshire : [2]

Mr. Martin made out a paper on the 25th of April for me ; which
he shew'd to Mr. Grenville the night before last ; and I *never* saw
'till this night. By this paper *my friends* begin to doubt whether the
second million is *absolutely* necessary.

This lays me under great difficulties ; the shame and reproach of
receding ; of yielding to Mr. Grenville and my Lord Bute in a point
merely relating to the Treasury. Whatever shall be done, my present
resolution is . . . to let the King know that *that* has pass'd in the
course of this affair which makes it impracticable for me to continue
long in the Treasury.

And the next day :

The secret is now out ; the *honest* Mr. Martin order'd the clerks,
yesterday, in the presence of some of the Lords [of the Treasury] to
make out an account of what saving there would be, if the troops
were recall'd and the German expence ended, at the end of June. . . .

Sure, after this, nobody can doubt a moment whether I should
make so pitiful a figure as to remain at the head of the Treasury. My
present thought is that I should remain in the Treasury 'till the
Parliament is up ; to make no bustle there this session. I beg this
may be a secret.[3]

Bute, Grenville, and Martin seem indeed to have acted in
an indecent and disloyal manner towards Newcastle, and the
bulky papers, wherein Martin has tried to justify his conduct,
confirm the impression that it was not easy to explain it away.[4]

---

[1] See above, p. 313.   [2] Add. MSS. 32938, f. 67.
[3] *Ibid.* f. 85 ; for a list of the queries set to the clerks, see *ibid.* ff.
140-3.
[4] Martin, on 29 July 1762, sent Hardwicke 'a paper, containing a state
of facts, such as (I hope) will sett me right in the Duke of Newcastle's
opinion, and in the opinion of the most worthy of his friends' (Add. MSS.
35597, f. 136 ; the paper, *ibid.* ff. 138-43). Hardwicke transmitted both
the paper and the covering letter to Newcastle on 4 August, and there are
copies of them in Add. MSS. 32941, ff. 96-107. Newcastle wrote to Hardwicke on 7 August (*ibid.* f. 177) : 'He (Martin) admits all the facts ; and
leaves it only to the interpretation of the reader whether those facts were
done with good or bad intentions.' Hardwicke replied on the 8th (*ibid.*
f. 187) : 'I barely acknowledged the receipt of it [the paper] . . . Mr.
Stone was in the right in saying that this paper admits every thing that he
had ever heard upon the subject.' A dossier on this matter is also among
Martin's own papers in the British Museum, and a few stray papers about
it are among the MSS. of Gilbert Elliot at Minto House, Hawick.

It must, however, be noted that, according to eighteenth-century ideas, Martin was not Newcastle's man — his connexion had been with Leicester House, he was brought into office by Pitt, and was never on close terms with Newcastle ; [1] and as for spying on Ministers through subordinates, Newcastle himself did it without shame or hesitation.[2]

When matters reached a crisis, Bute was, or alleged himself to be, confined to his house by illness. He wrote to Newcastle on 6 May :

Lord Bute is sorry to hear that nothing has been yet done in the vote of credit ; he hopes his Grace will take the King's pleasure so as to carry the message to-morrow, for he knows His Majesty to be very sollicitous to have an end put to this session.[3]

The next day, Newcastle, before going to Court, called on Bute, to acquaint him with what he intended to say to the King — 'for that I would by no means say anything that should be undutiful or disrespectful'. He told Bute that he still adhered to his opinion concerning the second million, but that even if the King concurred, he could not remain in office ; that he would acquiesce in Grenville's proposals 'to avoid everything that could give any disturbance or raise a flame just at the end of the session', but that the recent incidents made it impossible for him to remain at the Treasury, and he would therefore ask the King's permission to resign.

[1] When the Coalition was formed in July 1757, Martin was not restored to the place of Secretary to the Treasury which he had held under the Devonshire-Pitt Administration, but was offered financial compensation to the amount of £1500 p.a. 'Now, my Lord', wrote Martin to Newcastle on 30 July 1757 '(if your Grace will permitt me to deliver my simple sentiments frankly) I have long disapproved of this method of loading the publick for the gratification of individuals ; which seems to be peculiarly unfitt in a time of national distress. . . . I do not presume to judge your Grace, who are not to be tryed by my principles, and to whom I am beholden for seeking every expedient to serve me, but those principles such as they are, whether sound or whimsical, must govern me' (Add. MSS. 32872, ff. 393-4). Newcastle gave a polite answer to this harangue (5 August 1757, *ibid*. f. 463), and resented it only when he found that Martin had shown his letter to other people. 'I confess', was Martin's candid reply, '. . . that my part in the business with your Grace having been such as my own heart approved ; I was not sorry to have opportunities of letting my acquaintance know it, where I might without the appearance of ostentation and conceitedness' (Add. MSS. 32876, ff. 21-2). Samuel Martin was restored to his place in the Treasury in June 1758.

[2] See below, pp. 414-15.   [3] Add. MSS. 32938, f. 79.

My Lord Bute never said one single word to dissuade me from it ; to lament my going out, which common civility required ; to ask the cause of it, or to shew any disposition to remove it.

His Lordship only said : 'Your Grace will consider that your going out at this time may affect the peace,' (not as it would give encouragement to France to stand out ; that I suppose, he thought would be doing me too much honour). But his Lordship said, my friends would, from that time, be against the peace. I assured his Lordship to the contrary — that I should be as strongly and heartily for the peace when I was out as I was whilst I was in ; as I thought it absolutely necessary for the good of the nation. I said also smiling, I extremely approve *your peace* ; I wish, I could approve as much *your war* ; meaning his ridiculous maritime war. This ended our conversation ; we parted very civilly and seemingly both well pleased. But I believe it is the first instance, when one in my station had acquainted the King's Minister in the civilest manner, with his design of leaving his employment, that something civil was not said upon it.

Newcastle next went to the King, whom he found 'extremely gracious' ; he asked Newcastle whether he still adhered to his opinion, saying that this would have weight with him. Newcastle replied that he did, but that he would not press the point, and asked the King to direct Barrington to move 'one million only, as usual'. After that he informed the King of his decision to resign.

The King really seem'd good natured and affected. Said, he hoped I would think better of it ; that I had time to reconsider. His Majesty wish'd I would. That this thing was now over ; that he had a very good opinion of me ; that he always could depend upon my conduct, both in and out of employment ; and hinted, what he had once said before, that he had *always* been of that opinion.

I told His Majesty that I should always be a dutiful subject to King George the Third, as I had ever been to King George the First and King George the Second. But I adhered to my point. When he was signing the warrants, he then, of his own accord, repeated the same thing ; *that he hoped I would reconsider it and not persist in my resolution.* That was the purport ; to which I answer'd that I hoped His Majesty would remember what I had had the honor to say to him.[1]

[1] Newcastle to Devonshire, 7 May, 'at night' ; *ibid.* ff. 105-11.

In the account which George III gave of the same interview to Bute, 7 May, and which substantially tallies with that of Newcastle, no mention is made of the friendly or civil things which he had said to Newcastle; obviously he thought that indifferent or rude behaviour to one of the oldest and most faithful servants of the Royal Family would have been 'manly'.

The D. of N. has been here and to my great astonishment has waived his opinion but ended with resigning his office, that is to say when I may have made proper arrangements; his language was full of duty, and protesting he meant to support my measures with all his weight; the thing he most rested his opinion on was his Board's deserting him; this being the case I hope to see my dearest friend in a fortnight resign the Seals for the Treasury: then Government must be formed in a manner to continue, not a patch, believe G. Greenville is not right at present therefore cannot be too narrowly watched and sifted.

When Newcastle saw the King again, three days later (10 May), he perceived that it was Bute's resolution 'to force me out immediately'.

The King, who was very gracious the other day, said not one word to me, upon my own subject, a proof the party is taken. . . .

. . . The point now remaining to be considered is the time when, and the manner how, I should quit. As to the time, I should think about the rising of the Parliament, for I want some days, to make some little dispositions in the Treasury, for some people who have been promised. As to the manner, I would put it upon the last offensive act, of overruling, or rather intruding into the business of my office, of engaging my colleagues and my secretary in open opposition to me. . . . One favor . . . I ask of all my friends . . . is this, not to quit their employments, but to let every body know, that what I do, is with their approbation, and with some, by their advice, and that they shall continue to act with me, in the same conduct, as when I was in business, or otherwise, I am to be the scapegoat for the whole. The Duke [of Cumberland] says, the D. of Devonshire will go no more to Council. I should think, my friends should cease doing that, when I resign.[1]

In short, Newcastle wanted his friends, while retaining office, to enter into a semi-opposition and play the game which

---

[1] Add. MSS. 35421, ff. 259-60.

some of them had played for him in 1756–7 ; what he forgot
was that on the previous occasion the King himself had been
in semi-opposition to the new Administration.   Hardwicke
replied the same day :

> I don't much wonder at the King's not reviving today the subject
> of Friday's audience.   Your Grace knows that His Majesty never
> begins topicks that are matters of altercation or disagreeable to him-
> self.   The late King never did it, tho' so much more conversant in
> business. . . .
> I take it for granted that your Grace is absolutely determined to
> quit your employment ; but as *to the time and manner of doing it, and
> the reasons to be publickly assigned for it*, I beg you would not take a
> hasty resolution. . . . I will freely own . . . that my humble
> opinion is, that you must either go into opposition, or else absolutely
> retire from public business.   You say *that you would have your friends
> declare that they will continue to act with you, in the same conduct, as
> when you was in business* : they must do that either in opposition
> to measures, or in support of measures, and what is to be the
> consequence ?

For his own part Hardwicke was too old, had no office to resign,
and could not act the part he had acted in 1756–7.

> To be hanging about the Court ; harkning to the intrigues of it ;
> and watching the turns and openings that may play up, as things
> are now constituted, is what I can by no means undergo ; and with
> regard to yourself, . . . it will keep you in perpetual uneasiness, and
> can end in nothing material at last, but opposition.[1]

Newcastle was now taken at his word, and no opportunity
was given him any more to withdraw his resignation though
his friends tried their best to convince Bute of 'the danger he
was bringing himself into' by dropping Newcastle ; it was of
no avail.   The account given by Henry Fox, a jaundiced witness,
may perhaps be accepted on this occasion, as it coincides with
other evidence :

> The D. of Newcastle tells every body, and told Ld. Ilchester, that
> after he had said he would resign, the D. of Devonshire expostulated,
> and Lord Mansfield went a day or two after, and *pleaded* an hour
> without being able to extract a wish from Ld. Bute that he would
> stay.   'What then,' says he, 'can I do but go out ?'   It is strange

that his Grace should tell this. I told it Ld. Bute. 'Nothing,' says he, 'is more true.' [1]

Newcastle in his own accounts of the talks which Devonshire and Mansfield had with Bute, describes with exasperation Bute's attitude — he professed to believe that Newcastle had 'made his choice', was 'determined', and that 'the thing was over'; and 'did not give the least handle to either of them to endeavour to make it otherwise which . . . shews plainly that it had been *his determination* for some time . . . to make it impossible for me to continue in employment'.[2]

The King himself, wrote Newcastle to Rockingham on 14 May,

resorted to the language of the Minister, *the Duke of Newcastle is determined*; and never desired the Duke of Devonshire to endeavour to make me alter my resolution.

I believe there are few instances where such an indifference has been shew'd towards one in my situation, except where there had been an open and profess'd design to turn him out. . . .

I hope I shall always act as an honest man and as a friend to my country, and this Royal Family, and to my inseparable friends, the Whigs, but I shall take care that His Majesty shall know when I resign that I am at liberty to act, as I shall think proper, upon every occasion that may happen. I say this because my Lord Bute insisted with my Lord Mansfield that I would not oppose. That must depend upon their conduct and the opinion of my friends.

Thus Newcastle's thoughts were turning towards opposition, while 'their conduct' towards him did not improve. He added in a postscript dated 'Friday [14 May] night, past nine':

[1] 'Memoir' by Henry Fox, in *The Life and Letters of Lady Sarah Lennox* (1901), by Lady Ilchester and Lord Stavordale, p. 63. See also letter from Ilchester to Henry Fox, 18 May 1762, published by the present Lord Ilchester in *Letters to Henry Fox* (1915), pp. 149-51.—On 28 June 1762 Newcastle wrote to Hardwicke (Add. MSS. 32940, ff. 112-15): 'My Lord Mansfield . . . gave me an account of one or two conferences which he had had with my Lord Bute' who 'told him that Mr. Fox had told him, that the Duke of Newcastle had told Mr. Fox, that he had employed my Lord Mansfield to propose terms of accommodation to my Lord Bute, (what lies are invented *somewhere* !).' Newcastle points out that he had not even seen Fox — but was that not merely a confusion with Ilchester?

[2] Newcastle to Sir Joseph Yorke, 14 May, Add. MSS. 32938, ff. 239-249; see also Newcastle's letter to the Duke of Cumberland, 17 May, *ibid.* f. 306.

I was this day at Court. His Majesty was barely civil. . . . I desired the King's leave to attend His Majesty some day next week to settle my *private account*; [1] and that I hoped His Majesty would allow me to retire from my employment a day or two after the Parliament rose. His Majesty ask'd me whether I should go to Claremont ? I said, yes ; I might afterwards go to other places.

The King did not drop one word of concern on my leaving him, nor even made me a polite compliment — after near fifty years service and devotion to the interest of his Royal Family. I will say nothing more of myself; but that I believe never *any man* was so dismiss'd; but all this puts me more in the right. *C. Viry* told the Duke of Devonshire that the resolution was taken not to *ask* me to stay. [2]

And this is the account which George III gave of the same interview to Bute, 14 May :

The D. of N. has been here and said he is preparing his accounts that he may retire. I did not say anything more than that I hoped they would be full, he is to bring them next week : I thought it best not to mention his retiring next week as that would be giving him notice perhaps to [*sic*] soon, particularly as I have not heard the report of my dear friend's conversation with George Grenville.

The offensive remark, he 'hoped they would be full', was almost certainly a literary afterthought on the part of George III, for had he made it, Newcastle would not have failed to mention it in his plaintive letters to his friends ; still, even as an invention it is characteristic.

At first the intention apparently was that on Newcastle's resignation Bute should take the Treasury with Grenville for Chancellor of the Exchequer, a place for which Bute had named him at the time of Pitt's resignation, and for which he had still further qualified by his recent interventions in Treasury matters. But on 20 May, Rigby informed Fox that Charles Townshend had told him of Grenville having 'refused being Chancellor of the Exchequer', [3] and it is to this refusal that Bute seems to refer when writing to Grenville on 22 May : 'I have been forced to make an unpleasant arrangement where I

[1] The secret service accounts ; see *The Structure of Politics*, pp. 173-4.
[2] Add. MSS. 32938, ff. 262-4.
[3] See Ilchester, *Letters to Henry Fox, Lord Holland* (1915), p. 151.

am immediately concerned, on your mind revolting against what I had ever looked upon as fixed.'[1]   And it was probably at that juncture, between 15 and 17 May, that George III wrote to Bute about Grenville in a letter, undated as usual :

> I don't doubt but if he could, he would have some office where he could in his opinion figure more, than as an Assistant in a Board ; he is very far out if he thinks himself capable for a post, where either decision or activity are necessary ; for I never yet met with a man more doubtful or dilatory. . . .

Possibly Grenville's refusal of the Exchequer made Bute doubt for a while whether he could take the Treasury :

> . . . the thought of his not accepting the Treasury or of his retiring chill my blood [the King wrote to him probably on 19 May] ; is this a moment for despondency ?   No !   for vigour and the day is ours ; my dearest friend's sincerity when he talks of his own ignorance in business would be doubted by any man in this country but me . . . ; what I should imagine is, that if he cannot point out to me a good Chancellor of the Exchequer, he should see for an honest quiet man, and put his chief confidence in Oswald as to Treasury matters ; but to be short, take the Treasury and numbers will be with you.[2]

Bute's hesitations and fears concerning leadership and 'numbers' in Parliament were, no doubt, heightened by the fact that Newcastle was clearly drifting into opposition ; for, encouraged by some of the 'country Whigs',[3] Newcastle carried out his intention to let the King know that on resigning he reserved to himself freedom of action.

The D. of N—— has quite alter'd his language [wrote the King to Bute on 19 May], he says he hopes I will look on him as at liberty to act as his conscience shall guide him.   I reply'd that that is the language every man that opposes, uses ; but that his conduct was what I should form my judgement on the truth of the professions he has ever made me.

---

[1] *Grenville Papers*, vol. i. p. 446.

[2] Rigby, in the letter of 20 May, quoted above, wrote to Fox that Charles Townshend betted him 20 guineas that Lord Bute would not take the Treasury.   Rigby added : 'Some people yesterday named Lord Halifax and Legge for the two first at the Treasury Board, but I doubt that intelligence'.

[3] See, *e.g.*, letter from Lord Rockingham, 15 May ; Add. MSS. 32938, ff. 287-91, and from John White, M.P., 16 May, *ibid.* ff. 298-9.

The change in Newcastle's language was bound to react on the attitude and plans of the Court; none the less, on 21 May, Newcastle wrote to Hardwicke with something like pained surprise:

> I have had certain intelligence that *they* say their intention at first was not to turn out any one single man; for then they thought the Duke of Newcastle intended really to retire, and to have nothing more to do with publick affairs; (I don't know who told them so). But now they find, by the Duke of Newcastle's discourse to his friends, who are in place, that they should keep themselves clear as to any engagements for their future behaviour; and from what the D. of N. said to the King, that there is a design to force the D. of N. in again; they must fix their party and compleat their scheme. From whence I conclude, many of my friends will be turn'd out.[1]

Hardwicke, having four sons in politics and office, pointed out to Newcastle the unwisdom of talking in that way to friends who were to retain their places, and professed not to believe that 'any such discourse had been held to them *in general*' by Newcastle, though it closely resembled what he had said to Hardwicke.[2]

On 25 May, the day before Newcastle formally resigned office, the King spoke more graciously to him 'than he had done for some time past', said he was sorry to part with Newcastle, and desirous to do everything that should be agreeable to him. The meaning of this offer was specified in a talk with Devonshire:

> The King [wrote Newcastle to Cumberland on 26 May] . . . said that he knew what I had done for the service of His Family, that I had prejudiced my fortune by it; and therefore he wish'd the Duke of Devonshire would sound me, whether I would take a pension, in any shape, privately or publickly, in any manner I should like.

The next day the King was again very gracious, and pressed the pension on Newcastle, describing it as a debt owing to him; but Newcastle refused it.

> The King was pleased, at parting, to say that he could depend upon my support; to which I made a bow, and said nothing.

---

[1] Add. MSS. 35421, f. 263 (original), and 32938, ff. 381-2 (copy).
[2] *Ibid.* f. 394.

I have been so much misunderstood on both sides of that question, that I thought it was best to be absolutely silent, as I had twice declared to the King, that I could make no promises nor enter into any engagements upon that head.[1]

NEWCASTLE AT CLAREMONT

Newcastle, in the letter in which he described to Cumberland his leave-taking from the King, announced his intention of waiting on the Duke, who was assuming more and more the part of Royal leader of the opposition. 'It is little information I shall now be able to give, relating to publick measures, they keep every thing an absolute secret from me. . . .'[2] Cumberland answered the same day :

I most heartily rejoyce at the manner in which you received the Kings good intentions. Your friends must like it, your enemies will not dare to blame it. We shall meet at the Chapter tomorrow; if Court should be over in time, perhaps you may like to call on me afterwards, if not, the Lodge is not so far from Claremont, but that I may flatter myself with your company there some times, for we are become speculators, not actors, and have leasure to talk over past transactions, if precluded from the knoledge of fresh events. . . .[3]

Hardwicke, who for his own sake, for the sake of his sons, and also of Newcastle himself, did not want to see him engage in political intrigues, but wished him to retire for good, wrote to him on 28 May :

I heartily wish that the conduct in that quarter [the Duke of Cumberland's] had been allways uniformly agreeable to that sense, which is now so handsomely profess'd of your long, expensive, unwearied, and most useful services. . . . But . . . I cannot restrain my self from suggesting one word upon the great honour done you by the very gracious invitation to the Lodge. Your Grace has not been us'd to go there, nor do I recollect that you were ever ask'd . . . if you should now begin that resort, it will I fear give a handle to suspicions, insinuations, and malicious reports of caballing and concert, in order to opposition, and what will be traduc'd with the name of faction, however unjustly. I think the appearance of this would do no good to H.R.H., and great prejudice to your Grace.[4]

---

[1] Add. MSS. 32939, ff. 5-7. [2] *Ibid.* f. 6.
[3] *Ibid.* f. 1. [4] *Ibid.* f. 54.

But Newcastle was not to be convinced, and wrote to Charles Yorke on 2 June :

I differ . . . as to my visit to Windsor Lodge. As I am determined to do nothing without the advice and concurrence of my friends, I am safe as to my conduct ; I will not put it into the power of any body to say that I give the lie to my whole life : but I don't owe those gentlemen the regard, to be afraid of giving them the alarm; the more they are alarmed, the better for the publick.[1]

It is impossible to sum up in plain, reasonable terms what it was that Newcastle wished or expected ; his feelings were contradictory, a mixture of ambition and apprehensions, of the wish to make a figure and the fear of incurring responsibility, of sentimental 'regards' and the craving for being sentimentally regarded ; and his political thinking was naive and inane. He professed that opposition would 'give the lie' to his whole life, and yet was determined to keep himself free to enter it. He told his friends not to resign with him, but expected them, while retaining office, to show their deep regret for him, and their ill-humour with those on whom they now depended. When Bute seemed to contemplate dismissals, this was to Newcastle mean vindictiveness, while the contrary was evidence that 'my Lord Bute's plan is to get my friends from me'. He professed to be happy in his retirement and to have found relief in it, but wanted others to pine and clamour for his return. With intense jealousy he watched developments in London, and employed his friends, from men of ministerial rank such as Lord Barrington, down to Ancel, an office-keeper at the Treasury, to spy on his successors. Wishing to rival Bute's levees, he endeavoured to secure the greatest possible concourse of friends at Claremont ('the rains have made this place so pleasant that I am desirous that my best friends should see it in that situation'),[2] and resented it if any of them did not turn up. Among these was naturally his nephew, Lord Lincoln, always bored and indifferent. Newcastle wrote to him on 8 July : 'I much want your company here. Our *crowds*, thank

---

[1] *Ibid.* ff. 155-6.
[2] Newcastle to H. Stanley, Claremont, 28 June 1762 ; Add. MSS. 32940, f. 116.

God, begin to abate.'[1]   And while spying, scheming, and trying to emulate Bute, Newcastle was painfully astonished at not receiving official papers after having resigned office.

> There is one thing I think myself and my friends . . . have reason to complain of [he wrote to Stone on 30 May] ; which is that tho' the Duke of Devonshire, Lord Hardwicke and myself entirely concur'd in the orders which were sent by my Lord Egremont relating to the terms of peace ; not one of us have been spoke to either upon the first letters sent since to Lord Egremont . . . or know in the least the orders that are given since ; or the contents of what may have been since received.[2]

Hardwicke replied to a similar complaint, on 17 June :

> I do not think that it was to be *expected* that after having left the Cabinet Council such communications should be made.   They would embarrass both sides. . . .
>
> It gives me much pleasure that your Grace has so much reason to be satisfied with the regard shewn you by your friends.   I never doubted it, and am persuaded that you will find it encrease rather than diminish.[3]

It would indeed have increased prodigiously, even among Newcastle's friends at Court and in office, had they merely had the certainty that he would not embarrass them by attempting a return to politics and office.   They too tried to take him at his word ;   even before Newcastle had actually given up office, his friend Kinnoull declared to Egremont that he would support whomever the King put at the head of the Treasury, and that Newcastle had 'resolved to leave quietly and not meddle in affairs'.[4]   After Newcastle's resignation, Robert Nugent wrote a letter to Barrington, which Barrington promptly forwarded to Newcastle, 'because I think it will give you some pleasure'.[5] It reads like a joint petition to Newcastle not to haunt their world ;   Nugent thanks Barrington for having relieved him of the anxiety he felt

> from reports spread here [at Dublin], with all the air of authenticity, of circumstances attending our noble friend's resignation very different from those he communicated to you.   What really pass'd does

[1] Add. MSS. 32940, f. 284.   [2] Add. MSS. 32939, f. 102.
[3] *Ibid*. f. 386.   [4] George III to Bute, 17 May 1762.
[5] Add. MSS. 32939, f. 337.

honor to Majesty; and perfects the character of as able, faithful, and disinterested a Minister as ever served the Crown. . . . That the King may never want such a servant and that our friend may find in retirement and self-approbation an ample recompense for the loss of power is all that is now left for you and me to wish for with regard to both.[1]

In short, Newcastle's 'friends' were repeating what Bute had said — that Newcastle was 'determined' and that 'the thing was over'. But this was certainly not what Newcastle expected from them, and he resented their suggesting that it would be 'most honorable for me to retire *absolutely* from publick business . . . and that that is my intention'.[2]

But Newcastle found reason to be vexed with the behaviour even of those friends whom he valued most. He wrote to Andrew Stone on 30 May :

. . . my great friends, with whom I consulted and advised, have, I fear, been too cautious in approving my conduct, or blaming that which left me no choice, what to do. And the eagerness in my friends less informed and less material, to keep their employments, or exchange them for as good, or better than those, they had before. This leaves me as it were *alone*, separated and distinguished from the rest ; whereas, in truth, it was a common cause, and ought to have been treated as such, I don't mean altogether by resignations, but by manner of talking and treating the subject, rather than by silence, as, I believe, is pretty much the case at present.[3]

Stone answered with truth and common sense :

As to what your Grace mentions of the conduct of your principal friends, it does not seem difficult to account for it. Had it been the measure, to have quitted with you, I am persuaded they would have done it readily, and cheerfully : but your Grace always declared, and they understood, it was not to be so. And, that being the case, whilst they remain in office, they will hardly avoid an appearance of some complaisance to those, that govern ; tho' I doubt not, they will all (by *all* I do not mean any great number) be ready upon all occasions, to shew their real and steady attachment to your Grace.[4]

Presumably by '*all* occasions' he did not mean 'any great number' either.

[1] 5 June 1762 ; *ibid*. f. 339.
[2] Newcastle to Hardwicke, 7 October 1762 ; Add. MSS. 32943, ff. 90-1.
[3] Add. MSS. 32939, f. 102. [4] *Ibid*. f. 109.

Meantime Newcastle was happy at Claremont, yes, very happy — the whole world was to see how happy he was !

I am sure [he wrote to Kinnoull on 15 June] you will be glad to hear that (thank God) the dear Duchess of Newcastle and I are both in perfect health settled here, much to our ease and satisfaction. Company indeed we don't want ; for the house has been more than full ever since we came down ; and is likely to continue so for some time ; and I wish you could see any of the company and know from them whether they ever saw me more easy or in better spirits in my life.[1]

'His Grace', wrote Royston to Hardwicke on 20 June, after a visit to Claremont, 'keeps up his spirits in company, but I doubt his time hangs upon him when he is alone.' [2] Hardwicke replied the same day : 'The resort to him at present keeps up his spirits, but that won't last ; and I hope he don't count upon all that come as his firm friends'.[3]

The weather is very hot and fine [Newcastle went on to say in his letter to Kinnoull] ; and this place is very pleasant ; but we have had no rain : notwithstanding which I have as fine hay and corn as ever was seen. I can be a farmer as well as your Lordship. . . .

Indeed, what a delightful occupation 'farmering' would have been, if only it had not been disturbed by accounts of Bute's crowded levees, which Newcastle's late private secretary, H. V. Jones, was directed to send him, with lists of those present.[4]

The Great Man [wrote Newcastle to Rockingham on 2 June] . . . is in high spirits, and seems to carry all before him. I thank God, I have put it out of his power to carry me ; and I defy any thing he can say or do upon my subject.[5]

And the same day he wrote to Charles Yorke :

. . . nobody can be more pleased with a resolution he has taken, than I am with mine ; I feel the comfort, the honor, and the safety of it. My best friends thought I would not adhere to it. I did not think it worth my while to undeceive them ; I knew the fact would soon do

---

[1] Add. MSS. 32939, ff. 353-4.   [2] Add. MSS. 35352, ff. 242-3.
[3] *Ibid.* ff. 244-5.
[4] See, *e.g.*, Jones's letters of 9, 11, 12, 17, and 19 June, Add. MSS. 32939, ff. 246, 294, 307-8, 387, and 415 ; and the list of the levee of 2 June, compiled by Ancel, office-keeper to the Treasury, and forwarded by Jones, ff. 309-11.   [5] *Ibid.* f. 157.

it. . . . I found an universal clamour, in all my friends, at the monopoly of universal power in my Lord Bute ; I would no longer *submit* to it ; and, I don't in the least envy those who do. I don't mean by not quitting ; for there is a very effectual way of shewing their inclination, without directly quitting their employments.[1]

Still, in spite of Bute's crowded levees, the Court was uneasy at the possibility of Newcastle entering into opposition. They feared a junction between him and Pitt, which some common friends tried to effect, and the attitude of the Duke of Cumberland added to their uneasiness. On the death of Lord Anson (6 June), Bute meant to offer the Admiralty to Lord Sandwich, and began by talking to him about the general situation ; he

said the Duke of Newcastle is *unquiet* and *uneasy* ; and complains of ill usage tho' there was no foundation for it ; that, *that being so*, it was necessary for the King to know upon *whom* he could depend. Lord Sandwich replied 'If that question is directed to me the answer I must give is that my attachment is *to the Duke of Cumberland.*' Lord Bute did not make one word of answer nor ever mention'd the Admiralty.[2]

The Duke of Bedford, who wished to remove anything that might hinder the conclusion of peace, seemed similarly anxious concerning the line Newcastle was going to take, and when talking to him on 5 June, insisted

that he must and would constantly repeat his earnest advice, that I would give no disturbance. That the King had spoke to him upon it ; had talked to his Grace with great kindness and regard of me, etc. . . . I cut that pretty short and said, I could lay myself under no promise or engagement. . . .

His Grace pressed me much not to give any opposition and said, you will not oppose what you approved when you was in employment. I answer'd *most certainly not, my Lord.*[3]

Hardwicke, though looking at the matter from a different angle, agreed that this was not the time for opposition.

[1] *Ibid.* ff. 155-6.
[2] Newcastle to Devonshire, 10 June ; *ibid.* ff. 265-6.
[3] *Ibid.* ff. 264-5. For a previous letter, of 15 May 1762, in which Bedford pointed out the evil effects which Newcastle's resignation, especially if followed by opposition, would have on the peace negotiations, see Add. MSS. 32938, f. 285.

This new Ministry has enough upon their hands [he wrote to Newcastle on 17 June]; and, if they can't make their peace, will soon find themselves in the greatest difficulties. The unpopularity is rising fast enough. But I should not wish to do any thing at present to give them a pretence to alledge (as Queen Anne's Tory Ministry did, and as my Lord Bolingbroke has printed over and over) that the opposition they met with forc'd them to accept a worse peace than otherwise they should have been able to make.[1]

Newcastle, as usual, expressed his complete agreement with Hardwicke, whose advice he would follow; though he owned that such restraint placed him in a difficult position and that he was in danger of losing friends 'by not declaring' — for 'mankind are so made, that if they don't see something is to be done on one side they will engage on the other'. But the opposite policy would be 'improper and perhaps dangerous in itself'.

Make a *declaration*, of what? Of *opposition, to what*? To right measures, to the necessary support of the Government, I am sure nothing shall ever induce me to that. . . . But, on the other hand, I will enter into no engagements. . . . For, as, on the one hand I would not put it in the power of any one man living to say I intended *opposition*; so, on the other, if I was to declare absolutely *the contrary*, my Lord Bute's next levée would be twice as full as any he has yet had. Those levées have done a great deal of hurt; it is said, all the Duke of Newcastle's friends were there, and not one Cavendish, Manners or Walpole.[2]

On 19 June, Hardwicke saw Bute, who made certain general advances to him, for George III would have wished to draw Hardwicke from Newcastle; but possibly these advances were also meant by Bute as a tentative approach to Newcastle, for he seems to have realised by now the mistake he had made in not retaining Newcastle, when he practically begged for it.

[1] Add. MSS. 32939, f. 385.
[2] Newcastle to Hardwicke, 19 June; *ibid*. ff. 410-11. Henry Fox remarks in his 'Memoir', published in *The Life of Lady Sarah Lennox* (p. 65): 'None of his [the Duke of Devonshire's] friends go to Lord Bute's levée. All the D. of Newcastle's do.' And the King wrote to Bute on 1 June 1762: '. . . the list of those at the Cock Pit yesterday pleased me much, except none of the Duke of Devonshire's people being there, nor Ld. Coventry and others still in my service that cry up Mr. Pitt'.

He [Bute] already saw too much of the weight and difficulty of his new office [Hardwicke wrote to Newcastle]; that he had heard your Grace complain of it, but he saw more of it since he came into it; that it would require the assistance of all honest men to support the King's affairs and the necessary service of the nation.

Hardwicke replied with assurances of his duty and zeal for His Majesty's service, but reminded Bute that his friendship and connexion with Newcastle was of forty-four years' standing, and that he was not 'capable of doing any thing to weaken or depart from that attachment'. 'His Lordship's behaviour was very civil, decent and calm, without any *aigreur* at all, but I thought I could discern under it some apprehensiveness.'[1]

And again on 30 June, Hardwicke wrote to Newcastle :

I was told yesterday by one who, I believe, had it from pretty good hands, that my Lord B. is extremely embarrass'd and uneasy; tir'd already with his *new Secretary's* prolixity and prosing; and with the dryness and non-inventiveness of *the other*.[2]

At the end of July there was a meeting of the Charterhouse to elect a new Master, which gave Newcastle, one of its Governors, a welcome excuse for relinquishing rural happiness and coming up to town. Having previously complained to Devonshire of not hearing 'one word from your friend Viry, for my friend I can no longer call him',[3] he now advised Viry of his coming,[4] and once more received his visits and confidences.

I have seen C.V. twice [wrote Newcastle in a 'Memorandum' of 22 July]; yesterday and this morning. . . .
C.V. express'd great concern at my having resign'd my employment; that things must be made up, that there were misunderstandings on both sides; that he knew my Lord Bute's good inclinations towards me; and often repeated, and *for my family*. I cut him extremely short; that what I had done was upon mature consideration . . . that what he proposed was impracticable; and indeed, he proposed nothing but that I should *support the Court*; and all be made up between us. . . .[5]

---

[1] Hardwicke to Newcastle, 19 June 1762 ; Add. MSS. 32939, ff. 417-20.
[2] Add. MSS. 32940, f. 164.
[3] 23 June ; *ibid.* f. 46.
[4] *Ibid.* f. 401.
[5] Add. MSS. 32941, ff. 18-25.

The next day Viry returned to the subject of Newcastle's relations with Bute, placing the blame for what had happened on Grenville —

that my Lord Bute had told him lately that he should be glad to shew any publick mark of his regard for me ; and particularly again, for my family. . . . I told him that I had taken my resolution ; that all he said were but words. That I had not done, what I did, lightly ; and that I should adhere to it.

To prod Newcastle, Viry further reported, or invented, that Pitt had said 'he would enter into no opposition ; . . . that he had been twice united (*uni*) with the Duke of Newcastle ; but would never be united (or *uni*) with him again'.[1]

Hardwicke too was in town and, at Bute's request, went to see him (28 July). Bute now came closer to the point, and expressed his regret at Newcastle's resignation, with whom 'he thought he could have gone on longer and better . . . than with anybody else, for there was allways a good humour about him ; and he had not the starts and emotions, that some others were liable to'. If Newcastle, he went on to say,

should, at any time, think any office proper for his rank and age, the King would most readily confer it ; and it would give him (Lord B.) the greatest satisfaction. That, in respect of the D. of N.'s friends, he had never intended any hostility against any of them ; that he had carefully sought them out in the Treasury etc., in order to protect them.

Hardwicke replied that Newcastle was perfectly easy as far as his own person was concerned but placed the whole weight on public matters, wherein he adhered to the German war and the Prussian subsidy.[2]

---

[1] Newcastle to Devonshire, 23 July ; Add. MSS. 32941, ff. 36-9.

[2] Hardwicke to Newcastle, 28 July 1762 ; *ibid*. ff. 84-7. About that very time, Dr. Francis, Fox's scribe, was preparing a virulent pamphlet against the German war ; the 'Heads' for that pamphlet 'given by Lord Bute' are preserved among the Shelburne Papers at Bowood. Nor had the idea been given up of attacking Newcastle over the Treasury management of the war. 'With regard to the Commissariat', wrote Bute to Shelburne on 22 July, 'tho' I have not lost sight of it since I came into the Treasury, it is so tedious, so immense a machine, that I am as yet by no means master of the subject. I hope one day to have that most infamous and exhausting measure fairly stated to the publick' (Shelburne Papers).

The same day Bedford was at Claremont, and talked to Newcastle in such a way that 'one would almost suspect . . . his Grace had been *employ'd*'.

His Grace said, I must come *into employment*. I treated that (as I think it) impossible. I kept quite off, as to any future part, I would act ; that I was determined to keep myself at liberty. He then said, I am sure, you will do nothing to *hurt* the King and the Government ; *that you may depend upon*. . . .

As to employment, that is all chimerical ; I think, nothing would ever make my Lord Bute quit the Treasury or *me* take it. I am sure, I would not take the President [of the Council] for *many reasons*. My Lord Bute squinted at a distance at Mr. Pitt, but only at a distance.[1]

There can be little doubt as to Bute's reasons for wishing to regain Newcastle's active co-operation ; he wanted Newcastle to share with him the responsibility for the peace treaty, and, even more, he felt the need of having the support of that ultra-pacifist in the Cabinet to carry the treaty. For Grenville was proving obstreperous and 'had many struggles with Lord Bute upon the terms, which he was desirous to keep up higher than Lord Bute (who feared the negotiation might break off) could be brought to consent to'.[2] Nor were the other members of the Government much more compliant ; at the decisive Cabinet Council, on 26 July, when Bute thought peace with France practically assured, 'to his great astonishment he found himself single'.[3]

How grating must it be to Lord Bute, and what a prospect does it afford him, to find his Cabinet Counsellors, and many of them such as nobody but himself would have made so, differ from him in Council without declaring their minds to him first in private.[4]

After the Cabinet meeting, Bute wrote to Egremont :

I am not ashamed to own that I write this letter with a heavy heart, convinced in my own mind of two important truths ; the one,

---

[1] *Ibid*. ff. 108-10.

[2] George Grenville's narrative of the events of 1762, *Grenville Papers*, vol. i. p. 450.

[3] H. Fox in his 'Memoir' in *The Life and Letters of Lady Sarah Lennox*, p. 69. According to Fox the meeting was on Monday, 27 July ; but 27 July was a Tuesday — the day of the week, not of the month, is correctly stated.

[4] *Ibid*. p. 70.

that peace was in our power: the other, that we are about to lose an opportunity, we shall scarce recover again. . . . Possessing these ideas, you will not be surprized, my dear Lord, if the situation I have just been in, single and alone, alarms me; I feel most sensible, that I am from the King's known goodness to me, to stand at mark, for the long train of calamities, that the continuation of this war brings in my view.

He was prepared to forget 'Mr. Grenville's dissenting from me in word, look and manner through the whole examination of the Preliminaries', but realised that peace could not 'be made except by a perfect confidence between the French Ministers and the King's . . . I mean by Ministers your Lordship and myself. . . .'[1] Thus 'George' had ceased to count as a 'Minister'. 'If peace is not now concluded', wrote the King to Bute on 26 July, 'I must insist that my dear friend does not quit me, but at the same time I must insist on most of the Cabinet of this day being then dismissed.'

The fear of having otherwise to bear part of the responsibility for the peace treaty had played a notable part in Newcastle's original decision to resign. He wrote in his 'Private Mem^{ds}' on 12 May 1762:

The terms of peace — in my circumstances not taking it upon me.

.   .   .   .

They will fling the odium upon me.
In employment I ought to take my share.
Out of employment not obliged to it.
They will fling it all upon me.
If so, I had better get out beforehand.

By the time the offers of rejoining the Cabinet were made to him, there was 'more clamour' against Bute 'than there ever was against any man',[2] and fear of having to share his unpopularity, rather than pride, made Newcastle so surprisingly firm in resolutions which, at the point of realisation, had been practically imposed on him. Nor did Hardwicke encourage him to accept office — 'who would thrust themselves into the present entangled state of the negotiation of peace? It is only interested persons that are in such hast.'[3]

¹ Add. MSS. 36797, ff. 6-7.   ² Fox's 'Memoir', p. 76.
³ Add. MSS. 32941, f. 94.

But the negative decision not to accept office was hardly sufficient. 'I am solicited every day', wrote Newcastle, 'to know what party my friends should take' ;[1] 'our friends grow more impatient every day to know what conduct *we* intend to hold' ;[2] etc. When Newcastle, immediately on his resignation had started to 'resort' to the Duke of Cumberland, he chalked out for himself a line which pointed towards active opposition ; but though he admitted that in going to Windsor Lodge he acted contrary to Hardwicke's opinion, this did not prevent him from declaring, in the same breath, that he was safe as to his conduct because he would do nothing 'without the advice and concurrence of my friends'.[3] In other words, he was moving towards opposition, but insisted on having the formal decision pronounced by his 'principal' friends so as to make them responsible for his own actions. 'I have taken one resolution, to go *with my friends*, not one step forwarder or backwarder than they . . .' ;[4] 'for my own part, my party is taken, to act with my friends . . . and therefore it is for them to determine' ;[5] etc. But Hardwicke, who wished to secure an unhampered run in politics for his sons, and undisturbed rest from politics for himself, was reluctant to confirm Newcastle in his obvious inclinations.

As to the general and fundamental question *with whom* you should elect to unite [wrote Hardwicke on 8 August], I think it a very difficult one, and that it is not yet ripe for a decision. . . . A great part of the reasoning will depend upon the turn which our negotiation of peace shall take. . . .[6]

The next proposals of office were made through Lord Lyttelton ; the Presidency of the Council was offered to Newcastle, and the prospect of the Great Seal for Charles Yorke was held out to Hardwicke, which made him wish, more than ever, that if Newcastle did not resume office, he should retire altogether, and not injure the prospects of the young Yorkes by futile opposition.

[1] To Hardwicke, 29 July ; *ibid.* ff. 108-10.   [2] 20 August ; *ibid.* ff. 321.
[3] See above, p. 327.   [4] 11 August ; *ibid.* f. 206.
[5] 20 August ; *ibid.* f. 321.   [6] *Ibid.* ff. 185-8.

All . . . depends upon a general plan [Hardwicke wrote to New-castle on 21 August], which, notwithstanding the hast of some of your friends, cannot yet be decided upon. . . . If your Grace has determin'd, as you say, *to have nothing to do with the present Adminis-tration, or to show any thing but civility to them,* that puts all such considerations out of the case; and perhaps that may be the wisest part of all, provided it be done without going into a general, de-termin'd, factious opposition, which I know you detest as much as I do.[1]

In the talk with Newcastle, Lyttelton frankly admitted that Bute would have wished to carry on without him, but 'finding the impossibility of doing it', wanted to regain his support, while 'himself always remaining at the head of the Treasury'.[2] Newcastle replied

that . . . it was impracticable. That I was to come in to support my Lord Bute and his measures; to have all the odium thrown upon me; and I did hint to him, that that would not be a part much approved in the nation, and very improper for myself.[3]

Lyttelton's offers had undoubtedly been authorised by Bute; some three weeks later he acknowledged them in a way which could even be taken as an intimation that they remained open. Newcastle wrote to Hardwicke on 11 September:

Lord Bute told Lord M[ansfield] that there was a great intimacy between my Lord Egremont and my Lord Lyttelton, and seem'd fully *acquainted* with all, which my Lord Lyttelton said to your Lordship and me. And, I think, told my Lord M., that I had re-jected, or not enter'd into, what my Lord L. had flung out to me; but, as I had parted with the King as a friend, not an enemy, he thought I could not take it amiss, tho' I might not think proper to accept it.[4]

Hardwicke replied the next day:

I never doubted but Lord B. was fully acquainted with all that *the latter* [Lord Lyttelton] had said either to your Grace or to me, and what we had said in return. I think, what Lord B. said to Lord Mansfield was directly making himself a principal in what had been flung out to your Grace.[5]

---

[1] Add. MSS. 32941, f. 330.
[2] Newcastle's Minute of his conversation with Lyttelton, 24 August 1762; *ibid.* ff. 370-75.   [3] *Ibid.* f. 373.
[4] Add. MSS. 32942, f. 221.   [5] *Ibid.* f. 229.

On 3 September, Newcastle, as Chancellor of Cambridge University, went to Court with a congratulatory Address on the birth of a prince. The King whispered to him: 'I desire you would come into my closet after the Address is over'. The peace negotiations formed the main topic of the conversation; the King

began with some general accounts; and then said, he would talk freely to me; for he was sensible of my zeal for his family, duty and good wishes to him, and made me many compliments upon that subject; but said he would own to me that there were many *stories* about me which he would not believe; that I would *attack this*; and that I would *attack that*; that His Majesty had always replied, that he knew me, and my zeal for him; and that he would never believe any thing of that sort of me, *'till he saw it.*

Next he went through the proposed peace terms, mentioning among others that the French

would demolish all the forts etc. which they had upon the river Mississippi (His Majesty was pleased to say up to the Ganges, but I apprehend the King mistook the Ganges for some other river). As I am far from knowing exactly the state and limits of those countries I said nothing farther upon that head.[1]

When talking about Santa Lucia, the King tried to suggest that the restitution of the island had been agreed upon before Newcastle had resigned. Newcastle denied this, and further pointed to the change wrought by the recent British successes and the withdrawal of Russia.[2] 'I hope you will approve my behaviour', wrote Newcastle to Devonshire; 'and tho' I resolved to keep myself at liberty, I thought it honest and fair, to fling out the objections, that are universally made to the terms of peace.' [3]

But Devonshire apparently did not relish Newcastle's vicarious cavillings, so completely at variance with their own previous unreserved pacifism. He had written to Newcastle on 25 August:

I think the peace if made on the terms we have heard is a good one and therefore in justice to our own characters we ought to

---

[1] In a marginal note Newcastle added: 'His Majesty was here under a mistake, and confounded the boundaries of the Mississippi with what had been agreed with the French with regard to the East Indies'.
[2] September 4; *ibid.* ff. 145-57.   [3] *Ibid.* ff. 174-5.

support it, besides it is so very near what we ourselves approv'd of, that we cou'd not well do otherways ; . . . I am for a lasting peace . . . and the way to attain that . . . is not to force such a one upon our enemys as they shall set uneasy under.[1]

And how he took the 'objection' flung out by Newcastle on 4 September can be gathered from a note which the King wrote to Bute on the 6th : '. . . the Duke of Devonshire has seen the Duke of Newcastle whom he hopes will be quiet'.[2]

The Duke of Cumberland, absolutely independent and responsible to nobody, remained implacably hostile to his old opponents, Leicester House and Bute, and encouraged Newcastle's incoherent, half-hearted starts towards opposition, while the friends whom Newcastle had left in office were painfully aware of the contradictions and difficulties in which, by entering opposition, he was bound to land everybody, himself included. On 1 September Charles Yorke explained to him at Claremont, that if there was to be opposition, Newcastle's

own resignation must be followed by that, which he had hitherto disavowed, *the resignation of many of his friends* . . . that few of those who were young and going on in the world, would be forward to stake themselves upon a supposed personal point . . . that his friends had *made a mistake*, who thought he meant *retirement*; and that he had advised himself ill in going out; for he would have fought with more advantage *in* than *out*; free from the appearances or imputation of faction. . . . That if the work was to be done in this way, he might perhaps find it more tedious than he imagined.[3]

When Newcastle came to Wimple, on 7 September, Hardwicke framed his discourse 'entirely upon the plan' of Charles Yorke's letter — that the opposition could not succeed without Pitt, that there was no ground for it 'except such, as may arise

---

[1] Add. MSS. 32942, f. 9.

[2] Bute MSS. There is another letter from the King of 28 July reporting Devonshire's conversation about the forthcoming peace treaty :

He did not doubt but he could bring all his friends and also the D. of Newcastle to support it. I on this said I had still too good an opinion of the D. of Newcastle to think he would ever enter into opposition. He answered : that duke declares he is not bound to any party as yet and says he means to be at liberty and has refused the offers made by common friends of joining Mr. Pitt.

[3] Charles Yorke to Hardwicke, 3 September; Add. MSS. 35353, ff. 287-8.

from objections to the conditions of peace', and that the most material objections in 'the popular run' against the treaty would probably be on points agreed to by Newcastle and his friends 'whilst they attended the Council'. But even if they justified their changed attitude by the change in the situation, Newcastle's friends who were in office would have to resign, for they could not

go into a general opposition, possessed of the employments and favours of the Crown. That, tho' some of them might be induc'd to this, many of them would not; and indeed hardly any of them without shewing them hopes *in futuro*, and holding out to them some prospect of success in a new Administration.

This was to be the harvest; where were the labourers? I made the D. of N. go thro' the list of the House of Lords, and we could find very few hands, and fewer heads. As to speakers *to be depended upon* reduc'd almost to his Grace and my self.

And if the whole was 'gone thro' with the best success, Mr. P. would be at the head of the new Administration'.[1]

Still, it was no good arguing with Newcastle, who himself hardly knew what he wanted, or how to attain it, but could not 'be content, without returning to what he was'.[2] It pained him to be out of everything, to have no share in the appointing of bishops and tide-waiters, to have no say in public affairs, to receive no locked official boxes (which look impressive, whatever their contents), in short it pained him that he himself could no longer look and feel important. But how was his return to be effected?

Would he chuse [asked Charles Yorke] to come into Administration, and return to the Treasury, whilst Lord B. was absolute in favour? If so, in the nature of the thing, he could only return to his former state of uneasiness and indignities. Would he go into opposition with Mr. Pitt . . . in order to return with him into office? If so, Mr. Pitt must be the Minister.[3]

These questions had in reality been for some time before Newcastle without his ever being able to give a 'direct answer',

[1] Hardwicke to Charles Yorke, 9 September; *ibid.* ff. 292-3.
[2] This phrase was used by Charles Yorke, in a talk with Lyttelton, on 29 August; see letter from Charles Yorke to Hardwicke, 2 September; *ibid.* f. 283.
[3] *Ibid.* f. 288.

or, alternatively, to draw the obvious conclusions. When at the end of July, Devonshire, in his talk with Henry Fox, insisted that it was impossible for Bute to maintain himself, as '*nobody* would act with him', Fox said

that, if that was the case, my Lord Bute would return to the Groom of the Stole; and would renounce *the Minister*. The D. of D. said, who would act as Minister, when the Favourite could do, what he pleased with the K.? Mr. Fox then replied, it was hard indeed, if nothing would do, but tearing the King's Favourite from His Majesty's person.[1]

And this is Newcastle's account of his own talk with Devonshire on this subject : [2]

The D. of D. (I think) is of opinion, that some new system or plan of Administration must be form'd, and seems *rather* inclined to leave my Lord Bute about the King's person, than, in conjunction with Mr. Pitt, to carry things to the utmost extremity; [3] but his Grace was far from having any determined opinion at present. I often told him that I would not come into the Treasury, or the Secretary's office ; that, if I was to have an employment, the Privy Seal was what I would prefer to all others ; that I should insist that my great friends must make a principal part of any Administration to be formed ; and particularly to have *a Treasury of friends*.

In other words, Newcastle wished for an Administration which would concede to him influence and patronage without burdening him with responsibility, but he saw that he could not expect this while Bute retained his pre-eminence at Court, and his final comment on these projects shows more insight than he usually displayed in such matters :

[1] 'An Account of the Duke of Devonshire's conversation on Saturday, July 31st', Claremont, 2 August, 1762 ; Add. MSS. 33000, ff. 95-100.
[2] *Ibid.*
[3] As late as the beginning of September, Devonshire seems to have inclined that way. In the account which, on 9 September, Hardwicke gave his son Charles of his talk with Newcastle, he wrote (Add. MSS. 35353, f. 294) that they were both agreed that if Bute was left at Court, he 'would be Minister behind the curtain, and who would stake themselves to the public to be responsible upon that foot, after having thus offended or provok'd him ? And yet the D. of N. said that the Duke of Cumberland and the Duke of Devonshire, were of opinion for admitting of this ; for the former said the King must not be forc'd, nor the authority and dignity of the Crown violated ; and the latter was not for root and branch ; and they were both against letting in Mr. Pitt.'

This is all very loose talk, to amuse ourselves with, at present; but I am satisfied is very difficult, if possible, ever to be put in execution.[1]

When in the course of the next two months the popular run against Bute had become 'greater than could be imagined', and 'the whole united body of the Kingdom'[2] seemed against him, Newcastle was ready in a 'gentlemanly' way (and at a proper distance) to follow in the wake of the attacking forces, full of 'regards', unwilling to expose himself, disclaiming ambition, but determined not to be left out or neglected:

. . . no consideration upon earth [he wrote to Hardwicke on 7 October] shall make me a responsible Minister in any degree; or, at least, a principal one; and yet, I can't think of my being treated as an old piece of household stuff, that they may do what they please with. . . .

My real inclination and plan is this; I am far from saying, it will do. I should be very glad to be instrumental, in a proper way, and as a gentleman, to relieve the publick and my friends from the haughtiness and power of an absolute Scotch Minister, ignorant of business, and unacquainted with the necessary qualifications of an English Minister.

I should also rejoice to see such an Administration and such a Treasury settled, as might protect our old friends, without laying them under difficulties; and reward those, who are unrewarded at present, who shall be friends to, and recommended by us.

I should chuse to have *no employment*, but to be called to Council, and to be consulted with your Lordship and the D. of Devonshire, in the direction of affairs and disposition of employments. I don't see the impracticability of this scheme; but in this, both Mr. Pitt and Mr. Legge must be principal parts.[3]

Hardwicke replied on 9 October, 'with the freedom of sincere friendship':

I am thoroughly convinc'd that such a scheme is absolutely impracticable. For your Grace, or all three of us, to be call'd to

[1] 'An Account of the Duke of Devonshire's conversation on Saturday, July 31', written down by Newcastle at Claremont, 2 August 1762; Add. MSS. 33000, ff. 95-100.
[2] Expressions which, according to rough notes made by Newcastle, Temple used in a conversation with him on 23 September at Windsor, where they had gone for the installation of the new Knights of the Garter; see *ibid*. f. 116.   [3] Add. MSS. 32943, ff. 90-91.

Council is very practicable; but that any persons who are to be the responsible Ministers, will lay themselves under an obligation to consult . . . persons out of employment, in the direction of all affairs of State and more especially in the disposition of places and employments, is a thing not to be supposed. . . . And how does your Grace think Mr. Pitt would quadrate with it, if he were to be one of the Ministers ? [1]

Newcastle would not 'retire . . . from public business', nor let himself be discarded, but he would not be 'a responsible Minister' either ; what he wished for was a safe retreat in the most conspicuous place, a haven of rest at the centre of power. He would not join Bute, and he would not lead a determined opposition against him ; but he hoped 'his great friends' would 'decide', and others would fight, and something would happen, and the 'loose talk' he 'amused' himself with would somehow prove a 'practicable scheme'. Meantime he was fussing about in his muddling, shuffling, incoherent manner, and creating all the appearances of insincerity, and even perfidy. He who had recognised the King's right to choose his own advisers and condemned all attempts to force 'the closet' by means of a formed opposition, who had acknowledged Bute as *the Minister* and gone much farther than Bute in urging moderation with regard to the peace terms, now that popular passion and prejudice were threatening to overwhelm the King's favourite, talked about the need to free the nation of 'the Scotch Minister', and criticised the peace treaty. There was nothing for which Newcastle had to thank the King and Bute, and there was no reason why he should have exposed himself for their sake or felt tender regards for either ; still his refusal to resume a seat in the Cabinet, his disingenuous criticisms, and his opposition (rendered half-hearted by cowardice, and not by any romantic loyalties) stamped him as a common politician who played his own hand, and played it badly. Hence, when his feeble attempts foundered, the Court were justified in treating him as an enemy, whom in the hour of apparent danger they had

[1] Add. MSS. 32943, ff. 120-4. That this view was correct, Newcastle was to see three years later, when he became Privy Seal in the Rockingham Administration, and found, or felt, himself neglected by 'a Treasury of friends'.

courted in vain and could now afford to despise ; he was no longer what he could have claimed to be on 26 May 1762 — the faithful old servant of the Royal Family, who had given up most of his life and a great part of his fortune to their service.

FOX TAKES CHARGE OF THE HOUSE OF COMMONS

On 6 September, Bedford started on his unpopular peace mission to Paris, and Newcastle wrote with patent satisfaction :

Clevland told me yesterday, that the City is in the highest rage ; particularly with my friend, the Duke of Bedford, who goes to negotiate such a peace, and Mr. Fox, who is supposed to be the adviser and supporter of my Lord Bute ; and against my Lord Bute himself. Nothing can be stronger than the run is ; and indeed violences are to be apprehended from both quarters.[1]

'Such a peace' — would Newcastle have disapproved of it had he still been in office ? As Fox rightly remarked, the fury was directed 'against the man, not the measure, . . . and that by some who were more for peace than he is and in their hearts approve it more than he does'.[2]

. . . what will be the immediate consequence to Ld. Bute of this violence against him ? [wrote Fox in his 'Memoir', on 7 September] I say against him, because, before the terms of peace were guess'd at, it was as great as now, so that I am satisfy'd better or worse terms would neither lessen or increase it.[3]

That this was so, the opposition themselves would hardly have disputed. 'If even a *good* peace was made under this Adminis-tration', observed Rockingham, 'it would not be unreasonable to suppose that a *better* might have been, had the Administration had the appearance of being strong enough to have carried on the war'[4] — an argument legitimate enough in friends of Pitt, but not of Newcastle.[5]

[1] To Devonshire, 4 September ; Add. MSS. 32942, ff. 174-5. About the 'rage' in the City, see also Symmer's letter to A. Mitchell, 10 September 1762 ; Add. MSS. 6839, ff. 284-5.
[2] In a letter to his brother, Lord Ilchester, 5 September ; see Ilchester, *Henry Fox, 1st Lord Holland* (1920), vol. ii. p. 185. [3] P. 77.
[4] In a letter to Newcastle, 5 September ; Add. MSS. 32942, ff. 181-2.
[5] When on 1 October, Cumberland, who was convinced that Bute could neither conclude peace, nor continue the war, asked Newcastle whether he

Lord Bute is certainly in distress [wrote Newcastle to Rockingham on 20 September]; Mr. Elliot and some of his friends wish him to try it, upon his own bottom, by force of power; and I have been told that Fox advises the turning all my friends out, who wont comply with *them*. . . .

Some are for my Lord Bute's joining with Mr. Pitt; and that is supposed to be the inclination of Mr. Grenville, and Mr. Elliot. Others are for his joining with us; and that is certainly the wish of Lord Egremont and Lord Halifax.[1]

Fox was confident that a majority in Parliament could be secured for Bute and peace, provided the necessary measures were taken in time, and firmness and courage were shown 'without contempt of danger'. At the end of July, he declared to Devonshire that if Bute made peace 'the Tories, the Scotch, and the loaves and fishes might support him. . . .'[2] The Opposition, Fox wrote in his 'Memoir', would be embarrassed by being 'in their hearts for peace', and also by the pacifist declarations they themselves had previously made.

If then the Torys and Scotch stand by Lord Bute (which his enemys will I think force them to do), they will be joined by so many that his Lordship may possibly be sure of a majority. Let that appear, and the majority will be great.[3]

Still, he urged Bute 'to make sure of as many individuals as may be engaged between this [the middle of August] and the meeting of the House of Commons. And many may be more easily engaged than they can be after it is met'.[4]

Bute, however, was not the man who, on his own account, could have built up and cemented a Parliamentary 'system'. 'He talk'd of the loaves and fishes; and . . . that a young King would find friends, and would be supported',[5] but it was

'could get the money for carrying on the war upon the extended plan', Newcastle replied that he '*could not answer for it*', but that he 'was well assured my Lord Bute could not do it' (Add. MSS. 32943, f. 42).

[1] Add. MSS. 32942, f. 308.

[2] See Newcastle's 'Account of the Duke of Devonshire's conversation on Saturday, July 31st', Claremont, 2 August 1762; Add. MSS. 33000, ff. 95-100.   [3] 7 September 1762; p. 77.

[4] Fox to Shelburne, 16 August 1762; Fitzmaurice, *Life of William, Earl of Shelburne*, vol. i. p. 117.

[5] In a conversation with Mansfield; see letter from Newcastle to Rockingham, 14 May 1762; Add. MSS. 32938, ff. 262-4.

not in his nature to cultivate men or to engage in laborious and unpleasant pursuits ; and while himself ill-fitted for the management of the House of Commons, he would not readily concede it to Grenville,[1] his 'Minister' in it, possibly because of their disagreements over the peace treaty. On 18 September, Shelburne wrote to Fox in distress :

Our domestick affairs . . . are . . . reckon'd on without much certainty. The great body of the Torys are by no means assur'd, some of them are very much the contrary. Those under Government have not been asked their opinions, and there is no detail establish'd among Lord Bute's friends. . . . I have represented to Ld. Bute and continue to represent to him every time I see him, that there is not a moment to be lost, either in signing the peace or assuring himself of a competent majority in the House of Commons to support him and it, as one cause.[2]

[1] Grenville mentions in his narrative of the events of 9-11 October 1762 (*Grenville Papers*, vol. i. p. 483), the opinion he had declared

> some time ago of the difficulties to carry on the business of the House of Commons, without being authorized to talk to the Members of that House upon their several claims and pretensions, and having them communicated through me to Lord Bute and to the King, which was a circumstance that Lord Bute could not consent to. . . .

Information about these differences reached Newcastle, who, on 16 October 1762, reports to have heard

> that Mr. Grenville had insisted with my Lord Bute, that all applications for employments &c., from Members of the House of Commons, should come first and directly to him ; my Lord Bute said, he should like very well to be rid of all those troublesome applications, but that it could not be (Add. MSS. 32943, f. 275).

Horace Walpole, at the time, was disinclined to believe these accounts in view of Bute having conceded those very powers to Fox, a more dangerous man than Grenville (see Walpole's letter to Horace Mann, 20 October 1762). But in his *Memoirs of the Reign of King George III* (1894), vol. i. p. 153, he reproduces it, though in a rather different version :

> Grenville . . . aiming higher, had been unwilling to risk an appearance of honesty when it was not in his own cause. He had neglected to traffic with the members of the House of Commons ; had secured none of them ; and, being pressed by Lord Bute on that head, fairly owned he would not deal with them, unless the power was his own, and their dependence rested on him. Lord Bute was startled, and would have compromised, as himself was unacquainted with the men. . . . But Grenville was obstinate. . . .

Whichever version is more accurate, either tends to show that no systematic preparations had as yet been made when Grenville gave up the seals.

[2] *Letters to Henry Fox*, ed. by Lord Ilchester (1915), pp. 160-61.

The obvious man for the task was Fox who was clearly
drawing apart from his late patron, Cumberland ; this conduct
he justified by saying that he 'was not supporting my Lord
Bute, but acting according to his opinion',[1] and by accusing
Cumberland of being opposed to peace, merely 'because it
might establish Lord Bute', 'and to hurt Lord Bute . . . tho'
he approves the terms, he will join with the loudest in con-
demning them'.[2]   Still, even though relations between them
were getting more and more strained, an attempt was made by
Fox at the end of September to engage Cumberland's help for
establishing a coalition between Bute and Newcastle. In doing
so, Fox undoubtedly acted at Bute's request, but probably not
altogether against his own inclinations : for however much he
disliked Newcastle, he loathed Pitt even more, and by such a
coalition he must have hoped to avert a surrender of the Court
to Pitt,[3] and to avoid a final break between himself and
Cumberland. In a letter to Cumberland, on 29 September,[4]
Fox professed to have asked Bute whether he contemplated
a coalition with Newcastle or Pitt, and to have received an
emphatic denial ; but it seems that in reality it was Bute who
employed Fox to sound Cumberland.[5]

Upon reflection, Sir [wrote Fox to Cumberland], though I believe
he [Bute] has no thought of treating, yet I believe that he must, and
will be driven to it. If that should be the case, and that the King
tries to make your Royal Highness the mediator, it will be much
more worthy of you, than the character of the head of an opposition.
. . . If His Majesty must have a sole Minister made in the room c

[1] Add. MSS. 33000, f. 95.

[2] See his account of the visit to Cumberland, in the beginning of August ;
in his 'Memoir', p. 69.

[3] Attempts at gaining Pitt were made about that time ; Pitt told Thomas
Walpole, on 13 November 1762, 'that lately he had been applied to, by
persons of high rank, to concur with Lord B. for the publick good, with
offers much above his deserts. . . . He told those persons, Lord B. could
never expect, he would abett the transcendency of power, his Lordship was
arrived at. . . .' (Add. MSS. 32945, ff. 1-2.)

[4] Albemarle, *Memoirs of the Marquis of Rockingham* (1852), vol. i.
pp. 128-33.

[5] Hardwicke, with an acumen sharpened perhaps by his intense dislike
of Fox, wrote to Newcastle on 9 October (Add. MSS. 32943, f. 120) : 'I
thought the Duke [of Cumberland] had been convinc'd that that gentleman
had left him for my Lord Bute ; but he is very capable of being a double
spy, and in that capacity I presume he now acts.'

his favourite, no share of administration left with that favourite, His Majesty is lost, for as long as he sits upon the throne; and however it might please people now, on reflection the usage would be thought hard, and your Royal Highness not to have acted a very friendly part to the Crown.

The next consideration is this: may not Lord Bute (who being to continue in administration might prefer the Duke of Newcastle to Mr. Pitt for a colleague), if he is to leave administration quite, choose to give it up to Mr. Pitt, who would bring such popularity with him to the King as has never yet been seen. Drove to go quite out, I think this would be the case.[1]

On 30 September, Cumberland was with the King, to congratulate him on the capture of Havana. The King talked 'upon the present state of the peace', asked advice upon it, and 'nothing could be more *personally* gracious to the Duke than the King was, during the whole audience'[2] — which was remarkable, as he must have known that Cumberland openly declared against 'the sole power and direction of the affairs of this Kingdom', exercised by Bute. But while the King, Bute, and Fox seem to have thought of Cumberland and Newcastle as an alternative to Pitt, Cumberland was by that time 'much soften'd towards Mr. Pitt', Pitt was reported to have said 'that no one in this countrey is fit to be at the head of affairs, but the Duke of Cumberland',[3] and Newcastle was declaring that no Government was possible without Pitt, and continued his (justified) suspicions of Fox. When Cumberland talked of Newcastle's return to the Treasury, Newcastle protested that

were it practicable (which I don't see how) to make a thorough reconciliation with Mr. Pitt, without which, I think no man can undertake it, the objection of my age and the particular resentment of the King and my Lord Bute to me, daily work'd up by Mr. Fox would still remain.[4]

Meantime Bute's difficulties with his two Secretaries, Grenville and Egremont, reached such a pitch as to make him wish

[1] Albemarle, *op. cit.*, vol. i. pp. 131-2.
[2] Newcastle's 'Substance of a very material conversation, which I had the honor to have with H.R.H., the Duke of Cumberland, at Windsor Great Lodge, on Friday last, the 1st inst.', Claremont, 3 October; Add. MSS. 32943, f. 34.
[3] Newcastle to Hardwicke, September 30; Add. MSS. 32942, ff. 430-1.
[4] Add. MSS. 32943, ff. 44-5.

to be rid of them, at almost any price; on 30 September, Rigby wrote to Bedford about 'the cursed situation in which these two rascally Secretaries of State are disposed to plunge their master, your Grace, and their *friend*, the Minister',[1] and about the talk which, the previous day, the King had with them 'upon their scruples'.[2] The differences in the Cabinet were rendered still more acute by the capture of Havana and, on 2 October, the King wrote to Bute in a letter marked '53^{m} pt. 8':

It would appear very extraordinary at any other time but the present moment, off hand to fix the plan of Government; but so impending is the present crisis that there is no hour to be lost; cruel is my situation when I agree to a scheme that seems for a moment weakening my dear friends credit in this country: 'tis handsome and very noble in him to propose it; if he can suggest no other plan by morning I will consent to it for I think the Duke of Newcastle joint Secretary with Fox; both by mutual jealousies will be less formidable than were but one of the two parties to take office, and with proper management I don't doubt but, to hurt the other, both will strive to strengthen my friend's hands, thus perhaps in the end things may be better than at first it appears; to be brief, peace is the thing that is absolutely necessary for the well being of the country, whatever brings that without hurting mine and my dear friend's characters is to be adopted.

The Cabinet Council fixed for 4 October was cancelled, and Fox was summoned from the country. It was with a heavy heart that George III agreed to accept Fox for his Minister in the House of Commons; in March 1763, when Bute proposed him for his successor at the Treasury, the King thus summed up his view of the man, and the reasons which had prevailed with him in October 1762:

I have one principle firmly rooted in my mind from the many seasonable lessons I have received from my dear friend, never to trust a man void of principles, if any man ever deserved that character 'tis Mr. Fox; the seeing him at the head of the House of Commons was very unpleasant to me: but I consented to it, as that was the only means of getting my dear friend to proceed this winter in the Treasury. . . . His [Fox's] . . . bad character comes strongly into my thoughts whenever I hear him named; tis not prejudice but

[1] Thursday morning, 30 September; *Bedford Correspondence*, vol. iii. p. 130.   [2] Same date, evening; *ibid.* p. 132.

aversion to his whole mode of Government that causes my writing so openly my thoughts to my only friend.

Fox arrived in town on the 6th, and this was the account he gave of his talk with Bute, in a letter to Bedford, on 13 October :

I was . . . told that Mr. Grenville (half unable, half unwilling) could go on no longer. His Majesty was in great concern lest a good peace in a good House of Commons should be lost, and his authority disgraced, for want of a proper person to support his honest measures, and keep his closet from that force with which it was so threatened. I was that person who could do it : so called upon he had that opinion of me to think I would; and he knew not whom else he could call, if I declined it. I took no time to consider before I answered, that to be Secretary of State too, if the sessions was troublesome, would be impossible for me to undertake. I represented, as to the rest, that it would be adding unpopularity to unpopularity, of which there was enough; that my name might frighten Tories away, and that an experiment which should fail would make His Majesty's case very disagreeable indeed.[1]

Before joining the Government, Fox saw Cumberland once more. He wrote to his brother, Lord Ilchester, on 10 October :

[1] *Ibid.* pp. 133-4. See also letter from Fox to Devonshire, 12 October 1762, quoted by Lord Ilchester, from the Devonshire MSS., in *Henry Fox*, vol. ii. pp. 189-90.

It is a moot point when the offer was first made to Fox to join the Government. Lord Fitzmaurice writes (*Life of Shelburne*, vol. i. p. 120) :

The negotiation was at once entered on, and Shelburne before the close of the month [September] wrote to Bute that 'every step possible was taken to prepossess Fox in favour of what was proposed, and that he did not think he could refuse taking on him the lead of the House of Commons.

Lord Ilchester is convinced that no such offer had been made to Fox in September (*Henry Fox*, vol. ii. p. 191), and that the letter quoted by Lord Fitzmaurice 'was not written till the early days of October, *i.e.* after the King's offer'.

In 'The Register of Correspondence of the Earl of Bute', Add. MSS. 36796, a letter is noted from Shelburne to Bute, dated 28 September 1762 : 'Thinks Mr. Fox will accept the lead in the House of Commons.' If this letter is identical with that quoted by Lord Fitzmaurice (as it seems to be), his dating is correct, and still Lord Ilchester's thesis, that the offer to Fox was first made on 6 October, seems tenable ; Shelburne does not say, at least not in the passage quoted by Lord Fitzmaurice, that the proposal had been made to Fox, only that the thing 'was proposed,' and that he had prepared the ground for it (I take it that the 'he' in 'he did not think' is paraphrase, and refers to Shelburne) ; and as it was only on 2 October that the King agreed to Bute's scheme, a formal proposal is not likely to have been made at an earlier date.

'I shall see the D. of Cumberland to-morrow, and after that determine, which I believe will be as I have said; tho' the consequence may be a breach with him.'[1] And to Shelburne, the same day: '. . . my conversation with him shall remove all doubts, if there are still any, of my being warp'd up to his opinion'; 'I will not consider . . . the Duke of Cumberland further than to grieve that I knew him so little.'[2]

A discrepancy between the three accounts which we have of that interview seems to point to a quaint game having been played by Fox. In the report which Fox sent to Bute by word of mouth, through Shelburne, he appears to have alleged that Cumberland had suggested he should replace Bute at the Treasury; but Fox himself did not repeat that allegation in the written account he sent to Devonshire on 12 October. Nor is there any trace whatever of such a suggestion in the account of that interview which Cumberland gave to Newcastle — indeed the question with which he alleges to have challenged Fox, whether they would reinstate Newcastle at the Treasury,[3] seems to preclude it. With Fox's verbal message concerning the interview, Shelburne brought Bute a paper which Fox had received from a friend and dependant of his own, J. L. Nicholl, arguing that the proper solution was for him to assume the Treasury. If Fox, as Shelburne told Bute, 'never looked upon it as the thing in question, or to be considered of',[4] why transmit at all a letter from a clerk in the Paymaster's Office? But Fox had warned Bute against adding unpopularity to unpopularity, and now seems to have suggested a new way of avoiding such an undesirable accumulation. Bute, however, did not taste the idea; on 11 October he wrote to Shelburne:

I have considered the idea in one point of light only, . . . how far this or any other alteration in the plan proposed, could have more

---

[1] Ilchester, *Henry Fox*, vol. ii. p. 195.

[2] Fitzmaurice, *Life of Shelburne*, vol. i. p. 122.

[3] See below, p. 355. That Cumberland did suggest Newcastle's return to the Treasury seems confirmed by Fox's letter to Devonshire, on 26 October: '. . . when I think it is H.R.H. and yr. Grace's wish in this critical time to see the D. of N. Minister, I am astonish'd . . .' (see Ilchester, *op. cit.* vol. ii. p. 206). 'Minister', used in this way, meant in the eighteenth century First Minister.

[4] Shelburne to Fox, 'Monday night, October 1762'; Fitzmaurice, *op. cit.* p. 125. That Monday was undoubtedly 11 October.

effectually supported the Kings honor, facilitated his measures, and produced the peace . . . Upon the most thorough and disinterested examination therefore of this delicate point, I am satisfy'd that any deviation from the plan proposed will prove destructive to some of the purposes mention'd, detrimental to all; carrying with it an appearance of fear and timidity foreign to my heart, and most inconsistent with my situation; no, my dear Lord, if the storm thickens and danger menaces, let me stand foremost in the ranks, I claim the post of honor, and will now for the first time fling away the scabbard; next to my little experience of business, my unwillingness to punish has been no little drawback to me as Minister, I know it, I know the constructions put upon my conduct; few, very few indeed judge of me as I am, and even my noble friend may sometimes have imputed actions to timidity, which sprung from motives of a more generous nature; but now the Kings situation, the perilous condition of the countrey, the insolence of faction, demand a rougher rein, and I have taken my part.

He concluded by expressing his admiration for

the noble and generous manner, in which he [Fox] quits retirement and security, to stand with me the brunt of popular clamour in supporting the best of Princes against the most ungenerous, the most ungratefull set of men this countrey ever produced; . . . it corresponds so entirely with my own feelings, that I am certain that the warmest friendship will cement that union which publick principle has first produced.[1]

The first that Grenville heard of his having to surrender the leadership of the House to Fox, and the Secretaryship of State to Halifax, was in a message from Bute, on 9 October.[2] In the interview which followed on the 11th, Bute, with 'the warmest expressions of friendship' and earnest wishes for its continuance, informed Grenville of what had been decided for him and everybody else. When Grenville asked whether he had incurred the King's displeasure — he relates in his narrative —

Lord Bute would scarce suffer me to state this question before he interrupted me with the strongest assurances of the high opinion and good-will the King entertained of me; that this was at no point of

---

[1] Shelburne MSS., at Bowood. The letter as reproduced by Lord Fitzmaurice in his *Life of Shelburne*, pp. 126-7, is incomplete — the concluding paragraph is deleted without the omission being marked; it is reproduced in the copy of the letter in Add. MSS. 36797, ff. 52-3.

[2] See *Grenville Papers*, vol. i. pp. 451 and 482.

time in my life higher than in the present moment; that the King depended upon my services to his Government . . .; that he, Lord Bute, knew my zeal and attachment to the King, and had therefore always wished to see me at the head of the Treasury. . . .[1]

'Mr. Grenville entered his protest very strongly against the step the King was going to take', but declared that if the King 'thought it expedient . . . he should acquiesce'. Subsequently he 'held pretty near the same language to the King', who, according to Grenville, 'seemed pleased with his acquiescence'.[2] And this is the account which the King gave to Bute of that pleasing interview with the man who had never stood higher in his estimation:

I will not fatigue my d. friend with Greenville's language but only say it was perfectly agreable to what he had said in S. Audley Street; . . . we ended with his accepting the Admiralty, doubting whether he could get in for Buckingham, and declaring his firm intention to support Government with all his power; he seem'd on parting very low, and as if he had hop'd he should have convinced me of the impropriety of the plan to be enter'd upon.[3]

Meantime no progress was made with the offer to Newcastle; indeed, the inclination to make it was weakening. On 5 October, having received Devonshire's letter refusing to attend Council,[4] the King wrote to Bute:

I have no doubt but the D. of Devonshire is too timid to have taken such a step had not he known that the Ds. of C——d and Newcastle would approve of it; we must therefore turn our eyes some other way, and see whether by gaining Fox and Charles Townshend the House of Commons can't be managed without these proud dukes.

Fox, too, advised Bute not to treat with Newcastle, as 'a notion of Lord Bute's meeting in any way with him will weaken Lord Bute, and treating with him will end in nothing else, for he will be intractable';[5] and the King agreed with him — 'Fox is right when he discourages any steps towards the D. of Newcastle'.[6] Still, when Cumberland, in the talk on 11 October, taxed Bute with having driven out all the old Ministers,

[1] See *Grenville Papers*, vol. i. p. 484. [2] *Ibid.* pp. 451-2.
[3] The King to Bute, 11 October 1762. [4] See below, p. 370.
[5] Fitzmaurice, *op. cit.* vol. i. p. 121. [6] To Bute, 8 October.

Mr. Fox took up this last expression . . . and said, they *excluded themselves*; and then express'd the great desire of (the King I think, and) my Lord Bute, that there should be *a coalition*. . . .

Mr. Fox . . . said; they desire that we should all return to the Council or Administration; and particularly, that the Duke of New-castle might be Secretary of State, if he pleased, and have the sole disposition of all ecclesiastical preferments. His Royal Highness with great quickness replied, *Will they bring the Duke of Newcastle back to the Treasury again?* That was not to be thought of; I believe Mr. Fox rather shew'd it by his silence, than by any direct declaration.[1]

The two Ministers most anxious that Newcastle and Hard-wicke should return to Council were Egremont and Halifax. Clevland, who for many years had been secretary to Lord Anson (Hardwicke's son-in-law), and had been retained by Halifax at the Admiralty, told Newcastle that Halifax intended to come to talk to him upon it; but Newcastle professed him-self reluctant to offer an opportunity for such a talk. Still, when Halifax did come, on Saturday, 16 October, Newcastle, the moment he left, wrote to Clevland in great excitement:

Lord Halifax has been here. . . .
I am so desirous to hear from you, that I beg you would send what you have to say by any one you can trust. . . . Jones is the man I trust with every thing; . . . let him know what you have for me, and desire him to send it to me in a letter; nobody shall know any thing of it. . . .
P.S. Burn this letter.[2]

Clevland, who was ill, sent for H. V. Jones, and the same night Jones transmitted the following account to Newcastle:

On Monday last [11 October], my Lord Halifax acquainted Mr. Clevland, that he had, that morning, talk'd in the strongest manner to my Lord Bute upon the present situation of affairs, and particu-larly of the Administration; and had endeavour'd to shew him the impossibility of going on without the assistance of your Grace and my Lord Hardwicke; and offer'd himself to convey proper proposals to your Grace. Lord Halifax prevail'd so far with Lord Bute as to

---

[1] Newcastle's account, 'Substance of what pass'd with H.R.H. the Duke of Cumberland at Windsor Lodge, 19 October 1762', Claremont, 20 October 1762; Add. MSS. 32943, ff. 303-17.
[2] *Ibid.* f. 248.

obtain his consent to his (Lord Halifax's) speaking to the King upon this subject. His Lordship did so immediately; and was authoris'd by His Majesty to apply to your Grace. But on Tuesday, upon seeing Lord Bute, Lord Halifax found (with great concern) that things had taken a different turn; and that the intention then was to try what could be done with Mr. Fox. . . .

However, Lord Halifax said, he was determin'd to return to the charge; and to inculcate the necessity of bringing back your Grace and my Lord Hardwicke. . . .

Jones added that Clevland had obeyed Newcastle's order and burnt his letters, 'and desires, that this may be dispos'd of in the same manner'.[1] Fortunately such orders were not always obeyed.

What had happened between Halifax's interview with the King on Monday (11 October), and his talk with Bute on Tuesday, can be gathered from the letter which George III wrote to Bute on Monday at 6.30 p.m.:

I thank my dear friend for his account of the D. of Cumberland; Fox's already foretelling victory is most comfortable. . . .

Halifax . . . talked much of his desire to gain the D. of N—— to which I reply'd that I thought that might be right, but that I was for beginning with Ld. Hardwicke, he offer'd to take any step to bring this about; . . . I doubt whether Fox's intelligence won't make any step towards either of them improper; I hope when I see my dear friend to-morrow to hear what has passed betwixt him and Mr. Fox.

Fox saw Bute on 12 October, at noon, and the next morning he was 'declared a Cabinet Councillor, and His Majesty's Minister in the House of Commons'.[2] None the less, Halifax was allowed to proceed to Claremont and make a last attempt to gain the adherence of Newcastle. He declared that 'the King, Bute, and all the Ministers' wished Newcastle and Hardwicke to return to Court and the Council, and went into various aspects of the matter. He

fear'd . . . that H.R. Highness would set himself at the head of an Opposition; what a cruel thing it would be, to have the Royal

---

[1] Add. MSS. 32943, ff. 234-5.
[2] Fox to the Duke of Bedford, 13 October 1762; *Bedford Correspondence*, vol. iii. p. 134.

Family divided: and that *that* was another strong argument for his
wishing to have me return to the King's service.[1]

Further he said,

how much he wish'd it, for my own private ease and satisfaction,
that I might have a share in what was doing, and not be absolutely
excluded from all sort of business; that, if that should be the case,
my friends would be under this *dilemma*, either, they would abandon
me (which, his Lordship seem'd to think, might be the case of some
of them, and that that would justly and necessarily give me concern,
for which he should be very sorry;) or, they would lose their employments for adhering to me; and he was sure, that in many cases,
where their employments were very necessary for them, that would
give me the greatest uneasiness.

To this I answer'd, that I should never expect any thing wrong
or unreasonable from my friends, but that those dilemmas had often
happen'd, in similar cases; and, if disagreable consequences did
happen, one must submit to it.[2]

Newcastle's final reply was that he adhered to his resolution
'not to return to Council, or to accept any employment'.

Newcastle acknowledged that Halifax had behaved 'with
great friendship and regard, and, I am persuaded, sincerity, as
far as related to himself towards me', but complained that the
offers had been vague, and not 'specific'. Newcastle's advisers
agreed with this criticism. '*Coalition* is the favourite word of
Administration at present', wrote Cumberland on 17 October,
'but when press'd, it is always dribled down to more than a
share of odium, and hardly any power to serve the country'.[3]
And Hardwicke on the 23rd: 'No office hinted at; no specific
proposition made; only *pray come to Court and to Council*, and
help to support those, who have demolished you.'[4] Hardwicke
advised caution; he did not think that this was the end of the
offers and negotiations, and he wanted Newcastle to avoid the
inconveniences which had arisen 'from the too great haste in

---

[1] Add. MSS. 32943, f. 305. In the 'Narrative of what pass'd with the
Earl of Halifax, on Saturday, 16th October' (*ibid.* ff. 274-91), Newcastle
merely states that Halifax 'express'd the greatest hopes that H.R.H. the
Duke, would not countenance any opposition; and seem'd to think that
my coming to Council would be a proof of the contrary. . . .' But when
talking to Cumberland, on 19 October, Newcastle admitted 'that what his
Lordship had said was much stronger', and gave the above version of it.
[2] *Ibid.*   [3] *Ibid.* f. 266.   [4] *Ibid.* f. 369.

closing *at the beginning* of this reign, without any explicit stipulations made, or securities given'.[1]

In reality this was to be the last of the efforts made by the Court to secure Newcastle's return to office ; but, as a rule, in estimating the further actions of George III and Bute, hardly any account is taken of these three months of vain endeavours. Newcastle for once was really pleased with having adhered to his 'resolution', and had the full approval of his friends. Would they have felt the same, had they known how much the King had been averse to accepting Fox and his methods ? There had been more honest purpose in the attempts to regain Newcastle's co-operation than they would believe, and there was infinitely more stability in the new system than they reckoned with. 'I was never more surpriz'd at any domestic event in my life,' declared Hardwicke on 17 October. '. . . I will venture to pronounce beforehand, it will never do.'[2] And he added the next day that Bute 'must be very weak if he fancies that the making such a hackney as Mr. F. his conductor in the House of Commons will do the business'.[3]

NEWCASTLE DEFEATED

Newcastle much desired to trust those whom he chose to call his friends, and yet, subconsciously at least, he knew how little the 'friendship' of many of them was worth. No wonder that he was one of the first to appreciate the import of what the Court had done in placing Fox at the head of the House of Commons.

I take . . . the case to be this [he wrote to Hardwicke on 21 October]. My Lord Bute is determined to try to support himself by power *only* ; probably he has been encouraged by Mr. Fox to do so, provided his Lordship would put his power into *those hands*, who knew how, and had courage enough, to execute what was necessary to produce the full effects of that power.

My Lord Bute saw plainly, that Mr. Grenville was not the man, and, I suppose Mr. Fox soon convinced him that he himself was. . . .

My Lord Bute has now *fixed his Ministry* ; the sole real power *in himself* ; and the active and executive part of it, *in Mr. Fox*. . . .[4]

---

[1] Hardwicke to Newcastle, 17 October ; Add. MSS. 32943, f. 261.
[2] *Ibid.* ff. 258-9.   [3] *Ibid.* f. 261.   [4] *Ibid.* ff. 332-40.

And in even clearer terms Newcastle described the situation to Charles Yorke on 25 October : [1]

> I fear, our friends will find themselves extremely mistaken, as to the consequences of the very bold step, my Lord Bute has taken, in delegating, as it were, his sole power over this kingdom, to so unpopular a man, as Mr. Fox.

He too, at first, thought it an ill-judged measure, but 'upon reflection and observation', has completely changed his mind.

> My Lord Bute has the sole power of this Kingdom; he is . . . determined to exert it to the utmost, and depend singly upon it; . . . he has therefore . . . chose the man . . . who will stick at nothing; and is both willing and able, to try the full extent of that power. No man knows better, than he does, the *weakness*, and *wickedness* of mankind; or to make the best use of it. He sees already that power has *influenced* many, and stagger'd many more, whom he vainly flatters himself, he shall fix and determine, by the manner in which he (Mr. Fox) shall exert it.
>
> He publish'd every where, that the Duke of Newcastle's friends (many) are gone over to my Lord Bute; he names, tho' without foundation, particular persons; and whoever will be influenced by the extent of power, will know, it will be now exerted in earnest. He will begin, by sounding every body, and turning out some, for examples; he has agents working every where; he knows whom to employ; and how to work upon different dispositions and constitutions.
>
> These are the reasons, which make me think, that my Lord Bute has done *ably*, for his purpose, in the choice he has made. . . .

'They have taken their part,' wrote Newcastle on 21 October, 'and will go through with it, if they can. It is to be consider'd, whether they are to be suffer'd to do it.' If not, what were to be the counter-measures ? On 19 October, Newcastle consulted Cumberland on what, in his opinion,

> should be done upon the whole; for we must soon come . . . to some determination; or we shall lose all our friends by default, and they will afterwards alledge in their justification that they knew nothing of our determination; and this begins already to be the case. . . .
>
> The Ministers find, that every body is shy; and tho' there is the most universal cry against their persons and their measures, they see

[1] Add. MSS. 32944, ff. 18-19.

no one step taken to defeat them; or any inclination in any one single man to suggest or undertake anything for that purpose. . . .
. . . Some resolutions . . . must be taken without loss of time, or the whole is over.[1]

The first measure to which Newcastle directed his attention was, as it ever had been, the muster of friends at the opening of Parliament. Whatever turn events may take,

a true zeal for the interest of this countrey [he wrote on 3 October] . . . and that regard which many profess for those, who have been driven by my Lord Bute out of the Administration, should be sufficient to engage every single man, in either House of Parliament, who pretends or desires to be thought a friend, to be present the first day of the Session.[2]

But what directions should be given to his friends with regard to attendance at the preliminary meetings ? Naturally he was not going to 'insist upon their graceing Mr. Fox's meeting at the Cockpit'[3] — should he go further and try to dissuade them from attending it ?

To be sure [wrote Newcastle to Devonshire on 10 October], I could wish that there should not be great numbers; that would strike them more than any thing; but whether it is right to attempt to prevent it, or whether *curiosity* or some *management* for the Court, may not render any such attempt vain, I can't say.[4]

Moreover, as the Duke of Cumberland pointed out,

the absence of our friends in place, upon that occasion, would give my Lord Bute an occasion to closet every man early, to know what his future conduct would be with regard to the Administration; and to make early examples of those who would not give him satisfaction; that will follow sooner or later, but perhaps there may be some objection to . . . giving rise to it so soon.
I proposed to the Duke, as a middle way, to let those in employment, who chuse to be absent, be so ; . . . and to contrive that all our countrey, independant friends should know, that their not appearing at the meeting would, in our opinion, have a very good effect.[5]

Hardwicke, pressed by Newcastle for advice as to the general line of policy they should adopt, replied once more that it was too early to decide about it.

[1] Add. MSS. 32943, ff. 311-17.   [2] *Ibid.* f. 45.
[3] *Ibid.* f. 398.   [4] *Ibid.* f. 144.   [5] *Ibid.* f. 313.

It is impossible for you at present to open any particular specific plan of opposition to your friends, because that must depend upon events — *peace or no peace; and if peace, what shall be the conditions of it;* and, *if war, how proposed to be carried on.* Therefore my poor opinion is, to induce your friends to keep themselves free from engagements with those gentlemen, and to parry their closettings with general answers; to procure them to attend at the first meeting of Parliament; and, as to the meetings of both Houses the night before the Parliament, I like very well your *middle way.* . . .[1]

Was Hardwicke's advice truly objective, or was it coloured by the dislike he felt, and openly avowed, against being dragged back into politics, and especially into opposition politics, which, if merely for the sake of his sons, he very much wished to avoid ? Cumberland, from whom benevolence was expected towards his young, inexperienced nephew, could not assume an open and active part in opposition, such as in the past had been played by the heirs to the Throne, nor 'beat up volunteers'; Devonshire was timid, indolent, and ill; while Newcastle was utterly unfit to act on his own. There was no one in their group to take the lead. 'I am . . . clearly of opinion', wrote Newcastle on 21 October, 'that nothing right for the publick or ourselves, can be done but in concert with Mr. Pitt.'[2] But would Pitt concert his measures with them ?

On 25 October, Newcastle wrote to Charles Yorke in obvious despair :

I must . . . desire to know, what my friends will do. I can no longer keep in suspence, or amuse, those, who are ready to take part with us, if we have ourselves *no part to take.* I shall say this very plainly, to the Duke of Devonshire, and to my Lord Hardwicke; and, in a proper manner, to the Duke of Cumberland.

. . . What part Mr. Pitt will act, I know not. I hear, from good hands, that he says, *Nothing will be done* . . . the Duke of Devonshire is at the Bath, my Lord Hardwicke at Wimple; and the Duke of Newcastle will do nothing, (and there he is in the right) without those two; *is this an appearance of doing any thing ?* And I can't but say, Mr. Pitt reasons, as every man of sense will do, and must do.[3]

For the last two months Newcastle had been compiling his Parliamentary lists. There is one of the House of Lords, dated

[1] *Ibid.* f. 372. [2] To Hardwicke, *ibid.* f. 335.
[3] Add. MSS. 32944, f. 20.

26 August 1762,[1] in which 85 peers are classified as 'for' Newcastle and 104 as 'against'; of his friends, however, 24 are queried, and of the opponents 35, which, adopting the tripartite division of later lists, leaves 61 'for' and 69 'against', and marks 59 as 'doubtful'. The next list is dated 20 September,[2] and, after having been corrected, appears as a new list on the 24th;[3] this, for almost two months, seems to have served Newcastle as his map of the House of Lords. When he ceased using it — about 15 November [4] — the changes in it were so many that it can be treated as a fourth list. A fifth was drawn up on 6 December,[5] and a partial list, of the 'Sure Friends' only,[6] on 18 December. Here is the picture of the House of Lords as it appears in these lists :

	Sure	Doubtful	Against
August 26 . . .	61	59	69
September 20 . . .	70	47	72
„ 24 . . .	73	34	83
November 15 (?) . .	76	17	97
December 6 . . .	51	2	109
„ 18 . . .	44	—	—

The first survey of the House of Lords in two columns only — 85 'for' and 104 'against' — was distinctly unfavourable to Newcastle. By judiciously manipulating his doubts, he soon established a balance between the two sides, leaving, however, almost one-third of the House undetermined. By 20 September further corrections made the two sides appear very nearly equal, with about one-fourth of the House 'doubtful'. During the next two months, the gradual redistribution of that intervening group covers up, to some extent, the weakening of the Opposition ; but about 15 November, Newcastle already conceded to the Court a clear majority in the House of Lords, and by 6

[1] Add. MSS. 33000, ff. 107-9.
[2] Ibid. ff. 113-15. [3] Ibid. ff. 118-19.
[4] Lord Powis still remains in it in the column of 'sure' friends, although by 15 November, Newcastle had doubts concerning the line he was going to take, and by 20 November, the certainty of having been deserted by him ; see The Structure of Politics, pp. 283-5.
[5] Add. MSS. 33000, ff. 217-18. [6] Ibid. f. 238.

December a two-thirds majority. By 18 December he reckoned on 44 stalwarts only, 33 lay [1] and 11 spiritual peers. Newcastle is credited with the epigram about the fathers in God who 'forgot their maker', and yet he seems to have been unwilling to admit to himself how true it was ; and this in spite of the suave and evasive replies to his circular letter which he received from some among them whom he thought his best friends,[2] and even in spite of the very explicit statement made to him by the Archbishop of Canterbury exactly a month before he drew up the list in which eleven bishops are still classed as 'sure friends'. On 18 November, Newcastle put down in his 'Memorandums' : [3]

Arch-Bishop of Canterbury. Thinks the bishops, in general, desirous to give no disturbance, or express any resentment of any thing that has pass'd. Except some few who would certainly go with me.

I lamented my want of credit with them, as other Ministers have formerly had with those, whom they had prefer'd.

The first survey of the House of Commons is dated 27 September,[4] and takes the form of a 'List of Members to be sent to, to attend' (at the opening of the session) ; it comprises

[1] These were the Dukes of Cumberland, Devonshire, Portland, and Grafton, and Newcastle himself ; Rockingham ; Newcastle's old friends, Hardwicke, Kinnoull, and Grantham ; his nephew Lincoln, and three peers connected with the Pelhams by marriage, Sondes, Abergavenny, and Onslow ; two relatives of the Duchess of Newcastle, Jersey and Godolphin ; Bessborough, a brother-in-law of Devonshire ; Waldegrave and Albemarle, who were connected with Cumberland ; Bristol, a follower of Pitt (curiously enough Temple was forgotten, and does not appear in any of these lists) ; Archer, who was connected with James West, and Archer's son-in-law, Plymouth ; lastly, Ashburnham, Cornwallis, Edgcumbe, Ravensworth, Scarborough, Spencer, Stamford, Strafford, Torrington, Walpole, and Winchilsea.

[2] The Archbishop of Canterbury hoped that the bishops would attend 'and pay such regard to the sentiments of your Grace and your excellent friend Lord Hardwicke, as will most conduce to a general agreement in whatever measures the situation of the publick may require' (17 October 1762 ; Add. MSS. 32943, f. 268) ; the Bishop of Durham 'most heartily prayed' to 'find all honest men united in one view, for the preservation of this poor country. . . .' (Ibid. f. 299) ; etc.

[3] Add. MSS. 33000, ff. 163-4.   [4] Ibid. ff. 129-35.

317 [1] out of 558 Members.   This does not necessarily mean that Newcastle still hoped to have a majority in the House, but even though one can understand that some names should have been put down tentatively, the selection is remarkable.   From the list used for the 'circular letters' in October 1761, 66 names only were deleted, and of these at least ten were friends omitted by oversight.   The 56 Members who, I take it, were deliberately weeded out, include fifteen connected with Fox and eight with Bedford, men recently promoted by Bute (*e.g.* John Turner and George Rice), or who had quarrelled with Newcastle (*e.g.* Samuel Martin and Humphrey Morice), contractors favoured by the new Treasury, etc., etc.   No allowance was made by Newcastle for the wider workings of 'the attractive influence of power'; instead of asking himself on whom he could still reasonably count in his radically altered position, he merely omitted those whom he no longer could possibly treat as friends.   Even this was done in a way which points to a supreme desire not to face facts.   Relatives and dependants of some peers who, in the list of the House of Lords on 24 September, had been classed as 'against',[2] on the 27th appear among the Members of the House of Commons to be summoned by Newcastle;   Sir James Lowther, Bute's son-in-law, is omitted from the list but his nominees remain;   and even some Bedfords and friends of Fox are left in.   Where no degree of self-deception could have sufficed, negligence preserved Newcastle's list of friends in the House of Commons from being duly shortened.

To the 227 Members whom Newcastle retained from the list of the previous year, he added 40 — of these 7 were Tories, 4 followers of Pitt and Temple, 8 had been abroad in 1761 (and not all were back even now), and at the very least 12 were added without any valid reason.

Newcastle himself was to write to 145 Members [3] (but, as on previous occasions, many of his invitations were to be reinforced

---

[1] This figure includes three vacant seats which Newcastle expected to be filled by friends;   and also one non-existing Member, who seems to have come into being through Newcastle failing to decipher his own handwriting.

[2] The Dukes of Ancaster and Manchester, and Lords Darlington, Buckinghamshire, Gower, Bath, Hertford, Falmouth, and Bathurst.

[3] Add. MSS. 33000, ff. 147-50.

by letters from other leaders or patrons) ; 34 Members were
to be summoned by Devonshire, and 15 by Rockingham.
Cumberland, who had given up the command of the Army in
1757 and was not likely ever to hold it again, was to secure the
attendance of 19 Army officers, including Thomas Calcraft —
the younger brother of Fox's notorious assistant — and of John
Craufurd, who was on active service in Portugal and whose
brother was one of Bute's political agents in Scotland. The
Duke of Marlborough and Lord Northumberland, though
classed as 'doubtful' in the list of the House of Lords, appear
among the deputy-conveners,[1] while the attendance of Members
dependent on the Admiralty was to be secured for Newcastle
by Clevland, its senior Secretary !

Lord Lincoln does not appear among those whose co-
operation was to be invited — did Newcastle in reality lend
an ear to certain rumours, to which he professed to give no
credence ? On 1 October, Fox, when boasting to Cumberland
that 'many of the Duke of Newcastle's friends were gone over
to my Lord Bute', 'mentioned some few particular names'
which Newcastle did not 'chuse to repeat' ; but of whom he
claimed not to have 'the least suspicion in the world'.

It is very plain [he wrote] how my Lord Bute and his friends
reason. The D. of N. has refused . . . the advances that have
been made to him ; therefore the next thing to be tried, is to get
his friends from him ; and to circulate a belief, that *that* is, in some
measure already done. . . .[2]

. . . .

It is unfortunate, that the innocent conduct of some of my friends,
by their visits to my Lord Bute, and attendance at his levées, has
given too much ground for reports of the nature. . . . Opposition
and personal attendance are different things. One, might very
properly be refused, if thought to be attended with any incon-
venience to the publick ; but the other, can't be often repeated,
without some particular view.[3]

On 12 April 1762 Newcastle, in a lucid moment, had said
to Bute : 'My Lord, I don't know, *who are my friends* ; as will

---

[1] It seems, however, more probable that finally they were not applied to.
[2] Add. MSS. 32943, ff. 31-2.   [3] *Ibid.* f. 44.

be the case of every one, when he is in the situation, I am in at present'.[1] With the loss of office his case had become infinitely worse, but there had been no occasion for testing his friends, and Newcastle refused to face the facts of the situation. When, about 20 October, he heard that the Administration claimed to have 260-280 sure friends in the House of Commons, he thought this mere boasting;[2] so far he had positive knowledge of only very few defections.[3]

On 10 October, Newcastle wrote to Devonshire:

. . . they brag of having gained some of my friends and particularly, my Lord Lincoln, and with him would go, Offley, Brudenell, Jefferies, etc.—. . . Lord Lincoln is far from governing himself, as I would have him, . . . but he is as capable of robbing upon the way, as of *renouncing me*. . . .[4]

And again, on 21 October, to Hardwicke:

As to my Lord Lincoln, . . . his passion, his pride, and his blind contempt, of late, of the world, and what people say; . . . have, I am afraid, made him hold a very indiscreet conduct; and offer, very improper discourses. I have spoke my mind honestly and fully to him.[5]

Still, it is hardly to be supposed that Newcastle knew how far Lincoln went in those 'discourses'—of which the following, reported by the King to Bute on 5 September 1762, may serve as an illustration:

Lord Lincoln . . . desired to say a few words to me, they were to declare his attachment to and resolution to support my Government, that he thought it the more incumbent on him to speak out, because of his uncle's strange, unsteady conduct, whose opinion on any public measure could not be five minutes depended on; that it was with shame he remembered the language the D. of Newcastle had made him hold a year before the late King's demise to my dear friend,[6] wherein he had declared that whenever I mounted the Throne he

---

[1] See p. 314. [2] Add. MSS. 32943, f. 339.
[3] On October 14 Newcastle wrote to Devonshire that he had great reason to think that Robert Nugent 'has alter'd his manner of *thinking* and *acting*' (*ibid.* f. 206). Nugent carried with him three Members in the House — his son Edmund, and two relatives by marriage, T. E. Drax and J. E. Colleton. [4] *Ibid.* f. 145.
[5] Newcastle to Hardwicke, 21 October; *ibid.* ff. 339-40.
[6] See above, pp. 100-101.

would assist Government to his utmost, but only as a private man, and that now he is as fond of power as when he first enjoyed it and he feared will ever be restless. . . .

Such declarations made the Court hope for Lincoln's help in forming their 'system' in the House of Commons, and on 24 October he was summoned to the King.

Lord Lincoln [wrote the King to Bute] has been here, who is full of duty to my person, owns the right of the Crown to appoint what Ministers they please, and declares great regard for my d. friend, but as to the speaking to his friends, he has great difficulties owing to his attachment to the Pelhams and his great aversion to Mr. Fox ; . . . he looks on the Duke of Newcastle as determined to be noisy, and that he will never join men with such base intentions.

But this was the account which Lincoln gave to Newcastle of that conversation, and which Newcastle repeated to Cumberland :

His Majesty . . . expressed his great concern that my Lord Halifax had not succeeded with the Duke of Newcastle . . . repeated all the gracious things, which he had often said upon my [*i.e.* Newcastle's] subject ; and then concluded — My Lord Halifax says, the Duke of Newcastle will come into the House of Lords *undecided*, (which by the way I never said ;) But, said the King, I am afraid the decision is already taken ; and therefore my Lord Lincoln (loading him with all the professions and offers of grace and favor) I know you so well, and have that affection for you, that I hope you will assist me in my distress, and prevent my being forced in my closet, as there may be an intention to do. There are many friends of the D. of N., who were more friends of his brother, than his ; with these probably you may be able to prevail ; and I should be much obliged to you, if you would endeavour to get them, to come into my measures. . . .

My Lord Lincoln replied, Tho', Sir, perhaps my uncle and I may have differ'd upon particular points, what can Your Majesty think of me, if I was capable of acting this part to my uncle, to endeavour to get his friends from him, in this manner ; I am incapable of acting such a part ; or of leaving and abandoning my uncle. And tho' I should be very sorry, that it should happen ; I ought not to deceive Your Majesty ; I am afraid, incidents may arise, which may oblige me to desire Your Majesty's leave to resign my employment. . . .[1]

---

[1] 'An account of what passed this day, at Windsor Lodge', 2 November 1762 ; Add. MSS. 32944, ff. 210-11. The account which Fox had given

Newcastle was exultant —

> my Lord Lincoln . . . has behaved with the greatest firmness, and
> with the utmost friendship, affection, and attachment to me ; and
> has taken care to remove any vain, or unkind suspicion, they may
> have flatter'd themselves with, that any consideration whatever, can
> ever detach him from me, and my interest.[1]

As Lincoln would not canvass his friends for the Court,
Fox tackled them directly.   On 27 October, Newcastle wrote to
James Peachey, one of the King's Grooms of the Bedchamber,
whom he had returned to Parliament for Seaford :

> They have begun with my two very good friends, (as I thought)
> Mr. Brudenell[2] and Mr. Offley ;[3] and they have prevailed so much
> with Mr. Brudenell, that he immediately assured my Lord Bute,
> that he would support their measures in Parliament, without know-
> ing or enquiring, what those measures were, or consulting, or think-
> ing of me, who gave him his seat there.
>
> I cannot say, that I expected this behaviour from Mr. Brudenell ;
> . . . and no man should, for his own honor, tie himself down, in this
> manner, to the will of a Sole Minister. . . .
>
> Mr. Offley's answer was a much more manly one . . . (tho' even
> that, was not such a one, as I should have advised ;) viz. that he
> would support the King's measures, as long as he remain'd in the
> King's service. . . .
>
> . . . After what has happen'd, I can scarce be sure of any body.
> Could you find an opportunity to sound Mr. Fanshaw ?[4] I ask no
> more, than that they should not previously engage themselves, before
> they know, what I and my friends would propose to them ; or, even
> the Ministers, to whom they are to tie themselves, have to propose to

Cumberland of 'what passed in my Lord Lincoln's audience of the King'
(quoted in the same paper) seems to have been based on what Lincoln had
said on 5 September.

[1] Add. MSS. 32944, f. 106.

[2] James Brudenell, M.P. for Hastings ; at the general election of 1761
Newcastle had recommended him to the Hastings Corporation, stating that
he was a 'brother to the Earl of Cardigan and Master of the Robes to His
Majesty (an employment which gives him the honor of being immediately
about the person of the King)' ; see Add. MSS. 32920, ff. 368-9.

[3] John Offley, M.P. for Orford ; he was a Groom of the Bedchamber
and had moreover a secret service pension, but gave up both, and remained
loyal to Newcastle who in 1768 returned him for East Retford.

[4] Simon Fanshawe, M.P. for Grampound, and a Clerk Comptroller of
the Green Cloth ; another of Henry Pelham's official parasites, inherited as
liabilities by Newcastle, and as boon companions by Lincoln.   He promptly
deserted Newcastle.

the publick. I should be glad to know, if you have heard any thing
of my Lord Gage's [1] intention in this respect.[2]

'Ought not Peachey & Co. to be questioned by my dear
friend or Mr. Fox on the part they mean to act ?' wrote the
King to Bute on 4 November ; and before the month was out
Newcastle, in his list of the House of Commons, had to cross
out Peachey from the column marked 'for'.[3]

Fox in his Parliamentary campaign made use of every connexion he had, without regard to its origin. Lord Sandwich,
with whom he had been associated in serving the Duke of
Cumberland, was one of the first to be tried, and on 26 October
Fox informed him that he had come with Bute to the desired
'explanation',[4] and hoped the result would fully satisfy Sandwich. In the next letter, on 30 October, after Devonshire
had been dismissed, Fox offered Sandwich the post of Joint
Postmaster-General, relinquished by Devonshire's brother-in-
law, Lord Bessborough. 'The signal is now given and I
believe all thoughts of accomodation are over on each side.
You will take your party like a man, and do it soon.'[5] By
both sides the case of the Duke of Devonshire was now made
the test of men's allegiance.

Devonshire, by the half-measure of retaining Court office
after having withdrawn from the Cabinet Council, had placed
himself in a false position, and the irritation which during four
months of anxious, embarrassed discussions about the peace
treaty had gathered against the 'non-cooperators', naturally
turned against him who was still at Court. At the end of
September, Grenville, uneasy about the peace terms, suggested
that Devonshire, Newcastle, and Hardwicke should be summoned to the Council at which the decision was to be taken —
he obviously wanted to make them share in the responsibility ;
but Bute replied 'that not one of them would come : besides,

[1] William Hall, 2nd Viscount Gage, M.P., Paymaster of Pensions; he
was Peachey's colleague at Seaford and he too owed his seat to Newcastle.
With Newcastle he remained and lost his place.
[2] Add. MSS. 32944, ff. 105-6.
[3] See Add. MSS. 33000, f. 266.
[4] Sandwich MSS.
[5] *Ibid.*

he had no right to summon two of them . . .',[1] meaning that
Newcastle and Hardwicke were no longer in the King's service.
Devonshire was ; and on 3 October he received at Bath 'an
office letter from Ld. Egremont' saying that though he 'had
declin'd attending Council, yet as the final decision of the peace
was now to be taken', the King had no doubt but he would
attend and advise 'on so important an object'. Devonshire
replied by asking to be excused, as in his 'uninform'd situation'
he could not give any opinion, or make himself responsible for
measures that he had had no share in and was 'in a manner
unacquainted with'.[2]

'I shall be a little impatient to know how it is taken', wrote
Devonshire to Newcastle ; but Hardwicke did not think this
was 'a time for the Ministers to take any revenge for it' [3] — he
did not know to what an extent 'vigour' had become the *mot
d'ordre* at Court. Indeed, on receipt of Devonshire's letter the
King thought of sending immediately 'to Bath for the wand',[4]
and on 9 October, when planning a redistribution of offices,
treated Devonshire's as vacant ; [5] while Bute, the day Fox
joined the Government (13 October), hinted to Lord Denbigh
that 'this measure may probably, thro' the obstinacy and per-
nicious intentions of some people, be followed by others,
necessary for supporting the King's independancy'.[6]

Devonshire's removal from office was an agreed measure,
but the offensive manner in which it was done seems to have
been the King's own sudden resolution. On 28 October he
wrote to Bute at '38^{m} pt. 10' :

The great meeting my d. friend mention'd some days ago to be
held at Claremont I believe is to be held in town this day ; for I met
the D. of Devonshire in Hammersmith, and the D. of Newcastle
under the Terrace in his way to London ; how it galls that I meet
the Duke of Devonshire still bearing the wand, if he should come

[1] See Newcastle's account of his conversation with Cumberland, on
1 October, Add. MSS. 32943, f. 30.
[2] Devonshire to Newcastle, Bath, 3 October 1762 ; *ibid.* ff. 48-9 ; a
copy of Devonshire's letter to Egremont is among the Bute MSS., and
tallies with the account which Devonshire gave of it to Newcastle.
[3] To Newcastle, on 9 October ; Add. MSS. 32943, f. 120.
[4] The insignia of the Lord Chamberlain.
[5] Bute MSS.   [6] Add. MSS. 36797, f. 14.

to day, which I doubt from the D. of Newcastle's being on the road, he shall not leave the closet as Chamberlain.[1]

Obviously the King did not mean as yet to refuse admission to Devonshire ; but 'past 3' he wrote again to Bute :

The D. of Devonshire came here a little after one, I order'd the page to tell him, *I would not see him*, on which he bid him ask me *with whom he should leave his wand*, I said *he would receive my orders* ; . . . on the D. of Devonshire's going away he said to the page *God bless you, it will be very long before you see me here again.*

Fox, writing about the incident to Sandwich on 30 October, gave a plain and sensible statement of fact :

The D. of Devonshire resigned on Thursday and went to Chatsworth Fryday very angry. I am very sorry that he had so much reason given him to be angry. He would have resigned at all events, but perhaps without warmth, or drawing others to resign with him.[2]

But this was not how the story was to be told in future — attempts were soon made to blow it up into a constitutional issue, for big cries and sham heroics were much in demand on either side. Bute wrote to Rigby on 30 October :

. . . some of our friends lament the D. of Devonshire not being allow'd to resign, instead of treating him in a manner no person of his rank was ever treated before ; shall I give you the K—— own words : the D. of Devonshire in refusing to come to my summons treated me with a contempt never shown to a King before ; from the minute he did so, I was determin'd to dismiss him, rather than permit him to dismiss me, and therefore when he came before I had time to send him a proper message, I let him know that I would not see him ; are his brothers gone out, so much the better, will more great men follow, let them, I prefer six open enemys to two secret ones, to one false friend. This is the true state of the case which I wish, Sir, you would impart to the Duke of Bedford.[3]

---

[1] Bute MSS. Thus the story recorded by Horace Walpole in his *Memoirs of the Reign of King George III* (vol. i. p. 159), that the King 'coming from Richmond that morning . . . met the Dukes of Devonshire and Newcastle together in a chariot', is not altogether accurate ; still less, that 'at the moment the Duke arrived at St. James's' the King 'was writing to Lord Bute that *now was the time* . . .'

[2] Sandwich MSS.

[3] Add. MSS. 38200, ff. 79-80.

And on 2 November, Bute wrote to George Townshend with rising exaltation :

At the minute I write there exists the most factious combination of *soi disant* great men against the lawful right and liberty of the King that ever happened in this country. . . . The King has flung the last dye for his liberty and it promises success beyond my expectation ; the Duke of Devonshire having refused to attend the King's particular summons to the Cabinet, contrary to the oath of office, has been dismissed and many, they say, will follow him ; be it so ; ten open enemies are preferable to one secret one ; [1] even this has it's good, for these repeated insults have at last conquered the natural mildness of our young Sovereign, he has taken his part and 'tis determined to meet the sword.[2]

To Newcastle no less than to the Court, the incident came as a welcome occasion for an overt change of attitude and the reversing of measures. Having originally made the mistake of telling his followers not to resign with him, Newcastle had cast about for insults to friends over which he could wax virtuously indignant. When, on 21 June, Hardwicke was not summoned to the Council, Newcastle wrote to Hardwicke's nephew, H. V. Jones : 'Such presumption, I had almost said impudence in a Minister I never heard of before. . . . This treatment, my Lord Hardwicke may forget, but I shall ever remember it.' [3] Now Devonshire had been summoned and had refused, and the sequel came to Newcastle as the supreme occasion for friendship, wrath, and a call for resignations ; for he was at that time desperately short of a 'point' on which to rally a following that was visibly disintegrating and dispersing. 'We shall never have so proper an occasion as this of the ill usage of the Duke of Devonshire', Newcastle wrote to Rockingham on 1 November.[4] And to Lord George Cavendish on 31 October :

Nothing ever astonished, or provoked me more, than that did ; and by all I hear, it meets universally with the reception, it deserves. It has already had a wonderful effect with all my friends ; and indeed, I should never look upon them, as my friends, if they did

---

[1] Three days earlier it was 'six to two' — see above.
[2] Add. MSS. 38200, ff. 89-90 (Liverpool Papers) ; another copy of his letter is in Add. MSS. 36797, ff. 16-17.
[3] Add. MSS. 32940, f. 60.
[4] Add. MSS. 32944, f. 190.

not think upon it, and receive it, as I do. . . . Such treatment to such a man, and to such a meritorious family, is not to be bore.

Everybody was incensed, enraged, and 'in extreme good humour' (*i.e.* on the point of resigning); while Newcastle showed his friends, or gave them 'gently to understand', what was right for them to do.

I see, we shall have little difficulty to make our friends give up their employments [he continued in his letter to George Cavendish]; but it must be a measure; and we must consider, how low that should go. The resignation of great and considerable men is an honor to us; if it goes too far, it may be a burthen, and give the Ministers places to dispose of, to encrease their party immediately. . . .

In short, let us agree amongst ourselves what to do; and, I am persuaded, our friends will follow us. . . .[1]

On 2 November, Newcastle talked 'the matter over fully' with Cumberland, and they agreed that resignations should be restricted to 'persons of high rank, or of great distinction', such as the Duke of Rutland, Lord Powis, some Lords of the Bedchamber, etc.

My opinion was, and is, that, as we have no immediate object in Parliament, to try our friends upon, if there were not, upon this last event some resignations of persons of consequence, we should lose all our friends; and that they would not be to be recover'd afterwards. To that H.R.H. entirely agreed.[2]

George III, for his part, professed complete indifference to resignations whatever the rank of the people concerned, and viewed 'the factious methods' taken 'to increase the number of martyrs . . . with scorn and indignation' and 'a mind so determined, that no event will shake. . . .'[3] He wrote to Bute on 31 October :

After the Drawing Room Lord George Cavendish resigned his wand, but did not utter a syllable ; taking it I told him I willingly let every one quit my service who have lost the zeal to serve me, and then turned on my heel; thus the two brothers are gone; Lord

---

[1] *Ibid.* ff. 167-8.
[2] 'An account of what passed this day at Windsor Lodge', Claremont, 2 November 1762 ; *ibid.* ff. 206-15.
[3] Bute to Rigby, 30 October ; Add. MSS. 38200, ff. 79-80.

Rockingham resigns on Wednesday, whether any of the Bedchamber will follow his example is entirely unknown to me.

Similarly, when Rockingham resigned on 3 November, 'His Majesty's answer was short ; saying that he did not desire any person should continue in his service any longer than it was agreeable to him.' [1]   If Rutland, Lincoln, or Coventry were to resign,

I should think myself well rid of them [wrote George III to Bute early in November] ; force and steadiness will undoubtedly overturn this faction and I can't help hinting again what I did last night that every officer that votes against Government at a time like this ought to be made an example of.[2]

Thus it was the King himself, not Fox, who pressed for strong measures ; he wrote to Bute on 3 November :

I am provoked that Mr. Fox should every moment cry out for mildness, that at this minute would be pusillanimity ; the sword is drawn, vigor and violence are the only means of ending this audacious faction ; indeed I have but one man about me, that is my dear friend, the others are to-day angry, to-morrow perhaps soft, but now they must go on with spirit or else are unfit to aid Government at this hour of faction.[3]

On 3 November, at the Council, George III 'call'd for the Council Book declaring that it was to strike out the D. of Devonshire'.[4]   The same day Charles Jenkinson compiled a 'List of Privy Councillors struck off the Council List from the Restoration to the present time' ; [5] after the event, Bute anxiously searched for precedents.

On 5 November information that the preliminaries of peace had been signed in Paris reached the City, and the next day the Government.[6] 'Millions of thanks to my much beloved

---

[1] Rockingham to Cumberland, 3 November ; Albemarle, *Memoirs of Rockingham*, vol. i. p. 143.   [2] Bute MSS.   [3] *Ibid.*
[4] This is the King's own account in a letter to Bute of 3 November.
[5] Add. MSS. 38334, ff. 194-5.
[6] On 6 November, at 10.30 A.M., George III wrote to Bute that Selwyn, the banker, had brought Egremont

this morning the account of my d. friend had yesterday from Touchet ; Selwin's messenger was over taken by a servant of Mr. Rigby who was sent to the Duke of Bedford's broker who has bought 200,000 ; if this

friend for his most comfortable note, this will sink the impious hopes of faction', wrote the King to Bute on hearing the news ; [1] and he proceeded to discuss how to make the vacant offices serve that purpose. In the letter in which, on 3 November, he informed Bute of having struck off Devonshire's name, he added :

I approve so much of the D. of Rutlands getting instantly the wand as the only means of gaining him, and I am sure Granby is so much attach'd to him that if he goes right the son follows: therefore unless I find my d. friend has objection to the doing it tomorrow if he seems yielding I will instantly give it him.

And in the letter which Bute, with the King's approval, wrote to Granby on 5 November, he told Granby (who was still in command of the British troops in Germany) that the King would have immediately deprived Devonshire of his office 'but wished to know first, whether the Duke of Rutland, then in the country', was prepared to take his place.[2] 'Both friend and foe, put the whole upon the Duke of Rutland's quitting', wrote Newcastle on 13 November.[3]

At the levee, after the Council of 3 November, the King was 'remarkably gracious' to Rutland, who, when asked by Egremont whether he meant to resign his employment,[4] replied that 'he should take no resolution' without consulting Granby.[5] 'Lord Eg——t told the K.—— that the D. of Rutland says he won't oppose, but if his son is angry he must resign, . . .' wrote Bute to Shelburne ; and in a postscript — 'Should not His Maj. see the D. of Rutland as soon as possible ?' [6] So

is so, for his Grace's private profit, the public messenger has been detained. . . .

The King feared 'this to be true' but 'put on the face of doubting Selwin's intelligence' (Bute MSS.). In judging that report it should be remembered that Egremont was hostile to Bedford. [1] 6 November.

[2] Add. MSS. 38200, ff. 93-4. The statement was probably not altogether correct ; still, as early as 8 October, the King wrote to Bute : 'The proposal of the D. of Rutland for the latter [the Chamberlain's Staff] seems very proper'.

[3] Add. MSS. 32944, f. 354.   [4] He was Master of the Horse.

[5] See the account which Newcastle had from Rutland and which he sent to Granby on 5 November ; Add. MSS. 32944, f. 271.

[6] 3 November ; Shelburne MSS. The letter is printed in Fitzmaurice, *op. cit.* vol. i. p. 135, but this concluding paragraph and the postscript are omitted.

far the intention of offering him Devonshire's place had been conveyed to him through Calcraft only, 'and as an inducement . . . they told him there was now vacant in the Chamberlain's gift a place of 1200£ pr. an. . . .'[1] 'I will not fail to speak fully to him this day', wrote the King to Bute on the 4th. 'I would have done it yesterday had I known the weight Calcraft's language had with the Dutchess.' Rutland was sent for, loaded with compliments, and offered the Chamberlain's Staff.

The D. of Rutland has just left me [wrote the King at 1.15 P.M.], he was very civil but too silent, desir'd to remain where he is, yet at the same time I think if closely follow'd, I shall to-morrow have his assent, his last words were that he wish'd I would not press him to change before he heard from his son; I reply'd it was an office of too great importance, at such an hour to remain longer vacant, that I had waited till now purposely to bestow it on him; and that I must have his final answer to morrow.[2]

Newcastle expected Rutland's answer to 'be a negative', and hoped that upon that he would be 'turned out', 'for they want the Master of the Horse for the Duke of Marlborough'.[3] Rutland adhered to his previous resolution, but Newcastle's hope was not fulfilled. It was Fox's advice to make Granby 'more drunk with praise than he ever was with champaign', and thus to get the Rutland family 'to declare'; 'and we will with these simpletons distance the other old familys, those phantoms they talk of so much'.[4] 'Nothing can exceed the dutifull and noble language of the Duke of Rutland on this occasion', wrote Bute to Granby on 5 November; and added that the King felt sure of the line Granby would take — 'when the real truth comes to be opened, Lord Granby will be as jealous of his [the King's] honor and the disrespect shown him,

[1] Add. MSS. 32944, ff. 282-3.
[2] The contents of this letter were transmitted by Bute to Shelburne, 'near 2'. As only a copy of the King's letter can now be found among the Bute MSS., and this seems more defective than that in the Shelburne MSS., I quote from the latter.
[3] Newcastle to Devonshire, 5 November; Add. MSS. 32944, f. 281; see also his letter to Granby, same date, *ibid.* f. 273.
[4] Fitzmaurice, *op. cit.* vol. i. p. 136; and Shelburne MSS. Fox's dislike of the 'old families' was in a way genuine, for he was a snob, and had spent his life running after them.

as he is himself'.[1] The same day (5 November), Newcastle, too, appealed to Granby :

> The present case is the first of the kind, that has ever happen'd; and, if some disapprobation is not shew'd of it, in all probability, these measures of *terror* will be pursued; and God knows, when that will end; and what fatal consequences may arise from it. How then can this disapprobation be shew'd with the least inconvenience to the publick, but by the resignation of some of the most considerable persons in this kingdom? That would strike terror, and in the proper place, upon the Ministers who gave this advice; and prevent them from pursuing it; or, put it out of their power to do it. And . . . is there one man in this Kingdom, whose declaration, upon this occasion, would have more effect, than the Duke of Rutland's ?[2]

When Newcastle's letter reached Granby at Warburg, he was 'so ill . . . as not to be able to read it', but on 12 Decembei his chaplain had 'the happiness' to assure Newcastle 'that yesterday things took a more favorable turn, and last night Lord Granby slept very well'.[3] On 6 February 1763 Granby returned to England 'in perfect health' and, from Fox's point of view, 'in the best disposition'.[4] Meantime Devonshire's place had been given to Marlborough, Rutland remained Master of the Horse, and the Manners family voted with the Court.

Newcastle, engaged in a veritable hunt for resignations, wrote to Hardwicke on 9 November 1762 :

> I saw a great many people on Thursday last [4 November]. The shocking event, in striking the Duke of Devonshire's name out of the Privy Council, enrages, frightens, and alarms every body; and particularly my friend my Lord Kinnoull, who is come up . . . full of wrath, and resentment, without management, or disguise; determined to quit his Chancellor of the Dutchy [5] immediately; that the Ministers (Lord Bute and Mr. Fox) have *begun* these acts of violence; and they must take the consequence of it. This I dare say, we shall find the general language; except some few *rats*, who will do their own business.[6]

---

[1] Bute to Granby, 5 November 1762; Add. MSS. 38200, ff. 93-4.
[2] Add. MSS. 32944, f. 274.
[3] The Rev. Bennet Storer to Newcastle; Add. MSS. 32945, f. 276.
[4] Fox to Bedford, 9 February 1763; *Bedford Correspondence*, vol. iii. p. 190.
[5] Of Lancaster.   [6] Add. MSS. 32944, f. 333.

A few tried to rat and still remain friends with Newcastle. Lord Barrington, when appealed to by him, winced, pleaded a 'sense of duty', went away 'in the deepest affliction', was forgiven, and promised on every occasion to show his gratitude and his 'respectful affection' for Newcastle ; and to continue informing him of 'what happens here worthy your knowledge',[1] *i.e.* spying on his new chiefs and associates. And yet he was not mean, merely half-sincere, tolerant to himself, and accommodating to those in power.[2] On 13 December 1762 he wrote to Andrew Mitchell, M.P., British Minister at Berlin : [3]

You know my attachment for the Duke of Newcastle and for him only ; and you can therefore conceive how distressful it has been to me, that I should take a different part from him in publick affairs. I very early and very explicitly told him, that I thought support of Government a duty, while an honest man could support it : that I approved and even admired the peace which the Administration had concluded ; and that I had long agreed with his Grace in thinking, it was of the most dangerous and mischievous consequence to continue the war.

As for Newcastle, from whom 'personally I never can separate myself', he had

such offers several times in the summer, and particularly at the end of it, as I think he could not have refused, if he had not been govern'd and flatter'd by the Duke of Cumberland, who has undone him. . . .[4]

Newcastle had failed to take his chance ; what could his friends do for him now ? or what could he expect from them ?

[1] See letters from Barrington to Newcastle of 4 and 5 November ; Add. MSS. 32944, ff. 233 and 287.
[2] The following letter from Barrington to Mitchell, dated 23 March 1761 is characteristic of the man, no matter whether the modesty he professed was sincere or a pose :

Our Administration is at last settled : . . . the same strange fortune which made me Secretary of War five years and a half ago, has made me Chancellor of the Exchequer ; it may, perhaps, at last make me Pope. I think I am equally fit to be at the head of the Church and of the Exchequer . . . but no man knows what is good for him. My invariable rule . . . is to ask nothing, to refuse nothing ; to let others place me and to do my best wherever I am placed. (Add. MSS. 6834, ff. 29-30.)

[3] *Ibid.* ff. 41-2.
[4] Barrington to the Earl of Buckinghamshire, 17 December 1762 ; H.M.C., *Lothian MSS.*, pp. 244-5.

Barrington was the normal product of the Pelham school of Whigs.

On 13 November Newcastle still tried to seem hopeful, but could no longer hide his disappointment and anxiety. He wrote to Hardwicke : [1]

> I had above forty audiences, on Thursday last [11 November], and found great spirit and resolution in most of them; some few exceptions, (in the H. of Lords) with which I shall acquaint you. But the material part is, that our friend my Lord Kinnoull has executed his intention, by going to my Lord Egremont, and resigning his employment; but, not at all in the manner, which I had reason to expect . . . by his declarations. . . .

When Kinnoull saw Egremont, he forgot all his wrath and resentment, represented his resignation as 'a single act of his own, to make himself easy, in acting a part he owed to the Duke of Devonshire', and disclaimed opposition. Similarly he told Newcastle

> that he could not enter into opposition; that he had his jealousies etc.; that he found, people began to reason, that this affair of the Duke of Devonshire, was a private affair ; that they were sorry for it; but that it was not a reason for them, to resign their employments ; that I should find, that nobody more would resign; perhaps my Lord Lincoln, and my Lord Ashburnham; that there would not be one resignation in the Law; that he had heard, no one of my Lord Hardwicke's family would resign; and ran on in this unaccountable way.

The attitude of others seemed to bear out Kinnoull's contention.

> I found my friend, my Lord Coventry, in the strangest way imaginable ; he wants opposition ; he wants a *point* ; he wants Mr. Pitt; but he is against quitting: he has a great regard for the Duke of Devonshire ; but he has offered Mr. Pitt, to quit with him; and he can't be quitting every day.
>
> I have seen nothing of my friend my Lord Northumberland; but I hear, his Lordship blames the Duke of Devonshire; and says, he ought to have come up to Council, when the King required it. That is only a pretence. . . .[2]

---

[1] Add. MSS. 32944, ff. 352-3.

[2] On 23 December, after Northumberland had been appointed Chamberlain of the Queen's Household, Newcastle wrote to Devonshire :

> I had yesterday a long visit from my Lord Northumberland, in which I had as many strong professions from his Lordship, as ever I had in my

Everyone had some excuse for hanging back, and not the least remarkable was that which Ashburnham named to Newcastle :

The difficulty which he makes, (and others with less sincerity) is, this is quitting for the Duke of Devonshire, to whom he has no attachment, when he did not quit for me, to whom he is solely attached.

Newcastle, having started the letter with the 'great spirit and resolution' he had found among his forty politicians, finished by seeing 'interest and corruption prevail so far' that he 'despaired of doing any good'.

Hardwicke's answer [1] supplied cold comfort ; he, too, found people 'very sorry' for the incident with Devonshire, and censuring it 'strongly' ;

but it is a single act, and a private act, and the affairs of the public are not to be thrown into confusion on that account ; they are sure the Duke of Devonshire himself would not wish it. But, be that as it may, it is no reason for them to resign their employments. . . . I never doubted but it would be so amongst people in lower stations and ranks. For . . . I never thought that a measure of opposition could be founded on this act unless a number of the *great nobility* would take it up in a high tone and make it their own cause, in which case persons in the House of Commons, brought into Parliament by them or dependant upon them, would follow their leading. But by what your Grace tells me . . . I do not find that the great nobility (except the Marquis of Rockingham) seem at present disposed to hold that conduct.

As for his own sons — 'I perceive the view (a very right one) with which your Grace has inserted this passage in your letter' — his reply was that as they were 'all of years of discretion, capable of judging for themselves', he would '*not insist* upon their resigning', but let them 'determine for themselves'.

I find people in general, even our most particular friends, much inclined to peace and determined not to oppose upon that head, provided it comes out to be admissible. They alledge that in this point they followed your Grace when in ; that you instructed and

life. The account, or excuse, he makes for himself, is this, that, upon my going out, there was no plan or measure concerted ; that nobody resign'd ; that he knew nothing ; and that being at Court in one office, he thought, he could not refuse, changing it for another, when the King desired it of him so earnestly. (Add. MSS. 32945, f. 337.)

[1] 15 November ; *ibid.* ff. 15-18.

convinced them that it was absolutely necessary, and they cannot
contradict themselves.

And as for the 'corruption' of which Newcastle complained,

this cannot possibly be new to your Grace, who have been conversant
in Courts and parties above these forty years. Have not you all along
seen such motives to be the great hinges on which the generality of
people's conduct has turned?

He concluded by advising against immediate resignations.

None the less, Newcastle pressed for the resignation of
those whom he could determine. On 31 October Lincoln,
'incensed' over Devonshire's dismissal, had sent word that he
would 'resign his Lord of the Bedchamber upon it, whenever
it shall be thought proper'; [1] and he behaved 'like an angel'.[2]
On 14 November he wrote to Newcastle: 'I thought, you
knew me *better* than to think it necessary, to remind me of
doing what I promis'd'.[3] On 16 November Newcastle, after
having seen Lincoln and Ashburnham, wrote to Devonshire:

I shall honor, and love them, as long as I live. They had taken their
parts, like friends, and like men of honor and consideration in this
country. . . . They both declared to me without my saying one
single word to either of them, that they intended to go to Court, on
Friday next [19 November], and resign their employments. They
did it, in the most manly, the most proper and the most affectionate
manner, to me.[4]

On 19 November the King reported to Bute:

I never saw a man so hurt as Ld. Lincoln, he declares that the D.
of N. alone could have drove him to this step, that he out of the way,
his attachment shall be inviolable; beg'd I would not give ear to
what calumny might say against him; I assur'd him his conduct
should be the sole rule of my opinion; as to the other I shortly told
him I permitted him to resign.

And Lincoln wrote to Newcastle on 21 November: [5]

I am sorry you gave your self the trouble of writing so long a
letter; for God's ! sake, have done with your *thanks*, I dont want

[1] Add. MSS. 32944, f. 167.
[2] Newcastle to Granby, 5 November; *ibid.* f. 275.
[3] Add. MSS. 32945, f. 7.
[4] *Ibid.*, draft ff. 33-48, copy ff. 49-58.   [5] *Ibid.* f. 112.

them, your *suspicions only*, have hurt *me*, they are thank God totally removed, that is all I desire. . . .

A few smaller dependants followed Lincoln's lead.

Roberts' resignation [wrote the King to Bute] I took on as certain, Lord Lincoln having set him the example; Pelham also probably, little Jefferies I found from Lord Egremont was to be ordered by the D. of N—— to retire,[1] he must then starve being these many years a bankrupt; thus two or three base, designing men to distress Government ruin their dependants; courage my d. friend, go on as you have begun and they will soon see that their disgrace is the sole fruit of the impious conduct.[2]

Roberts resigned unwillingly, and reinsured himself with the Court by extreme complaisance in the matter of the two boroughs he had managed for the Treasury (Harwich and Orford); [3] while Jeffreys, a mere parasite, did not resign his sinecures in the Mint and the Parks, nor forgo his secret service pension, but now offered his homage to the Court; and his congratulations to Newcastle, when Newcastle resumed office in 1765.[4]

The 'great nobility', as Hardwicke had foreseen, did not take up a 'high tone', or make Devonshire's dismissal into 'their own cause'. Visions of a mighty array of nobles who joined (or should have joined) in a common cause were evoked by Bute and Newcastle; Burke has further developed that legend, and the Whigs have upheld it ever since. In reality, Newcastle and Devonshire had been so unfortunate as to tumble into an opposition which in no way suited their taste, Rutland carefully kept out of it, Bedford was with the Court, Marlborough joined it willingly, Sandwich (because of his attachment to Cumberland) 'with the greatest heart breaking'; and the Argyll interest was, at that time, represented by Bute, nephew and successor to the two Dukes who had ruled Scotland

[1] It seems doubtful whether this was true; in Newcastle's list of the House of Commons, marked 'corrected November 13' (Add. MSS. 33000, ff. 153-61), Jeffreys is transferred from the column marked 'for' to that of 'against', and never moved from there again.

[2] *C.* 20 November 1762.

[3] See chapter on 'Two Treasury Boroughs' in *The Structure of Politics*.

[4] About Jeffreys see the chapter on 'Parliamentary Beggars', *ibid.* pp. 402-6.

for more than fifty years. The maker of the so-called Whig opposition in 1762 was Cumberland, who during the best part of his life had been reputed a danger to the Constitution; while the noblemen who of their own accord were to enter into opposition were all very young men, and not of 'Revolution' lineage, Rockingham being descended from Strafford, Grafton and Richmond from royal bastards, Dartmouth from a Tory family, while Portland's ancestor only came to England in consequence of the Revolution. Indeed, the 'great nobility' of 'Revolution' origin were not to be scared or made to read grave portents into a silly incident; they felt perfectly easy about their future political standing, though not all of them felt the same about their financial position.

This was what drove Lord Sandwich into taking sides with the Court. He was in financial difficulties, and could not afford to resign the sinecure of Vice-Treasurer of Ireland; if anything, he had to add to his income. On 10 November he wrote to Cumberland that, to his great concern, he found it would be impossible for him 'to avoid taking some part in the present divided state of the government', and that in view of the 'confused condition' of his own affairs, he could not refuse the offers which were made to him.

Your Royal Highness's goodness to me has hitherto been so great, that I am not entirely without hopes, that you will think my case a particular one, and retain some indulgence for me if I find myself obliged to join in with the stream, which I am well convinced is much stronger than your Royal Highness has been made to believe.

It has been suggested to me that I may go Ambassador to Spain, which of all things is what I should like the most. . . .[1]

Cumberland answered the same day in a dignified and, on the whole, friendly letter : [2]

My Lord Sandwich, I return you many thanks for your letter of this morning; I am sure I should be very sorry that I should in any shape prevent or interfere with [what] you find so absolutely necessary for both yourself and family, and wish you joy of the embassy to Spain, where I don't doubt but you will be of as much service both to the King and public as you formerly were when employed. I remain your very affectionate friend,   WILLIAM.

[1] Sandwich MSS.   [2] *Ibid.*

On 6 November Bute had written to Shelburne :

I have a card from Ld. Sandwich desireing to see me to morrow. I wish I knew the present state of Mr. Foxes negotiation with him, for you dropp'd something yesterday, that by no means quadrates with H.M. intentions, I mean that of double office ; will it be too troublesome to let me have a little sense as Eton boys term it ?

Sandwich was obviously trying to retain his sinecure together with his new office. On 12 November Bute related to Shelburne the outcome of a further interview :

I was satisfied entirely with Ld. Sandwich, I hope he was with me. I saw he wish'd to commute at least his office into mony, but I fancy we shant dispute much about that ; for I will do every thing in my power to make him easy.[1]

The same day Fox wrote to Sandwich :

I judge from the King's conversation to day, that your Excellency has pleas'd, and is pleas'd, having deserv'd a most cordial reception, and met with one. I want much to hear from yourself that it is so. Pray, my Lord, send Mr. Major, Mr. Henniker, Mr. Stephenson and, if you can, Lord Clive to me next Tuesday. . . . Let him come, if you can and ask *one* thing, not two.[2]

With Sandwich three Members of the House of Commons immediately crossed over to the Court,[3] and three more were gained through his mediation,[4] but not Lord Clive and his family.[5] Nor was Clive brought over by Lord Powis, whose defection was a sore blow to Newcastle, on personal as well as on political grounds ; its ultimate effects in the House of Commons were not, however, as great as he had feared at first, for more than half of the 'Shropshire gang' refused to join Bute and Fox.[6]

When Newcastle decided to beat up resignations among

[1] Shelburne MSS.
[2] Sandwich MSS.
[3] Lord Carysfort, R. Jones, and T. Duckett.
[4] J. Major and his son-in-law J. Henniker, and J. Stephenson.
[5] About the attempts to g⁐in Clive, see *The Structure of Politics*, pp. 288-9.
[6] See the chapter on 'Shropshire Politics and Men' in *The Structure of Politics*, especially pp. 283-6.

friends holding important places, he drew up the following list, dated Claremont, 3 November 1762 : [1]

Principal Employments.

Ld. Ch. J. in Eyre	Duke of Leeds .
Master of the Horse	Duke of Rutland
Lords and Grooms of the Bed-chamber	Marquis of Rockingham
	Earl of Lincoln
Ranger of St. James's Park	Earl of Ashburnham
	? Earl of Hertford
	Earl of Coventry
	? Earl of Northumberland
	Lord Orford
Grooms	James Peachey
	H. S. Conway
	John Offley
	? Col. Fitzroy
Treasurer of the Household	Earl of Powis
Comptroller — has quitted	Lord George Cavendish
Clerks of the Green Cloth	Thomas Townshend
	Henry Bridgeman
	? Simon Fanshawe
Treasurer of the Navy	Lord Barrington
Secretary-at-War	Charles Townshend
Vice-Treasurer of Ireland	Earl of Sandwich
Chancellor of the Duchy	Earl of Kinnoull
Attorney-General	Hon. Charles Yorke
First Lord of Trade	Lord Sandys
Postmaster-General — has quitted	Earl of Bessborough
Lords of the Admiralty	? Hans Stanley
	Lord Villiers
	Thomas Pelham of Stanmer
Lords of Trade	Soame Jenyns
	Hon. John Yorke
	? John Roberts
Paymaster of Pensions	Lord Viscount Gage
Surveyor of Gardens	George Onslow, Esq.

NB. *Q*. Whether it would not be more advisable to stop at the Great Officers and not include the Boards of Admiralty, Trade, etc.

[1] Add. MSS. 33000, f. 141. I do not reproduce Newcastle's misspellings of names. The queries placed against some of the names signify doubts whether these men would resign.

Of the 33 Ministers and Court officials mentioned in the list, 17 retained their offices, or exchanged them against better ones ; George Cavendish and Bessborough had quitted before it was compiled ; Kinnoull, Lincoln, Ashburnham, and Roberts resigned under pressure from Newcastle ; Charles Townshend after various whimsical tergiversations, to which the world had become fully accustomed in his case ; Rockingham alone resigned on a political principle, and Offley of his own free will ; while Fitzroy, 'Tommy' Townshend, jun., Villiers, Pelham, Gage, and Onslow, all Members of Parliament, continued to adhere to Newcastle without resigning, and were subsequently dismissed for voting against the Government. These, the nucleus of the future opposition, were all, except Gage, young men of about thirty. The only outcome of the campaign for resignations was to expose Newcastle's weakness, and to enable the Court to provide immediately for its new adherents and for men they wished to connect more closely with Administration (*e.g.* for the Bedford, Marlborough, and Sandwich groups, for Lords Orford, Northumberland, Strange, etc.).

There are extant among the Newcastle Papers at least six complete surveys of the House of Commons drawn up between the middle of October and 25 November 1762.[1] The earliest draft, by George Onslow, M.P. for Surrey,[2] in its original form marked 204 Members as 'for' Newcastle, 90 as 'doubtful', and 264 as 'against'. Numerous corrections were made, and in each of the drafts some 50-80 Members were shifted from one column to another ; most of these transfers were mere shufflings, made without sufficient knowledge, and they approximately neutralised each other, leaving the figures at about 210, 88, and 260. Thus the same number of friends was assigned to the Court which, when reported as its own estimate, about 21 October, Newcastle had doubted, and a majority was conceded to it such as was not likely to be overturned by the

---

[1] For an analysis of these lists see Appendix B, pp. 491-3.

[2] This was the son of Speaker Onslow, married to a niece of Newcastle ; a cousin of his, bearing the same names, sat for Guilford, and is usually referred to as Colonel Onslow. During the years 1762-6, George Onslow, the Member for Surrey, supplied Newcastle with reports of debates in the House of Commons and with various lists of Members.

'doubtful'. In one list only, drawn up about 15 November,[1] the two sides appear as very nearly balanced — 238 'for', 71 'doubtful', and 249 'against'. This optimism may have been due to the hope then entertained of gaining the co-operation of Pitt, and of winning over many Tories to the opposition ;[2] it was short-lived — corrections made in the list during the next ten days changed the respective figures to 192, 97, and 269. Next, a new column of 'absent' was introduced, and the last complete survey of the House, drawn up apparently before the meeting of Parliament on 25 November, classified 176 as 'for', 34 as 'absent', 91 as 'doubtful', and 256 as 'against'. Even this forecast was soon to prove much too favourable to the opposition ; at Fox's meeting at the Cockpit, on the night of 24 November, 248 Members were present which, even though several were not supposed to have 'come as friends',[3] pointed to a total greater than 256 ; and there is in the Newcastle Papers an undated, 'List of Commoners, certain [friends] and all in town',[4] probably drawn up about 25 November (and corrected after 1 December), which even in its original draft contained only 142 names. The Government majority was established beyond doubt, and the question now was merely how to prevent a final collapse and disintegration of Newcastle's following.

Newcastle had realised from the first that he could no more conduct an opposition than carry on Government without Pitt, and in talking to Cumberland on 2 November, once more emphasised the imperative need for Pitt's co-operation [5] — 'but . . . how shall we get at him ?'

The Duke replied: In my situation, I can't be beating up for volunteers, or sending for Mr. Pitt; but if Mr. Pitt, by himself, or by any of his friends, shall desire to know my opinion, as to *persons*, or things, I shall very readily give it him.

---

[1] Add. MSS. 33000, ff. 261-7.
[2] The corrections in the preceding list (ff. 245-50) do not remove a single Tory from the column marked 'for', but add four to it from among the 'doubtful', and two from those 'against', while no less than eleven Tories hitherto classed as 'against', are placed among the 'doubtful'.
[3] See Barrington's letter to Newcastle, 25 November ; Add. MSS. 32945, f. 139.
[4] Add. MSS. 33000, f. 197.   [5] Add. MSS. 32944, ff. 214-15.

Approaches were now made through Thomas Walpole [1] and Nuthall.[2] Pitt declared to Nuthall on 5 November 'that a great plan was necessary' and that he 'was ready to concurr in measures with the Duke of Newcastle'; further, that he did not approve of the peace terms, which, if as reported in the papers, were 'inadequate to our present circumstances and successes'.[3] Still, on 13 November, he said to Walpole that 'he did not well see, what was to be done; that the D. of N., D. of D., and Lord Hardwicke had been so much disposed to a peace. The peace was now come, and seem'd to be final.' Moreover, in the forming of a new Administration he could not concur in the proscription of Tories who had supported him; and

tho' it was necessary Lord B. should be removed from the office he now held, he [Pitt] might not think it quite for His Majesty's service, to have the D. of N. succeed there; begging, this might not be thought to proceed from any resentment to the D. of N.

For his own part he did not wish to hold office again without being assured of the good will of the King.[4]

A meeting between Cumberland and Pitt was arranged for 17 November.

The Duke is determined [wrote Newcastle to Hardwicke on the 15th] to bring him to a point, if any thing is to be done now; or, to wait for incidents, as they arise. H.R.H. is ready, but not too forward; he wishes to be at the *French Peace*, tho' not without some probable hopes of success; and upon that he wants to know Mr. Pitt's thoughts.

The Duke does not dislike the account Tommy Walpole gives of Mr. Pitt's conversation; *it is the man*, and as such we must take him, if we will have him.[5]

When they met, they 'talk'd upon every point, freely and confidentially', and Pitt neither declaimed nor made speeches, but 'held his conversation in a proper manner':

[1] M.P. for Ashburton; a son of 'old Horatio', and a son-in-law of Sir Joshuah Vanneck, whose partner he was in the City.

[2] Pitt's solicitor and friend.

[3] 'Conversation between Mr. Pitt and Mr. Nuthall, 5 November 1762; as related to Mr. Walpole'; Add. MSS. 32944, f. 277; and letter from Nuthall to Walpole, 6 November 1762; *ibid*. f. 307.

[4] Add. MSS. 32945, ff. 1-2.   [5] *Ibid*. f. 25.

declared very strongly his opinion against my Lord Bute's transcendency of power, which could not be suffer'd . . . and express'd
a great desire and even determination, on his part, to do what might
depend upon him, to put an end to it.

But he (Mr. Pitt) must do it in his own way; he could not appear
to take that part, in order to bring in the D. of Newcastle; he would
come with his own handful of people; and, in short, (I think) disclaimed, at least at first, any connection, or open correspondence
with us.

He repeated that 'he must have regard' for the Tories, who
had acted with him, and added 'that he had promised them not
to be in the House the first day'.

Mr. Pitt was much against doing any thing, the first day; or,
making any opposition to their Address: and the Duke was much
of that opinion. . . . If that is so, . . . the consideration of giving
any opposition to *any part* of the address, is over; and indeed as
things stand, and 'till we can know a little more, than we do, of our
strength, I think, we must look about us a little before we do any
thing.[1]

Thus five days before the meeting of Parliament, no clear
decision had been reached by the opposition; their numbers
were dwindling, and there was no one to take the lead.

If any body had told me one year ago [wrote Newcastle], that
any of our friends, would have come into an Administration solely
directed by my Lord Bute, and Mr. Fox; . . . declaring, they
meant to support themselves *by power*, I should not have believed it.
And I still think, when our honest country gentlemen come together,
aided and assisted, as they will be, almost by the unanimous cry and
support of the City, and the whole Kingdom, it will be otherwise;
especially if Mr. Pitt will act, as he ought to do.[2]

Indeed Newcastle, who had always mistrusted independents
and abhorred Tories, now inclined towards them. On 2 November Cumberland had told him that

my Lord Grosvenor and his brother, . . . Sir Walter Blacket and
Mr. Noel had declared for us; that His Royal Highness had heard
that Sir Charles Mordaunt and several of the Tories would not
support this Administration. . . .[3]

[1] Newcastle to Devonshire, 20 November; *ibid.* ff. 83-92.
[2] *Ibid.* ff. 90-1.   [3] Add. MSS. 32944, ff. 212-13.

The same day Legge wrote to Newcastle in a similar strain about his own Tory friends,[1] and on 26 November, the day after Parliament had met, he informed Newcastle that Sir Charles Mordaunt, Prowse, and Bagot were 'in suspence what to do'.

> Sir Charles Mordaunt and Bagot [wrote Newcastle to Hardwicke] told Mr. Legge that they found themselves in a very disagreable situation — that if they were proscribed (meaning by us) was it to be expected, that they should assist in running down the present Minister for whom they did not shew any great regard. Legge wanted to have power to assure them that there was no such intention. . . . Jack White and old Tommy Townshend, who are good Whigs and wise men, think it would be madness not to authorize Legge to say so much, and would be flinging away men, whom the others would gladly receive.[2]

When George III and Bute spoke about the extinction of parties, they stood condemned in the eyes of the purveyors of loyalty on monopoly terms ; now the opposite was 'madness'. Devonshire wrote to Newcastle on 30 November :

> The D. of Cumberland and Ld. Hardwicke have no objection to our admitting those Tories as individuals that are ready to act with us upon our principals, but I have seen Mr. Legge and do not think that it will come to any thing.[3]

Reverting to this subject, Hardwicke wrote on 25 December : '. . . as to principles, I am really at a loss where to find them.' [4] But even now, although he thought Legge's friends 'the sounder part of the Tories', he did not expect much from them ; nor from anyone else. Administration was in the ascendant — 'when one considers *the motives*, which prevail in general, how can one wonder ?'

> And yet [he continued in his letter of 27 November] we ought not to deceive our selves. We ought not to ascribe the whole to such causes ; for I am persuaded, . . . that the burden and tedium of the war, and the desire of peace, are so strong in the generality of the Parliament, and of the nation (abstracted from the interested or wild part of the City of London), that the very name of peace is agreeable

---

[1] Add. MSS. 32944, ff. 223-4.
[2] 26 November ; Add. MSS. 32945, f. 153.
[3] *Ibid.* f. 219.   [4] To Newcastle ; *ibid.* f. 367.

to them, and they would have been content with terms rather lower than all we have yet been told of these Preliminaries.[1]

These were laid before the House on 29 November, but the ex-Ministers were still always in doubt what line to take. Even Newcastle was dispirited :

I have long doubted [he wrote that day to Hardwicke], both from observation, and reflection, whether it would be advisable for us, to give any opposition to the Peace. The evident reasons against it are, the fear of acting inconsistently with ourselves ; and that affects me more particularly . . . as I declared my opinion so strongly, that peace was absolutely necessary ; and, as I am quoted for it, by the King, and all his Ministers, and speakers in Parliament.

And there was also this 'most unsurmountable' objection :

I see so little disposition any where, but in some of our zealous friends in the House of Commons, to attack the *present* power in any shape, that I would not attempt the doing it, to give a pretence to our friends to say they voted *for the Peace*, and not for the *Minister*. . . .[2]

These 'zealous friends', intent on opposition, were a group of young men led by the Duke of Grafton.

The D. of Grafton, and our warm friends [wrote Newcastle on 27 November], press extremely the bringing on *some point*, immediately, or, we shall lose all our friends. The question only is, *what* that point shall be. Can any thing arise out of the Preliminaries, or the negotiation relative to them, which we can *properly* come into ? [3]

They urged Newcastle to take action, George Onslow informing him

that there appear'd, the first day, the greatest disposition in the House to shew spirit ; . . . that our friends are most pressing for some point to shew themselves upon ; and that they will not be easy without it ; and that, if nothing else can be found out, *they* will attack the Peace, which, they think, the most popular point, they can go upon.

But so far there was no trace of organisation on the opposition side, no coherence or proper team-work.

Our friends in the House of Commons [Newcastle was told by Onslow] are desirous of collecting themselves together, that they

---

[1] *Ibid.* f. 166.   [2] *Ibid.* ff. 196-8.   [3] *Ibid.* f. 160.

2 C

may know one another; for that purpose, they wish to have a meeting; they are sure, they shall be 180 at least. This deserves consideration. . . .

Otherwise the game was up.

Mr. Onslow says, *that if nothing is done*, and that soon, we shall not only lose all our friends; that they will think themselves *sacrificed*; that they have belonged to us, and will belong to us; but, if after all they have done, it is to end in nothing, *they must and will go elsewhere*: and that the Duke of Grafton is the *strongest* in this way of talking.[1]

On 30 November a group of these young men dined together at the Duke of Grafton's house; there were Grafton (aged 27), George and John Cavendish (35 and 30), Midleton (32), Thomas Townshend, jun. (29), Charles Townshend 'the Spaniard' (34), Villiers (27), George Onslow (31), and Richard Hopkins (33). Except Grafton and Hopkins,[2] they were all in the House of Commons.

I find by them as I do by others [wrote Onslow to Newcastle] the extreme discontent that every day encreases, at no step being taken to collect and unite us in a body, that no measure is taken that looks like any plan being form'd, much less like their being acquainted with it. . . .[3]

He went on to urge opposition to the preliminaries of peace;

a division should be had on that at all events; for without it, we lose all our ground, all our popular cry, . . . May not that throw things more than is to be wish'd into the hands of Mr. Pitt, . . . and may not people list under that banner that are now desirous of looking up to you as their head. . . . Determine on some plan to follow; call us together at a meeting and let us know it: that we may no longer continue in that unsettled ignorance which I find grows irksome to them all, checks their ardor, and will if continued make them think themselves neglected, unsupported, and by that means sacrific'd to the resentment of the most arbitrary Administration that this country ever knew, and who will boast if they succeed of having done so by what Lord Kinnoul says, 'intimidating and corrupting'.[4]

---

[1] Add. MSS. 32945, f. 200-1.
[2] Richard Hopkins, a close friend of Grafton, was returned to Parliament by the Rockinghams in February 1766 for the Government borough of Dartmouth, and continued in Parliament till his death in 1799.
[3] Add. MSS. 32945, ff. 227-9.   [4] *Ibid.* ff. 227-30.

But the old 'leaders' were no further now than they had been the last four months. The same day Devonshire wrote to Newcastle that Cumberland

is as well as every body else eager for a point, the only difficulty is where to find it, I begged Lord Hardwick to find out one, but he seem'd to think it very difficult.[1]

On 1 December the first division was taken, on a minor point — what day the Preliminaries were to be considered. Midleton and T. Townshend jun., moved an amendment; the figures were 213 v. 74. John Cavendish sent Newcastle a list of 52 of the minority, adding that 'the Tories all went against us'[2] — but his own list includes Grosvenor, Wilbraham Bootle, Staunton, and Sir Walter Blackett, all four Tories, and the complete list[3] adds to them another Tory, Dowdeswell, the future leader of the Rockingham Whigs. Still, most Tories, even Sir Charles Mordaunt and Bagot who had so recently negotiated with Legge, voted with the Court. But so did Hardwicke's youngest son John, George Adams, a nephew of Anson, and Soame Jenyns, a close friend of the Yorkes; and even others on whom Newcastle could count with better reason — 'there were several very good men in the majority that I dare say will not stay there', wrote John Cavendish.

On receipt of these reports, Newcastle wrote in his 'Memorandums':[4]

The division of yesterday.
No system — no plan — want a manager.
Bishop of Glocester — Mr. Pitt.

.   .   .   .

The attendance to-morrow.
Soame Jenning's discourse, and my Lord Royston's.

A last appeal was now made to Pitt, the Bishop of Gloucester conveying to him on 3 December an expression of Newcastle's friendly feelings;

that you had acted together, generally with the same, though sometimes with different sentiments; but that now, if your joint endeavours to serve the public should point the same way . . . you

[1] *Ibid.* f. 219.   [2] *Ibid.* ff. 239-41.
[3] Add. MSS. 33000, ff. 195-6.   [4] *Ibid.* f. 198.

should for the future have no reason to complain of his perfect accord and union with you.[1]

Meantime the Yorkes, especially the young generation, were prevaricating more and more. Royston had written to Charles Yorke on 27 October :

I do not think it will be for the D. of Newcastle's or Ld. Hardwicke's credit to set themselves at the head of a *weak opposition*, nor am I very fond of a junction with the D. of C. and truly as to Mr. P. I have tasted enough of him.[2]

Charles replied some time in November :

Our old friend the D. of N. is an entire stranger to any thing but the *ambition* of a Court, without *wisdom* to attain the *end*, or *opportunity* to create the *means*, of that *ambition*.[3]

On 2 December a meeting was held at Newcastle House to consider the line to be adopted in the House of Lords : [4]

Present.

Duke of Devonshire	The measure, which is proposed for our friends in the House of Lords is, to argue against such parts of the Preliminaries, as are liable to objection ; and to conclude, with opposing any approbation ; and by moving to adjourn.
Marquis of Rockingham	
Lord Hardwicke	
Lord Kinnoull	
Mr Attorney-General [Charles Yorke]	
Duke of Newcastle	

NB. This measure was proposed by the Duke of Newcastle ; the Duke of Devonshire and my Lord Rockingham entirely approved it, and shew'd the greatest earnestness to do something ; the others rather doubted about it ; but my Lord Hardwicke said, that, if I persisted in it, he would concur, and support it, as well as he could.

Newcastle still tried to persuade Mr. Attorney-General to take the lead in the Commons, but he replied on 7 December : 'Some of your friends *not in office* should begin the debate. My part will depend on the turn of the question, and the manner of debating. . . .' [5]

---

[1] *Chatham Correspondence*, vol. ii. pp. 195-6.
[2] Add. MSS. 35361, f. 33. [3] *Ibid.* f. 40.
[4] Newcastle's minute ; Add. MSS. 33000, f. 200.
[5] Add. MSS. 32945, f. 254.

The same day Royston wrote to Charles Yorke : 'My Lord [Hardwicke] dines to day at Newcastle House. I am very well satisfied not to be of their Cabinets, for *old folks* do not like *contradiction* or *doubts* from juniors.' [1]

On 8 December the eve of the first vote on the Preliminaries of Peace, Lord Midleton was still appealing to Newcastle for some lead :

> I hope that you will not think me too importunate in begging to know what is fixed for tomorrow, and who will be the person to object to the motion to be made by the Ministry. I must own that I think it of the utmost importance that something should be absolutely settled on this subject before we go into the House tomorrow.[2]

The day came, and they entered the House without any clear decision having been taken. Many accounts have been published of the debates which on 9 December took place in both Houses. I shall limit myself here to reproducing that which Barrington sent to Andrew Mitchell on 13 December [3] — it is short and, on the whole, accurate.

> The die is now cast. The Duke of Newcastle and Lord Hardwicke spoke against the Preliminaries in the House of Lords, where however there was no division. In the House of Commons 319 Members voted thanks to the King for the Peace he has concluded ; 65 only voted against those thanks. I look on the opposition as now declared. . . . Lord Hardwicke is supposed to join them no further than he has thought himself obliged to do, from his long friendship with the Duke of N. Lord Royston his eldest son voted in the House of Commons for the Address approving the Preliminaries ; the Attorney General in his speech [4] commended them on the whole, tho' he expressed a wish that some of the articles had been otherwise : neither he nor his youngest brother, who is in the Board of Trade [5] stay'd the division. Mr. Pitt came to the House on crutches, out of his bed, to which he had been confined for some weeks : he spoke three hours and 25 minutes standing and siting ; he never made so long or so bad a speech,[6] blaming the Preliminaries in general tho'

---

[1] Add. MSS. 35361, f. 41.   [2] Add. MSS. 32945, f. 262.
[3] Add. MSS. 6834, ff. 41-2.
[4] The next day, 10 December, on the Report.
[5] John Yorke, returned by Rockingham for Higham Ferrars.
[6] James Hayes, an adherent and admirer of Pitt, wrote, however, to R. N. Neville at 1 A.M. after the debate : 'I am just got home from the House of Commons, and though tired to death with a very bad debate,

he commended that part of them which relates to the cessions made by France on the Continent of North America. He was very moderate in his expressions, not at all abusive, declared he had no connections with others supposed to be opponents, and intimated that he should attend Parliament very little this session.

Pitt's disclaimer of any connexion with the Newcastle group, and his leaving the House before the vote was taken, had a discouraging effect; many thought that had he not said 'he was a single man, Charles Townshend, *cum multis aliis*, would never have voted for the Peace, and that it was impolitic to make that declaration when there was no occasion for it'.[1] None the less, the extent of the defeat can only be accounted for by the miserably bad management on the opposition side — even of the leaders of the zealous young set, the Cavendishes, Villiers, T. Townshend, Onslow, and Midleton, did not take part in the division. Grafton, in his *Memoirs*, states that the numbers of the minority were so small, because,

as it was given out that there would be no division, many of the Opposition left the House on that idea. About sixty or seventy of those who remained did divide, and complained much that they were deserted by their friends. This misapprehension caused some ill humour; and the absentees came down the next day to divide on the Report against the Address.[2]

But even on 10 December the numbers were 227 to only 63, as many who had voted in the minority the previous day did not vote again.

Newcastle ascribed the defeat, in a large measure, to the extraordinary behaviour of the young Yorkes. While Hardwicke in the House of Lords spoke against the Preliminaries, in the Commons Royston voted for them and Charles left the House without voting.

This gave such an alarm to all our friends [wrote Newcastle to Hardwicke on 19 December] that it was impossible to rally them

except the part Mr. Pitt took in it, who is always great, and, in some parts of his speech, upon this occasion, as great as ever he was in his life'; *Bedford Correspondence*, vol. iii. p. 168.

[1] Lady Temple to her husband, 17 December; *Grenville Papers*, vol. ii. p. 22.

[2] See *Autobiography and Political Correspondence of Augustus Henry, 3rd Duke of Grafton*, edited by Sir William Anson (1898), p. 24.

afterwards. Many immediately took their part upon it. My friend, Mr. Rawlinson Erle, and Mr. Cocks of the Ordnance and, I believe, Sir Wyndham Knatchbull [1] voted against us, contrary to what they had done the night before.[2]

Lists of the minority in the divisions of 9 and 10 December have been preserved, and were even published early in 1763. But there is usually a margin of uncertainty about the division lists of that time. There are no less than four in the Newcastle Papers for 9-10 December, all marked the same way — 'List of those who voted in either one, or the other, of the last questions' — and no two of them absolutely tally.[3] On 25 January 1763 Midleton wrote to Newcastle :

Wilkes's [4] list of the Minorities will be published this day, but is not yet out. He does not make the two amount to above 96 ; yet I do not think that he could controvert any of those who are on the list which your Grace read to me on Sunday. Wilkes would be very much obliged to your Grace for a copy of your list, for the sake of correcting any mistakes or omissions which may be found in his first edition, by a second.[5]

Newcastle replied the same day :

As to my list, I am very far from being sure, that it is so correct, that I dare send it to any body to publish. . . . I am very sorry, that an incorrect list should come out; it will hurt our friends. . . . I am sure you will take care, not to discourage Mr. Wilkes; if your Lordship should, in discourse, have occasion to mention my name, I beg, you would make my best compliments to him. . . .

---

[1] Cocks was a nephew, and Knatchbull a grand-nephew, of Lady Hardwicke.

[2] Add. MSS. 32945, ff. 313-14.

[3] Each of these four lists has been bound in a different volume of the Newcastle Papers. The earliest, in the handwriting of George Onslow (Add. MSS. 33035, ff. 50-1), contains 107 names (the numbering shows only 106, as the name of John Page is inserted but not counted). The next in point of time (Add. MSS. 33000, ff. 232-5) still contained in its original draft 107 names, but one was subsequently crossed out. The next list (Add. MSS. 32946, ff. 273-6) omits six names from the previous, and adds five new ones, and thus finishes with only 106 ; subsequently two names were crossed out in this list. These, and one more, are omitted from the next list (Add. MSS. 33002, ff. 476-8), which closes the series with only 103 names.

[4] He obviously means 'Wilkie's' ; John Wilkie was a bookseller and publisher in St. Paul's Churchyard.

[5] Add. MSS. 32946, f. 169.

P.S. Our friends might be extremely angry, if they knew, any list of their names, came from me.[1]

Wilkie's list appeared with only 98 names,[2] but it has this advantage over Newcastle's lists that it gives separately the names of the Members who voted on 9 December, and then adds the new voters of the next day. For the first night there are the full 67 (this includes the two tellers), but only 31 additional names are given for the second division.

On 9 December no less than 12 of the 67 were Tories,[3] who thus, on that crucial division, formed almost the same proportion among the minority opposed to the Court as in the whole House ; 12 were merchants [4] (one of these had, however, already been counted among the Tories) ; three 'East-Indians',[5] three Members connected with Pitt and Temple,[6] and two with Cumberland ; [7] besides a good number of independent 'country Whigs'.[8] It was only on the second day that the Newcastle group came up in better numbers — seven relatives of his,[9] two of his oldest and most trusted friends,[10] several dependants of his,[11] his City friends,[12] his new ally Legge with John Buller, three Cavendishes with G. V. Vernon, etc., etc.[13]

[1] Add. MSS. 32946, f. 206.

[2] It is reprinted in *The History of the Late Minority* (1765), pp. 85-8.

[3] William Beckford, T. Cholmondeley, Sir W. Codrington, G. Cooke, S. Egerton, R. Holt, Sir R. Long, James Long, E. Popham, H. M. Praed, D. Rolle, and T. Staunton.

[4] W. Beckford, B. Burton, J. and N. Calvert, B. Fisher, two Fonnereaus, F. Honywood, Sir R. Ladbroke, J. Mawbey, J. Thomlinson, and W. Willy.

[5] H. C. Boulton, Lord Clive, and J. Walsh.

[6] Bamber Gascoyne, James Grenville, and John Wilkes.

[7] Lord Ancram and J. Fitzwilliam.

[8] *E.g.* Sir G. Armytage, Sir J. Barrington, William Clayton, Sir G. M. Metham, Sir F. Vincent, etc.

[9] G. Onslow, T. Pelham, Sir F. Poole, J. Shelley, T. Townshend and his son, and Lord Villiers.

[10] John White and John Page.

[11] *E.g.* John Butler, Member for Sussex, James West, who had been Newcastle's Secretary to the Treasury, Andrew Wilkinson, his Yorks. agent, etc.

[12] William Baker, Joseph Mellish, and Thomas Walpole.

[13] With Newcastle's lists of the minority on 9 and 10 December appears an 'additional list' of other Members whom he still looked upon as friends. There are five copies of that 'additional list', again scattered among different volumes of the Newcastle Papers : the earliest, in the handwriting of George Onslow, Add. MSS. 33035, f. 52 ; the next two in the same volume, ff. 53-4 and 110-11 ; the fourth, Add. MSS. 32946, ff. 277-8, and the fifth and

The next day Newcastle, with a mind oppressed and chaotic, in a handwriting more illegible than ever, scribbled 'Memorandums', a mass of confused and sometimes incomprehensible notes, so that even his faithful chaplain, Thomas Hurdis, after many years of practice, was not able to disentangle two or three passages.[1]

Mems.   NEWCASTLE HOUSE, *December* 11, 1762.

Mr. Egerton — message to me — not to be carried by the Duke of Bridgewater and the Bishop of Bangor — I am to carry them.[2]

Mr. Rigby — omne quod exit in hausen [inausum ?] I detest — took pains to declare that the Attorney General was gone.

The Attorney General — Chaplin spoke against — Sir George Armitage, very well — Sir George Saville spoke — admirably well — grateful people — the poor, to be sure, crowded upon their knees to sue for peace.

Duke of Bedford.

Crabb Boulton with us — Major against us.

The Fonnereaus not there.

Onslow extremely well — Jack Shelley spoke extremely well — Solicitor-General strong and boisterous against — the Attorney General — spoke admirably well — Adams against us.[3]

most complete, Add. MSS. 33002, ff. 476-8. At the end of this last list appears the following calculation :

Voted	103	Additional List . .	49
X deduct . . .	13	Q. deduct . . .	10
	90		39
Additional List . .	39		
	129		

Voted					103
Additional List . . .					49
In all					152

The thirteen names among those who had voted in the minority marked with an 'X', are those of Lord Ancram who sold his seat to the Court, of the two Fonnereaus who sold their votes, and of Bamber Gascoyne who was on the point of accepting office ; and of nine Tories on whom Newcastle felt that he could not altogether rely.

[1] Newcastle's draft, Add. MSS. 33000, ff. 278-9 ; Hurdis's copy, *ibid.* ff. 223-4.

[2] The meaning of this seems to be that Samuel Egerton, M.P. for Cheshire, said that he could not be influenced by his relatives, Francis Egerton, Duke of Bridgwater, and John Egerton, Bishop of Bangor, but would adhere to Newcastle.

[3] John Chaplin, of Blankney, M.P. for Stamford, was a son-in-law of Lord Exeter, and connected in politics with the Duke of Ancaster ; Sir G. Armytage, M.P. for York, and Sir G. Savile, M.P. for Yorkshire, were

Next Question. A Commission of Accounts.

Q. Whether a Committee of Accounts is necessary — or a secret committee — Sir George Colebrooke.

I shall be with the majority.

All the Tories down.

Mr. Penton — the first night — Sir John Morgan with us — Cholmley of Chester — the Morgans absent.

Lord Grey with us — Duke of Portland strong with us — better times for your friends and mine — Whichcotte against us — Sir Ellis Cunliffe absent.

George Brudenell went away. [Subsequently added in the margin : 'against'.]

Burton ⎱ with us.
Joseph Mellish ⎰

People must be put under some direction.[1]

Here follow again the names of various Members, and notes as to whether they had been in the House, how they had voted, etc. ; and again some general reflections :

Some question must be thought of.

To be sent to Mr. Pitt for his approbation, angry at what past the first night.

Some resolution must be taken immediately.

'Rockinghams'; H. Crabb Boulton, M.P. for Worcester, an East India director, usually went with Clive ; J. Major, M.P. for Scarborough, had been won over to the Court by Sandwich and Fox (see pp. 329-30) ; the Fonnereaus who sat for the Suffolk boroughs of Aldeburgh and Sudbury, had voted with the Opposition on 9 December but, for the sake of contracts, joined the Court ; John Shelley was a nephew of Newcastle and his nominee for East Retford ; G. Onslow, M.P. for Surrey, was married to Shelley's sister. The Solicitor-General was Fletcher Norton, M.P. for Wigan ; G. Adams, M.P. for Saltash, was a nephew of Lord Anson, who had been a son-in-law of Hardwicke — Adams usually went with the Yorkes.

[1] Henry Penton, M.P. for Winchester, was a grand-nephew of Joseph Gulston, M.P. for Poole, who still adhered to Newcastle ; but Penton did not vote with the minority in either division. Sir John Morgan, M.P. for Herefordshire, and Thomas Cholmondeley, M.P. for Cheshire, were both Tories ; Cholmondeley appears in all the lists of the minority, John Morgan in none. The Morgans who were absent were Thomas Morgan, of Tredegar, M.P. for Breconshire ; his son Thomas, M.P. for Brecon Town, and his nephew William, M.P. for Monmouthshire. Lord Grey, the son of the Earl of Stamford, was M.P. for Staffordshire, and a Rockingham Whig. T. Whichcote, M.P. for Lincolnshire, had in the past been a follower of Newcastle, but went over to the Court with the Ancaster family. Sir Ellis Cunliffe, M.P. for Liverpool, B. Burton, of the Bank of England, M.P. for Camelford, and Joseph Mellish, M.P. for Grimsby, were merchants ; G. B. Brudenell, M.P. for Stamford, was a cousin of James Brudenell, a nephew of Burton, and a brother-in-law of Sir S. Fludyer. Burton, Mellish, and G. B. Brudenell adhered to the Opposition.

And in conclusion a note which I am unable to explain :

D.N. £5000 in two months — an unlimited credit.
1000 g. last week — 2000 yesterday and this day.

A plan must be formed, and some one must take the lead —
this Newcastle had repeated for a long time past ; but who
was to do it, and how ? All the men Newcastle could think of
were : the insignificant Legge, who until his sudden disgrace
at Leicester House, over the Hampshire election at the end of
1759, had never been a friend of Newcastle ; Charles Yorke,
who had clearly deserted him ; and Charles Townshend, who
invariably played his own hand (and, as a rule, played it badly).
In that middle generation who had learnt their politics under
Walpole and the Pelhams, and were now about forty or fifty
years old, there was not one man who was fit to lead an opposition. On 12 December Newcastle wrote to Devonshire :

I have had a long conversation with my friend Legge. . . . He
has talked very openly to me ; I think he has lost some part of his
courage. He despairs, as indeed almost every body does, of our
making a good figure. He is afraid of being the Leader *Designatus*,
as he calls it, of this opposition. . . .
He says, he is not qualified to be the sole Leader in the House of
Commons. That he shall have nobody with him ; . . . but . . . if
Charles Townshend (of whose good intentions for us, he much
doubts) and Mr. Attorney General, would undertake it with him ;
or, I believe, if the Attorney General would join with him, and assure
him of the concurrence of his family in the House of Commons,
Legge would do his part and act with courage.
I endeavour'd to shew him, that, if something of this kind could
not be established, the whole must be dissolved ; or, our friends
would be a rope of sand ; and expose themselves every day ; and
the principal argument I made use of, was, that his undertaking it
was the only way to hinder our friends from doing rash things, and
exposing themselves, and us every day.[1]

The same day Newcastle wrote to Thomas Walpole :

I always fear'd the attacking the Peace, and you know it. We
must go on, with spirit ; but at the same time, with prudence and
moderation. We are endeavouring to persuade Mr. Legge, and the
Attorney General, to take the conduct upon them, to whom our

[1] Add. MSS. 32945, ff. 280-1.

friends should resort for advice ; and my nephew Charles Townshend, (who never comes near me) may be at the head, if he pleases ;
and he will be sounded upon it. At present, we act like children,
and expose ourselves, and our friends : many of our friends are still
angry.[1]

But others were less sanguine as to the possibility of collecting the defeated, demoralised forces, especially if no better
leader could be thought of than Legge, or the problematical
Charles Yorke, or the impossible Charles Townshend. James
West wrote to Newcastle the same day (12 December) :

If there be any plan of opposition in general, I fear it will be very
uphill work, against such a majority flushed with success, and some
of our best friends, out of humour, others skulking, repenting, and
wishing for the loaves and fishes superior to any other attachment ;
unless Mr. Pitt was to set heartily in conjunction with your Graces
friends, on some fixed plan of Revolution principles, for tho' no man
has a higher opinion of the two persons mentioned, yet . . . [they]
will scarce obtain that following which is necessary to keep together
and to encrease the present Minority : and I should be very sorry to
see a character so respectable and so esteemed, as your Grace is at
present, except with some few violent persons, rendered less so by
an opposition to the measures of the publick, in trifling divisions,
which become contemptible, by violence being added to weakness.[2]

And Devonshire wrote to Newcastle on 14 December, after
a talk with Legge :

. . . it struck me that he was afraid to undertake the task, I agreed
with him that he alone wou'd not do, but that if Charles Townshend
wou'd undertake it and the Attorney Genl. give his assistance upon
proper occasions, something might be done, he did not seem in my
opinion to relish it ; and indeed, my dear Lord, I fear there is nothing
to be done. I look upon Mr. Pitt as gone, Mr. Townshend very near
the same, . . . and the Marquess [of Rockingham] agreed with me
that we had much better lye by for the present, otherways we shou'd
only show our weakness and expose ourselves. . . .[3]

Newcastle's political building was in ruins, and now he
knew it himself. He wrote to Hardwicke on 14 December :

Your Lordship will easily imagine that the contemptible figure
we make, (and myself more particularly) in both Houses, goes to my

[1] Add. MSS. 32945, f. 285.   [2] *Ibid.* f. 278.   [3] *Ibid* f. 287.

heart; and I don't see my way out of it. I must either abandon the few friends I have left; or leave them to themselves, to expose themselves, and us.

It is but too true, what Mr. Fox said, at first to the Duke of Cumberland, viz., my Lord Bute has got over all the Duke of Newcastle's friends. Never was man, who had had it in his power, to serve, to make, to chuse, so great a part of the Members of both Houses, so abandon'd as I am at present: but that which hurts me the most, (I say every thing, I think, to your Lordship) is, that, I find, it affects the dear Dutchess of Newcastle extremely; and that those very few friends, who have taken their fate with me, and resigned their employments; and those who, by their behaviour in the House of Commons, expect, every hour, to be removed, are most extremely hurt; and rather blame me, for exposing them, and feeding them up with hopes of support, where they found none.[1]

The Massacre of the Pelhamite Innocents

Newcastle wrote in his 'Memorandum' of 11 December: 'Next question — a Commission of Accounts'. He was afraid of a hostile inquiry into his financial conduct of the War — which had been perfectly honourable, though probably inefficient — and of consequent impeachment; whereas, with a little judgment, he ought to have known that he could safely leave the care of such an inquiry to the Paymaster-General of the Forces. 'Mr. F[ox]', wrote Shelburne, 'was most unaccountably afraid of it — insomuch that he could not conceal it from any body'; [2] Fox would probably have found it easier to account for his fears than for the money, but anyhow nothing came of that Commission, which (according to Shelburne) is the way of official inquiries. Still, Newcastle was scared, and started immediately to compile lists of 'sure friends', and of those he could trust 'on a personal point'. The first list, of 13 December, puts their numbers at 88 and 94; [3] the second, of 17 December, classifies 105 as 'sure friends', 20 as safe 'on a personal point', and 22 as 'absent'; [4] in the third, of 18 December, the figures are 112, 21, and 15.[5]

---

[1] *Ibid.* f. 289.
[2] See Fitzmaurice, *op. cit.* vol. i. p. 140.
[3] Add. MSS. 33000, ff. 226-8.
[4] *Ibid.* ff. 229-31.　　　　　　　　　　　[5] *Ibid.* ff. 241-4.

It was not, however, by the obsolete method of impeachment that the victorious party was to take its revenge ; what occurred at Christmas 1762 was a massacre of the Pelhamite innocents. Horace Walpole writes in his *Memoirs of the Reign of King George III* : [1]

A more severe political persecution never raged. Whoever, holding a place, had voted against the preliminaries, was instantly dismissed.[2] The friends and dependents of the Duke of Newcastle were particularly cashiered ; and this cruelty was extended so far, that old servants, who had retired and been preferred to very small places, were rigorously hunted out and deprived of their livelihood.

When Newcastle planned to 'strike terror' through resignations he was thinking of 'persons of high rank or great distinction' not of minor followers who, if unprovided for, would become 'a burthen' on him while their places would furnish the Court with additional patronage. But no Government could be expected willingly to provide for the servants, political or domestic, of the Opposition, and Newcastle vainly flattered himself that it would be left to him to decide who was, or was not, to relinquish his place. On 24 November Fox wrote to Bute that he would recommend 'a thorough rout' of Newcastle's dependants, and on the 30th he urged that Newcastle should be deprived immediately of his three Lieutenancies.[3]

---

[1] Vol. i. pp. 184-5.

[2] This was done by order of George III. He wrote to Bute on December 10, at 5.24 P.M. :

I thank my dear friend for his intelligence of this day's division ; I think . . . Col. Fitzroy, and Mr. Robinson can't be too soon dismissed, the latter is still Secretary to the Congress. Sir Alexr. Gilmour has no right now to what he wished in Ireland, for he had no occasion to attend Parliament this day he being on guard consequently was forced to ask my leave to attend the House this day, which was never before asked when intending to oppose Government.

And again on 11 December :

I think Fitzroy, Thomas Townshend and any other that have been with them cant be too soon dismissed, that will frighten others.

Thomas Robinson M.P., the son of Lord Grantham, had since June 1761 drawn a salary at the rate of £2800 a year as 'Secretary to the Embassy at the Congress of Augsburg', though it had been clear for a good long time that that Congress would never meet.

[3] Summarised in the 'Register' of Bute's correspondence ; Add. MSS. 36796, f. 168. None of Fox's letters of 1762 can be found among the Bute

The execution of these measures was, however, postponed till after the decisive victory had been won.

On 19 December Newcastle wrote to Hardwicke in naive consternation :

I saw, from the beginning, that *my* friends *in the House of Commons* were condemned ; that I did not, and do not complain of. . . . But their carrying their resentment so far, as to remove all my friends and relations from offices, not in the House of Commons, and where the objects of their resentment could not offend . . . is, I say, such a stretch of power, as is hardly constitutional.[1]

And to Devonshire on 23 December :

I hear . . . my friend Mr. Rigby says, the Duke of Newcastle would have turned out the King's friend, my Lord Bute ; why should not the King turn out the Duke of Newcastle's friends ? I have no objection to that ; but why should Mr. Fox turn out all those poor, unhappy men to starve, who have no demerit of their own, are in offices incapable of a seat in Parliament, and who have been, at any time, put into those offices by the Duke of Newcastle.[2]

. . . your Grace's old friend, my Lord Gower, said the other night, that *they* would turn out every Custom House officer in Sussex, down to offices of 50£ pr. an. only.[3]

The list of the proscribed was becoming longer and longer, and Newcastle, with rising indignation, was echoing the plaints and laments which reached him from all sides. He wrote to Hardwicke on 5 January 1763 :

Indeed, my dear Lord, these repeated instances of cruelty, and the miserable scenes, I see every day, of misery and destruction to all my poor friends, whom I have ever had an opportunity to serve, almost weigh me down ; and nothing but an active resentment in my friends can restore me. I believe, there never was, such an instance of cruelty and barbarity, to single out one man, and all his dependants and relations, in this manner.[4]

MSS. at present. — The same day Fox wrote to Shelburne urging the same point (the letter is preserved among the Shelburne Papers at Bowood) :

For God's sake take away the D. of Newcastle's 3 Lieut[cys] before Granby comes, who may be here to day or to morrow.

The enemy is at a stand. Why do we stand too ? Spirit and dispatch should go together, indeed will ; a dilatory pursuit will soon be no pursuit.

See also Ilchester, *Henry Fox*, ii. 214-15.

[1] Add. MSS. 32945, ff. 315-16.   [2] *Ibid.* f. 335.
[3] *Ibid.* f. 339.   [4] Add. MSS. 32946, ff. 67-8.

Charles Yorke, the Attorney-General, was undoubtedly one of the friends whom Newcastle expected to show 'an active resentment' — 'if that was the case, these violences would be soon stop'd'. Hardwicke, put on the defensive, answered with a gentle and justified counter-charge :

In truth, my dear Lord, this matter should have been more particularly consider'd, and attended to, before we went into an opposition against the approbation of the Peace. It should have been attended to how great a length of time your Grace had been in power, and had the filling up of almost all the places ; longer than any other Minister in our memories. It should have been consider'd that so many places during pleasure, fill'd up by you, were so many breaches, at which the enemy might enter, if they had inclination to do it. I am sure I pointed it out to your Grace in some of my letters, or conversations during the summer ; and my Lord Halifax particularly mention'd it to you as a consequence, that would give you great concern, in his last conversation with you at Claremont.[1]

Lists of minor officials, compiled with a view to eviction, are preserved among the papers of Charles Jenkinson, at that time Bute's Secretary to the Treasury. There is a 'List of Land Tax Receivers';[2] a 'List of several Persons holding Offices in the Customs by Patent during Pleasure',[3] a 'Supplemental List of Custom-house Offices with Observations',[4] lists of Surveyors-General,[5] of Auditors and Receivers 'of the King's Land Revenue',[6] and of officials in the Excise, Salt, Stamp, Alienation Offices, etc.[7]

Jenkinson's lists of December 1762 survey the whole field, Newcastle's of January 1763 show where the blows fell, or were about to fall — for he received secret information and warnings from Milward Rowe, the Chief Clerk of the Treasury, an 'innocent' who was not massacred ; 'whose name', wrote H. V. Jones on 5 February, 'it is unnecessary for me to entreat your Grace, not to mention, upon this occasion'.[8] There is a 'List of persons to be *removed* and *appointed*, January 23',[9] another of 5 February,[10] a 'List of Sussex gentlemen removed

---

[1] 5 January, 1763 ; Add. MSS. 32946, ff. 58-9.
[2] Add. MSS. 38334, f. 206.
[3] *Ibid.* ff. 211-12.   [4] *Ibid.* ff. 214-15.   [5] *Ibid.* f. 216.
[6] Add. MSS. 38335, ff. 43-4.   [7] *Ibid.* ff. 55-67.
[8] Add. MSS. 32946, f. 321.   [9] *Ibid.* ff. 179-81.   [10] *Ibid.* ff. 323-4.

from their places',[1] and lastly a paper drawn up with a view to restoration when Newcastle was on the point of resuming office in July 1765 : 'List of Officers removed in the years 1762 and 1763 whose appointments arise in the Treasury.' [2]

It is unnecessary, and would be tiring, to attempt an analysis of all these lists — one will suffice ; and I choose the Sussex list, although in it the political character of the appointments is, if anything, less marked than in some others — with Newcastle Sussex origin by itself ranked as a qualification for office.[3]

List of Sussex Gentlemen removed from their Places.[4]

Excise.

Mr. Poole, Commissioner
Mr. Steele, Comptroller of Accounts
Sir John Bridger, Commissioner of Appeals
Mr. Milton, Register

Customs.

Mr. Henry Shelley, Searcher
Mr. John Pelham, Inspector General of Exports and Imports
Mr. Milward, Surveyor of the Riding Officers for Kent
Mr. Battine, Surveyor of the Riding Officers for Sussex
Mr. Ferd. Poole, Petty Customer
Mr. Lambe, Tally Cutter in the Exchequer

---

[1] Add. MSS. 33001, f. 7.

[2] *Ibid.* ff. 23-4. I do not deal here with the lists of friends in the two Houses of Parliament, but only with the small fry of officials. The names of peers and commoners who had resigned their places, or had been dismissed, are given in a paper marked 29 August 1763, 'Lords and Members of Parliament removed, or resigned ; or who are to be consider'd' (Add. MSS. 32950, ff. 277-9). It should, however, be noted that the list includes also many who were to be 'consider'd', without having held any places in 1762.

[3] The following passage in a letter from Newcastle to Lord Deskfoord, dated 7 September 1754, sums up Newcastle's theory of appointments :

> We have lately given a great mark of our impartiality in England, having remov'd seven landwaiters and other officers in the port of Bristol, for making false returns of *weight of tobacco* ; tho' those officers were put in, one by me as a Sussex man, and almost all the others for being themselves, or their friends, useful in elections (Add. MSS. 32736, ff. 451-2).

[4] Add. MSS. 33001, f. 7.

Stamps.

Mr. Turner, Register in the Wine Licence Branch

Salt.

Mr. Michell, Treasurer

Alienation Office.

Mr. Courthorpe
Mr. Steele, Receiver General

Hawkers and Pedlars.

Mr. Coates
Mr. Tredcroft in the Customs and at Gibraltar

Who were these 'innocents'? and how had they come by their places?

Edward Milward, Surveyor of the Riding Officers for Kent (see under 'Customs'), wrote from Hastings, on 25 February 1761:

Had not a very great command of interest rested with me, the routs in the adjoyning Corporations [Winchelsea and Seaford] might have blown up a little dust here, but as matters stand I will carry the election for his Grace of Newcastle against all interest whatever.[1]

On 27 March he was able to report that Newcastle's candidates had been unanimously elected — 'I took the whole management on my self agreable to your Graces command'.[2] And on 16 December 1760 he had offered to help also in the county but hoped Newcastle would think him 'worthy of the same addition for extra services in Kent, as Mr. Battine is allowed in Sussex'.[3] This William Battine appears in the list of the 'Sussex gentlemen' as 'Surveyor of the Riding Officers for Sussex'.[4]

The name of Thomas Steele appears twice in the list. He was Receiver-General in the Alienation Office, the work in the

---

[1] Add. MSS. 32919, f. 281.   [2] Add. MSS. 32921, f. 109.
[3] Add. MSS. 32916, f. 133.
[4] When in December 1760 he and his father had been asked by Legge for their support in Hampshire, William Battine sen. inquired with Newcastle what he wished them to do 'as neither of us stur an inch in any election affairs without your Graces direction or approbation' (*ibid.* f. 45).

office being done by deputy and he drawing a net income of
£300 a year from that sinecure ; he had received it for his
electoral services at Chichester.[1] The other office — of Comptroller of Accounts in the Excise — Steele held in trust for John
Butler, Member for Sussex, a friend and nominee of Newcastle ; as places in the Excise were incompatible with a seat
in Parliament, Butler could not hold that sinecure in his own
name but received the profits, which amounted to £700 a year.

In 1761, during a Parliamentary contest at Seaford, a letter
was sent to Newcastle signed, among others, by H. Poole, H.
Shelley, and William Michell, who in the Sussex list appear
as Commissioner of the Excise, Searcher of the Customs, and
Treasurer of the Salt Office : 'There is not the lest reason for
you to be alarmed about the election. But upon a consultation
we are uanimously of opinion . . .'[2] This was Newcastle's
electoral board at Seaford. Michell was one of Newcastle's
chief political agents in Sussex, active both in the county and
in various boroughs — Lewes, Seaford, New Shoreham, etc.
Henry Shelley was mainly concerned with Lewes and Seaford ;
while Henry Poole's additional title to consideration and sinecures was that his mother was a Pelham — a first cousin of
Newcastle's — and that his father, Sir Francis Poole, was
Newcastle's nominee in the House of Commons for Lewes.
The Poole family were poor and when, by the loss of Minorca,
Henry Poole was deprived of his sinecure in that island he
wrote to Newcastle that without some help 'it would be impossible for Sir Francis Poole to continue at Lewes'. Consequently
Sir Francis's secret service pension was raised from £300 to
£500, 'the first vacancy' in the Excise was earmarked for
Henry Poole,[3] and his younger brother Ferdinando was made
Collector of Petty Customs (£150 p.a.). Well provided for at
the expense of the public, the Pooles were able to continue their
services to Newcastle in the House of Commons, in Sussex,
and in various Sussex boroughs.

[1] Steele's son, Thomas Steele jun., was Member for Chichester 1780–
1807 ; Secretary to the Treasury 1783–1791 ; Joint Paymaster-General
1791–1804 ; P.C. 1791 ; Commissioner of the Board of Control 1791–93.
[2] Add. MSS. 32920, f. 416.
[3] See *The Structure of Politics*, pp. 454.

Mr. Thomas Lamb, 'Tally Cutter in the Exchequer', was Newcastle's election manager at Rye. Thus, *e.g.*, on 20 March 1761 Phillips Gybbon, Member for that borough, wrote to Newcastle that its Corporation was nearly £1000 in debt and wanted to have it paid by whoever was to be Gybbon's colleague in the next Parliament; Mr. Lamb had received 'repeated directions from the Corporation to let the new candidate be acquainted with this circumstance that he may not be surprized when it is mentioned to him at Rye as it most certainly will be'. Mr. Lamb therefore 'begs he may know what your Grace would have him say when he returns to Rye in relation to this affair; he proposes to set out to morrow afternoon, which I beleive will be extreamly necessary to watch the motions of the adversary'.[1]

When in March 1761 Newcastle was threatened with an opposition in Sussex, his steward, Mr. Coates, sent him a list of those who had accepted the invitation to attend him at the county election and who would take charge of particular places.[2] This was Mr. Coates, Commissioner of Hawkers and Pedlars. His colleague, Mr. Tredcroft, was of a family which had long been established at Horsham and exercised a certain influence in its Parliamentary elections — this influence, in fact, survived far into the nineteenth century.[3]

The character and services of these officials, 'poor unhappy men . . . who have no demerit of their own', and 'are in offices incapable of a seat in Parliament',[4] are to some extent disguised in the lists which Newcastle drew up in January 1763

[1] Add. MSS. 32920, f. 366.
[2] Add. MSS. 32921, f. 179.
[3] See. W. Albery, *Parliamentary History of Horsham* (1927). When at the general election of 1747 the Pelhams supposed that Lord Irwin would not choose to return his son for Horsham, as he was still under age, they intended to suggest to him

> the bringing in some friend who might have a small employment and quit his seat when Mr. Ingram came of age. The person we thought of to suggest to you in that case was poor Mr. Tredcroft. He has a place in the West Indies and another provision which was thought both certain and profitable; but hitherto neither one nor the other have brought him in one shilling (*ibid.* p. 88).

At one time 'poor Mr. Tredcroft' was a candidate for a secret service pension; see Add. MSS. 33000, f. 83.
[4] See above p. 405.

but were well known to his successors at the Treasury, as will
be seen from the notes which Jenkinson placed against their
names.　Here are a few examples of how they are described in the
two sets of lists :

Newcastle's List.	Jenkinson's List.
(Add. MSS. 32944, ff. 178-81 ; 23 January 1763)	(Add. MSS. 38334, ff. 214-16 ; 18 December 1762)

Edward Milward. Surveyor of the Riding Officers for Kent, of Hastings ; a very good officer ; son-in-law of the late Mr. Collier and succeeded him in his office.

£250 a year. Appointed by the Duke of Newcastle ; his father was a manager for his Grace at Hastings and resigned in favour of the son who is likewise useful in that borough.

William Battine. Surveyor of the Riding Officers for Sussex, a most excellent officer ; . . . He is son to Major Battine, eighty years of age, who was recommended to this office . . . by Sir R. Walpole ; he and his son have enjoy'd it ever since ; and are, and ever were, most zealous and active friends to the Government.

Surveyor of Sussex. An election friend of the Duke of Newcastle's, lives in Sussex. £250 per annum.

Thomas Steele. Comptroller of Accounts, Recorder of Chichester, a zealous friend to the Government.

Comptroller of the Excise by patent during pleasure, 10 September 1756, has a salary of £2,120, for himself, deputy and clerks. . . . Steele is supposed to retain £700 p.a. for Mr. Butler's use and to pay the remainder to deputy and clerks and in taxes.

| William Michell. | Treasurer [of the Salt Office] known and beloved by all the gentlemen of Sussex ; many years *Under Sheriff.* | Cashier. For himself and clerks £430 p.a. A sinecure office. Mr. Michell was put in two or three years ago ; an attorney ; and a borough agent for the D. of N. ; lives in Sussex. |

The phrase which Newcastle used about some of these men — 'most zealous and active friends to the Government' — sums up their position, the dilemma in which they were now placed, and the contradictions inherent in Newcastle's own thesis. To whom did these men, appointed by Newcastle as First Lord of the Treasury, owe allegiance — to him, or to the office which he held no longer ? If they were indeed 'most zealous and active friends to the Government', and, in the words of one of them, were 'determined to support the interest of His Majesty and his Ministry against all opponents whatsoever',[1] they were left their places, but at the price of renouncing Newcastle, and were to him ungrateful wretches. But if they adhered to him, and were to continue looking after his electoral interests, could they still be described as 'most zealous and active friends to the Government', and was it reasonable to expect any Government to leave them where they were ?

Newcastle wished, as usual, to eat his cake and have it too, and counted on retaining the perquisites of office after having gone into opposition ; he tried to get away with Government property, and he failed. For men like William Michell, who remained with Newcastle [2] and were dismissed, did not, as a rule, represent much electoral strength, while among those who were in charge of organised borough interests Thomas Lamb of Rye was the only one to defy the Treasury. The letter which Edward Milward, the manager of Hastings, wrote to Newcastle

---

[1] The phrase was used by Griffith Davies, Collector of Customs at Harwich ; see *The Structure of Politics*, chapter on 'Two Treasury Boroughs'.

[2] 'I am so far from repenting that I spent the prime part of my life faithfully in his Grace's service', he wrote to Hurdis on 27 January 1763, 'that I rejoice at it, and would do the same if it came over again' ; Add. MSS. 32946, f. 228.

on 26 March 1763 [1] accurately describes the position in which men of his type were placed by Newcastle coming out against the Government :

I am truly sensible of the many civilitys I have received from your Grace for myself and friends and shall ever most gratefully acknowledge them, and your Grace may freely command me in all other matters (except in this particular at this time which must be attended with fatal consequences both to myself and friends). And it is not in my power to support an interest in this Corporation against the Treasury and Government for several years before an election without a very great expence to my self and more than I am able to support, all which I informed your Grace and friends in London. I beg leave to assure your Grace that nobody was more concerned at your quitting business than he who has the honor to be your Grace's etc.

A glance at the list of the 42 jurats and freemen of Hastings [2] explains Milward's difficulties ; 16 of them held places under the Government, of a joint annual value of £1580 (this includes Milward's own salary), and of the remaining 26, a good many were fathers, sons, brothers, etc., to the men thus provided for. If Milward had given up his place, how many of the others would have followed him ? They would have been 'much concerned' at his 'quitting business', and would have informed him that they could not afford to give up their places. Nor could the Government be reasonably expected to nurse Hastings for Newcastle at an expense of £1580 a year.

But the electoral aspect of Newcastle's civil service appointments is not the only justification of the 'massacre' of 1762–63. Whatever truth there may be in Rigby's assertion about the 'refractory' behaviour of officials appointed by Newcastle,[3] some of those who, if dismissed, would have figured among the

---

[1] Add. MSS. 32947, f. 325.   [2] Add. MSS. 33000, f. 289.
[3] See Rigby's letter to the Duke of Bedford, 3 February 1763, *Bedford Correspondence*, vol. iii. pp. 186-7 :

The Commissioners of all the Boards inferior and subordinate to the Treasury, such as Customs, Excise, Salt Duties, Taxes, &c., &c., had possessed themselves with a notion that Lord Bute could not maintain his ground, and that they should soon return under their old master. In consequence of this idea, they very foolishly and unjustifiably neglected not only even that civility which the First Lord of the Treasury had a right to expect from them, and they had been long enough used to pay, but also, in their official acts, demurred in their obedience to the

'innocents', can be proved to have gone even further, and to have played the part of Newcastle's spies against their new chiefs. The following letter of 26 August 1762, written by T. Ancel, the 'Office Keeper',[1] to Richard Turner, Newcastle's butler and 'Register in the Wine Licence Branch' in the Sussex list, may serve as an example :[2]

Dear Brother,

This evening arrived Mr. Dick from Russia, Mr. Lambe from the K. of Prussia, and Mr. Garstin from Prince Ferdinand together with one Dutch mail.

The heads of the news are. . . .

And here is another example of what Newcastle expected from men he had appointed : he was worried when in July 1762 he saw that the Treasury, so far from stopping payments, as he had foretold that it would, continued them even on an enlarged scale, without any obvious borrowing, and without putting an end to the German war. Anxious to know how they managed it, he wrote to Barrington on 5 August :

All the world is surprized at the payments made at the Treasury . . . and I am sure I am ; where they get the money. . . . Lord Bute told my Lord Hardwicke 'that . . . *it now appear'd* the Treasury had money enough to go on very well ; and that the Parliament would not meet 'till the usual time'. If this is so, your Lordship and, in consequence, myself, have been grossly imposed upon ; and shall make a very poor figure . . . to have laid so much stress upon a point which now comes out so strongly against us ; and to have carried it so far as to leave our offices upon it.

My honor is greatly concerned to have this matter entirely clear'd up. . . . I think, in justice I might desire of the Treasury themselves to know how this fact stands ; but I am sure, I have a *right* to demand of a clerk, whom I so lately put there, to have an account of the whole ; and if he had those qualities, which your Lordship thinks

Treasury orders. This was insufferable ; and no man can, with justice, blame any person in that high office for enforcing obedience to his orders. Such as continued refractory, therefore, have been removed ; and so absurd, cruel, and unaccountable has been the doctrine at Clare-mont upon this head, that, when friends and dependents of his Grace have been told, if they would only go to Lord Bute and ask their continuance of his Lordship as a favour, they should remain in their employments, they have been directed by the Duke of Newcastle not to do it.

[1] Add. MSS. 32942, f. 43.   [2] *Ibid.* f. 37.

he has, honor and gratitude would have engaged him to have given you information of it, without being called upon.[1]

Barrington answered on 12 August : 'I am endeavouring to find out the information your Grace wanted, by ways of my own, without applying to clerks.'[2] This did not please Newcastle.

I cannot agree with you [he wrote back on 15 August], that intelligence is not to be procured from clerks, provided those clerks owe their being such to them to whom they communicate any thing : Every clerk ought to trust his benefactor. It is *his* fault, if the publick suffers from such information ; and every clerk, out of gratitude for past favors does, and will reason, in that way. . . . But in this, you know, *we differ* ; and I believe, whatever the reasoning may be, the practice has always been on my side.[3]

But why then had Newcastle been so indignant at the behaviour of Samuel Martin, a Leicester House man ? or how could he blame a new Minister for dismissing clerks, however insignificant, if the supplying of information to their late chiefs was to be their 'practice' ?

When in 1765 Newcastle resumed office in the Rockingham Government, he pressed for the dismissal of the officials by whom Bute and Grenville had replaced his own nominees. Rockingham protested — 'I must say, my dear Lord, if your Grace expects me to act upon a spirit of retaliation — not of restitution — I can neither justify it to my feelings — nor to what I think in the end will prove politically right'.[4]

Epilogue

While Fox, with the King's consent, was ousting Newcastle's adherents from their places under the Government, the

---

[1] Add. MSS. 32941, ff. 160-1. The clerk was undoubtedly Thomas Bradshaw who had served under Barrington at the War Office and, in December 1761, had been transferred to the Treasury (see Treasury Books at the Record Office, T. 29/34, p. 206 : 'December 17, 1761 : Bradshaw : Admitted the fourth of the Principal Clerks of the Treasury to fill up the vacancy occasioned by Mr. Postlethwayte's death'). In 1767 Bradshaw became Joint Secretary to the Treasury, and in 1772 was made one of the Lords of the Admiralty. He sat in Parliament for Harwich, 1767-68, and for Saltash from 1768 till his death in 1774.   [2] *Ibid.* ff. 221-2.
[3] *Ibid.* ff. 245-6   [4] Add. MSS. 32970, ff. 226-7.

King dreamt of a very different purge, of which Fox himself would have been the first victim. Some time in November 1762, George III wrote to Bute, obviously in reply to an intimation from him that he wished shortly to resign the Treasury :

Now I come to the part of my dear friend's letter that gives me the greatest concern, as it overturns all the thoughts that have alone kept up my spirits in these bad times ; I own I had flattered myself when Peace was once established that my dear friend would have assisted me in purging out corruption, and in those measures that no man but he that has the Prince's real affection can go through ; then when we were both dead our memories would have been respected and esteemed to the end of time, now what shall we be able to say that Peace is concluded, and my dear friend becoming a Courtier, for I fear mankind will say so, the Ministry remains composed of the most abandoned men that ever held those offices ; thus instead of reformation, the Ministers being vicious this country will grow if possible worse ; let me attack the irreligious, the covetous &c. as much as I please, that will be of no effect, for the Ministers being of that stamp, men will with reason think they may advance to the highest pitch of their ambition through every infamous way that their own black hearts or the rascality of their superiors can point out.

Remember what Fox formerly said, we will give Lord B. a Garter and a Court employment and then we may do as we please.

Before long, both Fox and Bute were to withdraw from the political stage, disappointed and embittered men, leaving the fruits of their victory to George Grenville, for whom, at the time when the battle was fought, neither the King nor Bute, neither Pitt nor Newcastle nor Fox, had any use or regard ; and from whose tedious hectorings, two and a half years later, Cumberland and the Opposition Whigs were to be called in to deliver the King. But as for a 'reformation' of English political life, even the beginnings of it were to be delayed for twenty years — and what years ! And after that, very different hands were to undertake the work — a party of which the origin can be traced in December 1762, and of which the paternity is often ascribed to Newcastle, though in truth his part was 'done', and he knew not 'what *they* will do'.

*　　　*　　　*

I dined at my nephew Onslow's [wrote Newcastle to Devonshire on 23 December 1762], where were, the Marquess of Rockingham,

Lord Bessborough, Lord Frederick Cavendish, Lord Midleton, Lord Villiers, Tom Pelham, Tommy Townshend, Offley &c. They were all, except Offley, violent for a Club; Lord Bessborough as much as any of them; and, I think, at last the Marquess gave into them. They said, there was nothing to be done without it; that they must collect their friends; and they seem'd much elated with the effect, which the violences and persecutions have had every where.

I opposed, to the utmost, these Clubs or meetings; that they carried much the air of faction. One of them, (I think it was my Lord Villiers, or Onslow) said, they liked it the better; they were glad the Ministers should see, there was a faction against them. I then said, it would expose their weakness; for no one doubtful friend would come near them. I have done my part; what *they* will do, I know not.[1]

On 26 December 1762, Kinnoull, representative of the old gang of Newcastle's collaborators, wrote to him about these plans of the young men:

As to the Club proposed, it appears to me to be a measure attended with many bad consequences. . . . For my own part, I never will join in a measure which appears to me factious. But it is of little consequence what I do; I shall never be a favorite with the young men of spirit. . . . I do not consider myself at all in what I say; I consider your Grace alone, your character, your reputation, and the consideration due to your age, your experience and your abilities. . . . Your Grace's dignity and credit which is great both at home and abroad, must not be committed by these very worthy, very amiable, but very zealous and much heated young friends.[2]

The next move of the 'young friends' is disapprovingly mentioned by Newcastle in a letter to Hardwicke, on 31 January 1763:

My Lord Villiers, who is a very considerable, as well as amiable young man, and many of our young friends have proposed to me, that they should go in a body to Mr. Pitt. That I am entirely against. In the first place, such a publick application to him, would frighten him; in the next, it would not be proper upon many accounts.[3]

But when the results achieved by the Club became apparent Newcastle, probably in perfectly good faith, took to himself the credit for measures which he had originally discouraged; and

---

[1] Add. MSS. 32945, f. 341.   [2] *Ibid.* f. 385.
[3] Add. MSS. 32946, f. 264.

history has left to him a good deal of it, mistaking the survival of a name for an inheritance of personality and for a continuity of ideas.

The Society, which we had so successfully established by our dinners [Newcastle wrote to Kinnoull on 3 June 1763], of the most respectable persons in both Houses ; of which Mr. Pitt, and my Lord Temple, were principal parts, had given such a new spirit to our affairs, that soon shew'd itself in both Houses ; and particularly in the House of Lords, to such a degree, that in the opinion of every body, *that* was one of the principal causes of the sudden, and most surprizing retreat of the Minister.[1]

My next book, if ever written, will be on 'The Rise of Party'.

[1] Add. MSS. 32949, f. 15.

APPENDIX A

TORIES RETURNED TO PARLIAMENT AT THE GENERAL ELECTION OF 1761

England (104)

Robert Henley-Ongley	M.P. for	Bedfordshire.
Francis Herne	„	Bedford.
Henry Pye } Arthur Vansittart	„	Berkshire.
John Morton	„	Abingdon.
Richard Lowndes	„	Buckinghamshire.
William Drake } Benet Garrard	„	Agmondesham.
Samuel Egerton } Thomas Cholmondeley	„	Cheshire.
Thomas Grosvenor } Rd. Wilbraham Bootle	„	Chester City.
Sir John St. Aubyn, bart. } James Buller	„	Cornwall.
John Parker	„	Bodmin.
Jonathan Rashleigh	„	Fowey.
H. Mackworth Praed	„	St. Ives.
Sir Henry Harpur, bart.	„	Derbyshire.
Sir William Courtenay, bart. } Sir Rd. W. Bamfylde, bart.	„	Devonshire.
John Tuckfield } John Rolle Walter	„	Exeter.
Henry R. Courtenay	„	Honiton.
Dennis Rolle	„	Barnstaple.
George Pitt } Humphrey Sturt	„	Dorset.
Sir Gerard Napier, bart.	„	Bridport.
Richard Glover	„	Weymouth and Melcombe Regis.
John Tempest	„	Durham City.
Robert Lane	„	York City.
William Harvey	„	Essex.
Charles Gray	„	Colchester.

Thomas Chester ⎱
Norborne Berkeley⎰ . . M.P. for Gloucestershire.

Jarrit Smith . . . „ Bristol.
Charles Barrow . . . „ Gloucester City.
Sir William Codrington, bart. . „ Tewkesbury.

Sir John Morgan, bart.⎱
Velters Cornwall ⎰ . . „ Herefordshire.

John Symons . . . . „ Hereford City.
Chase Price . . . . „ Leominster.
Jacob Houblon . . . „ Hertfordshire.

Richard Milles⎱
Thomas Best ⎰ . . . „ Canterbury.

William Northey . . . „ Maidstone.
James Shuttleworth . . . „ Lancashire.

Thomas Lister ⎱
Assheton Curzon⎰ . . . „ Clitheroe.

Sir William Meredith, bart. . „ Liverpool.

Peter Legh ⎱
Randle Wilbraham⎰ . . „ Newton.

Nicholas Fazakerley⎱
Edmund Starkie ⎰ . . „ Preston.

Sir Thomas Palmer, bart.⎱
Edward Smith ⎰ . „ Leicestershire.

George Wrighte⎱
James Wigley ⎰ . . „ Leicester Borough.

John Michell . . . . „ Boston.
Coningsby Sibthorp . . „ Lincoln City.
George Cooke . . . „ Middlesex.

Sir Richard Glyn, bart.⎱
William Beckford ⎰ . . „ London.
Thomas Harley ⎰

Benjamin Bathurst . . . „ Monmouth Borough.
Sir Armine Wodehouse, bart. . „ Norfolk.
Thomas Howard . . . „ Castle Rising.

Sir Edmund Isham, bart.⎱
William Cartwright ⎰ . „ Northamptonshire.

Marshe Dickinson . . . „ Brackley.
Armistead Parker . . . „ Peterborough.
Sir W. Calverley Blackett, bart. „ Newcastle-upon-Tyne.
Sir James Dashwood, bart. . „ Oxfordshire.

Sir Roger Newdigate, bart.⎱
Peregrine Palmer ⎰ . „ Oxford University.

Robert Lee ⎱
Sir Thomas Stapleton, bart.⎰ . „ Oxford City.

Sir John Astley, bart. Richard Lyster	} . .	M.P. for	Shropshire.
Francis Child .	. . . ,,		Bishop's Castle.
Sir Chs. Kemys Tynte, bart. Thomas Prowse	} . ,,		Somerset.
Clement Tudway	. . . ,,		Wells.
Edward Southwell .	. . ,,		Bridgwater.
Simeon Stuart	. . . ,,		Hampshire.
John Jolliffe .	. . . ,,		Petersfield.
Henry Dawkins	. . . ,,		Southampton.
William Bagot	. . . ,,		Staffordshire.
Sir Robert Burdett, bart. .	. ,,		Tamworth.
Rowland Holt	. . . ,,		Suffolk.
Eliab Harvey .	. . . ,,		Dunwich.
Thomas Staunton .	. . ,,		Ipswich.
Sir Charles Mordaunt, bart. William Craven	} . ,,		Warwickshire.
Sir Robert Long, bart. Edward Popham	} . . ,,		Wiltshire.
Julines Beckford Edward Bouverie	} . . . ,,		Salisbury.
Peregrine Bertie	. . . ,,		Westbury.
John Ward William Dowdeswell	} . . ,,		Worcestershire.
Thomas Foley Robert Harley	} . . . ,,		Droitwich.
Edward Dering Thomas Knight	} . . . ,,		New Romney.

Wales (9)

Richard Price .	. . .	M.P. for	Beaumaris.
John Pugh Pryse	. . . ,,		Cardiganshire.
Herbert Lloyd	. . . ,,		Cardigan Borough.
Sir Lynch Salusbury Cotton, bart.	,,		Denbighshire.
Sir John Glynne, bart. .	. ,,		Flint Borough.
Herbert Mackworth	. . ,,		Cardiff.
Edward Kynaston .	. . ,,		Montgomeryshire.
Sir John Phillips, bart. .	. ,,		Pembrokeshire.
Edward Lewis	. . . ,,		Radnor Borough.

APPENDIX B

FIVE of the six complete lists of the House of Commons drawn up between the middle of October and 25 November 1762, are in Add. MSS. 33000, and one in another volume — I had it copied but the reference was omitted, and I have not been able to trace it again. This missing list, which I shall describe as 'X', is marked 13 November, and seems to come in between lists 'A' and 'B'. The following five lists are in Add. MSS. 33000 :

(A) ff. 153-61. In the handwriting of George Onslow, M.P. for Surrey ; drawn up between the 15th and the 27th of October, and marked 'Corrected November 13'. Lord Waltham, who died on 5 October, and Thomas Hales, who died on the 6th, are not in it, and the Nugents, of whose defection Newcastle heard about 14 October, were from the outset classed as opponents. James Brudenell, John Jeffreys, and Lord Barrington were first entered as 'for', but subsequently transferred to 'against'. Newcastle learned of Brudenell's change on 27 October, and of Barrington's on 4 November. But the corrections are not properly completed up to 13 November ; *e.g.*, the followers of Sandwich are not transferred from 'for' to 'against', though by 13 November Newcastle must have known that Sandwich had joined the Court.

(B) ff. 245-50. While this list was in use, three followers of Sandwich — John Stephenson, Thomas Duckett, and Robert Jones — were transferred from 'for' to 'against'. The names of the two Members returned for Eye on 1 December are inserted in Newcastle's own hand, but the list certainly ceased to be used long before 1 December. These entries would therefore help to date the list only if we knew what day Newcastle learned whom the owner of that pocket-borough, Lord Cornwallis, intended to put up at Eye ; Cornwallis had assured Newcastle, after Devonshire's dismissal, 'that he answers, that the two Members he is to chuse, shall, as well as himself,' be what Newcastle would have them (Newcastle to G. Cavendish, 31 October, Add. MSS. 32944, ff. 167-8).

In the binding the last folio of this list, on which the numbers of the various columns are added, has been detached ; it will be found disguised as f. 325.

(C) ff. 251-4. This is the same as 'B', only differently arranged ; and the last folio of this list, containing the end of the 'against' column, appears as f. 331.

(D) ff. 261-7. This list was drawn up before 20 November, for the name of Lord Robert Sutton, who died that day in London, was still inserted in its original draft, but was subsequently crossed out ; so was that of Lord Dungarvan, who on 21 November succeeded to the barony of Boyle. Also, when the list was compiled, Newcastle had as yet no certain knowledge of Powis's defection — this he obtained on 20 November ; the 'Shropshire gang' was originally placed under 'for', and transfers of its members to 'doubtful' or 'against' appear as corrections.

Ff. 326-30 are an earlier, incomplete draft of the same list.

(E) ff. 255-60. This list is a copy of 'D' corrected, but a new column is introduced, of those 'absent'. The list was compiled after 22 November, but probably before the 27th. Lord Clive and the two Foresters appear in it as doubtful, but when Newcastle had recovered from the shock of Powis's defection, and had presumably seen some of the Shropshire Whigs, he wrote to Rockingham on 27 November : 'Of Lord Powis's party, I think, we are sure of two Clives, two Forresters, Gen. Whitmore, and, I hope, Bridgeman' (Add. MSS. 32945, f. 162). This change of view does not appear, even as a correction, in list 'E'.

Of the incomplete lists for this period the most interesting is Add. MSS. 33002, f. 461 ; it must have been compiled at the end of October, and at the top of two parallel columns appears the suggestive question :

> May not the following Members   to be added to the
> be deducted from the Red List   Black List of 202 ? [1]
>   of 223

Among those to be transferred are James Brudenell and John Jeffreys, who in the first draft of list 'A' still appear as 'for' but by its corrections are transferred to 'against', and appear as such in list 'X' and lists 'B'–'E'. The paper can further be dated by the remark 'St. Clair dying' — he died on 30 November 1762. Yet this does not entirely resolve the puzzle : with the handwriting — not that of any scribe of Newcastle's — I am unfamiliar ; and in the Newcastle Papers I have never come across any reference to 'Red' and 'Black' lists. At the bottom of the paper stands the following summary :

$$211 \quad —^2$$
$$208 \quad —^3$$

---

[1] These figures signify the number of Members in these lists.
[2] This is the 'Red List' of Newcastle's friends after certain deductions have been made.
[3] The 'Black List' after certain additions have been made.

115	doubtfull
18	absent
5	more
1	St. Clair dying

Is it a preparatory sketch for one of Newcastle's lists, or, as seems to me more likely, a stray list from a different collection ?

INDEX

2 F